View from Zollernblick

Regional Perspectives in Europe

Professor Christopher Harvie

View from Zollernblick

Regional Perspectives in Europe:

A *Festschrift* for Christopher Harvie

edited by Eberhard Bort

Grace Note
Publications

View from Zollernblick -
Regional Perspectives in Europe:
A Festschrift for Christopher Harvie
edited by Eberhard Bort

First published 2013 by
Grace Note Publications
Grange of Locherlour,
Ochtertyre, PH7 4JS, Scotland
www.gracenotepublications.co.uk
books@gracenotereading.co.uk

Copyright © Contributors, 2013

ISBN: 978-1-907676-37-6 (PBK)

British Library Cataloguing-in-Publications Data
A catalogue record for this book is available from the British Library

Front cover: The figure of Venus in the Market Square of Freudenstadt was created by the Freudenstadt sculptor David Fahrner in 1954. Stretching out with one hand to grasp a better future, while pushing away the evils of the past with the other, the Venus is a reminder of the destruction of Freudenstadt in the Second World War and the subsequent reconstruction of the town. Some refer to her as the 'Mortgage Venus', as rebuilding the town was associated with a heavy debt burden.

Contents

4. Regional Politics and Policies

5. Regional Cultures and Cultural Connections

Appendix

List of illustrations, maps, graphs and tables

Acknowledgements

Thanks to all contributors to this *Festschrift*. Those who did not make the deadline will have to hope there will be a third collection of Freudenstadt papers in due time.

Thanks to Roddy Simpson and Allan McMillan for their photos, and to Julia Drechsel and Daniel Kälberer for their typing assistance.

We are particularly grateful for the support the Freudenstadt Colloquia receive from the Fritz Erler Forum in Stuttgart. And we appreciate how our hosts at the *Zollernblick* – or the *Waldhotel Zollernblick*, to give it its full Sunday name – make us feel welcome every July. We are, of course, grateful to the good burghers of Freudenstadt for organising their *Stadtfest* to coincide with our symposium.

A very special thanks to Chris Harvie for being Chris Harvie.

And last, but definitely not least, three cheers for Gonzalo Mazzei, Grace Note's publisher *extraordinaire*, who also designed the front and back covers of the book.

View from Zollernblick

Eberhard Bort

After *Networking Europe: Essays on Regionalism and Social Democracy*,[1] this is the second crop of papers from the annual gatherings Chris Harvie and I have organised at the *Zollernblick* in Freudenstadt since 1991. Originally, this symposium was a response to the regional partnership treaty signed between Baden-Württemberg and Wales in 1990, gauging the relevance of such regional cooperation in Europe. It soon developed into an annual conversation about European regional developments, with a focus on the evolution of devolution in the UK and Ireland. A collaborative effort between the University of Tübingen, the University of Edinburgh and the Friedrich Ebert Stiftung's Fritz-Erler-Akademie (now Forum), the Freudenstadt meetings have attracted academics, politicians, writers and journalists to the idyllic Black Forest for informal and usually pretty lively discussions, presided over by its 'spiritus rector', Christopher Harvie. So, this volume is also a *Festschrift* for Chris who will be turning 70 in 2014 – three days after the Scottish referendum on independence.

Of course, I am aware that we may disrespect every unwritten rule here. A *Festschrift* with the dedicatee as a contributor? But who could keep the, as Ian Jack called him, "ever-effervescent Chris Harvie"[2] out of such a venture? And we happily mix academic and journalistic pieces with essays and a dash of poetry, reflecting your man's interests as well as giving a flavour of the conversations at Hotel *Zollernlick*. And no, we'll not be offended if anyone calls it a bit of a *smörgåsbord* of a book. That's the way we wanted it…

The Ever-effervescing Christopher Harvie

When I returned back to Tübingen after a stint at Trinity College Dublin, the University's English Department had introduced *Landeskunde* (British & Irish Studies), tentatively at first, with Glaswegian Angus Munro, then, in 1980, with the appointment of Professor Christopher Harvie. I will not forget encountering Chris in is first lecture – how he drew the outlines of

---

[1] Eberhard Bort and Neil Evans (eds), *Networking Europe: Essays on Regionalism and Social Democracy*, Liverpool: Liverpool University Press, 2000.

[2] Ian Jack, 'A new sense of possibility shines on Scotland – but what will come of it?' *The Guardian*, 14 May 2011.

Wales and Scotland on the blackboard, his free-flowing style of lecturing, the myriad asides, the anecdotes, all a million miles away from the dry, much more stilted German style we were used to. Needless to say that, over his 27 years at Tübingen, the students simply loved him.

Each semester, Chris offered one lecture course, usually centring on a theme of 19th-20th century British history and politics, and two Pro-and-*Hauptseminars*, usually one dealing with an historical theme – 'industrialisation', 'urbanisation', 'imperialism', etc. – and another with a topic which enabled him to devise some sort of integrated introduction to work in recent politics, sociology, and contemporary history. HIs *Haupt-* and *Oberseminar* usually concentrated on areas within his own research interests, and acted as the basis for students to produce their own undergraduate theses in cultural studies.

'British & Irish Studies' was located in the English Language and Literature Seminar and was developed as a means both of broadening the curriculum for English teachers and of offering joint honours courses in English and Economics, English and Politics, etc. About half of Chris's students were studying for the *Gymnasium* Teachers' Diploma, and the remainder were either sitting the University Master and Bachelor's examination, or taking joint courses, chiefly English and Economics. The proportion in the latter two categories was increasing, and from 1986 Chris offered a Master's course in British Cultural Studies. After a long controversy with the education ministry in Stuttgart, Landeskunde was – in the reformed examination statutes of 1993 – recognised as the single most important subject in the Teachers' Diploma course, and candidates from then on had to take two courses instead of one before their examination.

Within this conspectus, he also offered one specialism in Scottish/British periphery studies every two Semesters. In the 2006 summer semester there was, for example, a lecture course on 'The Age of Victoria, 1837-1901', and seminars on 'Transport, Culture and Society and Britain and Europe'. Other seminars included 'MacDiarmid, Yeats and Cultural Revival', 'Province and Nation in Britain, 1745-1914', 'The Novel of Scottish Society, from Galt to Gray'.

In 1993, Chris founded, with a grant from the University and the British Council, the Welsh Studies Centre, which largely operates through Compactseminars organised by visiting Welsh academics: a pioneer project in Germany in that these produce a full certificate for the participants. Guest seminar-directors have included Prof Dai Smith, Prof Jane Aaron, Peter Lord, Neil Evans and Marion Löffler.

In all of this, his experience of eleven years at the Open University stood him in good stead.[3] In 1969, he had joined the OU at Milton Keynes as one of its very first staff members. He counted himself lucky to work with Arthur Marwick,[4] Clive Emsley, Henry Cowper, Cicely Havely and Anne Laurence. His

---

[3] See Henry Cowper's chapter in this volume; and Chris's Bibliography, which gives an overview of the areas covered by him at the OU.

[4] Chris was touched to be asked to give his eulogy at University College, London, in September 2006.

Tübingen *Mitarbeiter* included Helmut Schröder, Carola Ehrlich, Alex Böhm, Heidi Friedrich, Christine Frasch, Stefan Büttner, Katerina Magdou, and myself. Ever since our first meeting, Chris has been a huge support, and a friend. Sharing an office with him was an education and a half. We have collaborated on many a project, in Tübingen, between Tübingen and Edinburgh, and then in the Scottish Parliament – many a 'networking' lunch cadged in the Members' Restaurant!

In the Scottish Parliament and in his constituency office in Kirkcaldy, Dave Torrance (who won the constituency in 2011), Carol Lindsay, Catriona Elder and Alice Lowenstein kept an eye on him.

Chris was a member of the Labour Party from 1962 to 1989, when he joined the Scottish National Party. A seasoned Home Rule campaigner – co-author, with Gordon Brown, of *A Voter's Guide to the Scottish* Assembly in 1979 – he also joined, in 1991, Plaid Cymru. But he remained a member of the Fabian Society, the Centre for Scottish Public Policy (formerly the John Wheatley Centre), and the *Sozialdemokratische Partei Deutschlands*. After standing unsuccessfully as an SPD candidate in the local elections of 2004, no one was more surprised than he when, in 2007, as the SNP candidate for the Kirkcaldy constituency he found himself elected to the Scottish Parliament as a list member for Mid Scotland and Fife.

In late 2005, Chris had received a phone call from Alex Salmond, asking him to stand in the forthcoming Scottish Parliamentary election. The future First Minister hooked him in with a quote from the Marquess of Montrose:

> He either fears his fate too much,
> Or his deserts are small,
> Who dares not put it to the touch,
> To win or lose it all.

and eighteen months later, on 3 May 2007, he was elected.

He retired from Tübingen, but kept Compactseminars going throughout his four years in the Parliament, and after. And he also held honorary chairs at the University of Wales in Aberystwyth and the University of Strathclyde in Glasgow. He did enjoy his stint in the Parliament, not just the speaking opportunities, and his advisory role for Alex Salmond, the First Minister, and Michael Russell, the Education Secretary, but also working for his constituents.

In 2008, he got himself into a wee stushie over remarks he had made as a member of the Economy, Energy and Tourism Committee. Discussing Scottish tourism, he had described Lockerbie as a "dump", full of derelict shops and youths smoking and drinking. The tabloids had a field day, and 'outraged' politicians demanded an apology. Chris conceded that it was insensitive to use the Dumfries and Galloway town marked by the plane crash terror attack in which 270 people died in 1988. "I do apologise for certain comments. I certainly was wrong, I think, to use Lockerbie as an example." But the point of run-down small-town Scotland resonated. "There is the general problem of town centre dereliction," he insisted, "the problems of direction with kids, the problems with a booze culture."[5]

The episode reinforced the image of Harvie MSP. "Amid the serried ranks of assorted party hacks," opined Alan Cochrane in the *Daily Telegraph*, "and other forgettable mediocrities who make up the bulk of the members of the Scottish Parliament at Holyrood, the SNP's Christopher Harvie is, not to put too fine a point on it, something of an oddity."

> He is unfailingly polite, with an old fashioned, if sometimes dotty, courtesy that inclines him to listen to what others are saying, even if he disagrees strongly with them. And far from looking as if he has stepped straight from the Marks and Sparks fitting room, Chris Harvie has the audacity to wear felt fedoras, corduroy trousers, tweedy jackets and to have his specs hanging round his neck on a chain. I'm told, and I have no reason to doubt it, that one day last week he even wore plus twos – or knickerbockers, as those in the cheap seats have dubbed them - to the Holyrood chamber.[6]

"There are few more colourful characters wandering around the grey corridors of Holyrood than Professor Christopher Harvie," blogged the *Scotsman*'s David Maddox, who also hailed Chris's website 'The Intelligent Mr Toad' – "prove that there are still some politicians out there with a self deprecating humour."[7] Later in 2008, Chris won the 'Free Spirit of the Year' accolade at *The Herald* newspaper's *Scottish Politician of the Year* awards.

A life-long railway enthusiast, Chris has campaigned for the re-opening of the Borders railway line, and is Honorary President of the Scottish Association for Public Transport.[8] Even a cursory glance at his bibliography will show that he is a prolific writer. On top of his books and academic papers, he is a combative and thought-provoking presence among the commentariat, from *openDemocracy* to the *Scottish Review*. Had we attempted to list his journalistic pieces, we would have had to extend this *Festschrift* into a second volume!

Christopher Harvie was born in Motherwell on 21 September 1944. His father was a schoolteacher, and he grew up in the border village of St

---

[5] 'MSP sorry over 'dump' town jibe', *BBC News* Scotland, 27 February 2008, <http://news.bbc.co.uk/1/hi/scotland/south_of_scotland/7267022.stm>.

[6] Alan Cochrane, 'Christopher Harvie is the odd man out', *The Daily Telegraph*, 28 February 2008.

[7] David Maddox, 'The Musings of Mr Toad', Blog, 9 March 2009; <http://www2.jpscotland.co.uk/steamie/2009/03/david-maddox-musings-of-mr-toad.html>.

[8] See Christopher Harvie, *Deep-fried Hillman Imp: Scotland's Transport*, Glendaruel: Argyll, 2001.

Boswells, where the family lived until 1958. Thereafter he attended the Royal High School and University of Edinburgh, graduating with First Class Honours in History in 1966 and being awarded his PhD for a thesis on *University Liberalism and Democracy, 1860 – 1886*. Chris met Virginia Roundell in 1977 and was married to her from 1980 until she died in 2005. He has one daughter, Alison, who works for the Young Foundation in London.

Chris did not seek re-election in 2011 as an MSP, instead retiring to his home in Melrose, caring for his 92-year-old parents in the Borders and continuing to write. On 12 March 2012, he was awarded the Officer's Cross of the Order of Merit of the German Federal Republic in recognition of his lifelong contribution to German-Scottish understanding.

Chris has described himself as "a civic nationalist and greenish republican," whose "social beliefs owe much to Marxism as modified by Gramsci, the sociology of Patrick Geddes and a continually nagging if eclectic Christian socialism." He considers himself fortunate to have been able to teach – and learn from – excellent students in one of Europe's oldest universities; his loyalties lie "awkwardly between his homelands of Swabia, Scotland and Wales."[9]

In connection with the SPD's Friedrich Ebert Stiftung, he started in 1991 the Freudenstadt Colloquia on regional co-operation between Wales and Baden-Württemberg. Alfred and Gotlind Braun made us always feel welcome at the *Zollernblick*, and the cooperation continues to the very day with Sabine Fandrych and Silvia Wittig of the Erler-Forum in Stuttgart. Over the years, speakers have included Tom Nairn, Neal Ascherson, Dai Smith and Herta Däubler-Gmelin MdB, the former deputy-leader of the SPD, as well as Nuala O'Faolain of the *Irish Times*, Sarah Boyack MSP, Scottish Minister of Transport, Ron Davies, Secretary of State for Wales, John Osmond of the Institute of Welsh Affairs, Kenneth O Morgan, the historian and biographer, and many more. Some have become committed 'Freudies', taking part year after year, like Logie Barrow from Bremen, Helmut Doka from Stuttgart, Noel Spare, the Conlans, or Gustav Klaus. Every November since 2010, 'Freudenstadt ½' – an idea of Stefan Büttner's – has been added to the franchise – the *Zollernblick* at Edinburgh's Summerhall ...

The Ups and Downs of European Regionalism

In the early 1990s, at the first few Freudenstadt colloquia, the rhetoric of a 'Europe of the Regions' was brimming with optimism. And it was not just the ideas of Leopold Kohr[10] and E. F. Schumacher[11] and Patrick Geddes[12]

---

9 < www.guardian.co.uk/global/2007/jun/03/christopherharvie>.

10 Leopold Kohr, *The Breakdown of Nations* (1957), London: Routledge, 1986.

11 E. F. Schumacher, *Small is Beautiful: A Study of Economics as if People Mattered*, London: Blond & Briggs, 1973.

12 See Walter Stephen (ed.), *Think Global, Act Local: The Life and Legacy of Patrick Geddes*, Edinburgh: Luath, 2004.

that influenced the debates, Baden Württemberg – one of Chris Harvie's "bourgeois regions"[13] – was part of the 'Four Motors (a high-tech oriented regional partnership with Catalonia, Lombardy and Rhône-Alpes), to which Wales had docked on through its partnership treaty.

Alfred Geisel, then Deputy Speaker of the Stuttgart *Landtag*, expressed the widespread belief that we were *en route* to a much more federal Europe, and that the regions had to play a crucial part in the governance structures of this emerging Europe – with the Committee of the Regions developing into a regional chamber alongside the European Parliament.[14] Those were the heady days when Mitterand and Kohl and the Swiss President Delamuraz would meet in Basel to sign the *Déclaration Tripartite* and proclaim cross-border regions as the future building blocks of Europe.[15] In *The Rise of Regional Europe*, Chris Harvie argued that power was shifting from the traditional nation-state to smaller, highly-technologised, environmentally-aware regional or cultural-national identities. Yet, amongst all this optimism, his view from *Zollernblick* was also critical:

> 'Europe of the Regions'; 'Four Motors'; 'Arge Alp': was there not an element of wishful thinking in these beguiling concepts? Was the dominance of 'core regions' less a pattern for future development than a 'one-off'? With very little to do with the small-scale, self-regulating political and ecological systems of Kohr and Schumacher?[16]

Regional autonomies fully participating in European governance were still on the cards in the early 2000s, when RegLeg, the association representing and lobbying for the self-governing 'constitutional' regions of the European Union, was campaigning for access for the regions to the Court of Justice, for regions to become partners to the European Union institutions, and the reform and upgrading of the Committee of the Regions. In 2003-2004, Scotland's First Minister Jack McConnell was President of RegLeg. But he seemed caught between his commitment to regional solidarity across Europe and the regions' common interest to gain a seat at the top table in Europe, and constraints from London which had blocked the forming of a working group on the regions in Giscard d'Estaing's Constitutional Convention.[17]

The Final Declaration of the Second Conference of the Presidents of Regional Assemblies in Europe, which discussed the issue of a Charter of the

[13] Christopher Harvie, *The Rise of Regional Europe*, London: Routledge, 1994, p.xii.

[14] See Alfred Geisel, 'The Future of Europe: Federalism – Regionalism – Centralism?' in: Bort and Evans, pp.39-46.

[15] 'Der kurze Draht kam erst später', *Südkurier*, 23 January 2003.

[16] Christopher Harvie, *The Rise of Regional Europe*, p.65.

[17] See Eberhard Bort, 'The new institutions: an interim assessment', in Michael O'Neill (ed.), *Devolution and British Politics*, Harlow: Longman Pearson, 2004, pp.295-318.

Sabine Fandrych (Fritz-Erler-Forum) and Peter Friedrich (SPD, Minister für Federal, European and International Affairs in Baden-Württemberg) at Freudenstadt XXII (2012)

Freudenstadt 1/2 at Summerhall, Edinburgh November 2012

Regions in Europe, "signed by 197 regional Assemblies, the role of European regions in the enlarged Europe and in the ongoing process of enlargement, democratization at local and regional level, economic development and crossborder cooperation," stated:

> The Conference sees a clear role for the regional Assemblies contributing to the development of regional democracy and regionalism throughout the European continent, in the framework of a process of integration and enlargement, with increasing contact with 'new neighbours' and strives towards an active role for assemblies in the process of policy-making, active relations with the European Parliament, the European Commission and the Committee of the Regions and the Council of Europe and its Chamber of Regions.[18]

Symptomatically, these campaigns were largely unsuccessful and, although powerful regions with parliaments and governments are still a factor to be reckoned with in the evolving system of European governance,[19] the proposed – and long since abandoned – European Constitution might have recognises the existence of sub-Member State governance, but it would not have offered them a seat at the top table.[20]

The Committee of the Regions, composed of a wide variety of structurally uneven interests representing different local and regional levels, remained purely advisory. The failure to secure direct access to decision-making processes at the EU level has led some powerful regions to resist further transfers of power, as it would impair their autonomy:

> Under the current regime, regions have no 'hard' decision-making powers in EU policy-making other than those conferred upon them by the national constitutions in the formulation of the national position. They do, however, have recourse to a variety of 'soft' channels on both the domestic and the European level that allow them to shape EU policies through lobbying and argumentation. For legislative regions, the lack of 'hard' powers in EU policy-making may result in

---

[18] *Declaration of Arnheim*, Second Conference of the Presidents of Regional Assemblies in Europe, Arnheim, Netherlands, 9 July 2004.

[19] Paolo Dardanelli, *Between two Unions: Europeanisation and Scottish Devolution*, Manchester: Manchester University Press, 2005.

[20] Eberhard Bort and Christopher Harvie, 'After the Albatross: A New Start for the Scottish Parliament', *Scottish Affairs*, no.50 (Winter 2005), pp.26-38. See also Eberhard Bort, 'Scotland and Europe, or: Room at the Top for "Constitutional Regions"', *Romanian Journal of European Affairs*, Vol.4, No.2, 2004, pp.55-64.

disempowerment where traditionally regional powers are transferred to the European level.[21]

Meanwhile, Rhona Brankin, the Scottish Government's Environment and Rural Affairs Junior Minister, told the Freudenstadt Symposium of 2005 how dynamically Scotland's relations with Europe were developing under Devolution. It was the strategy of the Scottish Government, she said, to make Scotland one of the leading regions in Europe. In the first six years of the Parliament, Scotland had formed regional partnerships with four other European regions: Catalonia, Tuscany, Bavaria and North-Rhine Westphalia.

When Jack McConnell handed on the baton of the RegLeg Presidency to the Bavarian Minister of European Affairs, Eberhard Sinner, he called for its recognition to be enhanced as a means of linking the EU to its citizens: "The best way to do that is for devolved governments to have a stronger role in shaping and applying EU laws and regulations."[22] Unfortunately, that call fell on deaf ears.

Regionalism had been overtaken by the twin processes of EU enlargement and the move towards the single currency, which both centred on Member State governments.

The rationale of other regionalist movements was all about no longer wishing to share regional riches with less-endowed regions and about limiting immigration to the region, as the right-wing Flemish Bloc or the Northern League in Italy,[23] reactionary and distasteful, as vividly described in Michael Dibdin's Aurelio Zen novel *Dead Lagoon* (1994).

In the UK, the devolution process, asymmetrical from the start, progressed in Wales[24] and Scotland, and led, eventually, to remarkably stable government in Northern Ireland, but stalled in England. The Greater London Assembly, established after a referendum in 2000, was the only successful attempt to date to introduce devolution in England. In November 2004, a referendum on a Northern Assembly for Newcastle was rejected by 78 to 22 per cent.[25] And the 'provisional' eight assemblies in England, which were made up of councillors nominated to sit on them, but were seen as precursors for fully

---

[21] Anna-Lena Högenauer, 'The Impact of the Lisbon Reform Treaty on Regional Engagement in EU Policy-Making – Continuity or Change?', *European Journal of Law Reform*, Vol.X, No. 4 (2008), pp. 535-57, p.556.

[22] Robbie Dinwoodie, 'McConnell calls for European recognition', *The Herald*, 1 December 2004.

[23] For an analysis of the Northern League, see Giuseppe Sciortino, 'Just Before the Fall: The Northern League and the Cultural Construction of a Secessionist Claim', *International Sociology*, vol.14 (3), September 1999, pp.321-36.

[24] See John Osmond's chapter in this volume.

[25] 'North East votes 'no' to assembly', *BBC News*, 5 November 2004, <http://news.bbc.co.uk/1/hi/uk_politics/3984387.stm>.

elected regional assemblies, were abolished by 2010.

Tom Nairn increasingly saw "federalism, subsidiarity, devolved Regionalism" as "dodges of the bygone era" – echoing Gertrude Stein, he claimed that "self-government is self-government *is* self-government."

> With all its daft twists and turns, and hopeless exaggerations, globalization is providing new stimuli for nationality-politics. Not so much for 'national*ism*' in the late 19th and 20th century sense, but definitely for the emergence of new, smaller communities of will and purpose – the nations of a new and deeply different age.[26]

We have not heard much in the past few years of RegLeg and other attempts at coordinating European regionalism; we have heard a lot about regions striving for independence, from Catalonia via Belgium to Wales and Scotland. Their potential gain is, the flip-side, a weakening case for the Europeanisation process, of which a tier of regional governance ought to be an integral part:

> A new regional vision of Europe is demanding attention, one that challenges the current Europe of the nation states and is likely to do so more strongly in the coming century. If it is to be democratic, this new Europe must have strong local and regional governments.[27]

As most European legislation is actually implemented at the regional level, giving regions democratic access to European decision-making would be the obvious way of 're-connecting' citizens with the institutions of the EU, the stated intention of the aborted constitutional process. It is still the case that regionalism thus could help solving "a general problem confronting representative government – a decline in party membership, political engagement and voter participation," as Stanley Henig and Ulrike Rüb contended:

> This is sometimes described as a 'democratic deficit'. Effective regional government has been seen as one way in which the gap can be bridged and voters can be re-engaged with the political process. Related to this is the notion of better policy-making, based on the idea that decisions should be taken at the level which will best be able to respond to regional needs.[28]

---

[26] Tom Nairn, 'Globalization and Nationalism: the New Deal?', Edinburgh Lecture, 4 March 2008, <www.scotland.gov.uk/Resource/Doc/923/0057271.pdf>.

[27] John Osmond, 'The Welsh Assembly 1979 and 1997', in Eberhard Bort and Neil Evans (eds), *Networking Europe*, p.382.

[28] Stanley Henig and Ulrike Rüb, *Regional Devolution in Europe: Lessons for the UK?* (European Essay No. 31), London: The Federal Trust, 2004, pp.7-8

Regions and small nations can be leaders in innovative policies, be it education, transport or energy.[29] That is also an area where regional partnerships can play an exciting role. And, regional cultures in all their diversity have an important part to play in defining our European identity. That is why cultural contributions are an integral part of the Freudenstadt process – and is well presented in this symposium. It is often suggested that Jean Monnet said "if I had to do it again, I would start with culture."[30]

It has also become pretty evident that regions – like Baden-Württemberg – which managed to maintain a skills-based manufacturing sector rather than putting all their eggs into the one basket of financial services and call centres have been much more adept at weathering the shockwaves of the banking crash.[31]

But the financial crisis has also thrown some European regions into disarray. Not only has it put extra strains on centre-periphery relations in the wrangle over finances, it has also exposed regional profligacy as in Sicily, potentially facing bankruptcy,[32] and what has been dubbed the "regional extravagance" of Valencia.[33] Despite million-strong demonstrations for independence, the Catalan Prime Minister Artur Mas suffered a set back in November 2012 when his CiU coalition did not achieve an absolute majority – counter to expectations.[34]

Other small states experienced traumatic crises – Iceland and Cyprus spring to mind – which clearly gave food for thought for independence movements. But also raised eyebrows over EU crisis management. Just before the financial collapse, Kosovo declared its independence. But only 22 of the 27 EU member states recognised it. Spain, Romania, Greece, Cyprus and Slovakia held back, in view of independence movements and national minorities within their own borders.[35] The Turkish Prime Minister Recep Tayyip Erdogan called Kosovo's independence an example for Cyprus – but was conspicuously silent about the Kurds.[36]

---

[29] See the examples presented in this volume under the heading of 'Regional Politics and Policies'.

[30] See Cris Shore, '"In uno plures": EU Cultural Policy and the Governance of Europe', *Cultural Analysis*, vol.5, 2006.

[31] See Christopher Harvie, *Mending Scotland: Essays in Economic Regionalism*, Glendaruel: Argyll, 2004; and his contribution to this volume.

[32] Michael Braun, 'Sizilien ist pleite: Das Griechenland Italiens', *die tageszeitung*, 29 July 2012.

[33] David Gardner, 'Spain: Autonomy under fire', *Financial Times*, 15 August 2012.

[34] Ute Müller, 'Abschied aus der EU schreckt Katalanen ab', *Die Welt*, 26 November 2012.

[35] Reiner Wandler, 'Beispiel für Basken und Katalanen', *die tageszeitung*, 20 February 2008; Sascha Mostyn, 'Slowakei und Rumänien zittern', *die tageszeitung*, 20 February 2008.

[36] Jürgen Gottschlich, 'Vorbild für Zypern, nicht für Kurden', *die tageszeitung*, 19 February 2008.

Europe at the Crossroads

"The financial crisis that began in 2008 should have been a social-democratic moment," mused the *New Statesman*:

> After decades in which neoliberalism had held sway, here was an opportunity to rehabilitate the state as an economic actor and to win support for a more humane version of capitalism.[37]

But in the wake of the crisis, with capitalism in disarray, neoliberalism on the pillory, unrestrained banking and financial speculation being blamed, and working people and the poor footing the bill for bailouts and a sluggish recovery, the centre left held power in only six of the 27 EU member states. A puzzle? "Social Democracy, in one form or another, is the prose of contemporary European politics," was the historian Tony Judt's explanation.[38] Traditionally, the three great social democratic concerns, according to Judt, were to promote and protect social welfare, link states and markets, and extend democracy. But the left suffered, Paul Gillespie argued,

> from decades of adapting to the very forces which brought on the crisis. Ideologically its leaders bought into the neoliberal, efficient market consensus, promoting the deregulation which exploded two years ago. 'Third way' policies eroded the distinctions between left and right, as social democratic parties became more geared to consensual governing than representing alternative futures. Their links to the social classes, trade unions and other blocs supporting them were weakened without finding new social bases.
>
> As a result they lost their ability to fight defensive battles against the new insecurity or offensive political and intellectual ones for an alternative future. Liberal, green or radical left parties gained advantage, but the resulting fragmentation on the left throughout Europe has given easy victories to conservative parties in the European Parliament elections and a string of contests in larger and smaller EU member states.[39]

Is Social Democracy in terminal decline in Europe? In a symposium convened by Michael Keating and David McCrone, while accepting the dire state of

---

[37] 'Labour needs to find a response to Cameron's conjuring trick', *New Statesman* (Leader), 22 November 2010.

[38] Tony Judt, *Ill Fares the Land: A Treatise on our Present Discontents*, London: Penguin, 2011, p.143.

[39] Paul Gillespie, 'Social Democratic values need rethinking', *The Irish Times*, 14 August 2010.

affairs, the contributors insist that social democracy is not a single set of ideas or practices but a way of reconciling market capitalism with social inclusion and equality, still as relevant as ever, but in need of adaptation to the challenges the current crisis poses.[40]

These challenges are nothing less than the dismantling of social democracy, particularly in Spain, Portugal, Greece and Italy, but also in other countries, under the mantle of austerity.[41] The bailouts have seen billions diverted to ailing banks, while budgets and wages have been cut and social and welfare rights have been eroded – to a degree that seemed unimaginable even during the neoliberal decades leading up to the crash. Obscene bankers' bonuses, while millions of young people have no jobs; the return of economically forced emigration, while austerity strangles economic recovery.

Europe is at the crossroads. Socially, and constitutionally. Will the crisis lead to further integration – or will it lead to disintegration? Fact is that the losers of the crisis tend to be the poorest and the least educated. Those who are least likely to vote, particularly in European elections. Those were the focus of a remarkable speech by Michael D Higgins, the (social democratic) President of Ireland, before the European Parliament on 17 April 2013, which merits an extensive citation:

> Today, citizens in Europe are threatened with an unconscious drift to disharmony, a loss of social cohesion, a recurrence of racism and an increasing deficit of democratic accountability in some decision making of an economic and fiscal kind.
>
> We cannot, however, ignore the fact that European citizens are suffering the consequences of actions and opinions of bodies such as rating agencies, which, unlike Parliaments, are unaccountable. Many of our citizens in Europe regard the response to the crisis in their lives as disparate, sometimes delayed, not equal to the urgency of the task and showing insufficient solidarity with them in their threatened or actual economic circumstances.
>
> - They feel that in general terms the economic narrative of recent years has been driven by dry technical concerns; for example, by calculations that are abstract and not drawn from real problems, geared primarily by a consideration of the impact of such measures on speculative markets, rather than driven by sufficient compassion and empathy with the predicament of European citizens who are members of a union, and for whom all of the resources of Europe's capacity, political, social, economic and intellectual might have been drawn on, driven by the binding moral spirit of a union.

[40] Michael Keating and David McCrone (eds), *The Crisis of Social Democracy in Europe*, Edinburgh: Edinburgh University Press, 2013.

[41] Oliver Nachtwey, 'Der Nationalstaat lebt', *die tageszeitung*, 28 February 2013.

- In facing up to the challenges Europe currently faces, particularly in relation to unemployment, we cannot afford to place our singular trust in a single hegemonic model to the exclusion of others that might engage best problems such as unemployment in a version of a logistical, economic theory whose assumptions are narrow and questionable and largely indifferent to social consequences in terms of their outcomes.

- Instead of any discourse that might define the European Union as simply an economic space of contestation between the strong and the weak, our citizens yearn for the language of solidarity, the commitment to cohesion, for a generous inclusive rhetoric that is appropriate to an evolving political union that is anxious to reach a future of peace, prosperity, inclusion, and in a sustainable way.

- This is a serious challenge, not least because if we were to fail we run the risk of an economic crisis leading to a crisis of legitimacy for the Union. A Union that in its founding treaties is fundamentally founded on values – respect for personal dignity; freedom; democracy; equality; the rule of law and respect for human rights.

- The Union draws its legitimacy from the support of its citizens. That connection with the citizens – their belief that the European Union is of them and for them – is fundamental. Without it, we are adrift and citizens need an appeal to their heart as well as their reason. They need reassurance now that the Union will keep faith with its founding treaties.

- It is many years since Jacques Delors declared "Europe needs a soul", but it remains just as true. We should never forget that we are the inheritors of a profoundly important set of European values – Greek democracy, Roman law, the Judeo-Christian tradition, the reformation, the enlightenment, the great democratic revolution that began in France. Europe is therefore more than an economic space of contestation in which our citizens are invited or required to deliver up their lives in the service of an abstract model of economy and society whose core assumptions they are assumed not to question or put to the democratic test in elections.

- As we face into the future, we need to draw strength from the founding values of the Union and these include cohesion and solidarity – among Member States, among the citizens of our Union, and between the European Union and the rest of the world. We need to work together to apply ourselves to building a better future together – as Jacques Delors also said of this present crisis "Europe does not just need fire-fighters, it needs architects too".

- A first and urgent task must be to get Europe back to sustainable and fulfilling employment and a return to real growth. There is nothing more corrosive to society and more crushing to an individual than endemic unemployment, particularly among the young. Today there are 26 million people across the Union without work, 5.7 million young people, and 115 million in or at risk of poverty and social exclusion. We cannot allow this to continue.[42]

He received a standing ovation in Strasbourg. Not only centre-left parties should read the Irish President's speech carefully. It was a worthy contribution to the intellectual debate about the future of the European Union, which has engaged intellectuals from Umberto Eco to Jürgen Habermas in response to the present crisis.

Geert Mak, the Dutch writer, while peddling a good number of well-worn clichés, gets his main thesis right. As the European peoples and their parliaments are disenfranchised by the crisis management of the European Council and the European Central Bank, both lacking direct democratic legitimacy, he demands that in Europe politics and democracy must be put back at the centre.[43] Jürgen Habermas, Julian Nida-Rümelin and the economist Peter Bofinger responded to Sigmar Gabriel's request for a submission to the SPD's 2013 manifesto. They saw a clear link between the 'Euro crisis' and the anti-democratic tendencies which drove the "creeping transformation of a social civic democracy into a market-conform democratic façade." The only remedy, they argue, is a "transnational democratic deepening of the EU."[44]

The irony is that those who lament loudest about the democratic deficit at the heart of Europe are very often the same who block every attempt at such a democratisation of the European institutions, while stubbornly defending national sovereignty. Umberto Eco put a British reporter in his place when he used the 'unelected' governments of Lukas Papadimos in Greece and Mario Monti in Italy to warn against a supranational Europe. "All democracies know unelected institutions," he retorted, and mentioned the British monarchy and the American Supreme Court. "Nobody seems to question their legitimacy." Eco puts his trust in culture which, he hopes, will see Europe though its present crisis.[45]

---

[42] <www.president.ie/speeches/address-by-president-michael-d-higgins-towards-a-european-union-of-the-citizens-european-parliament-strasbourg-wednesday-17th-april-2013-2/>.

[43] Geert Mak, *Was, wenn Europa scheitert*, Munich: Pantheon, 2012

[44] Peter Bofinger, Jürgen Habermas und Julian Nida-Rümelin, 'Kurswechsel für Europa: Einspruch gegen die Fassadendemokratie', *Frankfurter Allgemeine Zeitung*, 3 August 2012,<www.faz.net/aktuell/feuilleton/debatten/europas-zukunft/kurswechsel-fuer-europa-einspruch-gegen-die-fassadendemokratie-11842820.html>.

[45] Gianni Riotta, '"Nur die Kultur verbindet uns": Umberto Eco über den Zusammenhalt in Europa', *Süddeutsche Zeitung*, 26 January 2012.

Ulrich Beck argues for a 'European Spring': the Europeanisation of the resistance against austerity. That trade unions in Spain, Portugal, Greece, Italy, France and Ireland organise strikes and demonstrations is in his view not a vote against Europe. But they send a clear signal. "We do not need bailouts for banks but rather a social lifeboat for the Europe of individuals, … solidarity with workers, the sections of the middle class threatened by the crash, well qualified young people who have no prospects of permanent employment, old people whose pensions have been cut…" This "new social contract" must provide "more social security through more Europe" and "protect the great cosmopolitan freedom from meddling by orthodox adherents of the nation-state."[46]

The original German title of Jürgen Habermas's *The Crisis of the European Union* is more playfully ambiguous: *Zur Verfassung Europas* means both 'On the state of Europe' and 'On Europe's constitution'. In his view, the crisis management of the European leaders threatens to turn "the first attempt at a democratic, judicial supranational community" into "an arrangement for the exercise of post-democratic-bureaucratic authority." His emphasis is no longer on the past, on the way the EU as a 'peace project' was born out of the horrors of two World Wars, but on a 'concrete utopia' (*pace* Ernst Bloch) of the European Union as a building block towards a "cosmopolitan rule of law", the EU as "an important stage along the route to a politically constituted world society."[47]

Bernadette Andreosso-O'Callaghan and Joachim Fischer recommended a refocusing on the purpose and achievements of European integration which now are threatened:

> It is time for all EU citizens to engage in building a democratic federal Europe, based on the principle of a fair society. This may mean a return to and rescuing of the achievements of the pre-neoliberal era which distorted the EU's greatest achievement, its social market economy, and to democratic political structures which saw a profound value in it.[48]

As to the present fortunes of social democratic parties, there are conflicting stories. Despite celebrating its 150th anniversary this year, the SPD seems to flatline in the polls at 25 to 28 per cent as the federal elections of September 2013 approach.[49] As Thomas Leuerer points out in his chapter on the Bavarian SPD, the Social Democrats cannot gain much by pandering to the right, and on the left there is competition from the Greens and from the Left party. Labour in the UK has a solid, if not stupendous lead over the Conservatives, but there

---

[46] Ulrich Beck, *German Europe*, Cambridge: Polity Press, 2013, p.82.

[47] Jürgen Habermas, *The Crisis of the European Union*, Cambridge: *Polity Press*, 2012, p.2.

[48] Bernadette Andreosso-O'Callaghan and Joachim Fischer, 'Ireland must embrace a federal Europe', *The Irish Times*, 4 February 2012.

[49] <www.wahlrecht.de/umfragen/index.htm>.

are still doubts about the leadership of Ed Miliband. Accepting the Cameron government's welfare spending cuts, and questioning the sustainability of universal benefits, does not breathe enthusiasm into potential Labour voters who are sick of austerity. Labour is broadly pro-European, but it seems split on the question of an in/out referendum. Scottish Labour struggles against a dominant SNP.

And in Ireland the familiar pattern of Labour suffering in coalition seems to repeat itself, as the party shares responsibility for the drastic austerity programme meted out by the government on the behest of the 'troika' – the EU Commission, the European Central Bank and the International Monetary Fund. Hollande's Socialists in France face a 'hot' summer over pensions reform. The trade unions have already spoken darkly of 'war', and ministers have been warned there will be little time for summer holidays.[50] François Hollande surprised the SPD when, at their anniversary celebration, he praised Gerhard Schröder's 'Agenda 2010', which saw reductions in health care benefits, the restructuring of labour regulations, tax cuts and an overhaul of the pension system – and cost the SPD at least 100,000 members, while giving rise to *Die Linke*.[51]

In autonomous Greenland, the social democratic Simiut party celebrated a stunning victory under Alequa Hammond, having campaigned for a more restricted exploitation and selling off of natural resources.[52] In Iceland, on the other hand, the electorate kicked out the centre-left government that had consolidated the country after the crash and instead returned the very parties that had steered the island state into the abyss. Highly ironic, given that none of the crisis countries in Europe has been nearly as successful in recovering from the crash. The red-green government had left the welfare state more or less intact and implemented policies that produced the lowest unemployment rate in Europe and remarkable economic growth. [53] At least the new/old rulers will not be able to repeat their calamitous policies, as the red-green government successfully shackled the banks. But EU membership seems doomed, as the Social Democrats were the only party left that advocated the Icelandic application.

Beyond the Referendum

We are, of course, in the run-up to the independence referendum in Scotland, addressed in several contributions in this collection. Given the relative stability

---

[50] Hugh Carnegy, 'François Hollande prepares to tackle pension reform', *Financial Times*, 13 June 2013.

[51] Patrick Donahue and Brian Parkin, 'Hollande Lauds German SPD's Courage for Welfare-Cutting Agenda', *Bloomberg*, 23 May 2013, <www.bloomberg.com/news/2013-05-23/hollande-lauds-german-spd-s-courage-for-welfare-cutting-agenda.html>.

[52] Reinhard Wolff, 'Gegen den Ausverkauf', *die tageszeitung*, 13 March 2013.

[53] Hannes Gamillscheg, 'Wenig gelernt', *Stuttgarter Zeitung*, 29 April 2013.

of opinion surveys over the past two decades (see Graph) – up to a third for independence, but clear majorities for devolution, preferably with increased powers for the Scottish Parliament, the absence of a question on the ballot paper representing this wish of the majority seems a strangely undemocratic way of going about a plebiscite.[54] Both the YesScotland and the Better Together campaigns have so far not set the heather ablaze. And the SNP's 'indy lite' – let's not rock the boat, keep the pound, keep the Queen, stay in Nato, share the welfare system, etc is causing those who advocate independence as a radical departure towards a fairer, greener, more equal Scotland, more akin to Nordic democracies, a headache.[55]

There may well be a No vote in September 2014. The constitutional preferences of the Scots have been very stable, despite all kinds of events and shocks to the political system, from the advent of the Parliament through various forms of government (coalition, minority, majority), the breakthrough of the SNP in 2007, trumped by the absolute majority of 2011, the financial crash, the change of government at Westminster, the 'Edinburgh Agreement' on the referendum... you name it, it did not significantly impact on the polling figures. Yes, the SNP was way behind at the beginning of the 2011 election campaign, and swept the board on polling day, but in 2014 the Scots are not voting for a government they can vote out of office four or five years later. The trend is, if anything, regressive.[56] And, surprisingly, young people seem to be even less in favour of independence.[57] I suspect that the minds of many Scots are made up about how they will vote in September 2014. Of course, I could be wrong. The campaigns clearly think that there is still all to play for.

Regardless of the result of the referendum, the status quo is already consigned to history.[58] The Scotland Act 2012 will provide greater powers (particularly fiscal powers) for the Scottish Parliament, and the 'unionist' parties are developing their models of 'Devo More' or 'Devo Plus' or 'Devo Max', all going beyond the Scotland Act. As John Osmond argues in his contribution, referendums develop their own dynamics. They 'accelerate history'. We may well live in the early days of a better nation.

---

[54] See Joyce McMillan, 'Scotland wants nae skinking ware', *The Scotsman*, 25 January 2013.

[55] See the contributions by Lesley Riddoch and Robin McAlpine in this volume; also: Gregor Gall, 'Yes campaign must unite people around a cause', *The Scotsman*, 13 March 2013.

[56] Polls in May 2013 register 31 or 32 per cent backing for independence, down by 3 per cent since the beginning of the year. See Eddie Barnes, 'Poll drop in Yes backing', *The Scotsman*, 10 May 2013.

[57] Scott MacNab, '60% of young voters say no', *The Scotsman*, 3 June 2013.

[58] See James Mitchell's contribution in this volume.

Constitutional Preferences 1997-2012

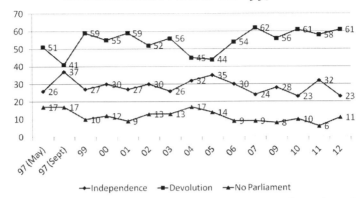

Source: Scottish Centre for Social Research: 'Ready for independence?'[59]

As if that was not enough excitement, there is also a fascinating interplay between the Scottish referendum and the proposed UK referendum on EU membership. Could the situation in September 2014 indicate that, as Alex Salmond claims, "a vote for independence is now the 'only way' to ensure Scotland's continued membership of the European Union.[60]

One thing is for sure: we will not run out of topics for debate at Freudenstadt in the foreseeable future – the trials and tribulations of regions and regionalism in Europe, the (mis-)fortunes of social democracy, and the evolving constitutional patterns across Europe, and especially in these isles, will provide plenty of discussion material. Just as a wee memento that we should, every now and then, try and transcend the Eurocentricity of our debates, we slipped in Sarah Boyack's Malawi diary – to show the internationalist reach of a 'regional' Parliament.

Freudenstadt has become a marque. A credit to our 'spiritus rector' – or, occasionally, Lord of Misrule – Chris Harvie. I hope this *potpourri* of a *Festschrift* gives a flavour of the colloquia in its kaleidoscope of regional perspectives, viewed from the vantage point of the *Zollernblick*.

---

[59] <www.scotcen.org.uk/study/scottish-social-attitudes-2012>.

[60] Eddie Barnes, 'EU stay "needs" Yes vote', *The Scotsman*, 15 May 2013.

'The Ever-effervescing Christopher Harvie'

War is the Continuation of Golf by Other Means (a round for Chris)

Peter McCarey

"The tweed's the thing"
Says Polonius. His baby
(He picks a three wood)
Teethes on his lapel.
Oot owre the rough he tees off
Into the trees
That promptly march on Dunsinane
Across the fairway. Cut!
To teas and ices for shiftless teens.
Alone they tweeze expression
Tease out sophistication for the rout,
For dual teams and peer review
Then it's rain that teems Leyland Atlantean windows
In pinball surface tension, butting through
The tears of things.

******

Eighteen is not a theological number.
It's seven sacraments times the three
Persons, less the Trinity – id est nothing.
The rough, not roughage, isn't purgative,
The fairway neither paradise nor primrose
Path to the sandy pit. His nephew
Is equally clueless with cruets and woods,
So let's admit the caddy IS an acolyte
And that - so hotly denied it's likely true —
His bowling parishioner's right arm
As he genuflects, moves stiffly back.
Does HE, though, clasping the crafted stem,
Bowed intent on that little white diameter,
Think of Mass? Unlikely. If he ever did
He'd put it, like this, aside without a grimace
And go on to concede his old pal Paddy Tierney
A two-inch putt for par.

******

I gowfed with the board at Carnoustie
Goosed a waitress at the 19th hole
Haw haw. We groused at Pittenthing
With the Chiseler of that Ilk, who grouched
About gormless Pictish beaters
Grouped on the sphagnum
Under a golf umbrella. Grout:
Urinal drip by drip deposited
In between his joints,
Gout and spite that came with the territory.

******

The Bruce at Cardross
In rough by the links
Attempts a long-range putt and drops another.
Right. From the sword-rack extracts
A double-fisted broad sword bigger than him
Hunkers down like a Cossack – oi! –
And helicopters bracken. He docks nettles,
Doffs thristles and dots the garth with hacked-off
Limbs and fronds. I mind Cardross.
Not a challenging course. They would say
It's a doss! It's a skoosh! For the Fair
We could stay in the steadings –
Gooseberries and pea-pods under glass.
Cobbled yards, linoleum, iron beds
The dross from coal briquettes
Sugar on sour days.

*****

De Bruis and de Bohun : two brutes
Whose grandfaithers squabble at meat in Valhalla.
The bloops of the bog and the brooks
Of the bickering burn. With the armies in order

de Bohun, mailed fist and missile ranging in,
Boots up. The charger boosts him through his pawns
At the shirt-sleeve king, who ought to leave
But jouks the lance-head, stirrup-stands
And deals the knicht twa beauts to the heid.
Game over.

'If you want to know how to get from Edinburgh to Peebles or to Melrose by public transport, don't consult the internet: ask Chris.'

Wolfgang Mössinger

First Minister, Members of the Scottish Parliament, Members of the German Bundestag, Professor Engler, dear guests,[1]

There is no doubt that Christopher Thomas Harvie is a true Scot. Having lived and taught for many years in Tübingen, the question is of course, has he also become a Swabian? Let us explore this a little. It is said that Swabians and Scots have two major traits in common: they are thrifty and grumpy. Well, some things might change over time: Parliament buildings and trams on the one side, and railway stations on the other; and what about grumpiness, for which Chris is certainly *not* a good example? As a long time resident of Tübingen in Swabia and having been involved in politics at both ends, Chris knows something about both their mentalities. So, he certainly understands the meaning of the Swabian saying "Not moaning is enough praise!", which epitomises the grumpiness for which the Swabians are known. And because we most definitely have nothing to moan about Chris, we could leave it at that and proceed directly to the formalities of handing over the Officer's Cross and then enjoy German wine and beer and Scottish food.

For those less familiar with German regional intricacies: Swabians share their region Baden-Württemberg with the people from Baden. These people are much more generous, less grumpy and generally good humoured, after all they share a border with France and Switzerland. And, fortunately for you: I am one of them. I am a Badener. So, in good Badisch-Scottish friendship, I will not leave it at that by simply not moaning, but will praise Chris for his outstanding contribution to the mutual understanding between Germany and the UK in general and, of course, Scotland in particular.

Born in Motherwell and raised in the Borders, Chris graduated from Edinburgh Royal High School and read History at Edinburgh University. One could say he is a born historian. There is very little in life, of which Chris

---

[1] This is the text of the *laudatio*, delivered by the German Consul General, Wolfgang Mössinger, on the occasion of the conferral of the Officer's Cross of the Order of Merit of the Federal Republic of Germany on Professor Christopher Harvie, at Summerhall, Edinburgh on 12 March 2012.

could not tell you its history. And he is also a born teacher: he has taught at Edinburgh University and then at the Open University, where he was instrumental in consolidating and expanding the History Department.

In 1980, he took a decision that changed his life and that of his wife Virginia: he accepted a call to become Professor of British and Irish Studies at Tübingen University. There, he managed to develop and extend the range of the English Department at the University by opening it for inter-disciplinary study and research. However, he never lost sight of his native Scotland. The logical consequence of this was that he developed a curriculum that included economics and – most importantly – regional studies. He built up an enormous network of connections from Tübingen via Aberystwyth in Wales to Edinburgh. Only recently, he lectured in the United Arab Emirates, I presume on regionalism.

He has always put this network to good use for his students who benefited from exchanges, seminars and many other opportunities to widen their horizons. Proof of that dedication is the fact that many of his former students from Tübingen are now here in Scotland working, for example, as lecturers or as parliamentary assistants. I am delighted to welcome Professor Engler, the Principal of Tübingen University, who will elaborate on this later. So, to cut a long story short (and it would be a long story, if we told you all his achievements during his time in Tübingen which is, by the way, not over yet: there are still PhD candidates in Tübingen tutored by Chris), I would like to continue by telling you a little about my personal experience of Chris.

When I met Chris for the first time, he was already a regional MSP for Mid Scotland and Fife, having stood as an SNP candidate in Kirkcaldy. We met at the members' restaurant in the Scottish Parliament at a lunch that Chris hosted for the then Minister for Science and Universities of Baden-Württemberg, Professor Peter Frankenberg. This first meeting was very typical for Chris's role in the Scottish Parliament. He was at one time (after his term in Parliament) dubbed by one critic as 'the Member for the Düsseldorf constituency'. This is of course deeply unfair, because Düsseldorf is in Northrhine Westphalia and, geographically as well as politically, very far removed from Tübingen. But what this critic inadvertently highlighted was that Chris widened the Parliament's horizon by looking for examples of good practice not only in Anglophone countries with a strong Scottish diaspora, but also elsewhere, and particularly in Germany.

A field which lent itself perfectly for this kind of benchmarking, was public transport. Chris, from a very early stage a keen railway enthusiast (he is a life member of the Scottish Railway Preservation Society), sought to bring together decision makers from the public transport sector. He organised the first visit of a Scottish minister to Germany by inviting the then Transport Minister Sarah Boyack to one of his legendary Freudenstadt seminars, where she met officials of Karlsruhe City Council, one of the cities in Germany which has developed an integrated tram, rail and bus system. He invited the manager of the Hohenlohe Eisenbahn to Edinburgh, to present to the Scottish railway community how he managed to revive a derelict local railway in Baden-Württemberg. It is to his credit that some of his fellow MSPs knew more about Germany's transport system than they knew about their own. Chris's knowledge of train and bus timetables is legendary, and if you want to know how to get from Edinburgh to Peebles or to Melrose by public transport, don't consult the internet: ask Chris. That is far more reliable and more pleasant.

A word about the Freudenstadt seminars. Freudenstadt (literally translated: 'town of joy') is a town in the middle of the Black Forest, a politcally motivated foundation by the Duke of Württemberg in the late 1500s to secure the benefits of mining in that area bordering on the territory of a much bigger enemy, the Habsburgs. (Don't draw too many conclusions from similarities with the Borders: it is all pure coincidence!). Every summer, for over 20 years, Chris and Paddy Bort, a lecturer at Edinburgh University and graduate of Tübingen, have convened an international gathering of regional politics enthusiasts there. They discuss similarities and differences between the UK, Germany and other countries with multi-layer governments. I had the honour to attend once (only once) and was impressed by the variety of subjects covered over a weekend. Admittedly, the venue is so secluded in the Forest, that you can't do much else than discussing politics – apart from having walks in the Forest, which is, in Chris's case, not mutually exclusive. It is thanks to Chris that people with a heavy workload and a full diary are persuaded to take the time to go to Freudenstadt. I see some of the 'Freudies' here today. I am sure they can confirm that the time there is always well spent: replenishing soul and mind and, as far as I remember, due to the 'Stadtfest', plenty of replenishing the body as well.

Constantly moving between Scotland and Germany, Chris Harvie has built bridges between our countries for over 30 years, bridges over which countless students and fellow researchers have walked and which have brought us closer to each other. It is, therefore, more than fitting that the Federal Republic of Germany recognises Chris's achievements. I quote from the document, signed by the President of the Federal Republic of Germany:

> In Anerkennung der um die Bundesrepublik Deutschland erworbenen Verdienste verleihe ich Herrn Prof. em. Christopher Thomas Harvie das Verdienstkreuz Erster Klasse des Verdienstordens der Bundesrepublik Deutschland; Berlin den 3. Februar 2012.

> In recognition of his merits for the Federal Republic of Germany, I bestow upon Prof. em. Christopher Thomas Harvie the Officers' Cross of the Order of Merit of the Federal Republic of Germany; Berlin, 3 February 2012.

It is my honour and pleasure to hand over the Cross to Chris, with my deepest personal gratitude.

Bundesverdienstkreuz o'Clock

Alison Harvie

Dream Harvie scene for a Sunday morning. I am on my way to Scotland.[1] The scenery is maybe not quite as dazzling as that of a few months back – on our trip from Denver to San Francisco – but this is a banker of a journey. East coast, via memories of seven years' schooling in York, three University years in Newcastle and an entire lifetime of visits to the Scottish family.

It is a very special family visit this time. Tomorrow my dad gets awarded the *Bundesverdienstkreuz*. I will confess that my knowledge of the German honours system was (is) scant but – according to wikipedia and any passing German I have been casually dropping this into conversation with – it is quite the thing. Unlike the UK, with our knights, dames and commanders, Germany only has the one state award. Which of course has allowed me to tweak its comparative importance according to how grand I want to sound. I *could* get away with claiming the Prof is being made the German equivalent of Sir Harvie, but in reality it would seem to be on par with an OBE. Important, though awarded to quite a few people every year.

Still – that is not to denigrate the honour. I am *wildly* proud. The invitation (which brilliantly I haven't actually received yet still nevertheless signs off with 'Dr Harvie and his daughter Alison look forward to seeing you there') states that he is receiving this for "services to education and cultural co-operation in Germany, Scotland and the British Isles". Some might call it cultural cooperation, members of the Scottish Parliament would probably remember it as the Honourable Member for Central Scotland and Fife (2007-2011) standing up frequently in the chamber to point out how we might learn something from how Germany tackles XXX (insert current topic of debate).

There's no denying Dad loves Germany. He headed there in 1979 – possibly in a fit of nationalistic pique as, despite his and a certain G Brown's best efforts[2], Scotland had just said no to devolution, and he had been offered his first Professor post at the University of Tübingen. He was already going out with my mother, and family legend has it that his romantic request to her went along the lines of "I've been offered a job in Germany, I'd very much like you to come with me, and for tax purposes it would probably be best if we were married".

People often do threaten to leave countries if politics doesn't go their way, for some reason Paul Daniels in 1997 comes to mind, but Dad stood by his word and wasn't to live permanently in the UK again for almost thirty

---

[1] Originally published as a Blog on 11 March 2012; see <http://evereffervescing.wordpress.com/>

[2] Gordon Brown and Christopher Harvie, *A Voter's Guide to the Scottish Assembly and Why You Should Support It*, Dunfermline: David Watt & Sons, 1979.

Chris Harvie and his daughter Alison at Summerhall, with Bundesverdienstkreuz (March 2012)

years – until politics had not only gone his way but also offered him a seat in the process. In the meantime he set up academic shop in Germany, wrote books, gained honorary professorships from Aberystwyth to Strathclyde (though as yet not the coveted PhD that would allow him to tell dreadful "doctor doctor" jokes), even stood as a local SPD councillor and made a home and a family in Tubingen.

I was born in Germany (all too) nearly thirty years ago. My mum obviously chose to overlook Dad's rather careless style of proposal and agreed to marry him. However, in her classic strong-willed (family trait alert) fashion, she only did so with the caveat that they would always keep a place in London. In a decision that must have made sense to two slightly elderly and possibly sleep-deprived parents I was then sent to primary schools in London and Tubingen *at the same time*. Until I was eleven I merrily swapped back and forth with my Mum every three months between education systems and languages. Primary school in Islington in the mid 1980s consisted of learning an awful lot about the workings of the local Victorian canal system, whilst in Germany I learnt long division two years ahead of my London counterparts, finished school by 12 every day and in the summer spent every afternoon at the local open air swimming pool.

That childhood, and a year spent in Leipzig after a decade of a slightly-less-itinerant education at school and university in the UK, means that my love of the country almost equals my father's. And I love it all the more for recognising him with this gong. To go with it he gets to throw a party and the man has been as busy planning as a prospective bride, to the extent that I threatened to rename him a Bundesverdienstkreuzilla as I was rung for the nth time to discuss potential venues. And so, to quote the invitation I have not yet received, but been copied in on a number of times, a hundred odd of us will gather at "the Summerhall culture centre, formerly the Dick Vet. A delegation from the Bundestag in Berlin will be present and the Consulate will also launch its new Facebook site." Brilliant. A party of German politicans, social media and a venue with a name that would definitely not stand up to SFW googling. News on the other side.

A Scottish Clerisy?

David Walker

Thinkers have been tempted into politics ever since Plato set sail, in the opposite direction to King Agamemnon and the Achaean fleet, for Sicily and the court of royal Dionysus. The despot turned out not to be the philosopher king of Plato's imagining, and his attempt at tutelage ended badly. Thinkers are as attracted by pelf and preferment as the next person, but also want to speak out, which tends to get them into trouble.

So it was 'back from Syracuse?' when Martin Heidegger laid down his Nazi-tainted rectorship of Freiburg University,[1] the Baden-Württemberg neighbour of the University of Tübingen where Chris Harvie has spent such happy and fruitful years. But Heidegger remained in the despot's party for years to come, believing in at least some of the precepts of Hitlerian National Socialism both before and after his short stint as book burner and excluder of Jews.

Philosophers like to say that power, now as then, has a limited appetite for truth, which, so their legend goes, it is they who utter. But thinkers and politics stand in a much less binary relationship than the conventional account implies. Take Plato himself, a serial flirter with power, by all accounts. He had had his fill of politics in Athens, long before he accepted the invitation to Syracuse – yet was tempted again. Political action, it seems, retains its lure for those vocationally wedded to thinking and writing; often the two become the same.

It would be hard to find a less Platonic figure than Chris Harvie: what could be more material and less spiritual than the type of document on which he lavishes so much loving attention, the railway timetable? And yet a large theme in his writing has been what he once called the 'intellectual torso' of Britain, and Scotland too: a belief not just in the power of ideas but of Jungian, archetypal ideas associated with such Harvie favourites as Halford Mackinder and Patrick Geddes, combined with the belief that writing is a species of political action.

Chris's simultaneous life in thought and politics shows how complex the relationship between the two can be – especially when, in his case, it was crowned by a spell as a parliamentarian, being a (to him) surprise beneficiary of Scotland's proportional voting system.

Left-inclined but founder of his own clubs, he is a man hard to pin down. And that is literally so, given his marathon journeying from Swabia to Islington to the Borders and into the depths of Wales, making Machynlleth Junction and Edinburgh's bus depot behind St Andrew Square unwitting sites of Europe-wide political engagement. How, before mobile communications came on

---

[1] See Jürg Altwegg (ed.) *Die Heidegger-Kontroverse*, Frankfurt: Athenäum, 1988

stream, would he have managed to put his time on coaches (St Andrew Square to Galashiels many times and often) to such fruitful use? Would he, like his revered Trollope writing while on horseback,[2] have devised some way of balancing a notebook while bouncing around in the back of the bus?

Chris is hard to place in another sense. This federalist and nationalist and student of the periphery[3] has also penetrated deep within the British establishment; he has flown close to 'the centre of things'. His thesis was examined by Lord Annan and you can hardly get deeper or more central than him.[4] Similarly, the invitation to Chris Harvie to contribute to the official history of the University of Oxford under the editorship of Michael Brock, the warden of Nuffield College, is hardly evidence of marginality,[5] even if that institution was just about to consign itself temporarily to political darkness by refusing Margaret Thatcher her honorary degree.

The Harvie biography also takes in his years of commitment to a principal example of all-British modernisation in Wilsonian mode, the Open University.[6] It is true that, despite its distinction and research excellence, the OU still struggles to find its identity and relationship to mainstream higher education, but it was not as if Chris was teaching in a … polytechnic. Yet his attachment to uncomfortable, interstitial figures (from Thomas Carlyle to Thomas Nairn) showed a certain edginess, which took dramatic form in 1980 with the beginning of self-exile in Swabia.

Politically, Chris's journey looks straightforward enough, from a Labour commitment to modernisation and social enlightenment to the realisation of the same values but within the carapace of an independent Scottish state. But where does his dislike of cultural modernity fit or his eagerness to rub shoulders with Tories such as Allan Massie, or his thudding disappointment, now with the standards and horizons of the metropolis, now with the standards and horizons of the Athens of the North?

The Republican elections adviser David Frum put down a new book from his erstwhile Republican soul mate David Stockman saying "as an insight into the gloomy mindset that overtakes you in older age, it's a valuable warning to those still middle-aged that once we lose our faith in the future, it's time to stop talking about politics in public."[7] Chris, it has to be said, has a lot of

---

[2] Anthony Trollope, An Autobiography, Oxford: Oxford University Press (Oxford World Classics), 2008, p.102.

[3] See Christopher Harvie, A Floating Commonwealth: Politics, Culture, and Technology on Britain's Atlantic Coast, 1860-1930, Oxford: Oxford University Press, 2008

[4] See Noel Annan, Our Age: Portrait of a Generation, London: Weidenfeld and Nicolson, 1990.

[5] See M.G. Brock and M.C. Courthoys (eds), The History of the University of Oxford, Vol. VI, Part 1, Oxford: Oxford University Press, 1997.

[6] See Jeremy Tunstall, The Open University Opens, London: Routledge & Kegan Paul, 1973.

[7] Financial Times, 6/7 April 2013.

faith in the past's futures, but little in how they turned out and less in what beckons now. "In 1979," he wrote longingly,

> Scotland still had 30 per cent of GDP in manufacturing instead of today's 12 per cent, the bounty of the oil, literate newspapers with three times today's circulations, a visual culture which produced *The Cheviot* (1973) and *Local Hero* (1983). Teachers saw their schools as missions; finance could be trusted; a common conversation hadn't yielded to the jabber of 'social media' and 'reality TV'; sport had talent and community, not silly money; there were high streets, not malls.[8]

So, the historian becomes a rueful recounter of the paths not taken. A *Floating Commonwealth* and much subsequent writing registers failure – the failure of Scotland's capitalists to anticipate trends in technology, work organisation and markets; the failure of policy makers, in Edinburgh no less than London, to spy out success and emulate it, especially in federal West Germany.

Some thinkers have become courtiers, the Syracuse option, joining the entourage of a big man, and seeking to shape him. Not all advisers are close in. Some write their books and pamphlets in buoyant expectation that the prince will pick them up. Others penetrate the inner sanctum and acquire the status of guru. For all the weakness of Toryism in Scotland, we have several rightwing examples of professorial dabbling in advice. They include, at a distance, Norman Gash, supplier of historical identity to a Tory party ever anxious to have historians clothe its naked protection of the interest of the rich and powerful in talk of a 'conservative tradition'. There is Norman Stone, for a while Mrs Thatcher's in-house intellectual, and the now deflated figure of Niall Ferguson – a particularly dark *bête noir* for Chris Harvie.

Perhaps in some alternative past future, Chris might have had some analogous role had Gordon Brown in power been more like the radical Scotsman he had been, especially when collaborating with Chris.[9] Instead of his vapid efforts to brand Britishness by encouraging householders to put out a flag,[10] the Harvian Brown might have continued thinking about a federal solution for the UK.

---

[8] Christopher Harvie, 'Comment: impact of the 1979 devolution referendum', *The Scotsman*, 8 May 2013; <www.scotsman.com/the-scotsman/opinion/comment/comment-impact-of-the-1979-devolution-referendum-1-2921522> .

[9] See Gordon Brown and Christopher Harvie, *A Voters' Guide to the Scottish Assembly*, Dunfermline: David Watt & Sons, 1979.

[10] Polly Toynbee and David Walker, *The Verdict: Did Labour Change Britain?*, London: Granta, 2010.

Chris has thought long and hard about the representation of politics[11] (and the hinges of political change).[12] Having diagnosed 'weakness of British political imagination' might he have filled the gap, either by himself supplying that turnkey work of political fiction that allowed the play of possibilities that conventional political action could never accommodate? Or might he himself have led the way, mounted the podium and spoken the words. But which words? The fate of politicians, as Chris Harvie realised long ago, may be repetition, "endlessly repeating some proposition in 'graspable' terms."[13] Or, as an alternative to clarity, woolliness.

That is often turned into a criticism, as if ambiguity had neither its uses nor justification. Max Weber decreed the vocation of politics was about combining a doctrine of ends with pliability; he omitted the necessity of opacity. Democratic politics – in societies where interests are multiple and competing (all of them?) – requires coding, displays of the linguistic trick of not quite saying one thing in order to prevent the division that happens when names are named.

Describing Lockerbie as a one-horse or one-supermarket town may have been factually accurate but pejorative labels make for a story. This intrepid phrasemaker started attracting attention in a chamber where colourful language was rarely spoken. Later, he said ruefully:

> A Carlyleian social-critical riff before a Holyrood committee studying tourism – flaying Tescotowns, loutish yoof, booze alleys – got me simultaneously on the front-pages of the *Sun* and the *Daily Record*, fully clothed and not a footballer. Not bad going.[14]

That was the trouble. Even in his heyday, the sage of Ecclefechan would not have made much of a parliamentarian. And that is not just because of media superficiality. Political speech is purposeful: it is action in words, in the style of Austin and Skinner. You say something to create an impression. Ill-dressed or boozing youth would be ready targets for political speech engendering reform in housing or training or job opportunities or, on the other side of politics, the construction of prisons and employment of more police officers. Carlyleian riffs from an SNP member had implications – not least about the Scotland the nationalists wanted to set free. Not that Chris Harvie lacked

[11] See Christopher Harvie, *The Centre of Things: Political Fiction from Disraeli to the Present*, London: Unwin & Hyman, 1991

[12] See Christopher Harvie, *The Lights of Liberalism: University Liberals and the Challenge of Democracy 1860-86*, London: Allen Lane, 1976.

[13] Christopher Harvie, *The Centre of Things*, p.5.

[14] Christopher Harvie, 'Comment is free?', *Scottish Review*, issue 68 (2008); <www.scottishreview.net/ChrisHarvie68.shtml>.

such a vision, of possibility and individual (and class) emancipation.[15] But the words expressed by the supporter of a governing party carry weight of a kind no academic work nor even controversial opinionating in pamphlet or website could ever.

His social criticism won admirers, understandably from the right:

> Set amongst the boring suits and the career politicians, desperate always to suck up to the party bosses by never straying from the uncontroversial, Chris Harvie may well appear to be an eccentric. There used to be a place in public life for such individuals, and politics, especially, was all the better for their presence.[16]

But Chris the controversialist also won critics. 'Harvie is a great man,' opined Anthony Barnett of OpenDemocracy,

> who unlike many political commentators on the left is also a formidable academic and has gone into politics as well. I have huge respect for this amazing three-fold combination. But in this case it seems to have brought together the notorious self-indulgence of politicians with the verbosity of a high intellectual and the petulance of a free-lance journalist.[17]

What is the balance between influence and intervention, between essay writing and blogging and 'physical' political action? Chris had discussed how the 'lights of Liberalism' had been warned not to rush into the arena of politics themselves, but "rather to work inwardly upon the predominant force in our politics – the great middle class – and to cure its spirit."[18] Chris has never given up on spiritual cures and, leaving his representative career till late in life, cannot be accused of rushing.

In any taxonomy of the relationships of thought and power / professional writers and politics, a special place should be reserved for those who made or tried to make their way in elective politics. Whispering in Dionysus' or Margaret Thatcher's ear is one thing; standing on the hustings, knocking

---

[15] Jimmy Reid, Christopher Harvie and Alasdair Gray, 'Scottish independence? No fear', openDemocracy, 30 November 2006, <www.opendemocracy.net/globalization-institutions_government/scottish_independence_4141.jsp>.

[16] Alan Cochrane, 'Christopher Harvie is the odd man out' The Daily Telegraph, 28 February 2008, <www.telegraph.co.uk/comment/columnists/alancochrane /3555519/ Christopher-Harvie-is-the-odd-man-out.html>.

[17] Quoted in Christopher Harvie, 'Comment is Free/', Scottish Review.

[18] Matthew Arnold, 'The Nadir of Liberalism' (1886), quoted in Christopher Harvie, The Lights of Liberalism, p.9.

on doors and soliciting votes is something else. The political life is a play of circumstance: opportunities arise and demand a response. So Chris Harvie became a candidate for the Scottish Parliament that he had agitated and campaigned for – in company with, among others, Gordon Brown. Canvassing the schemes of the 'Lang Toun' and getting rain dashed on the Esplanade is a lot harder than specially advising a minister. So professors and writers can become the people's choice, and sojourn in legislative halls, among them our dear Chris.

He joined the band of legislators who can be considered thinkers and intellectuals, a small crew, before and after the presence in the Westminster parliament of the wartime generation marked by Crosland and Jenkins and, on the Tory side, by Ian Gilmour and Ian Macleod. Not many people had needed to vote for Arthur Balfour – his elections were more a matter of influence and tradition. But this Scots grandee offers a reference point, not because he combined philosophical musing with repression of the Irish, but because his sustaining intellectual life appeared to have very little to do with his service in the House of Commons or ministerial jobs.

Some have viewed parliament as a means of realising the objects of their research – a characteristic (and a delusion?) more evident on the left. Take TH Marshall, the sociologist, who stood as a Labour candidate for the safe Conservative constituency of Farnham in Surrey at the general election of 1922, in order to exemplify his interests in citizenship and class. Beaten, he returned to Cambridge knowing (says Chelly Halsey) he was not suited to a career as a politician, but intent on elucidating his political interests in his studies.[19]

Before him, Mill's account of his brief spell as the people's choice for the Westminster constituency is edgy and unexuberant. He entered the lobby for unpopular causes but it is hard to reconcile his experience, and rejection by the voters in favour of a Tory, with the unbounded confidence of his aphorism "if you can inform the passion of the multitude against the self-interest of a few, you have the right to await the outcome with confidence."[20]

Thinkers have made the political grade, among the Scots John P Mackintosh who, before his early death, split time between the Westminster parliament and the lecture halls of the University of Edinburgh, though perhaps more to the advantage of the latter than the former. The political life does not usually repay thought, because thought produces harsh judgements of futility – the aphorism from Enoch Powell about the universal end of political careers might outlast memories of his racism. Rare are the professors who have gone in, prospered as parliamentarians (not the same as being preferred

---

[19] A.H. Halsey, A History of Sociology in Britain, Oxford: Oxford University Press, 2004, p.50.

[20] Quoted in Harold Lasky, 'Foreword', in J.S. Mill, Autobiography, Oxford: Oxford University Press, 1924, p.xv.

as ministers), and come out the other end better political scientists – Tony Wright stands out.[21]

And then, again, there stands the academic *manqué* Gordon Brown, a Chris Harvie interlocutor for many years. How could (a question for Brown's erstwhile political friends) this thinker, this explorer of ideas become the barren doctrinaire of his chancellorship, and the mindless prime minister of his political decline?

Chris's tenure as a list member for Fife was, his friends and admirers would admit, relatively undistinguished. He graced some interesting committee sessions and livened the lives of note takers and journalists (see above) but, he would be the first to admit, did not connect with the vital pulse of his party or the parliament.

Much is made, these days, of the 'professionalisation of politics' – the growing proportion of members of legislatures, notably the Westminster House of Commons, who have no vocational experience outside politics itself. The phenomenon is not new – neither Gladstone nor Palmerston, among the Victorian political giants, had ever done anything but politics, for all Gladstone's dabbling with the church. Professional politicians generally understand the game – the interplay of media, interest, parliamentary procedure and (often a long way down the list) policy.

In Hegelian terms, the world spirit has fetched up at Holyrood, leaving Chris nicely situated on history's side. But you would not infer victory from his writings, both during and after his service as a Scottish National Party member – he is a *Kulturpessimist*, except when talking and writing about transport, especially travel in Germany – *der Eisenbahnoptimist*.

One reason might be a nagging sense that statehood for Scotland and the political triumph of Nationalism may not be the emancipation he might once have wished. In his study of the Victorian liberal reformers, he concludes they got it wrong. The people let them down. "They did not anticipate that a revived national homogeneity would provide the matrix for the politics of economic manipulation, welfare and class."[22] Translate that into the twenty-first century: can revived nationhood address environmental rot, capitalist doziness and 'these islands' insularity? Chris's period as MSP gave few signs the answer could be affirmative.

Another may be that Chris is a Coleridgean. He came of an educational-political-cultural time when – the Open University its institutional expression – Leavisite beliefs were still held: cultural improvement could and must go hand in hand with political emancipation and material progress. Remember his description of a clerisy. Distributed throughout the country these resident guardians and instructors would

---

[21] See Tony Wright, *Doing Politics*, London: Biteback, 2012.

[22] Christopher Harvie, *The Lights of Liberalism*, p.13.

preserve stores and guard the treasures of past civilization, and thus to bind the present with the past; to perfect and add to the same, and thus to connect the present with the future; but especially to diffuse through the whole community that quantity and quality of knowledge … and to secure for the nation, if not a superiority over the neighbouring states, yet an equality at least, in that character of general civilization, which equally with, or rather more than, fleets, armies, and revenue, forms the ground of its defensive and offensive power.[23]

Coleridge democratised, a Scottish clerisy: how magnificent has been that Chris Harvie ambition, and how far it is yet from realisation.

---

[23] S T Coleridge, quoted in Jonathan Bate, 'Introduction', in Jonathan Bate (ed.), *The Public Value of the Humanities*, London: Bloomsbury Academic, 2010, p.12

The Material and the Moral: Chris Harvie on Culture

Tom Hubbard

Soon after the sudden death of Duncan Glen, *The Scotsman* e-mailed me to commission an obituary. He had been poet, editor, literary scholar, publisher, graphic designer and university teacher; at his funeral I met his brother-in-law who was aware of him as none of these, but simply as a brother-in-law. For the purpose of a clinching descriptor, how could I possibly sum up Duncan Glen? Not easy. Then I hit on it: he was a cultural worker. We had social workers (I am married to one), so surely we had cultural workers. Glen's last book arrived at his home on the day of his fatal stroke: he never handled the final product to which – as he had told me only a month or so before – he was eagerly looking forward.

This monograph, on the Kirkcaldy architect William Williamson, was later invoked in the town's Beveridge Suite, at a public meeting to discuss the uncertain future of the former Station Hotel building. Glen's celebrant was Chris Harvie MSP. It was a poignant moment: Harvie had never met Glen, but his widow Margaret was in the audience, and I was glad to have the opportunity to make the introductions.

Harvie on Glen on Williamson came to mind when, for this essay, I re-read Harvie's *Cultural Weapons: Scotland and Survival in a New Europe* (1992), and came upon his account of a visit to the Drachenburg, a nineteenth-century extravaganza high above the Rhine. It is off one of the stops on the rack-railway that climbs up from Königswinter to the summit of Byron's "castled crag of Drachenfels" among the Siebengebirge. Harvie evokes the Drachenburg as "like a Victorian station hotel (!) transplanted by a Wagnerian magician from, say, Middlesbrough." The mockery is affectionate, wistful even. Kitsch the Drachenburg may be, but Harvie takes us through its melancholy vicissitudes beyond the post-unification Nibelungen-obsessed 1870s into the Hitler years, the building's share of the consequent débâcle, and its dubious restoration thereafter. He speculates on the Drachenburg's possible future as a museum of *Gründerzeit* (= "Victorian") architecture, and concludes: "Meanwhile Herr Ehnes [who showed him round] remains Castellan, cropping the lawn ecologically with his flock of sheep, shooing them off the parterres and keeping the roof watertight."[1]

He continues, in like lyrical vein, to contrast German and Welsh/Scottish/English attitudes to the "great houses" while also citing Hermann Muthesius

---

[1] Christopher Harvie, *Cultural Weapons: Scotland and Survival in a New Europe* (Determinations) Edinburgh: Polygon 1992: pp.50-52.

as an advocate of the more modest English country-house as a model for German architects to follow

> for an unobtrusive sense of well-being and social solidarity. Scarcely a German town is without its suburb of Anglo-German villas, half timbered or harled, with details out of Rennie Mackintosh or Baillie Scott.[2]

In Scotland today, academic specialisation is based on the latter-day "one thing needful", which may explain why we have many little-boxy academics and few public intellectuals. I recently had a book proposal rejected by Glasgow University-based editors on the grounds that it was too "generalist" for their series.[3] I was not surprised at the rejection, given that "generalism" has become no more than a culturally-correct mantra within Scottish literary academic comfort zones, a concept worthy (oh so worthy) of labial tribute but not of practical support.

So we are not supposed to expect a political/economic historian (Chris Harvie) to write knowledgeably and eloquently on architecture. Two of our man's cultural heroes – John Ruskin and Patrick Geddes – found themselves in receipt of similar pusillanimity. How dare Ruskin, an art critic, venture into economics with his *Unto this Last*![4] Then there was that presumptuous Geddes, a botanist, straying into sociology, street theatre, cultural journalism, his "city design" notions and the Lord knows what else. To which Geddes would reply that "watertight compartments are useful only to a sinking ship".[5] All this, then, amounts to much of the intellectual pedigree of the annual Freudenstadt colloquia run by Chris Harvie and Paddy Bort: these weekends in the Black Forest bring together academics, journalists, creative artists and others from across the subject spectrum, leading to collaborations that are unforeseen and would not otherwise happen.

It should not be surprising, then, if Geddes's 1884 pamphlet, *John Ruskin, Economist*, reads at times like an overture to both Geddes's own activism and that of Chris Harvie. The proto-Harviesque motifs are there: the unselfconscious coalescing of apparently diverse disciplines, the wit at the expense of received opinion (notably those economic doctrines which exclude human values), the exhilarating cheek of it all. Geddes will have no

---

[2] *Ibid.*, p.53.

[3] It was to be a literary-historical survey of 'wandering Scots' among our authors, as also in the subject-matter of their work, from the middle ages to the present.

[4] From his Kirkcaldy constituency office, Harvie MSP cheerfully dished out copies of a strip cartoon version of Ruskin's thesis that what we called "wealth" was really "illth".

[5] Quoted in Hugh MacDiarmid, *The Company I've Kept*, London: Hutchinson, 1966, p.83.

truck with conventional dismissals of Ruskin as an airy-fairy arty-farty; to him, Ruskin combines hard-headed economic analysis with sturdy ethical commitment.

Geddes's Ruskinian call for "that union of material and moral order which is the task and problem of life"[6] finds an echo in his friend Hugh MacDiarmid's "A' that's material and moral - / And oor new state descried".[7] It is in this spirit that Harvie, in the course of his own analysis of Scotland's economic "illth", breaks into a deeply moving appreciation of Brahms's German Requiem and Bruckner's Te Deum.[8] The quest for the integrative vision, the seamless garment: we can trace this through Ruskin, Geddes and MacDiarmid to Chris Harvie.

Indeed, much in Harvie's thought and practice is underpinned by his scholarly work on the nineteenth century in a general sense. His The Centre of Things (1991) is his most sustained encounter with the Victorian "sages", notably Carlyle, and the "social-problem" novels of the 1840s and ensuing decades (e.g. Disraeli's Sybil, Kingsley's Alton Locke, George Eliot's Felix Holt, the Radical), right up to H.G. Wells and beyond. The book investigates territory similar to that of Raymond Williams's Culture and Society 1780-1950 (1958), but owes much to Harvie's own pedagogic activity with the Open University, prior to his transfer to Tübingen. Williams posited an antithesis central to the long Romantic-cum-Victorian period: the mechanical versus the organic. Carlyle's strictures on cash-payment as society's sole nexus, and on "mechanical" mindsets, feed into Harvie's own polemics against the reductivism of our own times. Ruskin had developed Carlyle's thinking in relation to the visual arts, suspicious as he was of mathematical measurement as against trusting to organic (as it were) coordination of eye, hand and instinct – in a word, artistry. (This would go back even earlier than Carlyle, to Blake's Urizen dourly clasping his rulers and dividers.)

However, Ruskin was also the exponent of an alternative but practical economics, and Harvie echoes Geddes's respect for the forensic mind behind Unto this Last. An early Harvie article on Kipling[9] takes the story forward in a direction that is crucial to our man's later activism: transport, and its contexts both technological and ideological. This relates intimately to his cultural concerns, given his tacit awareness that good public transport and computer technology can make possible many books, articles and conferences (such as Freudenstadt) that would not otherwise happen, or

[6] Patrick Geddes: John Ruskin, Economist. (The Round Table series.) Edinburgh: William Brown, 1884, p.43.

[7] Hugh MacDiarmid, Complete Poems 1920-1976. 2 vols., London: Martin Brian & O'Keeffe, 1978, p.325.

[8] Christopher Harvie, Mending Scotland: Essays in Economic Regionalism (Discussions series), Glendaruel: Argyll Publishing, 2004, pp.57-58.

[9] Christopher Harvie, "'The Sons of Martha": Technology, Transport, and Rudyard Kipling', Victorian Studies, 20 (3) (Spring 1977), pp.269-282.

that at least would make greater demands on time, labour and money. Along certain lines discussed above, Carlyle and Ruskin are continued by William Morris, but there is a strong implication, in Harvie's Kipling essay, that with Morris – but not with Ruskin – a dissociation of sensibility has set in. On the one hand, Morris, more of a "mediaevalist" than Ruskin, takes arts-and-crafts into non-industrial (pre-industrial?) utopianism; on the other hand, it is left to the imaginative but hard-nosed Kipling to assert machine technology (and technocracy) against a debilitated aestheticism. It is as if the necessary unity of the "material" and the "moral" has come unstuck.

This is what one can read between (as well as along) the lines of the essay on Kipling. It may seem curious that Harvie, given his ideological leanings, can appreciate Kipling's unlovely insights more respectfully (if guardedly) than those of his fellow-socialist Morris. However, let us contemplate this: the dissociation of sensibility can be grotesquely (if flippantly) brought into focus if we consider that it never occurred to the soi-disant "socialist" GDR authorities to decorate their side of the Berlin Wall with Morris designs.

Harvie cannot accept a Morris-like dismissal of technology, given his strong support for public transport and his admitted nerditude when it comes to trams, trains and timetables. His knowledge of the integrated transportation system of Baden-Württemberg is legendary, especially to those of us who are regulars at the Freudenstadt weekends. When he was MSP for Central Scotland and Fife from 2007 to 2011 – during which period I was one of his constituents – he expressed his enthusiasm for a reopening of the railway between Thornton and Levenmouth, via the now-melancholy ghost of a station at Windygates (once convenient for the Cameron Brig hospital and distillery – yes, you read that juxtaposition right). As a local, I was impressed by his detailed knowledge of Fifeana that I had taken for granted.

His campaigning for an improved infrastructure for our area would slide effortlessly to and from the county's (and his) cultural concerns (see Kirkcaldy's Station Hotel and local architect Williamson, above), on which he elaborated in his leading article, "Reimagining Fife", for the new online magazine *The Pathhead Review*.[10] This piece grew out of a talk which Harvie gave to the Fife WEA, and portions of it are worked into his book *Broonland* (2010). Its expansive treatment of Adam Smith and other writers and intellectuals of south Fife origin curiously echoed Richard Demarco's guest lecture, in 1995, at the then Fife College, just across the road from St Bryce Kirk, the venue for the Harvie talk.[11] A chronically-provincial and inwardly-

---

[10] Christopher Harvie, 'Reimagining Fife', *The Pathhead Review*, issue 1 (Spring 2011), pp.7-12. http://www.scribd.com/doc/52992764/Pathhead-Review or http://www.ravenscraigpress.co.uk/ and click on the link indicated.

[11] Richard Demarco, 'Kunst = Kapital, Art = Wealth', reprinted in part in *Fringe of Gold: the Fife Anthology*, edited by Duncan Glen and Tom Hubbard, Edinburgh: Birlinn 2008, pp.78-79.

parochial Kirkcaldy needed as much of this galvanising as it could get: between them, Demarco and Harvie reminded us of the European reach of Fife culture and history.

Harvie has a knack of making plausible connections between diverse coastal areas that would tend to be dismissed as belonging to the sticks. He will argue that they can be livelier, intellectually and spiritually, than vast centres such as London (which he has called a "gilded coffin"). To Harvie, *en province* can be more promising, more exciting, than *la métropole*. Given his readiness to salute the Kipling devil for having many of the best tunes, I suspect he would go along with Kipling's remark, from the turn of the nineteenth century, that "London is egotistical, and the world for her ends with the four-mile cab radius. There is no provincialism like the provincialism of London."[12]

Through his utterances on coastal areas that have more in common with each other than with their respective capital cities (be they London, Dublin or Edinburgh), Harvie offers us latter-day examples of the Ruskinian-Geddesian "union of the material and the moral order". The subject has come up in informal discussions at his former Kirkcaldy constituency office, but he develops it in print in an essay for the Cork University Press journal *The Irish Review*.[13] At the heart of Harvie's regionalism – that central concept of the Freudenstadt meetings – is a solidarity of those very regions and their capacity to learn from each other. Harvie's *Irish Review* essay links John Hewitt, Naomi Mitchison, Patrick Geddes, Walt Whitman (his "Sea-Drift" as germane to international and coastal connections), Joyce Cary, Arnold's "Sea of Faith", Adam Smith (on Mediterranean shipping "breaking out into the Atlantic") – the whole essay, in its veritable cascading of references, again recalls Richard Demarco in full flow (literally), not least in the latter's "expeditions" between "the Hebrides and the Cyclades".

When I showed this essay to the sculptor Kenny Munro, he remarked that it brought together so many motifs from his own intellectual and creative career. Munro, now based in Kinghorn – just south of Kirkcaldy, with splendid views across the Forth estuary – has himself been engaged with coastal projects linking Fife with other parts of the world, as documented in his own essay in *The Pathhead Review*, coming as it did not long after Harvie's piece in the same periodical.[14] It is here, however, that we come to an influence which does not feature in Harvie's *Weltanschauung*, and it is more than a

---

[12] Rudyard Kipling, *Letters of Travel (1892-1913)*, Paris: Nelson's Continental Library Edition, n.d., p.52.

[13] Christopher Harvie, 'Garron Top to Caer Gybi: Images of the Inland Sea', *The Irish Review*, no.19 (Spring–Summer 1996), pp.44-61.

[14] Kenny Munro, 'Discovering Myself in Fife: the Creative Energy of a Place Attracts'. *The Pathhead Review*, issue 1 (Spring 2011), pp.28-36. http://www.scribd.com/doc/52992764/Pathhead-Review or http://www.ravenscraigpress.co.uk/ and click on the link indicated.

little odd that it does not. Munro owes much to the German artist and "social sculptor" Joseph Beuys (1921-86), who had previously made an impact on Munro's friend and mentor George Wyllie (1921-2012) whose own Fife coastal connections were featured in the Aberdour Festival of 2011. The following statement by Munro, one would think, seems to accord with much of the foregoing account of Harvie's cultural concerns:

> Through research I've drawn comparisons between Beuys's innovative work and philosophy with the pioneering activities of the Scots polymath Patrick Geddes (1854-1932), whose international efforts examine the equilibrium within communities. In other words the relationship between FOLK-WORK-PLACE, the components within every society, urban or rural. It is interesting to realise that although Geddes and Beuys were a generation apart, they both were influenced by the philosophies of [Rudolf] Steiner and Goethe and recognised the value of the arts as a fundamental form of energy which can motivate all peoples in a constructive way, and to enhance quality of life in every sphere. The value of extending their philosophies cannot be overstated.[15]

Harvie's *Cultural Weapons* (1992) dates from a time when its author was well-settled in Tübingen, and the book revolves around his experience of living in a newly-unified Germany in the wake of the fall of the Wall. Beuys had been a major force in cultural, political and ecological debate in postwar Germany, but one suspects that Harvie had been put off by perceived whiffs of cultishness and charlatanry. I do not know this for certain, and Harvie may have changed his position over the past two decades. In the 1992 book, however, he has this: "A little of Joseph Beuys goes a long way".[16] Sure, it is possible to have too much of, say, the likening of yellow light-bulbs to lemons, but there is a lot more to Beuys than apparent gimmickry. Chris Harvie could do well to take another look. What is Freudenstadt but a form of Beuysian "social sculpture", bringing together its luminaries from diverse fields? The Open University veteran, one would have thought, actually has much in common with the man who, with Heinrich Böll (together, later, with others such as Mary Robinson), founded and developed the "Free International University"; witness this, from its 1972 manifesto:

> Whereas the specialist's insulated point of view places the arts and other kinds of work in sharp opposition, it is in fact

---

[15] Kenny Munro, 'Testimonies', *Cencrastus*, issue 80 (Joseph Beuys in Scotland), (Spring 2005), p.31.

[16] Christopher Harvie, *Cultural Weapons*, p.69.

crucial that the structural, formal and thematic problems of the various work processes should be constantly compared with one another.[17]

This surely continues the Ruskinian-Geddesian "union of material and moral", and indeed a comparative study of the F.I.U. with Geddes's proposals for a more-than-university at Scotland's former capital, Dunfermline (*City Development*, 1904) would yield much to be acted upon: Geddes's book, in effect, could form the basis of a localised, regionalised case study of an ethos not dissimilar to that of the F.I.U. More generally, Kenny Munro's comparison of Geddes and Beuys more than hints at potential wealth (in the Ruskinian sense of the word) for Scotland's intellectual discourse and social practice. One suspects that this could prove enharmonic with the multifarious activities of Chris Harvie.

A decade ago, in the course of an article on Richard Demarco, I wrote:

> It was in Northern Ireland – a periphery only too familiar with man-fragmented – that Beuys found his image of integration. [...] There exists dramatic footage of Beuys striding across the Giant's Causeway, its interlocking hexagons so palpable a metaphor for the unity-in-diversity informing the F.I.U. and its Demarco outposts.[18]

It is the coastal vision again, as intuited by Chris Harvie and Kenny Munro. But Beuys had also enjoyed a strong cultural relationship with a part of Europe far from any coastline, a part equally (if not more) familiar to Chris Harvie. Beuys's installation *Das Kapital Raum 1970-1977* deals with Celtic migration, by way of his knowledge of the lower Rhine region and his experience of working in Scotland during the 1970s. In Basel, aware of the historic presence of Scottish and Irish monks in mainland Europe, he added new rituals to the work. "Not far from there [Basel]", writes Christa Lerm-Hayes,

> places of insular religious mission are located. Perhaps it is no coincidence that Beuys installed *Das Kapital* at Schaffhausen within the geographical triangle of Neuchâtel or La Tène, Hallstatt and St Gallen, where the monks had returned to the roots of their own culture, enriched by Christianity. Beuys followed their lead.[19]

---

[17] Quoted in Caroline Tisdall, *Joseph Beuys*. London: Thames and Hudson, 1979, p.278.

[18] Tom Hubbard, 'The Road to Nowhere', *The Scottish Review*, no. 22 (Summer 2000), pp.75-82.

[19] Christa Lerm-Hayes, 'Migration in Beuys' Work and Joyce's Nomadic Language'. AICA, Derry 20.9.1997; Ulster Museum, Belfast 19.11.1997. Photocopy of a document

In conversation, Chris Harvie has spoken to me of that north-Swiss area which is to the south of Baden-Württemberg; the first time was when he gave me directions (by rail of course) from Tübingen to Schaffhausen, where I wanted to spend the free day following my 1990 guest lecture at his campus. It was clear to me then that Harvie identified the route as marking a broad but distinct transnational region – indeed one at the geographical heart of Europe: "It's the area," he pointed out, "between the sources of the Danube and the Rhine."[20]

The Scottish monks have been succeeded by more recent migrations of their compatriots, not least Harvie himself in Tübingen, Patrick Geddes's Scots College at Montpellier, and those of us who have gone out to teach Scottish studies at universities in Lyon, Grenoble and Lausanne, as well as at other mainland European locations. The results of these energies need to be better known in Scotland itself, which can only too easily become locked within jealously incestuous conventicles – the "small country" syndrome if you like.

Against all that – and "small country" could also include the spectacularly insular United Kingdom of South-East England (the essence of Tom Nairn's "Ukania"?) – Harvie opts to document the work of the "small platoons", and here he is talking about a different kind of smallness – as opposed, say, to David Cameron's "Big Society" vapourings. Harvie has argued that during the period between the two Scottish home rule referenda (1979-1997) it was certain cultural groupings – innovative, committed, but as often as not ill-funded, informal and ad hoc – which kept us going during the dark days. A political future was being shaped by a cultural present.

Chris Harvie and I first met during 1984, in the Scottish Poetry Library, an entity which at that time was new but with a low life-expectancy. The arts were skint (as, indeed, they are again – as if it were ever otherwise …). One of his first questions to me was if I were related to the post-war Labour MP for Kirkcaldy Burghs; he had recently written about my grandfather's 1944 by-election victory, in the course of a scholarly article on Labour in Scotland during World War II.[21] As we discussed shared international interests and an academic overlap as far as Victorian studies were concerned, a rapport was inevitable. It is that last field of interest which might take us to a fitting conclusion. As always, the questioner of Scottish received opinion and the literary canons that formulate around such, Chris Harvie has argued that the Kailyard "school" of fiction, usually glibly dismissed as nothing more than sentimental tosh, was an integral part of a movement towards literary

---

in the Archive of the Demarco European Art Foundation, 1997, p.2.

[20] It is also, interestingly, an area well known to Ruskin, whose verbal evocations of the Rhine Falls at Schaffhausen match Turner's visual equivalents of that haunt of the [post-] Romantics.

[21] Christopher Harvie, 'Labour in Scotland during the Second World War', *The Historical Journal*, 26 (4), 1983, pp.921-944; p.934.

regionalism. This included work by a good number of challenging writers from the peripheries – men such as Bedfordshire's Mark Rutherford, Arnold Bennett of the "Five Towns", and Ulster's George Birmingham.

> [T]he regional novel enabled middlebrow writers to put across reformist messages to a large readership. Its assumption was that a local "sense of community" could at least mitigate the asperities of the cash-nexus and class-conflict.[22]

Almost thirty years on, he might well have added – in view of his more recent utterances[23] – that a strong regional culture can also mitigate the dominance of vapidities in our High Street bookbarns and pile-'em-high festivals.

As an Aberdeen graduate, I have been especially heartened by his championing of Scotland's great (and unpushy) Victorian rural realist, William Alexander of the 1871 classic *Johnny Gibb of Gushetneuk*. Literary commentators in the Central Belt tend to give it a wide berth: the Doric speech is too much for them, and their anti-Kailyard reflexes come too easily into play. Kailyard it is not; neither does that label attach to Alexander's other novels, and we are all indebted to William Donaldson for resurrecting them from newspaper files and making them available in book form. Harvie follows Donaldson in viewing Alexander as a realist of the age of Zola; having discussed in *The Centre of Things* the mid-Victorian "Condition of England" novels of Kingsley et al, our man seems (in effect) to situate *Johnny Gibb* and other Alexander novels as "Condition of Scotland" counterparts. *Johnny Gibb* turns on the struggle of tenant-farmers – small platoons, we might call them – against landlords (and their hirelings) who are determined to exert politico-religious as well as class power against those who actually work the once-stubborn terrain of north-east Scotland. Harvie does concede that the deployment of Doric scares off potential readers outwith the north-east, but that problem is by no means insurmountable; I have found it possible, by means of an English translation of an extract from its most resonant chapter, to convey the gist of *Johnny Gibb* to overseas students. Linguistically curious, and free of the anti-Scots language baggage that bedevils Scotland itself, they are quick to discuss the original passage, which I also provide and read out to them. Moreover, the ill-division of power in rural areas is a condition recognisable to people worldwide. It is as if William Alexander (though he would have modestly denied it) was himself a one-man small platoon. Of him and his Victorian contemporaries elsewhere in Scotland and Ireland (Harvie also cites *Knocknagow* [1879] by Co. Tipperary's Charles Kickham), our man

---

[22] Christopher Harvie, 'Drumtochty Revisited: the Kailyard', *The Scottish Review*, no.27 (August 1982), pp.4-11.

[23] See, e.g., Christopher Harvie, 'Duncan Glen at Seventy-five', in *A Festscrift for Duncan Glen at Seventy-five*, edited by Tom Hubbard and Philip Pacey, Kirkcaldy: Craigarter Press, 2008, pp.57-63.

concludes: "Political fiction in such areas could remain a combination of the popular and the universal, but its closeness to the people excluded it from the metropolitan market."[24] On both counts, yes, precisely, but for Harvie it is the metropolitan markets, for all their present power, that come and go; what may revive and endure, though with appalling difficulty (if at all), is the congruence of "popular and universal" with "material and moral" – these two unities as one. The poet and folklorist Hamish Henderson makes essentially the same point when he writes of Antonio Gramsci's "union [...] between his inner vision and external human need".[25] Take this, too, from Henderson's notorious colleague, friend and adversary: "To be yersel's – and to mak" that worth bein' / Nae harder job to mortals has been gi'en.'[26] Step forward, Chris Harvie, cultural worker – and (probably also) social existentialist.

---

[24] Christopher Harvie, *The Centre of Things: the Political Novel from Disraeli to the Present*, London: Unwin Hyman, 1991, p.104.

[25] Quoted in Corey Gibson, '"Gramsci in Action": Antonio Gramsci and Hamish Henderson's Folk Revivalism', in *Borne on the Carrying Stream: the Legacy of Hamish Henderson*, edited by Eberhard Bort, Ochtertyre: Grace Note Publications 2010, p.253.

[26] Hugh MacDiarmid, *Complete Poems*, p.107.

Constitutional Futures:
Scotland, Wales, Northern Ireland, Baden-Württemberg

Momentous Decisions Ahead for both Scotland and the United Kingdom

Paul Gillespie[1]

A cloud of uncertainty hangs over the United Kingdom as Scotland decides on independence next year, followed by a further decision on whether the (remaining or intact) UK will stay in the European Union. The calendar is pregnant with political linkages. On the outcome hangs Britain's future international role and influence. As its closest neighbour, Ireland has a huge interest in what happens.

The latest polling shows a 50:30 margin against independence and a surprisingly larger 74:26 one against among Scottish teenagers as 16-year-olds prepare to vote for the first time. But many are undecided and demand more information with 15 months of campaigning to go. The Yes side is confident it can close the gap and is sure an insensitive London-centred No campaign will help.

Difficult questions

Advocates of independence have many difficult questions to answer. Most concern economic issues like the currency, pensions and interest rates. The Scottish National Party wants to keep sterling and hopes to negotiate a currency union with London. This would give it greater flexibility than simply accepting the imperatives dictated by England's scale and Conservative policies, which it rejects.

The treasury vehemently opposes such a union, mindful of the euro's difficulties. While the political and economic logic of independence might drive Scotland towards euro membership, current preferences would not allow it win the referendum that way. So sterling joins the lengthening list of links an independent Scotland would keep to the 'rest of the UK', alongside the monarchy, the BBC and a general culture of Britishness the SNP says it is part of.

---

[1] This piece first appeared in *The Irish Times* on 15 June 2013 and is here reproduced with the kind permission of the author.

Agreed separation

Independence has many other implications, as became clear at a recent Ditchley Foundation conference[2] involving senior Scottish, British and international participants. Legally much depends on whether the rest of the UK is the continuity state and Scotland a new one or if continuity is shared. But politics would trump the law, in that an agreed separation between Edinburgh and London, as both claim to want if Scottish voters do, would be accepted by most international partners.

EU membership would be sought by Scotland and Brussels could be pragmatic faced with such a consensus. But all member states would have to agree, including a Spain facing Basque and Catalan demands for independence, though it could lose access to Scottish fishing grounds if it vetoed. An intriguing scenario if Scots vote No might be the reinforcement of demands – possibly led by a UK now committed to deeper devolution – for a stronger regional voice at the EU table.

Great uncertainty

This is assuming the UK remains in the EU if Scotland stays in the UK, another great uncertainty. Polling shows a roughly 50/50 split on withdrawal, with a large swing group depending on negotiating outcomes. The uncanny resemblance between the unionist case for keeping Scotland in the UK to preserve access and influence and the case for the UK staying in the EU has been too little aired. Polling in Scotland shows a swing group moving to vote Yes if they think the UK will leave the EU.

The calendar shows the anti-EU party Ukip doing well in next year's European Parliament elections, three months ahead of the Scottish vote. The UK general election in May 2015 will still give Scottish MPs a role in forming a government – even after a Yes vote. And if it is a No, a UK vote on EU membership in 2017 would reopen the independence question.

Defence is a huge issue. The SNP wants to stay in Nato, but not to keep the UK nuclear submarine fleet in Scotland. That may change; but the US is worried by the inevitable weakening of its main ally after a Scottish Yes; emerging powers would then demand the UK's permanent seat on the UN Security Council.

Irish reconfiguration?

Structural change in the UK's internal and external relations could dramatically reconfigure Ireland, North and South, by putting unification on the agenda in quite unexpected ways. This would not respect the current public preferences in both parts of the country for the status quo of a highly

---

[2] See <www.ditchley.co.uk/conferences/future-programme/scrm---future-of-scotland>.

porous border and Northern powersharing. A UK without Scotland and out of the EU would be much less likely to stay together because England would be less willing to sustain transfers to Northern Ireland and Wales.

All the more reason why a self-interested official Ireland still recovering from financial crisis might want the UK to stay in the EU, London continue to subsidise Northern Ireland and see an independent Scotland as a potential competitor for investment more than a Celtic soul-sister.

Searching for the Democratic Intellect in the Scottish Parliament: MSPs and the Harvie Question

Klaus Stolz

If a Scottish Parliament comes, it must be able to advance firm, fair, well-informed and open argument beyond the boundaries of the state; with a culture of 'civic virtue' which secures a reservoir of enlightened and incorruptible expertise for co-operative regional politics in Europe.[1]

This vision of a Scottish Parliament championed by Christopher Harvie in his classic *Scotland and Nationalism* in 1994 is by no means a modest one. Fairness, expertise, virtue and even enlightenment – it is, above all, moral and intellectual qualities he was looking forward to. Harvie's own contribution to the debates about and the realisation of such a Parliament has been threefold. First, as an historian he has comprehensively analysed the role of intellectuals in Scottish national politics over centuries. Second, as a nationalist intellectual himself he was actively campaigning for this Parliament throughout the latter part of the twentieth century. And finally, when the Parliament was eventually set up, he got himself elected a Member of the Scottish Parliament (MSP) in 2007, and was actively involved to bring this body a little closer to his ideals of intellectual debate.

This article is an attempt to contextualise Christopher Harvie's academic analysis, political evaluation and personal trajectory by linking them to the broader debate about the quality of representation in the Scottish Parliament and in modern parliamentary politics in general. It will set off with a discussion of the peculiarities of the Scottish self-government movement and the expectations raised in this particular situation (I). In the second part I will contrast these expectations with empirical reality, i.e. with the personal, social and political properties of the Members of the Scottish Parliament (II). Having discovered a stark discrepancy in this respect, I will finally put the sobering findings into a more favourable perspective (III).

---

[1] Christopher Harvie, *Scotland and Nationalism: Scottish Society and Politics, 1707-1994*, (2nd ed.), London and New York: Routledge, 1994, p.215.

I

The Scottish self-government movement, it has been said, has always been a radical democratic movement.[2] It should be added that it has also been quite heterogeneous. At the centre, there was a nationalist party – the SNP – with oscillating electoral fortunes; as important support act there were devolutionist elements within the established unionist parties (especially among the Liberals, later Liberal Democrats, yet more importantly also in the Labour Party); furthermore, there were institutional forces like some of the Labour-run regional and local councils; there were devoted individuals, radical fringe groups and all sorts of organisations belonging to what was then quite awesomely called 'Scottish Civil Society'. All of them were united in their demand for Scottish self-government. How this should be achieved and what this self-government should actually consist of, however, remained not only largely controversial between the various components of this movement, it also underwent significant changes over time.

The major turning point in this respect was the ill-fated referendum of 1979 and the subsequent experience of Thatcherism. With the SNP still infighting and busy licking its wounds, the Labour Party reorienting towards socio-economic questions, and the Conservatives showing not the slightest inclination to honour their pledge to prepare a better devolution proposal, the issue of Scottish self-government – at least in terms of party politics – seemed stone dead. Any attempt to keep it alive or any initiative to revive the national question had to come from elsewhere. One major force that rather unwittingly mobilised the non-partisan elements at that time was the ideology that questioned the very existence of Scottish society: Thatcherism. Margaret Thatcher's ideological rejection of society as a meaningful concept (in her infamous 'sermon on the mound'), her very concrete onslaught on the pillars of the Scottish economy (to be observed in the closures of coal mines and steel mills) and society (attacking the Trade Unions and local councils, later also teachers and the health sector) and her readiness to implement highly unpopular policies in Scotland despite lacking electoral support north of the border were perceived, in the words of David McCrone, as "an attack on Scotland itself".[3]

This attack revitalised the urge for Scottish self-government in broad sections of Scottish society. Chris Harvie and others have highlighted the role of intellectuals and the cultural sphere in this process. As Harvie argues,

> ... the 1980s saw a nationalist stance become general among the Scottish intelligentsia [...]. The orthodoxy is now that the

---

[2] James Mitchell, 'Consensus: Whose Consensus', in: Gerry Hassan and Chris Warhurst (eds), *A Different Future: A Modernisers Guide to Scotland*, Edinburgh: Centre for Scottish Public Policy, 1999, pp.28-33; p.32.

[3] David McCrone, *Understanding Scotland: The Sociology of a Stateless Nation*, London and New York: Routledge, 1990, p. 172.

revival in painting, film and the novel, in poetry and drama –
staged and televised – kept a 'national movement' in being.[4]

One could extend this analysis to other fields of cultural production, like
popular music, where bands like Runrig, Hue and Cry, the Proclaimers and
others not only introduced Scottish elements into pop and rock music, but
also articulated major social and political grievances of Scotland, in particular
its lack of self-control. Some of them actively supported the national
movement financially.

This cultural revival had pronounced effects far beyond the cultural
sector itself. As Lindsay Paterson argues, it was crucial in providing the
middle classes in Scotland with a respectable national identity: "Being
Scottish is no longer seen as being culturally parochial – indeed it is seen as
a way of regaining access to the international culture by escaping from an
increasingly parochial Britain."[5] This growing national self-esteem coincided
with Thatcher's attack on the very institutions that symbolised Scottish
autonomy within the Union, i.e. education, law, the health sector, but
also local government and the devolved administration. As a result, large
sections of the managerial middle class – both from the traditional elements
of law and education and from the more recently established institutions of
the welfare state – whose members were used to running Scottish affairs
at least semi-autonomously, felt threatened in their privileged position.[6] No
wonder that by the late 1980s the support for Scottish independence in this
group had increased significantly.

The peculiar Scottish experience of the representational deficits of the
British political system under an uncompromising Prime Minister in the
1980s also strengthened strands within the self-government movement
that advocated a radical break with the British model of democracy. The
acknowledgment that "Parliamentary government under the present
British constitution had failed Scotland,"[7] in combination with the Scottish
cultural revival depicted above, opened up a debate about distinctive
Scottish democratic traditions that should inform any future constitutional
settlement. The new task was not only to establish a Scottish Parliament,

---

[4] Christopher Harvie, 'Nationalism, Journalism, and Cultural Politics', in: Tom Gallagher
(ed.), *Nationalism in the Nineties*, Edinburgh: Polygon, 1991, pp.29-45; p.30.

[5] Lindsay Paterson, 'Ane End of Ane Auld Sang: Sovereignty and the Re-Negotiation of
the Union', in: Alice Brown and David McCrone (eds), *Scottish Government Yearbook
1991*, Edinburgh: Unit for the Study of Government in Scotland, 1991, pp. 104-122; p.114

[6] See Lindsay Paterson, 'Are the Scottish Middle Class Going Native?', in: *Radical
Scotland*, 45 (1990), pp.10-11; and Tom Nairn, *Faces of Nationalism: Janus Revisited*,
London: Verso, 1997.

[7] This quote is from the first paragraph of the famous 1988 document 'A Claim of
Right for Scotland', produced by the Constitutional Steering Group of the Campaign
for a Scottish Assembly.

but to build one that was more democratic than the one down in London. In this debate the archaic English concepts of 'parliamentary sovereignty' and the 'Crown in Parliament' were contrasted with Scottish notions of 'popular sovereignty'. Another notion that strongly influenced this debate was George Davie's 'democratic intellect.[8] It is this perspective more than any other that has informed Christopher Harvie's vision of a Scottish Parliament quoted above. This link becomes even more transparent in the following passage:

> The Scottish intellectual tradition – with its emphasis on ideology, its transmission and application to government – is more than the myth of Scottish democracy. The elitist oligarchy which has dominated politics in the south is absent; ideas and criticism still have an independent value. The problem is to integrate them into the governmental process.[9]

The question, how to integrate this intellectual tradition into Scottish self-government – what could be termed the Harvie question – was discussed in the small intellectual circles of Scottish civic society in the run up to the Scottish Parliament. The answer, however, was rather mixed. Apart from a number of institutional devices – most notably a PR electoral system, but also the idea of a second 'civic' chamber – the solution was widely seen in a new personnel. The 'new politics'[10] Scotland was supposed to pursue had to be accomplished by "a 'new breed' of politician".[11] Expectations with regard to this new Scottish breed had been raised throughout the 1990s. While Chris Harvie's concern that the numerical expansion of the publically rather low esteemed tribe of politicians might be held against devolution seemed accurate in 1992,[12] the overwhelming endorsement of the Scottish Parliament in the second devolution referendum in 1997 has been correctly read as the very rejection of the 'old system' made up of "senior politicians

---

[8] See George Elder Davie, *The Democratic Intellect. Scotland and her Universities in the Nineteenth Century*, Edinburgh: Edinburgh University Press, 1961.

[9] Christopher Harvie, *Scotland and Nationalism*, p.215.

[10] See James Mitchell, 'New Parliament: New Politics in Scotland', *Parliamentary Affairs*, 53 (2000), pp.249-73; also Lindsay Paterson, Alice Brown, John Curtice, David McCrone, Alison Park, Kerstin Hinds, Kerry Sproston and Paula Surridge, *New Scotland, New Politics?*, Edinburgh: Polygon, 2001.

[11] Mark Shephard, Neil McGarvey and Michael Cavanagh, 'New Scottish Parliament, New Scottish Parliamentarians?', *Journal of Legislative Studies*, 7 (2001), pp. 79-104; p.79.

[12] Christopher Harvie, *Cultural Weapons. Scotland and Survival in a New Europe*, Edinburgh: Polygon, 1992, p.35.

and political elites of civil servants".[13] The civic, non-partisan element in the self-government movement had moved the goalposts.

One problem with this idea about Scotland's new political personnel was that it was part of a negative consensus formulated against the status quo.[14] While the Westminster system and its protagonists (partisan career politicians) were rejected, it was rather less clear with what and whom they should be replaced. A rather moderate position in this respect was the demand that the new system should redress the most obvious representational deficits of particular social constituencies, such as women, ethnic minorities and the lower social and educational strata, in order to provide a closer match of social and personal characteristic between representatives and represented. Such a vision was not necessarily directed against the established model of the professional party politician.

A more direct challenge to this model had come from two different directions. On the one hand, the notion of Scottish popular sovereignty – affirmed by the Scottish Constitutional Convention in its Claim of Right and encapsulated in its chairman Kenyon Wright's famous dictum, "... politics is too important to be left to the politicians"[15] – generally pointed towards an egalitarian, strongly plebiscitary model which would allow only for nondescript citizen politicians.

A more vocal part of the self-government movement, however, envisaged a Scottish Parliament with a strong role for civic Scotland. This concept had much more of an elitist overtone. Scottish civic society, with its social-democratic ethos and its newly won home rule stance might have been the natural – and widely trusted – opponent of an intransigent conservative and centralist British government, yet Scotland's civic institutions neither represented a paragon of popular participation nor did they constitute a particularly disenfranchised social group. No matter how broad the term 'civic' might be defined, the concept still smells of paternalistic nineteenth-century liberalism and the idea that politics should be left to the morally good and intellectually capable.[16]

There are two reasons why these rather different models, despite their inherent contradictions, were hardly perceived as conflicting in the Scottish self-government movement. The first one constitutes a practical reconciliation, as most commentators – among them Christopher Harvie – actually advocated a mixed system where different representational principles would govern distinct chambers of a bicameral parliament. The idea of a senate or civic forum as an initiating, drafting and/or scrutinising

---

[13] James Mitchell, 'Consensus: Whose Consensus', p.32.

[14] For this line of argument see James Mitchell, 'Consensus: Whose Consensus'.

[15] Kenyon Wright, *The People Say Yes: The Making of Scotland's Parliament* (ed. by Harry Conroy), Glendaruel: Argyll Publishing, 1997, p.20.

[16] For this position see Tom Nairn, *Faces of Nationalism: Janus Revisited*. London: Verso, 1997.

second chamber of non-partisan and non-bureaucratic experts was highly popular among the strong non-partisan, non-bureaucratic element in the movement.[17]

Theoretical reconciliation was to be achieved via the notion of the democratic intellect or, as Harvie had put it, the Scottish intellectual tradition. From this perspective, Scotland's anti-elitist tradition in education and public discourse (in spite of the former's decay) offered the hope that a broadening of the social recruitment base might not necessarily conflict with 'civic virtue' and that, in fact, such a broadening might represent the very precondition to secure a "reservoir of enlightened and incorruptible expertise" a Scottish Parliament seems so desperately in need of. While Harvie is quite aware that the Parliament cannot rely on "the 'kenner' – the speculative and imaginative intellectual – [who] is almost by definition remote from day-to-day politics,"[18] he seems to argue that, to a certain extent, Scots are all intellectuals now, or at least, they could be. Once the qualities of "a firm, fair, well-informed and open argument" where "ideas and criticism still have an independent value" are not exclusively located in one social class – and that is what the notion of democratic intellect claims –, the differences between nineteenth-century liberalism and modern concepts of popular sovereignty become marginal. Both would point towards pluralistic recruitment and an effective decoupling of parliamentarians from group or party interest.

II

A close look at the elected members of the Scottish Parliament since its inauguration reveals, however, that these expectations and ambitions were only partially realised. The most striking feature of MSPs' personal background has been the close approximation towards gender parity. Successful affirmative action policies, especially within the Scottish Labour Party, resulted in a share of 37 per cent of women in the first Scottish Parliament. This ratio increased to nearly 40 per cent in 2003 before dropping to 32 in 2007 and 35 per cent in the Parliament elected in 2011. In international comparison this is rather high.[19] These numbers are also much higher than those for Scottish representation at Westminster, which have been notoriously low (15 per cent and below) until 2010 when they rose to the European average of 22 per cent. While these results have been

---

[17] Christopher Harvie, *Scotland and Nationalism*, p.215; see also Lucy McTernan, 'Beyond the Blethering Classes: Consulting and Involving Wider Society', in: Gerry Hassan and Chris Warhurst (eds), *The New Scottish Politics. The First Year of the Scottish Parliament and Beyond*, Norwich: Stationery Office, 2000.

[18] Christopher Harvie, 'Nationalism, Journalism, and Cultural Politics', p.45.

[19] The world average for single or lower houses is currently at 19.5 per cent (22 per cent for Europe). See Inter Parliamentary Union website, <http://www.ipu.org/wmn-e/arc/world310511.htm> (retrieved 01. August 2011).

heralded as a great success, the lack of any representation from the ethnic communities in the first two parliaments had been widely lamented. In 2007, however, Bashir Ahmad (SNP) became the first MSP with an ethnic minority background, and in 2011 the number doubled, bringing its ratio in line with their overall share of the Scottish population.

An assessment of the educational and occupational background of MSPs is much more complicated, as categories are not always easily defined. However, all studies on MSPs seem to agree that representation in the Scottish Parliament closely reflects the general representational deficits to be found in most other advanced democracies. While the election of a university professor – like that of Christopher Harvie in 2007 – is still the rare exception, Shepard et al. reported that roughly three quarters of the first cohort of MSPs held a higher education certificate.[20] This share seems to have further increased at the election of 2003.[21] With regard to the occupational background of MSPs, the two most striking (yet inter-related) results are the clear over-representation of the professions and an under-representation of the working class. According to Keating, almost half of all MSPs in 2009 (48%) came from a professional background, which is much more than amongst Scottish (37 %) and still more than amongst non-Scottish (44%) Westminster MPs (of 2005).[22] Following general European trends these MSPs are much more likely to have worked as school teachers or in the health and social welfare sectors than in the traditional politics facilitating sectors of law and higher education.[23] At the other end of the occupational scale, former manual and routine clerical workers provided only 14% of MSPs, a figure much lower than that for Scottish MPs (20%), though not as low as that for non-Scottish MPs (11%). As the middle class professional background identified above is particularly prominent amongst women MSPs, it seems not unreasonable to state "that gender equality ... has been achieved at the cost of social representativeness."[24]

---

[20]   See Mark Shephard, Neil McGarvey and Michael Cavanagh, 'New Scottish Parliament, New Scottish Parliamentarians?'.

[21] Keating and Cairney (2006) report 90% for Labour, 92.9% for the SNP, 77.8% for the Conservatives, and 82.5% for the Liberal Democrats (yet they do not provide figures for the smaller parties or an aggregate figure for all MSPs).

[22] See Michael Keating, *The Government of Scotland: Public Policy Making after Devolution*, Edinburgh: Edinburgh University Press, 2010.

[23] See Maurizio Cotta and Heinrich Best, 'Between Professionalization and Democratization: A Synoptic View on the Making of the European Representative', in: Heinrich Best and Maurizio Cotta (eds), *Parliamentary Representatives in Europe 1848-2000: Legislative Recruitment and Careers in Eleven European Countries*, Oxford: Oxford University Press, 1999, pp.498-9; Michael Keating, *The Government of Scotland*, p.126.

[24] Michael Keating and Paul Cairney, 'A New Elite? Politicians and Civil Servants in Scotland after Devolution', *Parliamentary Affairs*, 59 (2006), pp. 43-59; p.51.

So while social recruitment can hardly be said to have become more pluralistic, these middle class professionals may still represent a broader section of Scottish society than the old style parliamentarians consisting of machine politicians and party hacks. A first glance at the trajectories of the newly elected MSPs in 1999, though, points to the contrary. 20 per cent of the first members of the Scottish Parliament had already served at Westminster, while as many as 40 per cent had at least stood for election to the UK Parliament.[25] Also 40 per cent (and thus just 6 percentage points less than at Westminster at the same time,)[26] had previously held a local government office.[27] Even more importantly, an astonishing 80 per cent had held an elected party office before their election to the Scottish Parliament. Taken together, only 10 per cent of MSPs in 1999 had no prior political experience in an elected public, party or interest group office (ibid.). This strong career political background is also reflected in the complete lack of representation from the non-party political element of the self-government movement. Prominent figures either did not intend to stand (e.g. Campbell Christie), failed to secure party political nomination (Isobel Lindsay), or lost out at the election as independent candidates (Kenyon Wright). The most telling story with this regard is perhaps that of the late Stephen Maxwell – a well-respected nationalist intellectual and civic leader, yet a rather free-spirited and inconvenient party member, who was denied a candidacy for the SNP because he refused to sign a statement of party loyalty requested by his party.

A look at the parliamentary careers of MSPs since 1999 further underlines this argument. With an average membership turnover of 31.5 per cent per election,[28] Scotland's incumbency re-election rate (68.5 %) is rather inconspicuous in comparative terms.[29] This means that the Scottish Parliament does not deviate from the general tendency of rather long-term parliamentary careers. This becomes most obvious when we look at the original intake of 1999. Almost a third of this cohort (41 if we discount technical breaks of less than a year) is still holding on to their mandate, which means that by the end of the current electoral period they will have concluded 16 years in the Scottish Parliament. Another 8 MSPs of this cohort

[25] Ailsa Henderson and Amanda Sloat, 'New politics in Scotland? A profile of MSPs: part 1', *Talking Politics*, 12 (1999), pp. 243-46; p. 245.

[26] Mark Shephard, Neil McGarvey and Michael Cavanagh, 'New Scottish Parliament, New Scottish Parliamentarians?', pp.93-4.

[27] Klaus Stolz, *Toward a Regional Political Class? Professional Politicians and Regional Institutions in Catalonia and Scotland*, Manchester: Manchester University Press, 2010, p.61.

[28] Author's own calculation after 4 elections. The next two paragraphs are based on the author's own dataset.

[29] Matland and Studlar (2004) in their cross-country analysis of turnover rates in 25 democracies report an average of 32.3 (and thus an average re-election rate of 67.7).

had lost their mandate at the 2003 election (or in the case of Alex Salmond had given it up voluntarily), yet by 2011 they had found their way back into the Scottish Parliament. In 2011, Scotland had 75 MSPs and former MSPs with a parliamentary tenure of 9 years and more (having served in at least 3 parliamentary sessions), 42 of them still holding a mandate. A further 42 MSPs have accumulated 8 years (two full session), with 12 of them still sitting.

As stated above, these longtime careers in professional politics traditionally come after an apprenticeship in local and/or party politics. A rather new, yet an increasingly frequented pathway into the Scottish Parliament is currently developing with the recruitment from paid staff positions (researchers and advisers at party headquarters or within the Parliament). Already 14 per cent of the current MSPs (2011) have come this way. 12 of the 129 MSPs – and thus almost ten per cent – have even progressed from a research assistant position in the very Parliament they are now serving as elected members.[30] This form of in-house recruitment constitutes an even more secluded self-reproduction of the political personnel than the old style model.

Finally, we have to evaluate any potential influx of civic Scotland via specific institutional devices and the consultation process. At first glance, the picture looks quite bright. The idea of a second chamber of Civic Scotland did find its way from the self-government movement into the deliberations of the Constitutional Steering Group and from their recommendations into the final institutional set up. However, the Scottish Civic Forum, finally established in early 2000 and largely funded by the Scottish Executive (together with Scottish Parliament Corporate Body), could not fulfil the ambitious role preconceived for it. Underfunded, with no institutional clout and without a public profile, it struggled to provide the Scottish voluntary sector with a strong voice in the formal decision making process before it was quietly abandoned in 2010. Despite the best of efforts of the people involved, this body was never – and was never meant to be – a serious challenge to the realm of professional parliamentary politics.

A second, altogether more realistic parliamentary gateway for civic Scotland had been seen in the newly designed Scottish committee system. And indeed, early studies have acknowledged a very wide-ranging consultation practice and the granting of special status to the non-profit voluntary sector.[31] Yet the overall judgment nevertheless seems to confirm the critical voices of Tom Nairn and others. Resourceful and well organised

---

[30] This pathway has become particularly popular in the SNP now. 17% of their first-time members in the 2011 Parliament had been research assistants in the Scottish Parliament before. An interesting inversion of this model can be observed in the Scottish Labour Party, where former MSPs are hired as parliamentary research assistants (The Herald, 12 June 2011) probably both in order to make use of their experience and to offer them a – temporary – fall back position to smooth their way out of their job.

[31] See Norman Bonney, 'The Scottish Parliament and Participatory Democracy: Vision and Reality', The Political Quarterly, 74 (2003), pp. 459-67.

interests, like the National Farmers Union or the Law Society, are much better placed to make their influence heard than small community groups. If this was "participative democracy at work", Norman Bonney commented, "it was ... the participative democracy of organised interests".[32] With regard to securing "enlightened and incorruptible expertise" many committees have also been consulting with leading academics in their field. Yet, the recent scandal about the improper cross-examination of two Scottish economists suggests that even this attempt to "advance firm, fair, well-informed and open argument" seems to have fallen victim to the general dominance of party politics in the Scottish Parliament.[33]

Thus, taken together, the figures and interpretations provided above do point to a rather bleak conclusion: The Scottish self-government movement and its intellectual project have been "hijacked".[34] They have been hijacked mainly by professional politicians who have developed into a distinct Scottish political class,[35] which has successfully absorbed the privileged positions in the decision-making process.

III

Yet all is not wrong in the people's republic of Scotland. While evidence in support of the hijack-scenario is too overwhelming to make any last minute retreat, in this concluding section I will provide three arguments that might at least help to put it into perspective.

First, I want to start with a truism that seems nevertheless worth repeating: party political competition and professional politics are highly functional in modern democracies. In terms of democratic theory, professional politics causes a dilemma. Professional politicians who are striving to make a living and a long-term career out of politics are clearly at odds with the basic democratic idea that everybody should be able to participate in decision-making, or at least that nobody should be allowed to permanently occupy decision-making positions and thus exclude others from them. However, the trend towards political professionalisation is part of a much wider long-term societal process, which has seen an increasing division of labour and social differentiation – a trend that is simply irreversible. In the course of modernisation, politics, too, is becoming ever more complex. Interests have to be aggregated at some point, majorities have to be organised, coalitions and compromises have to be forged. In almost all advanced democracies

[32] *Ibid*, p.465.

[33] James Mitchell, 'Holyrood on display as new politics is laid to rest', *The Herald*, 24 January 2011.

[34] James Mitchell, 'Consensus: Whose Consensus', p.32.

[35] See Klaus Stolz, *Toward a Regional Political Class? Professional Politicians and Regional Institutions in Catalonia and Scotland.*

this task is allocated to experienced specialists, i.e. professional politicians, supported by reliable agencies of coordination, i.e. political parties. While the democratic norm may remind us to keep the access to this profession open and to facilitate some form of cross-over from other social spheres, a complete deprofessionalisation would be counterproductive both on democratic and on functional grounds. Historically political professionalisation was a project of the Labour movement, enabling their clientele to actively engage in politics. Today, a parliament of well-intended, open minded and intellectually superior political amateurs and civic leaders might provide stimulating deliberation, but it would almost certainly tip the balance of power even further to those groups in society that are organised, and to those organisations that do have professional expertise at their disposal, i.e. bureaucracies and interest groups. If Scottish self-government is meant to be more than the traditional managed autonomy, Scotland better had come to terms with political professionalisation as an "inevitable nuisance",[36] rather than treating it as the central obstacle that has to be overcome. Similarly, party politics may rightly be criticised for some of its pathological degenerations, but should not be dismissed in principle.

Second, the emerging Scottish political class is neither completely devoid of 'civic virtue' nor has it completely debarred Parliament from less conventional representatives and more inspirational contributions. Within the ranks of the established parties (Labour, SNP, Conservatives and Liberal Democrats) we do not only find disciplined party soldiers, but also quite a number of distinguished debaters and free-spirited mavericks. Chris Harvie's own election and contribution to the Scottish Parliament, which earned him the *Herald*'s 'Free Spirit of the Year' award in 2008, is perhaps the best testimony in both respects. In the free spirit category other names like John McAllion and Elaine Smith of the Labour Party, Dorothy Grace Elder from the SNP as well as Donald Gorrie (Liberal Democrats) and Brian Monteith (Conservatives) immediately spring to mind, while skillful, intellectually stimulating and sometimes even colourful interventions have certainly come from the likes of Michael Russell (SNP), Wendy Alexander (Labour), Tavish Scott (Liberal Democrats) and David McLetchie (Conservatives).

The most obvious evidence with regard to the widening of representation, though, is the number of independent MSPs and of members from minor parties. In its second legislature (2003-2007) the Scottish Parliament contained not only representation from the four Westminster parties, but also seven Green MSPs, six from the Scottish Socialist Party (SSP), one from the Senior Citizen's Union Party and three non-aligned MSPs (although two of them were disgruntled party politicians, rather than non-party activists). It is to these sources that we owe some of the initiatives concerning the most vulnerable and underprivileged sections in Scottish society, like the

---

[36] See Jens Borchert, *Die Professionalisierung der Politik: Zur Notwendigkeit eines Ärgernisses*, Frankfurt: Campus, 2003.

debates and bills about assisted suicide, prostitution tolerance zones, the abolition of warrant sales, or free school meals. As the 2003 election has clearly shown, the Scottish electoral system does not preclude radical groups and minority interests to gain representation. The implosion of the SSP since then, however, has also revealed the dangers of depending on outstanding (in whatever respect) individuals rather than a more solid party base.

My third claim is that the high and mainly unrealistic expectations of a 'new Scottish politics' have actually undermined a more accurate evaluation of the institutional renovation of democracy in Scotland that really did take place. For, the Scottish Parliament has not only successfully resolved a crisis of democratic legitimacy in Scotland; it has also already accomplished some significant institutional innovations that will enhance the quality of public debate both inside and outside the chamber, in a way that might indeed help to preserve and strengthen the 'independent value' of 'ideas and criticism' within the political process. The first of these innovations is the extreme transparency – especially compared to the traditional working of the Westminster Parliament – it has provided for Scottish public life. This concerns the daily work of MSPs, debates in plenary and in the committees, as well as such sensitive areas as their expenses. While this has already led to a few casualties on the parliamentary benches (though far less than at Westminster), the lesson to be learned from the misconduct of a few individual MSPs is not about the collective greediness of Scotland's political class, but about the proper functioning of transparency rules and the close public scrutiny they allow. Moreover, with the implementation of its Freedom of Information Act of 2002, the Scottish Parliament has installed a Public Information Commissioner[37] who is responsible for opening doors to information from a wide range of public authorities in Scotland. The frequent usage that has been made of this legislation has already improved public discourse in many different areas.

A second important institutional innovation that directly concerns representation is the introduction of the Single Transferable Vote (STV) system for local elections in Scotland. Implemented by a Labour/Liberal Democrat coalition, this reform can be seen as a direct consequence of the Scottish Parliament's own crucial deviation from the Westminster path, with its adoption of a proportional electoral system. In its first instance, at the 2007 local elections, STV produced a much more pluralistic representation. Even in the West of Scotland, the traditional model of one-party domination – i.e. the Labour Party running councils due to their inflated majorities almost without any opposition – was replaced by a large number of different forms of coalitions. The effective number of parties increased from 3.81 to

---

[37] A post that has been filled with Kevin Dunion. Here is how to make good use of your civil society home rule activists.

4.44, indicating a clear deconcentration of the party system.[38] Moreover, by increasing electoral competitiveness and reducing the number of safe seats, STV has enhanced the role of citizens in the electoral process. With local politics fulfilling an important function of political socialisation, potential changes both with regard to the debating culture as well as with regard to voters' behaviour are also highly likely to have significant and lasting repercussions for the national level. While this local electoral reform might not be a panacea, it certainly does point into the right direction.

The high expectations of a new Scottish politics and a new political personell had been raised in a very particular climate. Organisations of civic Scotland and Scottish intellectuals have been important driving forces in this movement, significantly shaping its discourse. Yet, as Harvie stated in 1994: "The factors which have propelled Scotland towards self-government are not necessarily those which will make a settlement work".[39] And indeed, the introduction of Scottish democratic intellectual traditions into the process of self-government – and thus the resolution of the Harvie question – is not to be achieved by prescribing the sort of people who should represent the nation. Neither a reduction of professional politicians nor an increase of intellectuals, women, ethnic minorities or working class people in the Parliament, nor an exact socio-demographic match of population and representatives will do the trick. If we agree that political professionalisation is indispensible, yet the emergence of a self-serving and ring-fenced political class is detrimental for the advancement of 'firm, fair, well-informed and open argument,' then reformist efforts should be directed towards opening up the policy process as well as the election and – perhaps more importantly – the candidate selection processes to the public. Social closure in a representative democracy is not manifested in a lack of descriptive representation but in a lack of voters' choice and influence as well as in the high hurdles imposed for anybody willing to actively challenge an emerging cartel of incumbents.

---

[38] Klaus Stolz, 'Goodbye to the Westminster Model? Institutionalising Scotland's New Democracy', paper presented at the 28th Annual Meeting of the German Association for the Study of British History and Politics, Mülheim/Ruhr, 22-24 May 2009.

[39] Christopher Harvie, *Scotland and Nationalism*, p.217.

Being Scottish[1]

Lesley Riddoch

It is more than 300 years after the Treaty of Union.

Britain PLC has partly de-merged its acquisitions.

Scotland has regained a parliament and feelings of Scottishness abound. No wonder. It would be hard to think of a nation with more visible, durable and internationally accepted calling cards of identity -- Tartan, Bagpipes, Auld Lang Syne, Haggis, Burns, Whisky, Golf.

And yet.

Do Scots identify with these Balmoralised symbols of nationhood?

Disconnected from the environment that created them, kilt wearing, single-malt quaffing, Pringle wearing, golf-mad Scots seem strangely inauthentic. Like an identikit picture on a 'Wanted' poster – each piece may be accurate, but the whole face does not look like anyone real.

Nonetheless, at some point every Scotsman will have tried to pour himself into the part. Like 90 minute Christians who appear in church for marriages and funerals only, 90 minute Scots 'turn out' for Burns Nights, Stag nights, Rugby matches, Tartan Army events, weddings, funerals and barmitzvahs. When identity is demanded or ritual is required, the kilt comes out, a few poems or songs are dusted down, bawdy sideways snipes are made at women and serious drinking helps lads focus on the only point of male Scottish identity that seems to matter.

Not being English.

Not indulging in pedantry, moderation, village greens, New Labour, house-price discussions, real ale, cricket or morris dancing.

It is easy to sneer. But if this describes the English – what does it make the Scots?

Immoderate, excessive, concrete-jungle tolerating, Old Labour, vodka drinking, football-worshipping, hard men? The current working definition of Scottishness is male to the core and ties a nation psychologically and symbiotically to a neighbour it purports to despise.

And if anyone had not noticed, the English are currently on a quest of their own –driven to self-discovery by the apparently resurgent Celts. Jeremy Paxman, Kate Fox, David Starkey, Simon Schama – the bookshelves are groaning with attempts to scrape together a DNA of the English that does not rely on Empire, Good Queen Bess, 1966, Dunkirk and Eastenders.

---

[1] Parts of this article were first published in *Perspectives* magazine (March 2011).

If being English is currently a puzzle – being not English is an absolute nonsense. Expressed succinctly in Renton's speech, by Irvine Welsh in *Trainspotting*:

> Ah don't hate the English. They're just wankers. We are colonised by wankers. We can't even pick a decent, vibrant, healthy culture to be colonised by. No. We're ruled by effete arseholes. What does that make us? The lowest of the fuckin low, the scum of the earth. The most wretched, servile, miserable, pathetic trash that was ever shat intae creation. Ah don't hate the English. They just git oan wi the shite thuv goat. Ah hate the Scots.[2]

It is no wonder young Scots want out – into a bigger or smaller world where identity can be defined by sex, drugs, music, shoe size, MSN messenger connection, podcast preference, anything other than the dull, out-dated strait-jacket that accompanies the geographical accident of being Scottish.

And yet.

Try believing Scots are not a distinctive group but just self deluded northern Brits surfing the net and watching MTV in a globalised world devoid of local cultural reference. Andy does. This earnest Scottish TV researcher came over to chat after a BBC discussion show in which I was the only person to think Scottish independence was a perfectly reasonable political choice. The comment seemed to bother him. Like I had otherwise been on or near his wavelength but with one apparent endorsement of Scotland as a meaningful entity, had jumped straight onto another political planet.

The whole exchange that followed could easily have been avoided by adding that I am not a card-carrying Nationalist. But looking at this well meaning, background-denying, socialised but uneducated product of the British state, it seemed like time for some mischief.

Like.

Was Andy watching MTV in a terraced house – the traditional unit of "British" housing?

Nope – he lived in a tenement.

Did he take A levels like most British students? Nope – he took highers.

Did his parents own their house – like most Britons?

Nope, and unlike most English students he had stayed in their council house during university. Cheaper.

After MTV, would he be staying in to watch the Ashes followed perhaps by the Vicar of Dibley?

Nope. Unlike anyone south of the Border he would be listening to a witheringly sarcastic phone-in about the day's football (Off the Ball), watching a sitcom about two auld geezers on a bleak housing estate (Still

---

[2] Irvine Welsh, *Trainspotting*, London: Vintage, 1994, p.100.

Game), and would stay in guzzling lager because he could not afford to buy a round.

Ever thought of going out and just buying a pint for yourself, Andy?

Dinna be daft. Oh yes and he disnae quite speik English at hame either.

Alright. Did you vote for Britain's painting of the year –Turner's 'Battle of Trafalgar'? Or the best British poem – Rudyard Kipling's 'If'?

Nope – Andy's top marks would go to Dali's 'Christ of St John of the Cross' (a picture Andy knows in great detail because unlike the average British gallery, access to Scottish public galleries has always been free). And on best poem he would be torn between 'Tam O'Shanter', MacDiarmid's 'A Drunk Man Looks at the Thistle' and McCaig's lines about his best poem being two fags long.

And yes, before I ask, his dad did die prematurely from lung disease, lived in a council house, refused to buy it on principle, voted Labour until the shipyards closed, switched to the SNP, decided they were Tartan Tories and then supported Tommy Sheridan until the Parliament Building costs overran at which point he stopped voting altogether.

Andy, catch a grip.

The Scots are not just what happens when you vary England's default settings – less winter daylight, more poverty, more hills, less warmth, fewer people, less ethnic diversity. Though these basic physical truths have certainly helped shape identity and behaviour.

Scots are not just intemperate versions of our more measured southern cousins. We do not live in the same houses, laugh at the same jokes, read the same books, or share the same life expectancy. We do not have the same capacity to commercialise ideas. We do not have the same informal rules about collective behaviour. We do not speak quite the same language, and we do not (publicly) aspire to the same social goals. We do not have the same history, the same weather, geology, bank notes, education system, legal system or levels of home ownership. We do not vote the same way, we do not die the same way.

Scots are no more just northern variants of the English than the Irish are just western ones. Indeed, our mission may be to offer the English a new (if currently undesired) identity as southern Celts.

Despite its contradictions, the Scottish identity is not just a bundle of remnants – a set of random behaviours by mindless contrarians welded together into a dangerously unstable and unpredictable personality. Although on a bad day it can feel that way.

Scots are quite obviously different from the neighbours – English, Irish or Norwegian. But different enough?

Scots are (characteristically) in two minds.

Many believe important national differences must be as strong as primary colours, as absolute as gender, as non-negotiable as the Iron Curtain.

In practice, this 'high bar' of distinction is not louped by many neighbouring

European states either. And yet, the Scots demand it – instead of lowering the bar and accepting similarities exist across many borders, Scots exaggerate superficial differences that hardly matter.

The Nordic nations differ by only a few shades of grey. The Low Countries have pastel coloured borders. And yet, try suggesting Spain and Portugal, the Netherlands and Belgium, Norway and Sweden should all merge. Try it – and stand well back.

On mainland Europe, slight but important points of cultural distinction have become the cornerstones of each nation state.

I remember interviewing the Sinn Féin leader and former IRA man Martin McGuinness for Channel Four's *People's Parliament* just after the bizarre period in the 1980s when his voice was 'banned' on TV and radio. If Sinn Féin got their wish and Northern Ireland became part of the Irish Republic, I asked, what would be visibly different to the casual onlooker.

He thought for a while and then said, "the street signs would be in Irish Gaelic."

The same thought occurred to everyone listening – is that all? Could such a tiny change possibly justify those long decades of death, grief and violence?

And yet, travel to Norway from Sweden and street signs are often the only visible means of distinction. Start in Germany and travel to Holland. Are important social distinctions always accompanied by a host of visible differences?

In fact, Scotland does look immediately different – there are virtually no terraced houses in Scottish cities and virtually no tenements in English ones.

And yet we speak the same language, share institutions and share recent centuries of history with our southern cousins. So the Martin McGuinness question arises again. Does a very different history once upon a time justify change today? Do small social and cultural differences justify calls for independence?

Probably not without oil.

Almost everything written about Scottish independence eventually rests on the Black Gold. Will a new state crash and burn or wash its face with the 80-90% of remaining fossil fuel reserves which lie in Scotland's share of the continental shelf? Will that cash be safe in Scottish hands – or did the banking collapse suggest Scotland cannot rely on its own institutions to stand alone? Can Alex Salmond guarantee Scots will be better off in an independent Scotland?

Of course he cannot. And if Scots need such a guarantee, the country will remain a grumbling part of the UK forever. None of our small, independent neighbours broke away from larger states to be better off. Far from it. When Norway announced independence from Sweden in 1905, it immediately became the second poorest nation in Europe, replaced by Ireland a few decades later. The tiny independent nation of Iceland was brought under Norwegian control in the thirteenth century, when settlers felled every tree and turned Iceland into a northern desert dependent on the Norwegians for wood to provide boats, transport and fuel for heating and house building. Still, this tiny population – smaller than Coventry – seized its chance to declare independence without a moment's hesitation when Stepmother Denmark was occupied by Germany in 1944.

Back then, Iceland had not learned to harness its vast reserves of geo-thermal power, nor had it fought and won the Cod Wars with Britain or gambled and lost everything thanks to a bunch of cocky young bankers.

The urge to break away from any union – political, marital or financial – is rarely rational, or economically prudent. There may be preparation, debate and plans – but eventually caution becomes an anchor.

No Nordic state became independent to be better off.

Of course, the Scots may be the exception that proves the rule. Of course, history does not repeat itself.

And of course Scotland approaches the independence question with another big current running – localism. It may not be necessary for Scotland to prove its people are dramatically different to those further south to argue that 5 not 55 million people is the ideal size for government.

Culture, oil, history and size. Scotland has as many reasons for seeking independence as any other restless nation – although currently the argument convinces more voters south than north of the border. A majority of English people polled by YouGov in 2011 said they support Scottish independence. Some – like English socialist and nationalist Mark Perryman—think the departure of the Scots would be the making of the English. Others – like ex Sun-editor Kelvin McKenzie think their ungrateful northern neighbours are whingeing, handout-dependent, subsidy-junkies and cannot wait to stop the gravy train heading north.

Mind you, a lot of southerners think the same about Yorkshire.

Scottish independence could have opened up a debate about how best to manage indigenous cultural difference within these islands. It could have – but it has not.

Instead, Scotland's endless agonising over our constitutional status has become a right royal pain. Do we want more powers, don't we? A bit... no, a bit more... no, that's too much ...no maybe it's fine ... what about a referendum first ... or a Commission to decide on the question ... and a review panel to appoint the Commission maybe...

It has been easy to scoff and regard Scottish independence as Alex Salmond's personal problem.

After all, Scots are hardly Britain's cultural revolutionaries.

Take Wales. Gubbed by the English in 1283, they have been forced to dance to their neighbour's tune ever since – in education, health, local government, housing and outlook. Welshness has been kept alive by culture – the Methodist Chapel, male-voice choirs, Welsh language schools, S4C, and campaigns against incomers and their holiday homes.

Like defiant prisoners whistling 'Home of our Fathers' as the firing squad takes aim, the Welsh have had no structural way to defend their identity (until devolution) – none bar their culture. The Scots have always had more.

No offence to speakers of Gaelic and Scots, but neither language can fully define nor resurrect a nation. Law abiding, rational, dour-old bodies that we are, Scots are defined by institutions, not language. By an education system that seeks breadth, not specialism. By a legal system based on statute, not precedent. By a Kirk not led by the Head of State. By housing policy not based on sale, but (for better and worse) for rent. By an economy based not on private enterprise, but on the state. And of course by our two public holidays at Hogmanay.

We do things differently north of the border but we do not ask why.

As a result we prop up what doesn't matter and ignore what does.

Any day the family silver could be gone for good –we do not know what it looks like or where it was buried. No wonder.

Scots have spent too many years trying to look modern, trying to deny a peasant past, forget the cruelty of industrialisation, ignore the underclass it created and escape (into the ever-accessible world of alcohol rather than the distant and exclusive world of nature).

Occasionally we catch the scent of a blossom that has been taken from the room – like Hugh MacDiarmid's little white rose of Scotland that "smells sharp and sweet – and breaks the heart."[3]

What is it?

It is not the Scottish football team – however convenient a repository that is for outpourings of emotion.

It is not – sadly – radical thought or communitarian endeavour.

Scots do not do co-operatives, credit unions, local energy companies, community trusts or local asset ownership (at least not on the scale of our neighbours). We do not do truly local. We do not do trust.

It is not a tradition of healthy living.

We do not do the body as a temple, exercise, eating vegetables or getting outdoors.

We do not live in nature. We do not build in wood.

Our national dish is Chicken Tikka Masala washed down with Irn Bru or super lager.

We reassert our collective proletarian identity with every curry we order, every sun-bed we occupy, every triple voddie we demolish in the name of a 'good time', every year of life expectancy we lose.

All to prove we are not posh and therefore not English.

This pointless behaviour has become self-harming on a national scale.

If Scots have different values, we should defend them. If we have distinctive ideals, we should articulate them. If we have important customs,

---

[3] Hugh MacDiarmid, 'The Little White Rose', in *Complete Poems*, Vol.1, edited by Michael Grieve and W. R. Aitken, Manchester: Carcanet, 1993, p.461.

we should maintain them. Every other nation does – whether subsumed within a larger whole or independently governed.

Instead, we struggle to look traditional and go-getting – like former First Minister Jack McConnell with his bold pin-striped kilt.

We cling to a tough-talking, self-mocking, cynical world outlook instead of recognising such gallows humour for what it is – a coping mechanism from days of appalling poverty and unfairness (which many still endure). We ignore the paradox of an empty rural landscape in which there is apparently no room for expansion. The resulting sky-high property prices are blamed on wealthy incomers seeking second homes instead of the underlying land scarcity which has kept city and country divided, with no cabin culture – unlike every other country at our latitude, east or west.

We replicate the landowners' aesthetic of the empty glen through 'democratic' planning procedures. We validate the industrialist's degradation of landless labour by walling up the underclass in vast, disempowered housing estates.

We hobble our democracy and we shame ourselves.

What we cannot accept is what we already know.

Scottishness springs from one four letter word – Clan.

Who you are, who you know, what family you come from and where they live still matters more than anything else at every level of Scottish society.

On the plus side – it is levelling. For Scots, what you earn is not necessarily more important than who you know and where you were brought up.

"See you later" is exchanged every waking moment of the day by people who will almost certainly never meet again. Even in a corner shop 300 miles from home, the illusion of inclusion in a never-ending conversation or relationship must be maintained. We are all kin. We are all Jock Tamson's bairns. The sense of connection feels good.

My husband – brought up in Canada, born on the Isle of Wight – often feels uncomfortable when Glasgow taxi drivers ask where he is from. Fearing anti-English remarks if he tells the truth, he usually changes the subject. Mistake.

Scots pride themselves on having a connection with any place you can mention – north, south, east or west of the border. Thus, a talkative Scottish taxi-driver will feel compelled to make a place-based connection so passengers can be temporarily added to the Clan.

Conversation is the goal. Exchange is the means. Place or family detail is the missing ingredient. Once in place and once an Aunty Jeannie or a friend of a friend who once worked in Aldershot has been identified, other possibilities are unlocked -- all sorts of fascinating conversations can begin.

But not until that vital connection has been made.

This quest for belonging and connectedness underpins almost every aspect of Scottish language and behaviour.

On the minus side ... Clannish behaviour is conformist. All things collective are believed to be good per se – unions, public sector. Individual private success is frowned on as a threat to group cohesion.

Gangs operate as the new city clans – Football has become a clan battleground. Sectarianism survives because it helps define and consolidate clans. The ultimate clan value – loyalty in battle – can justify territorialism and a desolate, violent macho urban environment where women have no place. Clan loyalties obstruct democratic progress. But as a product of clan culture, Scottish politicians have failed to identify clannishness at work.

Individual success is frowned on as a threat to group cohesion. Tall poppies must be scythed.

Alex Salmond is unquestionably Scotland's tallest poppy. And yet, far from scything him down, Scots across social, sectarian, class and geographical divides abandoned the voting habits of several lifetimes to give him an overall majority in the Scottish Parliament – a feat hitherto considered impossible by the constitutional experts.

Over four years running Scotland, the minority SNP administration had remained optimistic, upbeat and confident – breaking or bending almost every rule in the miserable Little Book of Calvin.

Could Scotland's chronic drink problem be tackled fast – the prevailing wisdom said no. Years of education and changing habits and more education and dah de dah de dah...

The SNP said yes – raise prices on the types of booze most quaffed by big drinkers and watch 'em cut down on what they drink. Will it work? Who knows. Is it worth a try – yes.

Could Scotland cut its massive prison population – we imprison at three times the rate of our Irish and Nordic neighbours, with roughly the same crime rate. The wise old men and women of Labour said no. Years of education and changing habits and being tough on crime and the causes of crime and ASBOs, even though they criminalise nuisance behaviour and more education and dah de dah de dah...

The SNP said yes – I was on the Prisons Commission they set up which recommended a switch to community payback orders, not jail. Has it worked? – Youth crime is down and the population of Scotland's youth jail is down. But prisons are still full, money is committed to bricks and mortar, and it is hard to switch out to community services. Is it the right direction of travel? Of course it is.

Was there a bonfire of the quangos? – Not really.

Has the scrapping of business rates for small business resulted in more being set up? Not really.

Was the scrapping of bridge tolls consistent with setting the greenest energy targets in the world? Not at all.

Half of Aberdeenshire sang hallelujah when Alex Salmond called in the Trump Towers golf proposal Aberdeenshire Council rejected. The other half said they would never vote SNP (but clearly did).

Like them or loathe them, the SNP have been decisive, evidence based and quick in their decision making. As if time's a wasting. As if anything may indeed be possible. As if people can be trusted. As if we were indeed living "in the early days of a better nation".[4]

And the normally dour, downbeat, easily scared voters of Scotland have responded.

A system devised by Labour to prevent an overall majority for any party in Holyrood's proportional Parliament failed to kick in on 5 May 2011. The list vote designed to compensate loser parties with votes but no seats just delivered more seats for the SNP – against all expert prediction.

The Labour stronghold of Greater Glasgow – home of the pioneering socialist Keir Hardie – ousted 'weel kent' Labour faces for relatively unknown SNP candidates. Even the candidacy of 'Gorgeous' George Galloway did not deflect left-wing voters in their headlong flight from Labour to the SNP.

The official opinion polls were wrong. The gut instincts of commentators were wrong.

The SNP landslide terminated the political careers of Scottish Labour leader Iain Gray, Scottish Lib Dem leader Tavish Scott and Scottish Conservative leader Annabel Goldie.

Five-years of impotent thumb-twiddling beckon for Alex Salmond's new political opponents. No power-sharing. No coalitions. No wee deals – but also no excuses if the SNP fail to deliver on generous pre-election spending commitments viewed as rash and irresponsible by some supporters.

The pioneering proposals voted down by Holyrood's old unionist majority will soon re-appear -- like minimum alcohol pricing, local income tax and of course, the independence referendum. Scottish politics will be anything but boring.

In a few hours of voting in May 2011, the rigid electoral certainties of generations were swept away.

In Scotland you could bet your shirt on a few basic truths.

Workers used to vote Labour, employers did not.

The west voted Labour, the east did not.

Leafy suburbs voted Tory, leafless urban areas would not.

The north voted Lib Dem, the south did not.

Nationalists voted SNP, unionists did not.

The old faultlines that divided Scotland once looked as formidable and enduring as the Berlin Wall. Then they disappeared.

Seismic political change was only been possible because seismic cultural change has been happening north of the border too.

Each nation has a set of national personality traits. Scotland's set changed.

It seems Scots are able to ignore scaremongering, reward bold ideas and genuine effort and believe change might be for the better.

That is not to say the path ahead will be easy. The SNP has undoubtedly

---

[4] Salmond's memorable line after winning against the odds in 2007 – which came from Alasdair Gray's *Lanark* (1981), taken from a poem by the Canadian author Dennis Leigh.

over-promised. Spending cuts, job losses and a stagnant housing market mean support could ebb from the SNP just as swiftly as it flowed there in 2011.

But that is the point.

The dam of voting convention has burst.

How many other redundant outlooks and old hostilities will the floodwaters carry away?

Until now the Scots have generally viewed private as bad and public as good. All things collective are supported. All things sitting in the middle (co-operatives, social entrepreneurs, community assets) are viewed as odd, wafty – perhaps a way to undermine public sector jobs.

Clannish behaviour has long justified nepotism, supported the status quo and undermined equality. It has meant Scots can openly prefer family, kin, long-held allegiances, and local fiefdoms to anything newer, bigger or more diverse.

It has created a social conservatism that trumps common sense, fairness and even basic democracy. Teams are more versatile than clans – more inclusive, less macho, more rational and less defensive. But Scotland does not do teams. It does clans.

And that is our guilty secret.

Look at Scotland as a connected, community centred and family focussed country compared to England – and you can source that behaviour past Queen Victoria, past the Balmoralised faux-Highland society she created, past the horror of Culloden to the informal rules of the Gaelic-speaking Scottish clans.

Look at Scots as a suspicious people with myriad defensive groupings based on kin, not logic – and you are back at the same point of origin.

Look at Scots as masters of anecdote in the release of drink and private company, but servants of silence in the formality of public speaking – and you hear the centuries' long echo of the banned Mother Tongue.

Look at the self destructive nature of unemployed male Scots and you see a culture of masculinity modelled on the Clan warrior's ability to withstand damage – adapted now in the absence of clan or even class conflict to a masochistic culture of withstanding self harm.

Look at the proudest moment in the opening of the Scottish parliament when Burns's masterpiece, 'A Man's a Man for a' that' rang out from the temporary premises in the Kirk's Assembly Hall. "The rank is but the guinea's stamp, the man's the gowd for a' that."[5]

Where did such deep seated notions of equality and fraternity arise? Burns spoke French and supported the Jacobin values of the Republicans in France and America. He spoke no Gaelic. And yet his lowland culture – like the

---

[5] Robert Burns, 'For a' That and a' That', in *Collected Poems of Robert Burns* (Wordsworth Poetry Library), edited by Tim Burke, Ware: Wordsworth Editions, 1994, pp. 330-31.

American Declaration of Independence itself – was based on the expectation of equality that arose not from feudal England with its hierarchies, vassals and serfs, but from the non-feudal culture of the clan.

Millions of Scots are unwittingly acting out values created centuries ago by Gaelic speaking Scots with whom they believe they have no connection.

But as products of this culture, most Scottish politicians cannot identify the forces of the clan at work, even though whole parts of Scottish cities are gang/clan based and very territorial.

Violent male behaviour legitimised by the clan creates status – and that has created a destructive macho urban environment copied by young women who see no other/fairer values at work in their world.

What is the urban gang if not the reincarnation of the modern clan – young men bound together by loyalty whose acceptance, approval and identity depends on violent defence of territory?

In Scotland's huge housing estates public servants keep the peace by day.

By night they are urban battlefields.

Just as the polite burghers of Belfast tried to avoid the 'Troubles' by burying their heads in the bunkers of some very lovely golf courses, so middle class Scots barely recognise and hardly care about the plight of the underclass.

We need to face ourselves – not stumble on.

Time and again, I have marvelled at the massive social and emotional burdens Scots will neither fully embrace nor abandon.

Often, the prospect of living elsewhere seems attractive.

Time and again the physical beauty of the country, the power of its musical culture and the survivor cheek of its people have brought me back.

Will the SNP's landslide victory act as the final spur to change?

It must.

Common Weal and a State of Disorientation

Robin McAlpine

Voltaire's contention that "we look to Scotland for all our ideas of civilisation" is a quote that Scots reach for when they feel the need to experience national pride.[1] And yet it has become something almost sorrowful, like an age-worn sign stating that your local shop once won an award but which indicates only that it has declined so much old glories are all the only glories it has.

There is much about Scotland that remains globally valuable – the world does still look to Scotland for many of its ideas on bioscience, on energy engineering, on Higgs Bosons. Our creative arts are globally recognised. And the world still trades with us on luxury – our whisky, our seafood, our textiles. But civilisation? Who looks to Scotland for civilisation? English liberals perhaps, and some former colonies with strong Scottish ties. But these represent a low threshold.

There are, however, signs of change. In fact, Scotland might again become important to notions of civilisation. This is, as always, the result of a collision of a variety of social, economic and political factors – identity, prosperity and austerity, Thatcher's legacy, abuse of power in London and so on. But mainly it is a outcome of the fact that we face a referendum in 2014 that will decide whether or not Scotland remains a part of the United Kingdom.

Because, whatever else it brings, the constitutional debate in Scotland has altered political horizons and created new intellectual space. And with new space comes new building. This three-way relationship – opportunity, perspective, action – may be the beginning of a fundamental shift.

The opportunity comes simply from having a real, practical debate about a nation state that does not exist. Most of the great discoveries of human history stem from engineering as much as from thinking. So, for example, it is the idea that makes an understanding of bacteria possible but it is the microscope that makes the idea possible. Likewise, cosmology is a largely theoretical exercise but built on information gained through a fundamentally practical and solid piece of apparatus – the telescope. It is the capacity to use new perspectives and information to regenerate old thinking that propels human kind forward. This is true of social thinking every bit as much as scientific thinking, and the need to argue for or against an imaginary nation has provided the equivalent of a microscope with which to examine where we are now and a telescope with which to gaze forward. This is a structural framework which makes thinking possible in a way that the day-

---

[1] See Arthur Herman, *The Scottish Enlightenment: The Scots' Invention of the Modern World*, London: Fourth Estate, 2003, p.116.

to-day management of a continuing state does not. It provides perspective.

Along with this we have a comparatively 'protected space' in which to explore. The concept of 'protected space' is one that has been pushed to the background of our thinking by the market economy approach to all things. In fact, the really important things do not happen in markets but in protected spaces, places where the market is restrained, tamed, excluded. Universities are protected space. So is national defence. Or space exploration. In each case, the market simply would not deliver because the returns are either very long term or intangible. So the state steps in to create the protected space instead. Which is why almost every major innovation in the last 100 years of human history has occurred from anywhere except the free market.

It may not feel like it for those engaged in the increasingly bitter and polarised constitutional debate in Scotland, but this still represents a comparatively 'protected space' in which to think. Because what is being debated in the constitutional campaign is largely predicated on a fresh start. Yes, there has been a drive to make the debate about the narrow transitional arrangements, the details of the immediate future. But still, it has been impossible to prevent people thinking about and thinking for a future not defined solely by the present. This has created opportunity.

Finally, we have a process of building. This is the emergent aspect of Scotland's constitutional debate, and it is too early to be conclusive about what will result. But despite the first year of the campaign being aggressively corralled by parts of the No campaign and parts of the media into an effective dead end of arcane constitutional detail, as of the summer of 2013, real thinking is starting to bubble up from many places.

What is interesting is that this 'bubbling up' has most certainly not been controlled or planned, least of all by the Scottish National Party. In fact, SNP policy, so far as we have heard it, seems to be the equivalent of 'unthinking' – arguing that Scotland must be independent to escape misrule and then unthinking that again by proposing much the same form of misrule in an independent Scotland's future. Anyone sitting on planet earth in 2013 who has watched the moral and economic implosion of the City of London and its financial institutions and then concludes that the future is to sustain the regulatory framework that created this implosion has some pretty difficult explaining to do.

That does not mean individuals in the SNP have not begun a serious process of thinking. And it certainly does not apply to thinking in and around the independence-supporting Scottish Green Party, the socialist parties, the Radical Independence Campaign (a loose and very large coalition of socially progressive voices campaigning for independence as a route to a better future), many in academia, groups like the National Collective (a collection of mainly young artists and thinkers challenging a conservative view of nations and politics), think tanks like the Jimmy Reid Foundation and Nordic Horizons, blogs and websites like *Bella Caledonia* and, perhaps the most encouraging thing of all, lots of individuals who are writing or blogging or asking "couldn't we try…?"

And what is most important about all this bubbling up is that it is becoming clear to all that these bubbles are not random. In fact, they all stem from the same fissure; that the socio-political philosophy of anglo-capitalism is failing. As of summer 2013, these bubbles are starting to join up. It is starting to resemble the beginning of a movement, simultaneously loose but specific. And it has developed a name; 'Common Weal', a traditional Scots term with the meaning of both 'wealth held in common' and 'our shared wellbeing'.

Why is this important? Or more specifically, why is this important for anyone outside Scotland? Well, potentially, because of the difference between existence and transformation. A truly dreadful comedy from the 1990s was set in a bio-dome, a hermetically sealed, carefully controlled environment locked off from the outside world as a biological experiment. Except two idiots accidentally end up locked inside and proceed to destroy the ecosystem by smoking, drinking and generally destroying things. Then the unfeasibly sexy scientist running the place wakes them up to their actions and, in the last act, they montage their way to a restoration of the environmental balance in the dome. The point, the film implies in its low-rent way, is that it is all very well to take a pristine environment and protect it like a museum exhibit. It is another altogether to take a polluted mess and transform it into a pristine environment. The former is a curiosity, the latter is an inspiration.

In the UK in particular but more places beyond, this has been the problem with the Nordic nations as a guide for others who aspire to a more just society. The Nordics have managed much of what neoliberal economics takes to be impossible – high tax and high growth, mutual governance with workers and trade unions in powerful positions but without industrial disputes, high pay and yet competitive businesses, wonderful and extensive public services with no means testing, high rates of gender equality without targets or quotas. And so on.

The dominant political powers in Britain have been very keen to promote 'Nordic exceptionalism' – that Nordic countries are the exception that proves the rule, that there was some strange historical quirk that caused this but cannot be replicated, that there is just something fundamentally 'weird' about the minds of Swedes, Danes, Norwegians and Finns, that it could only happen if we have another world war or whatever. Anything to show that this is not possible again. (In the US, they do the same with Canada.)

And where the anti-Nords have an advantage is that no other nation has 'become Nordic'; in fact, even the extensive welfare states that emerged in Europe after the Second World War have not triggered other emerging economies to follow that model. There is little evidence that the world has become more 'European socially democrat', never mind more Nordic.

Which is where Scotland can become important again. If a nation deeply embedded in the anglo-economic tradition can break free and pursue a transformational process that rejects neoliberal market dogma and does something else instead, if it works, what then for London? If Scotland can develop a model of Common Weal that makes us more prosperous, more productive, a better global neighbour, happier, healthier and kinder to our environment, in a nation with healthy public sector finances despite an expanded welfare state, how then will this political approach be denied?

It is in the potential for Scotland to pioneer transformational political approaches which challenge the monolithic view of reality promoted by the IMF, the central banks, the financial markets and all the rest that its future role as a significant nation state on the world stage lies.

But what does this all mean?

Why possibility exists in Scotland

In reality, the last 50 years of Scottish history have been about mitigating change, not leading it. This is most obviously seen in the reaction to Thatcher and throughout the early devolution era. In this latter period some have implied that Scotland passively refused to adopt the market-dominated social policies of the Blair years. That is wrong; the process was not passive, and much energy was exerted in actively choosing to insulate Scotland and take some tentative steps in the other direction.

Of course, one of the biggest battles being fought at the heart of the debate over Scotland's constitutional future is the battle for meaning. Many who incline to see Scotland as fundamentally part of Britain have articulated Scotland purely as a response to Margaret Thatcher, one mirrored in the north of England. This is an anglo-centric analysis, seeing Scotland as a reaction. In fact, the differential Scotland/England voting patterns began well before Thatcher and were dominant by the 1970s.[2]

An awful lot of effort has been expended to battle for this particular meaning; is Scotland's differential voting patterns an indication of fundamental difference or not? For those unfamiliar with recent Scottish history, there has been an unwavering pattern of parties unwilling to sign up to a socially democratic agenda being unelectable, at least as potential governments. From the late 1960s to the dawn of devolution, Scotland returned a fairly unbroken block of Labour MPs to Westminster. The Tories had a few heartlands, but in Scotland they were a minor party, sniffing power only on the back of the politics of the south of England. In the post-devolution era, no serious challenge has been mounted for a place in government by any party unwilling to proclaim its social democratic credentials.

So what does this 'mean'? The most straightforward assumption would be that 50 years represents a pattern solid enough to suggest that, as a

---

[2] See Alice Brown, David McCrone, Lindsay Paterson and Paula Surridge, *The Scottish Electorate: The 1997 General Election and Beyond*, Basingstoke: Macmillan, 1999.

whole, Scotland is indeed politically different from England. The battle against this has deployed a number of techniques. One is to fragment the political geography – the north of England votes more like Scotland than England, 'proving' that Scotland is not fundamentally different. However, as soon as you have to resort to creating your own geographical entities to disprove geographical differences, you have nowhere to go. Already, the right wing media is trying to find a village – one village, anywhere in Scotland – with a handful of UKIP voters which will then 'prove' that Scotland is not hostile to UKIP. This is propaganda, not reality. If Scotland is an entity and England is an entity then you compare them by the collective or total act of each entity. On this basis, Scotland as a whole behaves markedly differently than England as a whole. It is then for England to have a debate about how different it has become from itself.

The other way the question of Scottish difference is manufactured is by social research and opinion poll. The new fashion among the conservative voices in Scotland is to prove that reality is not real because an opinion survey is inconclusive. The 'myth' of egalitarian Scotland, we are regularly told by people who seem to have little social science experience, is debunked by social attitude surveys that show Scottish attitudes are not all that different from English attitudes. Sort of like the way a tree's DNA is not all that different from a human's. It would take a chapter this size to properly dismantle that argument (thresholds, the question asked, a control group to show the maximum variation of view to see how different is different and so on). But mainly, this clever-clever poll-waving has a problem with reality. If we are not different, why do we make such clearly different electoral choices?

The failure on the part of the difference-deniers is that they do not engage with the material from which nations are built – identity, identification and inclination. Identity is an element of how we define ourselves, identification is a sense of who we trust and who we align ourselves with, and inclination is about what we hope for and our aspiration. I am, I am like, I want.

The problem for the UK is that England (and indeed many Scottish unionists) seem unable to get beyond the identity question, believing the crisis of Britishness is a question about 'who am I'. This is the traditional territory of the 'cultural nationalist', but it is a long time since this was a dominant strand in Scottish politics. Over the 1980s and the 1990s (and despite the efforts of parts of the Scottish establishment), most Scots became intensely comfortable with being Scottish. The violence of 1970s 'football nationalism' was long gone, and in its place emerged a Scotland in which people routinely describe themselves as Scottish. The biggest visible change can be seen at a Scottish wedding; as recently as the 1970s, a Scot in a kilt was assumed to be making a point. Now, a wedding is a whirl of plaid spinning at complete ease with itself. Identity politics have been resolved.

In parallel with this we find a process of de-nationalisation of independence, the cry of "I'm not a nationalist but..." Some suggest this shows that Scottish identity is not driving the debate. That is probably true, but because identity is largely resolved, not because it is insignificant. This is about the other two elements – identification and inclination.

Inclination is more straightforward to understand. London still thinks Scottish voting is an aberration, an unsophisticated electorate wailing in anger about a woman who is no longer there. That it might be a political choice is virtually dismissed. In fact, in this Scotland really is more like Britain – most people do not really like the neoliberal revolution, its poor quality, low pay jobs, its debt-fuelled vacuity. It is just that in Scotland we have developed a political culture that has responded, whereas in England the aim has always been to maintain but disguise the status quo. Again, Scotland has no hesitation in voting left, no conflict. In terms of inclination, Scotland has made its choice.

What appears to be an increasingly problem for the British State is identification. During the Queen's Jubilee in 2012 it was common to hear commentators emphasise that Scotland has no more of a republican movement than England. But this ignores the fact that when polled across Britain, 80 per cent of the English claim to be proud of the Monarchy, while only 40 per cent of Scots say the same thing[3]. And try as you might (the BBC really, really tried) you would have found very little fervent interest for the Jubilee on this side of the border.

In understanding Scotland, too few people have discussed this element, not the question of 'who am I and what do I want' but 'who do I trust, who is like me?'. The South East of England seems to continue to hold firmly to identifiers of the British State and the British Establishment – the Monarchy, the armed forces, the City of London – in a way that seems alien to many Scots. This, much more than any love of tartan or hatred of Thatcher, is the real problem for the UK, at least on its northern fault line. We simply do not feel particularly British on a day-to-day basis, and we do not particularly miss it because its primary identifiers do not resonate with us.

To understand this, consider Cameron's 2012 nationalist justification for a banker-driven veto of Europe. It was predicated on the idea that 'no-one likes bankers, but we'll back our bankers over their bankers'. Unless I completely missed it, this had no resonance in Scotland at all. If anything, we probably feel more hostile to the private school City of London bankers than we do to European Central Bankers of whom we are barely conscious.

It is important to understand this to understand why the roots of a Common Weal are established in Scotland. It is not because we are endlessly different than our neighbours in England. It is not because we are all the same on one side of a fence and they are all the same on another. It is because a process of historical and political transformation in Britain over the last 50

---

[3] Andrew Gimson, Rachael Jolley, Sunder Katwala, Peter Kellner, Alex Massie and Richard Mirada, *This Sceptred Isle: Pride not prejudice across the nations of Britain*, British Future, 2012 , <www.britishfuture.org>.

years has created two genuinely different nations. We vote differently, we feel differently, we identify differently, and we no longer worry about any of this.

A different set of cultural identifiers, a diverging sense of identification with the British State and a different political inclination have created a philosophical vacuum. The politics of Britain no longer match the politics of Scotland. The desire for 'something else' is strong.

A State of Disorientation

Britain is a surprisingly parochial country when it comes to sources of inspiration and measures against which to assess ourselves. For a long time Britain (often as a direct result of campaigns by the right-wing media) has tried hard to obscure Europe from us. The story became always about 'what's wrong with Europe' and why we would not want to be like them. Straight bananas and all that. At the same time, this story has been curated almost literally to disorientate us – orientate originally meaning to find east. Instead, we have had a strange distorting medium between us and things to the north and to the east. The US has far too often become our chosen frame of reference. This is partly linguistic, partly cultural, but mainly political. For generations, Britain saw itself as a bridge between Europe and the US, possibly more in delusion than reality. In the second half of the twentieth century, Britain was an important US asset in Europe, but the intellectual traffic was one way. We learned much about America's obsessions (small government, laissez faire, individualism) but evidence that they learned much about Europe's is much more limited.

The outcome of this has been that Britain has remained stubbornly unwilling to learn political lessons from anywhere to its east or north – as discussed above, Scandinavia has always been dismissed sniffily as a 'peculiar and specific' social model. In fact, if you listened only to the UK view of things, the European social model is one we think belongs separately to Britain. It is as if we are an island broken off from a continent, an island in which political evolution took a different course from the mainland, producing a unique and self-contained social order. This is not true; it was very much part of a continent that was struggling its way into a post-war settlement that could do nothing other than build something better among the ruins. We just do not see it that way. We imagine Britain to be self-contained.

To my eyes, this mindset seemed to reach its turning point in Danny Boyle's Olympics opener. That we took so much pleasure in hundreds of underpaid nurses dancing for free for corporate sponsors while the pernicious deregulation of the NHS in England was ploughing its way through Parliament seemed to me to present a major disjuncture. This was not a birthday party; we were not celebrating something in rude health. It was not a funeral; we were not mourning the loss of a loved one. It was like we were dancing round the room dragging a corpse with us. We were celebrating the ideal of the NHS at the very point where its founding principles were being discarded.

As the post-war ideal slips away before our eyes, in its place is the awareness that Britain is the fourth most unequal country in the world, and it is getting worse. As the horizons of the debate are stretched, unwillingly, from our island up to the north and out to the east, light is cast on our social democracy. And it is not a sympathetic light. Almost three out of four people in Scotland get by on less than £24,000 a year[4]. That is the average salary. Two out of five people get at least 40 per cent of their income from benefits and welfare. More remarkably, four out of five Scots get at least 15 per cent of their income from benefits and welfare. Poverty has never been properly tackled and is now getting worse. In fact, there are only four ways we could end up worse; become Turkey, Russia, the US or a third world country.

The other dark corner of British self-certainty that is suffering from exposure to light is our economic performance. When I was younger, when I had graduated in sociology but had not yet learned the details of economics, I can recall the certainty that Britain was outperforming Europe on all economic measures. Except productivity (which few people really understand and which was partially dismissed). And in industrial production (which we knew was old fashioned anyway). And in trade in goods (same). And in research and development (which we were told was wrong anyway because it did not include 'innovations' being carried out by investment bankers).

It was only much later that I realised this is a function of a pseudo-state media. On the economy it was an unwritten rule right up until the financial crash of 2008 that to 'talk down' the UK economy was like a small act of treason. Any Chancellor of the Exchequer who said "we're doing better than Germany" was taken at face value, and no-one in the media or political classes had an incentive to disagree. To look back now over the period 1984 (the 'Big Bang' in the City of London) to 2008 (the moment when the shockwave from the Big Bang brought the house down), mainstream commentary questioning the orthodoxy that all was well with Britain's economy is hard to find. And that despite it containing two economic crises and a sequence of declining indicators of economic health. We could niggle to our heart's content about the NHS or education, but we were not to ask if our leaders of industry knew what they were doing.

However, we can now stop and look back with a little more perspective. This is what economists Jim and Margaret Cuthbert did in two papers published by the Jimmy Reid Foundation assessing 40 years of the UK economy.[5] The findings are alarming – there is barely a measure which

---

[4] Not By The People: The Launch of the Commission on Fair Access to Political Influence, Biggar: The Jimmy Reid Foundation, 2013, <www.reidfoundation.org>.

[5] Jim Cuthbert, The Mismanagement of Britain: A record of the UK's declining competitiveness – and its implications, Biggar: The Jimmy Reid Foundation, 2013,

looking at it now indicated things were going OK, other than GDP and tax take, resulting from unsustainable hijinks in the financial services sector. One wonders, looking back now, how no real question was raised at the time. The statistic that hit me most was on industrial production. The following are the rates of change in industrial production for a range of comparable nations: Austria plus 99 per cent, Belgium plus 34 per cent, Canada plus 36 per cent, Denmark plus 23 per cent, Finland plus 84 per cent, Germany plus 34 per cent, Ireland plus 362 per cent, Netherlands plus 33 per cent, Norway plus 12 per cent, Sweden plus 54 per cent, the US plus 51 per cent. Oh, and the UK? Minus 1.2 per cent.

The United Kingdom has been in a state of disorientation for two generations. It has refused to look east or north, it has compared itself mainly inwards, it has floated on a sea of self-propaganda, it has faced crisis after crisis without reform. It appears to have only a mirror where it ought to have a geopolitical compass. Anglo capitalism has failed, and only now are we properly waking up to this truth.

What is Common Weal?

The strange thing about Common Weal is that it is simultaneously new and distinctive in terms of Scotland's political debate, and yet familiar and well understood in terms of individual policy approaches. Common Weal is in part a trick of branding, a means of uniting in an understandable way a range of policies that are pushing towards the same ends while propelling themselves away from the same root problems.

As with most matters in human relations, language is a good indicator. We can take two statements which each represent a dominant view on the source of economic growth, one from the anglo model and one from the Nordic model. For anglo-capitalists, no precept can reach higher than the belief that we must 'cherish the wealth creators'. It is a belief that a small minority possess special powers and that these powers apply in a market with minimal regulation, guided solely by profit as the source of national wealth. And it is complete rubbish and demonstrably so.

That is true, in part, because the economics do not sustain it, but true even more, because events do not sustain it. This dominant economic belief has swept all aside in its control of policy in Britain for three decades. And what is the result? A fundamentally unstable economy, massive income inequality, low productivity, low industrial production, poor balance of trade in goods and services, increasing debt and deficit in the pubic sectors, low social cohesion. On the up side? Quite a lot of very rich people.

Compare and contrast: "to build more we must share more." This is much closer to the dominant idea in Nordic politics, one shared by both right and

<http://reidfoundation.org/wp-content/uploads/2013/04/Mismanagement.pdf>; Margaret Cuthbert, *The UK Economy: a strong and secure UK?*, Biggar: The Jimmy Reid Foundation, 2013, <www.cuthbert1.pwp.blueyonder.co.uk>.

left. In fact, this is a loose translation of Norwegian Prime Minister Jens Stoltenberg who said "Vi må dele mest mulig likt, for å kunne skape mer."[6] A more accurate translation of which is "we must share as equally as we can, in order to create more." There, too, they have had a number of decades to test out that alternative thesis.

The outcome? Income and wealth inequality are low and social cohesion is high. Pay is higher, poverty is very low, and a much lower proportion of jobs are in unskilled, routine sectors. Total tax take and collection is higher, and this enables significant redistribution and strong public services, but without endemic debt and deficit. The welfare state is strong and public services are extensive, well funded and generally universally available. Finance is seen as a means of sustaining industry and providing financial security for individuals, not as a speculative means of profit maximisation. Economies are diverse with a much more balanced portfolio of industry sectors, much more emphasis on product innovation, a much larger medium sized industry sector exists, there is a much more diverse ownership profile (including more extensive public and community ownership and cooperatives), and a much more mutual and coordinated approach to economic development is taken. Society is generally more inclusive, with better gender and other equality in politics, on boards of governance, in leadership positions, etc. And there is an assumption that active democracy is beneficial for all, whether that is a very highly democratic structure of local government or industrial democracy that values the input of employees in the governance of enterprises.[7]

At heart, the Common Weal project aims to do only one thing; give people a choice between these two visions for Scotland's future. Even now, even after all that has happened to financial markets, the wider economy, household incomes, despite this, at a UK level we do not have an option of choosing between these approaches, only two versions of the first. Labour has presented Keynesianism as a means of getting back to good-old Dragon's Den Britain where we can all shop with abandon again, while admiring the thrusting brilliance of retail and property entrepreneurs. An industrial policy, the quality of people's jobs or an interest in industrial production do not come into it. Labour thinks markets will still sort out our problems, if only we hand a big wedge of cash to the construction industry.

Now, this last point is not to take away the importance of using investment infrastructure to stimulate growth, but this is presented as if it is only the act

---

[6] *Dagens Nyheter*, 13 February 2013.

[7] It is perhaps worth noting that as this is being written there is simmering social unrest in Sweden, a markedly non-Nordic state of social cohesion. Then again, Sweden has had more than ten years of a more neoliberal attitude to government from a right-of-centre administration which has broken down aspects of the Nordic social model. A breakdown in cohesion is precisely one of the outcomes that would be predicted as an outcome of this.

of building infrastructure that matters, not the infrastructure itself. Builders' labourers get jobs, they buy new sportswear, which creates some checkout jobs for the women. The profit creamed off by the construction company will make tax receipts look better than they really are. In fact, economically, it is hard to differentiate this from paying people to dig holes and fill them in again – assuming that hole-digging had been monopolised by multinationals that creamed massive profits off per hole dug.

The alternative approach? Yes, build the infrastructure, but with two major differences. First, integrate the injection of investment with an industrial policy. Let me give an example; Scotland has world-class expertise in both nanotechnology and thin film technology. Both of these have applications in the field of advanced construction material manufacture. So, have a five-year programme of building, but use research and development opt-outs from procurement rules in such a way that every new building will have self-cleaning glass which is sourced from Scottish manufacturers. Rather than hoping the market will reallocate the capital investment (which it does – straight into corporate profit and retail spend), make sure the investment is reallocated to where it actually makes a real difference.

The second difference is to stop equating large enterprise profit with economic success. Rather than compiling construction tenders for infrastructure in whatever way is easiest to deliver by the smallest number of bidding enterprises, work out what allocation of contracts is most likely to target real economic progress as assessed against real economic problems – not just tax, GDP figures and gross employment but indigenous industry development, high-quality jobs and greater income equality. In the case of social housing, for example, it would be massively less effective to contract a big consortium to knock down a housing estate and rebuild it (the profit-maximising model they favour) than it would to create social enterprises that would renovate existing housing stock while creating local employment and retaining the largest possible proportion of the capital investment in the communities that are supposed to be being helped.

These represent only a couple of examples of what a Common Weal approach might mean in practice. The 'movement' (if movement it turns out to be) is in its infancy and must grow up quickly. But even at this early stage there is a clear agenda. A group of academic economists, working with others, have identified a transformational agenda involving six key reforms.[8]

Firstly, tax reform and a real programme to address inequality. Both as a social and economic policy it is important we move towards taking a larger proportion of GDP in tax. This both enables stronger public services and (through the redistributive effect of taxes) much greater social and economic

[8] These are expanded in a Reid Foundation discussion paper – 'The Common Weal', available on the Foundation website: <www.reidfoundation.org>. Among the economists who worked on this are Professor Andy Cumbers, Professor Mike Danson, Professor Ailsa McKay, Professor Christine Cooper, Dr Geoff Whittam and Jim and Margaret Cuthbert. Many others were involved at various stages.

equality. It also helps to stimulate the economy and even out swings in the economic cycle. However, this is combined with higher pay and much less prevalence of low-skill, low-pay work, which means that, even with higher taxes, people have higher take home pay. However, in tandem with this it is important to pursue strategies to increase pay and to structurally reform the economy so it is much less dominated by low-skill, low-pay work.

Secondly, a completely different approach to welfare. In the Nordic countries the phrase 'Folkshemmet' is used to refer to what we call the welfare state. The literal translation is 'the People's Home', which outlines a very different attitude to welfare than the one developing in Britain. To move in that direction, Scotland should set out a set of criteria to underpin the welfare state – that public services and cash benefits are part of one seamless system, that this is then delivered on universalist principles from the cradle to the grave and from each according to ability to pay to each according to need etc. This should then be redefined not as a relationship between the state and the people but a contract between the people themselves, delivered through the state. The principles underpinning that welfare state will then enable a discussion about how it can expand.

Thirdly, reforming finance. Scotland needs a proper national investment bank for industry with proper governance. It must be run on mutual principles (including all stakeholders in the economy working together to set long-term strategic approaches) and must under all circumstances be prevented from drifting into a role similar to the existing banks (run on the lines of profit maximisation). This should be linked to national strategies for industry development. The investment bank should look very seriously at using pension funds as a foundation for creating investment capacity. There is also a very strong case for either that bank or a national social enterprise investment bank to function as a major lender to social and community enterprises (which might include local authorities) and to cooperatives and mutuals. We must also repair our private banks and rediscover the tradition of real financial innovation that made Scotland such a strong banking nation prior to the Big Bang.

Fourthly, we need to rethink ownership. The ownership of Britain's industry is monolithic and, by many measures, failing. It has led to a massive 'hollowing-out' in the middle of the employment spectrum, with the dominance of low-pay sectors (often large foreign-owned multinationals) at one end, and high-pay 'executive' jobs at the other, with little in between. There are pitiful levels of investment in research and development and staff development, and there is a general lack of long-term reinvestment. Reversing this requires a much more diverse economic ownership profile. More domestically-owned medium sized enterprises with a long-term ownership strategy focussed on innovative and productive enterprise (along the lines of the German *Mittelstand* industries) are key to this, not least because they pay tax. Equally, there are many parts of Scotland where good-quality employment is almost entirely unavailable. Social and community-owned enterprises must be supported as a long-term key structural part of the economy, particularly where the private sector has failed to generate quality employment opportunities. Mutual and cooperative industries at a large scale also have an important effect of 'countercyclical economic balance' since they do not tend to disinvest during economic downturns in the way large private enterprises do. Finally, the British rejection of the concept of nationalised industries is harmful. Models of public ownership have moved on from the 1970s model of large, centralised industries remote from customers.

Fifth, we need a programme of economic diversification. The massively damaging impact of over-reliance on financial services is now well known and the social and economic dangers of over-reliance on the housing market are also understood. The retail and personal services sectors are also proportionately too large in Scotland and must also be diversified (these are a large part of the structural cause of low pay). To do this we need to create more enterprises involved in modern industrial production which better use the skills of the Scottish workforce, create real export markets and produce better-paid jobs. The key sector is the medium sized enterprise sector. Scotland's economy should of course continue to seek inward investment but unless industrial strategies can develop a strong, productive, innovative domestic economy, economic precariousness and low-skill, low-wage employment will continue to dominate.

Sixth, we need a revolution in democracy and governance. The concept of participative democracy and diversified governance are important to the strategic themes outlined above. Industrial democracy (including strong trade unions working collaboratively with employers not only on employee remuneration issues but also on strategic management issues) has the effect of improving the economic performance of enterprises and avoids the monolithic 'group think' failures that have been revealed in the UK economy. Employee representation on management boards is welcomed by Nordic industry and is an important part of governance arrangements. Strong trade unions in a mutual rather than conflict relationship are also key to income and wealth equality. Generally, achieving more diversity, equality and representativeness across public and private life is seen as key – on boards, in politics, in leadership and so on. At the national level, greater participation by citizens in governance helps to mitigate the stultifying effect of unchallenged corporate political influence. It helps to produce better decision-making, less captured by producer interests. At the local level, it is essential that Scotland has significant democratic reform to move local decision-making into local communities.[9]

---

[9] See Eberhard Bort, Robin McAlpine and Gordon Morgan, *The Silent Crisis: Failure and Revival in Local Democracy in Scotland*, Biggar: The Jimmy Reid Foundation, 2012, <http://reidfoundation.org/wp-content/uploads/2012/04/The-Silent-Crisis1.pdf>.

And so...

This is a programme of thinking and policy development that the Jimmy Reid Foundation has helped to kick off. I can say, without any hesitation, that in 20 years of political life I have never been involved with a project which has generated so much interest so quickly and from such a diverse range of sources. The Nordic model may look like some left-wing fantasy from the confines of Westminster, but in the Nordic countries it manages to encompass everything from right-wing anti-immigration parties to far-left anarchist parties. They agree on very little, other than that their social and economic foundations must not be messed with.

And so it is that we have had enthusiastic contact from right of centre small businesses and distinctly left socialist groups. It is a process of seeking to tie together the interests of the many groups who have been let down by the British system. It is an open and plural approach, not owned or controlled by anyone. Then again, at the time of writing the phrase has been in existence for less than two months.

Still, two things remain as important legacies even of what has happened so far. The first is that the idea of a 'contested debate' is already alive. People have been writing in a number of different places saying 'we now have an option, an alternative'.[10] That such an alternative has an identity is helpful.

The second takes us back to Voltaire. This idea of Common Weal emerges out of a rethinking of Scotland and its place in the world. While the British establishment has sought to identify the independence movement in Scotland (and those who may not be full independence supporters but hope for something better than the Britain we have) as some sort of narrow, self-interested nationalists, nothing could be further from the truth. This is, in part, a rediscovery of the belief that it is possible to build a very bright light on a very small foundation. Scotland may be little more than five million people, but enough of them – given the space to think about it – want to do something better and different to the orthodoxy of the European elite. Where Greece has responded in anger and Italy in despair, Scotland is seeking to respond through hope.

We are not now a source of all the world's ideas of civilisation. But, in the belief that we can transform ourselves into something better, we may offer the world something even better; one really good idea about how civilisation can be torn from the grasping hands of the elite and returned to citizens.

---

[10] See, e.g., Joyce McMillan, 'Healthier view of social democracy', *The Scotsman*, 3 May 2013; 'At last, a vision for independence' (Editorial), *The Herald*, 5 May 2013; and Tom Gordon, 'An Agenda for change', *Sunday Herald*, 16 June 2013.

Scotland's other constitutional debate

James Mitchell

The debate on Scotland's constitutional status has a number of dimensions. One view is that it is a clash of competing nationalisms: Scottish *vs* British/ UK. There is little doubt that on either side there are combatants – and this does indeed appear to be their self-perception – who will support their country, whichever it is, right or wrong. These are people less concerned with what kind of Scotland or UK exists than the flag to be flown over public buildings – who either refuse to engage in outlining the kind of state and society they envisage or simply use instrumental arguments instrumentally. From a principled nationalist perspective, the integrity of the national state or the independence of the nation is all that matters. This is not to disparage such a perspective but we should recognise these positions as irreconcilable.

But an alternative perspective exists and, though it gets little airing in the media, it is important and deserves attention. A space or, rather, spaces are opening up in which the constitutional debate has been broadened out. This is not an inter-nationalist debate, as it were, but a full constitutional debate in which ideas citizenship are central. The central focus on citizenship makes the choice of which state people in Scotland should belong to an empirical question rather than a principled matter. There has long been ample evidence that support for constitutional reform was contingent rather than springing from the view that a nation has an automatic right to become a state. While the parties and the media engage in endless, arid argument over whether international treaties have to be renegotiated or are inherited, the appetite amongst the public is for some sense of how constitutional change will affect their daily lives, if at all.

In this debate, the questions are:

- what kind of Scotland/UK will we live in?
- who will belong to this Scotland/UK?
- what rights, privileges and responsibilities people will have in Scotland/UK?

This is a debate about the kind of state we want, and also who has the right to belong to the state. In this sense, this is a debate within a liberal democratic framework that focuses on an observation about liberal democracies made by Hannah Arendt, one of the most important philosophers of the twentieth century. Arendt wrote about having the "right to have rights,"[1] and "a right to belong to some kind of organized community"[2] in her classic work, *The Origins of Totalitarianism*. Arendt forces us to consider the most inconvenient aspect for both sides in this debate. Liberal democracies espouse thinking associated with the Scottish Enlightenment of universal individual rights. But liberal democracies are organised into sovereign states, with each state permitted considerable autonomy in defining these rights and who should have access to these rights. State sovereignty allows states to deny rights to individuals or categories of individuals, to turn away refugees from other places. It is hopelessly dishonest for either side to argue that their preferred constitutional arrangement is *per se* a step closer or further away from the achievement of universal rights. The test is not whether the integrity of the UK or an independent Scotland takes us towards or away from the Enlightenment ideal. The focus must be upon the kind of rights and for whom these rights would accrue in determining which approaches this ideal rather than the polity itself.

From one perspective, rights are seen as a matter for the political parties to argue over and not a constitutional issue. However, this is a rather dated view of constitutional politics. The days when a constitution was concerned purely with institutional politics – the relations between different levels of government and between legislatures, executives and the judiciary – are behind us, at least across most of the world. Modern constitutional deliberation is concerned with rights – the negative rights of earlier times, but also increasingly with positive rights. If a constitution is to do more than outline formal institutional relations and attempt to outline what citizens should expect, then positive rights need to be incorporated into the debate.

This has become even more pressing at a time of economic difficulties. All too often those who lose out in such circumstances are those most reliant on the state for protection. The question to be asked is what, if anything, does a constitution offer to entrench rights and outline responsibilities? What protection does a constitution offer for the weakest in society? Or are constitutions only to be designed, as in the past, for the protection of negative rights – freedom not to be subjected to actions of others including arbitrary government actions – or for the protection of positive rights – including social security, broadly defined? It may be that what this debate offers is a very limited focus on negative rights. If so, we should not be too surprised if this fails to engage the public or if the result is determined purely on the basis of an inter-nationalist battle for loyalty.

There are five key issues at stake:

---

[1] Hannah Arendt, *The Origins of Totalitarianism* (1951), London: Andre Deutsch, 1986, p.296

[2] *ibid.*, p.297.

i. One of the most fundamental issues at stake is who belongs? Who will have citizenship under either constitutional status is not a given in either case. In Hannah Arendt's terms, refugees are the 'most symptomatic group in contemporary politics'.[3] Who is able to claim citizenship is central to this debate.

ii. No side in this debate can, nor should be expected to, outline the nature of rights in detail, though we should expect some sense of the kind of state and society envisaged by both sides. We have a sense of what the constitutional status quo offers, but that will not be static. This is an opportunity to ask not only what kind of polity is the United Kingdom but also what it might become. It is obviously also an opportunity to consider what alternative, if it is an alternative rather than simply the UK writ-small, an independent Scotland would become.

iii. This is a debate about choices and capabilities. Each potential future will involve making choices about the kind of state and society we live in, but within our capabilities to deliver. Ideals are important and a sense of direction, as mentioned immediately above, is important, but we need to have a sense of whether we have the capabilities to bring about the kind of society and state envisaged.

iv. Capabilities also involve choices. Wealthy states – as Scotland or the UK would both undoubtedly be – must decide on how that wealth is distributed. We want to have our cake and eat it: we want high levels of welfare and low levels of taxes – this is primarily a *choice*, though one bounded by other considerations.

v. The status quo in terms of rights is not an option. The one certainty is that whatever decision is made in September 2014, we are moving into a period of change in rights.

I.   Who Belongs?

It matters less to any individual which states exist in the world than whether she belongs to one. The rights and obligations that follow residence, whether that residence is temporary or permanent are matters of singular importance.

---

[3] *ibid.*, p.277.

Indeed, gaining any form of residence was, for Arendt, a fundamental issue. We should be thankful that in this debate there is little to separate the two sides. Each is committed to a broadly liberal interpretation of belonging, though some might question just how liberal. The test arises in the hard cases. It is also notable that membership of the European Union affects this, as indeed any of the other considerations discussed in this chapter. The EU provides a framework within which questions of belonging occur and might be seen as offering some, albeit small and extremely limited, step towards universalism. It is extremely small in the context of world politics, an obvious point, but one that requires repeating. A large polity such as the EU is no less capable of parochialism than a small polity, and a Fortress Europe would offend notions of universalism more than that available in a more open-bordered small state. It is limited in that the determination of who belongs and of rights associated with belonging in the EU, though significant by almost any measurement, remain under development.

An interesting aspect of this has arisen in debates on who should be permitted to vote. This has a number of aspects, and answers to each are at least indicative of the kinds of rights likely to exist in different polities. The franchise in the referendum has been extended in respect of age. Those aged 16 and 17 will have a vote, and this has generated more comment than other aspects of the franchise. Included amongst those who will be able to vote are all EU citizens. There is, however, no appetite for allowing prisoners to vote amongst key figures on either side of the debate, despite developments in other European states including Denmark, Finland, Germany, Ireland, Sweden and Switzerland. The European Court of Human rights recently adjourned a hearing on voting rights for prisoners in the UK, pending the outcome of consultation within the UK, but following an ECHR judgment in 2005 criticising the blanket ban on prisoners' voting in the UK. This formal position appears informed more by a desire to avoid confrontation with the UK Government in its current mood of antagonism towards anything emanating from any European institution that might be presented as either challenging the UK's mythical Parliamentary sovereignty or moving it in a more liberal direction.

It has been suggested that Scots resident outside Scotland should be permitted to vote in the referendum. It is possible to be charitable in interpreting this proposal for an ethnic-based franchise. It is likely that it was simply partisan and unserious. Alternatively, its proponents may not have thought through its implications either in terms of its implementation – involving as it would significant costs in terms of identifying such electors – or, far more significant, the need for some ethnic definition of citizenship.

But beyond questions of who should vote which might offer a guide as to understandings of citizenship, there are other considerations that focus on the Arendtian issues of belonging. To what extent would an independent Scotland have a more open asylum and refugee policy? This is a key test if we measure any polity in terms of how it treats the most vulnerable in its care. In its report considering the various options available for the creation of a humane policy in this area, the Scottish Human Rights policy set challenges to partisans in the current debate that contribute to this wider notion of a good polity.[4] The challenge to both sides is to ask that all refugees seeking protection in Scotland should be welcome, treated with dignity and respect and be able to achieve their full potential. A wide range of matters are at stake in raising this challenge. These get closer to the heart of constitutional politics from the perspective of the most vulnerable in our keep than almost any other matters. Even before considering the kinds of positive rights that will be available, there is the prior question of who would have rights to these rights.

II. The Kind of State/Society Envisaged

We should expect some idea in broad terms of the kind of state and society envisaged under either future scenario. Both sides of this debate support some form of welfare state, but welfare states come in different shapes and sizes. We have witnessed significant changes in the provision of welfare in the UK over time, and there will be further changes in the future. Much is unpredictable under either constitutional scenario. Indeed, anyone making precise claims should be treated with suspicion. If we have learned one lesson in recent years, then surely it is the need for a greater degree of humility in forecasting in the social sciences – especially regarding economic developments. But we should expect some sense of the direction from both sides of this debate.

All we can say with anything approaching certainty is that what we have now will change. This is not a debate between the status quo and change after independence. This is a debate between two forms of change in terms of positive rights. The simple-minded assumption that the constitutional status quo equates with the welfare status quo should be dismissed.

In 1999, no-one could have predicted the policies pursued by the Scottish Parliament with anything approaching precision. One-dimensional public opinion surveys failed to capture the kind of changes that emerged and failed to predict the kinds of changes that occurred. Created as a means of 'stopping Thatcherism at the border', Holyrood developed its own welfare logic. In detail, it was unpredictable, but in broad terms it was highly predictable.

Devolution debates were closely associated with debates on welfare issues. In these debates, as I argued at the time, people in Scotland expressed

---

[4] The author was involved in drawing up the report which makes no recommendation as to how people should vote but raises challenges for all sides. The report, *Improving the Lives of Refugees in Scotland after the Referendum: An Appraisal of the Options,* can be found on the Scottish refugee council website: <www.scottishrefugeecouncil. org.uk/policy_and_research/research_reports>.

support for continuity. But they wanted continuity of the welfare state, not necessarily the way the UK was structured constitutionally. Whether that was provided by a centralised or devolved state was, for many people, secondary. That has not changed significantly – many Scots want to retain the state to which they owe most loyalty – not the UK state, nor a putative Scottish state, but some – ill-defined – welfare state.

There was much naivety in the early years as to what devolved government could do – an expectations gap existed between what it could do and what people wanted from it. This was largely hidden in the first decade of devolution, due to the phenomenal rising levels of public expenditure across the state. This public financial backdrop meant that decisions were made piecemeal and on an implicit assumption that spending levels would be maintained.

III. Choice and Capabilities

This is about a choice between the direction of travel towards potentially different types of social welfare. It may be that an independent Scotland and the UK would travel in the same direction at different speeds, though this seems unlikely. Choices will be constrained by a number of factors. Three are of particular relevance to this debate: available political support, public finances, and spill-over implications.

- Political support: what is very clear is that Scotland has diverged from rUK in public policy terms within the existing framework of devolution, and that seems unlikely to change with more powers.

- Public finances: The extent to which Scotland could afford to pursue more generous welfare remains a matter of contention, though the old assertions about Scotland's inability to afford basic welfare are now only made by the most partisan. It should also be noted that there remains considerable scope for using existing spending much more wisely – short-term decision-making over many decades, especially appalling during periods of significant increases in spending, has resulted in Scotland failing to make the necessary shift to preventative spending. That shift will prove difficult to make in the current situation, but needs to become a priority as soon as is feasibly possible.

- Spill-over implications/externalities: It has been suggested that the current constitutional arrangements create few incentives to prioritise growth, but instead encourage spending on services. That will change with independence or possibly under alternative models of devolution. Devolved government added a democratic layer to the Scottish Office – a system that was a highly efficient lobbying voice for Scotland within government. It has not made it as responsible as it might have done.

IV. Capabilities also Involve Choices

One of the paradoxes of Scottish politics has been that its two main parties – the SNP and Labour – are both instinctively social democratic, yet there is a marked reluctance to face up to the challenge of explaining how welfare would be funded into the future and under any constitutional scenario. Scotland is one of the most unequal liberal democracies with wealth heavily accumulated at the top end and parties seem remarkably reluctant to address this.

We could afford generous welfare under either constitutional scenario, but the marked reluctance to confront this has limited this debate. There is a need for a healthy and open debate on the balance of tax and spend – informed by the kind of society we want, rather than allowing any group to limit possibilities by claims – and that is all they are: claims – that some scenarios are not possible.

V. The Status Quo is not an Option in Terms Of Welfare

What is clear is that the welfare state as we know it is changing. The nature of employment has changed and is changing. The demography of Scotland is changing. Our needs as a society are changing. This is being incorporated into the debate. We should not delude ourselves into thinking that welfare can remain as it has been. Regardless of the constitutional status of Scotland, welfare provision will change.

Devolution had small 'c' conservative support – a defence against the prospect of a capital 'Conservative' Government rolling back the welfare state. There may be little agreement (within the Government, far less within the NO camp) as to the extent and manner in which the welfare state is changing now, but there seems little doubt that it is changing. The constitutional status quo means uncertainty as far as welfare is concerned. The questions that will have to be answered by supporters of independence as far as welfare is concerned are at least as relevant as far as the constitutional status quo is concerned.

But there are other real world developments that should not be ignored as attention focuses on the implications for welfare on the debate on independence. Considerable innovation is occurring in everyday practices throughout Scotland as the recommendations of the Christie Commission[5] are implemented.

Against the backdrop of the adversarial debate on the constitution, considerable work is taking place implementing at least some aspects of the Christie Commission's recommendations. It may not have been noticed by those focused on party politics or the Holyrood village – and how disappointing, if hardly surprising, it has been that we now have our own equivalent of the Westminster village here – but much is happening and much needs to be done. There is little danger of the many people involved in this work losing sight of this activity, but it would be useful to those with a narrow focus on the 'history making' debate on the constitution to occasionally raise their heads and become more acquainted with these 'day to day' developments.

Conclusion

The main difference between today's debate and the constitutional debate in the 1997 referendum is the greater degree of uncertainty surrounding welfare in the years ahead, regardless of how Scots vote in 2014. This will make voting difficult, at least for those basing their vote on something other than the self-evident truths of British and Scottish nationalism. Such information as exists is all too often suspect – often coming from players in the game masquerading as umpires. Whatever is decided, it will involve a leap of faith. There can be no definitive answers. There never are in liberal democracies. But there can be serious debate. That is required if we are to begin to understand the differences between the "right to rights" and questions of "who belongs" between our choice of states.

Hannah Arendt had been concerned that the liberal democratic contradiction would undermine "rights" (though for her especially the rights of stateless people). This constitutional debate allows us to consider this liberal democratic contradiction on rights – welfare rights – in terms of choices and capabilities between competing territorial and potentially welfare states.

---

[5] *Report on the Future Delivery of Public Services by the Commission chaired by Dr Campbell Christie*, Edinburgh: Scottish Government, 29 June 2011, <www.scotland. gov.uk/Publications/2011/06/27154527/0>.

The Man in the Next Room: Jeremy Bentham and Confederal Salmond

Christopher Harvie

I Bentham on Sentry Go

By May 2011, 'Salmondite politics' had evolved: not necessarily because of its positive qualities. Ideology seemed to be outweighed by a mix of operational rationale and 'human touch': a functional debt to Lloyd-George-in-Whitehall, 1906-22 – the 'faithful chelas' of the Bute House kitchen cabinet, the media and civil society familiars, the mid-Atlantic celebs. Salmond at Princeton in April 2013, speaking to five hundred on Adam Smith, conveyed a pragmatic, almost poetically *Scottish* sense of old traditions breeding new chances.

Such practicality (in terms of accepted ideology) let him beat Gordon Brown: his tactics had worked, evaluating key players in terms of price/position, not bribing but *getting on-side* qualities and functions. No fuss. Despite Scotland's limitations – non-confronting, dull Chamber, monolingual, self-satisfied, middle-class 'Scots Estatesmen', initiative long dampened – Salmond seemed, in contrast to Westminster, to have energised 'the speak of the place', and terminally short-circuited Unionism. Could things *really* be 'Better Together' with Nigel Farage down south?

Salmond was Bailie Nicoll Jarvie, not Rob Roy. His caution, balanced against the flair of a betting man, seemed to have worked. Occasional use of 'Braveheart' tropes came with a distrust of rhetoric and enthusiasm, a compact cabinet in which trusties outweighed imaginators, an issue-by-issue approach.

The problem is what I call 'the man in the next room', because back in 1972 he happened to me. When I was examined on my PhD thesis 'University Liberals and Democratic Politics, 1860-86' by Noel Annan at University College London, Jeremy Bentham was sitting in a sentry box in the lobby. He had been there, stuffed, since his death in 1832. The man whom Engels saw as the 'absolute bourgeois' became, in his own words, an 'auto-icon'. After 1972 he watched his intellectual world collapse, in as black a farce as Lenin's posthumous career.

Bentham has since completely dropped away from our discourse. He and his self-proclaimed successor Professor Albert Venn Dicey, prominent in my thesis, figure centrally in the ideas of our best constitutionalist, Professor James Mitchell, in *Conservatives and the Union* (1990) and *Governing Scotland* (2003), but hardly anywhere else. Bentham's utilitarian calculus refined

Adam Smith's sometimes elusive principles by evaluating them in terms of material results and, when imprecision meant they tripped each other up, imposed administrative *force majeure*.

In 2013-14, Salmond's main problem is the Independence Referendum and, within that, its *materiality*. It will not be won by couthy familiarity, or a daud o' Braveheart, but on the continuing energy/environment issue, segueing from dwindling if pricey oil to marine renewables, with appropriate legislative policy backups. True, there are imaginative, well-publicised gambits like the £10 million Saltire Prize for generating devices, but can Scotland *without* a dedicated ministry – or a well-equipped, competent industry – transform prototypes to production-line models? Sentry Bentham would say: *no way*.

In Holyrood there was an adequate 'state of the UK' debate – compared with London, where politicos' eyes seldom lifted from blogs or polls. But under a 'block grant' form of devolved constitution it tended to repetition and (after the bank collapse) was weak on the political economy of countering climate change, getting finance from the European and world economy and working out a price mechanism to cope with the fuel crisis. A consultative network existed, but to mollify interest groups rather than to determine long-term reconstruction.

Scottish Cabinet life lacks the 'dignified parts', the dancing-master presentation of the Benthamite machine, by Walter Bagehot and Anthony Trollope, both born technocrats. Their 'efficient' Westminster balance between supply and spending ministries instead appeared as 'talky' and 'silent' ministries: Education and Health versus Environment (*de facto* AgFish) and Infrastructure. Supposed 'decision-makers' were chatted up, while much executive authority was schlepped to 'arms-length agencies' varying from harmless to pointless, financed by Bute House in the hope that they might gradually colonise the subjects 'reserved' to Whitehall.

On the union side, Tony Blair and Gordon Brown had played around absent-mindedly with the London end: a situation not helped by Scotland being, in terms of the fateful Granita Compact, 1993 (which wrecked the Bagehotian cabinet), a 'Gordon Thing'. In 1997-2007, when Scotland was run by New Labour 'Shuttlefolk' from the VIP lounge at Heathrow, Tony talked to Jack McConnell, Gordon did not. Whitehall was supposed to dwindle even more under the tax powers contemplated by the Calman Commission. Dover House ought to have been a live issue for the 'Better Together' lobby but, emptied by Salmond *and* Cameron, ended up an echo-chamber.

II Scotland for sale?

The paradox of devolved Scotland has been that, as political authority moved north, capital control moved out. In the inter-war period the Lithgows and Colvilles provided, as suggested by Dicey in his *Law and Opinion* lectures of 1904, a sort of devolved governance *within* the public and financial sectors. Forty-three Scots-based businesses were valued at £1m and more in 1978

– in Knox and Wilson's useful *Scotland '78*. All but a handful had gone by 2007. Most manufacturers sold up by 1990: Guinness swallowed Distillers disgracefully in 1986. Britoil, formerly BNOC, lost its Glasgow HQ when bought by BP; British Steel at Ravenscraig was dead by 1992. Transport was the exception: Stagecoach and First Group transformed themselves from dour Scottish-state concerns into lonely, unwieldy megafirms, controlling (for the time being) international networks from Scotland. By the disused Greyhound bus stop in Laramie, Wyoming, a wee notice tells you to complain to First Group, Larbert, Scotland ...

Manufacturing dwindled (from 30% per cent of GDP in 1979 it fell to 20 per cent in 1996 and 12 per cent in 2012) with the rise of Chinese factories and Danish freighters after 1995, aided by the big Scots banks, *and* the Hongkong and Shanghai Banking Corporation (HSBC) with its strong Scots connections. Royal Bank of Scotland (RBS) and Halifax Bank of Scotland (HBOS) made up Salmond's world. He still probably believed in September 2008 that Fred Goodwin's bank was the same as Charlie Winter's, only bigger. Indeed Gillian Tett's *Fool's Gold* suggested that RBS's prestigious Whitehall board hadn't a clue about what its dealers were up to: a classic Benthamite 'sinister interest' created by handheld computing and opaque international 'instruments' had to be bailed out by Brown and Darling and moved south. Most of Salmond's network vanished, even if in May 2010 it took Brown with it.

Deindustrialised countries need – but do not produce – technicians 'trained on the job': the famous German 'dual-system' has to be 75 per cent works-driven. Nor is numerical adequacy sufficient. Experts matter when development schemes have to fight off dissenters at public inquiries; *and* when these fail and have to be clinically dissected and reformulated to get future financing. Scottish industry was already technically decadent, before the banks died. Salmond took power after the Edinburgh Parliament disaster (verdict: Dewar and Miralles, both dead, had slipped up ...). The Edinburgh tram disaster followed (verdict: overpaid Transport Initiatives Edinburgh had slipped up ...), but so far no inquiries, no Benthamite sanctions of 'consistency and ferocity'. Whitehall's super-carriers are now revealed as carrying only 12 planes and incapable of operating in tropical conditions. They waste our rare skilled men: 1500 and counting ...

Infrastructure is low-tech 'joabs on the tar' stuff like the east-of-Glasgow motorways, whose vast contortions lead nowhere in particular, Donald Trump's embarrassing golf course, and the second Forth Road Bridge. Salmond had wanted a tunnel, which could have been converted to high speed rail when the oil goes; of the £1.5 billion invested in it, only £36 million will be spent in Scotland. This *galère* gives the sense of pre-referendum goodies being scattered before the Scots 'advanced motorist' (*de facto* a wifi-less primitive, but likely to vote) rather than a logical investment.

There remains Scotland's 'geotechnic' future; it exists, has life-chances, and Salmond gets this wrong at *our* peril. Bentham was never far from purposeful people and things: his naval architect brother Sir Samuel (developing the hydrodynamic sailing ship, which fetched and carried up to the 1880s), James and John Stuart Mill from Kincardineshire (governing and modernising India), the 'Panopticon' prison and workhouse (grinding rogues honest), or New Lanark with Robert Owen (scientific management and co-operation).

Patrick Geddes's 'geotechnics' can deploy the country's historic coastal investment – from fisheries and war to oil – in quays, buildings, railways, roads, anchorages, lighthouses. Scotland's science and medicine still count, although attempts to apply them commercially (see particle physics, animal genetics, software) have been fairly ineffective. But Scotland accesses 25 per cent of Europe's low-carbon power – according to Chris Smout in his 'Land and Sea' essay, 12,000 million coal-tonnes *annual* equivalent – off a coast five times longer than Germany's useless 'Wattenmeer' (dry for much of the day) and tideless Baltic. Arctic ice-loss is opening up new east-west navigation channels, cutting 7000 kilometres off the China/Japan trip, needing break-bulk ports. We even have (uniquely?) expanding freshwater supplies.

But such 'lab-technology' advances need link-ups – with Norway, Germany, China, the Middle East. London interest, expressed by British Trade International, has been episodic, generally low. By 2013, some radical initiatives – from the giant EMEC lab of Scapa Flow to Edinburgh's multidisciplinary Summerhall – were underway, but have we yet a driving rationale?

Salmond: fair game for Wall Street and Hollywood? That pair, with their icons – *Bravehearts, Braves*, etc. – out-lured the others, despite long traditions of Scots overseas involvement. A take from France, Sylvain Chomet's touching animation *The Illusionist* (2010) showed a muted 1950s Scotland, distinct culturally from any other part of Europe. The visitor currently approaches Holyrood through a canyon of tartan tat, yet maybe its cheery Sikhs are closer to the bailies and chapmen of Walter Scott's day than the Microserfs of the call-centres, the Amazonian helots, the mid-Atlantic bureaucracies of arms-length Scotland?

The same goes for the old estates: commerce, kirk, law, burghs, colleges, sport. Manufacture was raced to the bottom by a Kirk dropping to English levels of impiety, and scandal on the Catholic side; lawyers and police have together obscured the 'black economy' of the West, charted by John A Mack and Hans-Juergen Kerner in *The Crime Industry*, 1975. Was bank-death the last act of the 'Luxury and Corruption' both Adam Smith and Bentham distrusted? John Galt's Provost Pawkie in *The Provost* (1822) becomes the local oligarch on the Board with the six-digit salary blethering for a ritual ten minutes on 'the team last Saturday' before telling you that your scheme for whatever hadn't a chance? Do 'Tartan Noir's best-sellers – Rowling, Rankin, Welsh – taking off from dysfunctional societies, make 'civic society' people confidently righteous, or just give up?

Scotland's cultural confusion is still less than in the south. But might it be inflamed by the referendum? Do 'big folk in bad new houses' reflect deals cut in Scotland within a torpid establishment: supermarket shopping, unimaginative education, urban blight? An anorexic media obsessing over high-cost *footballismo*, gone from international to bankrupt?

The churches lapsed by ignoring feminism. Might they recover through incorporating it? Most ministerial candidates for the Kirk are women; Catholics, lacking this resource, are in deeper crisis. A 2011 project for a Scottish tapestry found as female candidates only Saint Margaret, Lulu, and Dolly the cloned sheep. It hit financial problems and changed. Scotswomen, bored by most of the above, are at last taking over official life: 35 per cent of Holyrood MSPs in 2012, including two party leaders, against only 4 per cent at Westminster in 1992. Of leaders in Holyrood, Patrick Harvie (Green) and, less predictably, Ruth Davidson (Tory) are gay. Outside, Kathleen Jamie wonderfully combines the 'two Chrisses': Christian Johnstone 'Meg Dods', nineteenth-century novelist, cook and editor, as well as Chris Caledonia Guthrie, badly needed as 'Commemorating 1914' slouches into view. Will this leaven work? It had better.

III Uncharted waters

There is some sort of capital/politics balance in Scotland, unlike the situation in Ferdinand Mount's *New Few* (2011) which revealed the extent to which British institutions were not just affected by the control of the European Union but of European firms (private and state) and the sovereign wealth of far countries. See (and multiply) James Meek on the end of British-owned electricity in the *London Review of Books*. The Scots on their 'my enemy's enemy is my friend' principle have always looked sympathetically on Brussels and Strasbourg, also Paris and Berlin. 'A free Scotland in a united Europe' brought Salmond in 1987-92 to the head of the SNP. He was associated with equating small (though not micro-) states with dynamism. But the travails of the Euro and the fragility of other present or former 'Union States' (Spain, Italy, ex-Yugoslavia, ex-Comecon) have problematised Scotland's reception, while the 'arc of opportunity' (from Finland to Ireland) proved in 2008 tempting to tax-haven sharks and 'moral hazard'. Could Scotland follow the Norwegian route, using renewables like oil? Good. But did this also mean following Norway into Nato? The SNP was only just convinced.

Excitement and possibility persist in Scotland, noticed abroad if not in London. Salmond's role, accepted even there, contrasts with the *impasse* of his rivals. In 2013 Cameron-Clegg gets only 22 per cent backing in Scotland (15 per cent Conservative, 7 per cent Lib Dem) against 42 per cent in the UK. But this does not suggest a walkover. Holyrood has yet to outpoll Westminster. 63 per cent voted in the 'no change' Westminster election of 2010; only 50.4 per cent in the Scottish *bouleversement* of May 2011.

Bentham's and Thatcher's old union is now off the map. The limits to Devo Max or federal proposals are twofold: (1) the weakness of Britain's experience of federalism and its conventions (we have nothing like the institutional mattress of German 'co-operative federalism), and (2) the Britain-plus problem of toxic deindustrialisation. Self-sustaining industry (oil and renewable) and commercial relations require 'power and manoeuvrability', a phrase from the brave days of the 1970s oil boom: or, going further back, the precedent of the autonomy got by Norway for its huge merchant fleet in 1905. Immigration is essential, to increase skills and sustain an ageing population. Both will cause friction with the South. Can Salmond gain the necessary trade-offs? Or do his manoeuvres towards 'devo-max' and Nato imperil the progress so far made?

Could the solution lie in 'full' sovereignty, downloading the Benthamite machine to manage a new, clean-energy-based, technology, with feedback mechanisms in place. Plus a 'strong confederal' series of treaties with rUK, covering exchange, communications, transport, anti-terrorism, and joint judicial tribunals, with a Council of the Islands (like the Nordic Council, and based in Dublin) replacing the Lords?

Do Salmond's remarkable links with the Monarchy (Strichen speaks to Balmoral, probably about horses) suggest a workable confederal settlement at Bagehot's 'dignified' level? Scots autonomy would be contained by a development of the British-Irish agreement, with Ireland back in the 'New Commonwealth' it invented with De Valera's external association principle; reindustrialisation will impose its own inspectorate. Grinding the rogues of Lichtenstein or the Caymans honest, this will serve the common interests of The Islands better than federalism or 'devo-max'. What matters is the efficient level, and this must be created – from Scotland, from the archipelago and its waters, from Europe and from immigrants. The Scottish establishment, viewed close-up from the Scottish Parliament's Economy, Energy, and Tourism Committee, has proven ill-briefed and complacent. To grab another Benthamism and a neologism of oor ain: 'sinister interests' are hoaching in the Numptocracy; too many 'tsars' and 'icons' adorn our media as it swirls doon the pan.

A complex industrial adaptation will impose its own criteria. Renewable energy gives us the lever to bring back the clinicians and technocrats, on our terms. We cannot re-sit this.

References

The Bentham of A V Dicey's *Law and Opinion* lectures of 1904 (Macmillan, 1904) is brilliant and blunt. Dicey and Robert Rait's *Thoughts on the Union* (Macmillan, 1923) ought to be read with Dicey's 1886 aside in mind: "If I were an Irishman I should be an out-and-out nationalist". See the present author's *The Lights of Liberalism* (Allen Lane, 1976, Ch.VIII) and 'Scotland and Wales' in *The Oxford Handbook of British Politics* (OUP, 2009). He echoes in James

Mitchell's *Conservatives and the Union* (1990) and *Governing Scotland* (2003). These brought back to mind a vintage monologue about De Valera and the Commonwealth from Garret Fitzgerald in a Lancaster bar in 1974. *The London Review of Books* has atoned for the blandness of Linda Colley with Neal Ascherson and Tom Nairn at their percussive best – and fine historical accounts such as James Meek's 'How we happened to sell off our electricity' in LRB vol.34, no. 17, 13 September 2012. The 'Tapestry of Scotland' saga figures in the *Scotsman*, 21 December 2012, redeemed by Kathleen Jamie's 'Destiny Bag' in the lively pro-secession symposium *Unstated* (WordPower, 2013); Chris Smout's key environmental essay is in Devine and Wormald, ed., *The Oxford Handbook of Modern Scottish History* (OUP, 2012, Ch. I). My *Broonland: the Last Days of Gordon Brown* (Verso, 2012) depended greatly on Mack and Kerner's dystopic *The Crime Industry* (Council of Europe, 1975). Don't take my word for it, read Eric Ambler's *Send No More Roses* (1977, Fontana, 1988).

Autonomy, Community and the Kirk in Devolved Scotland

Tom Gallagher

A recurring theme in Christopher Harvie's writings is the desirability of communities to aspire to acquire autonomy from a centralising state and powerful economic forces. Scots acquired the practice of governing themselves in one important realm, long before the arrival of any democratic age. This was in religious matters, following the sixteenth century Reformation. The election of the elders and ministers by the membership of the Church of Scotland and the election of representatives to a national General Assembly "gave the Scots experience in making their own choices as to who should govern them."[1] Representative government thus became a norm for Protestant Scots in one important department of their lives. With the decline of religious observance and the rise of a multi-purpose state which often seeks to promote its own moral perspective as it manages people's lives, the reach of the Kirk has diminished. But it still seeks to engage with, and influence, the outcome of major national debates. Thus, on 23 May 2013, the Rev Sally Foster-Fulton, Convener of the Church and Society Council, urged Church members to become fully engaged in the debate on whether to remain in, or else quit, the United Kingdom, something to be decided by a referendum in September 2014. The Kirk remains neutral, but this high-profile office-holder embraced change: she hoped for the publication of a draft constitution and stated that "this is a unique opportunity to imagine, mould and nurture a vision of the kind of country we want to be regardless of the outcome..."[2]

Christopher Lasch (1932-1994) was an American social critic who warned about the harm being done by powerful social institutions as they snatched much of the autonomy enjoyed by individuals and wider family groups. He criticised both the political left and right for their headlong promotion of untrammelled capitalism or else the big state as frameworks for organising humanity. He argued that the outcome was problematic for society as whatever degree of freedom and autonomy existed in communities was gradually extinguished.[3] He argued that people were falling prey to harmful dependencies, those linked with corporate capitalism on the one hand and a heavy-handed bureaucracy with a controlling agenda on the other.

[1] Wallace Notestein, *The Scot in History*, London: Jonathan Cape, 1947 edition, p. 150.

[2] Church of Scotland Communications Department, 23 May 2013, <www.churchofscotland.org.uk>.

[3] Sean Collins, 'Scourge of the elites', *The Spiked Review of Books*, March 2013, <www.spiked-online.com>.

The imposition of free-market ideas on Scotland in the 1980s and beyond means that most intellectual writings about the modern Scottish condition emphasise the danger emanating from unbounded capitalism first, and the state sometimes a distant second. Chris Harvie is certainly no exception.

It is noteworthy that the Church of Scotland offered the most resounding challenge to Margaret Thatcher's free-market blueprint for Scotland which she presented in what became known as her 'Sermon on the Mound' when she addressed the General Assembly on 21 May 1988.[4]

Kirk ministers were already prominent in the Campaign for a Scottish Assembly and the Constitutional Convention which emerged from it in 1989. A primary goal of this drive for autonomy was to shield Scotland from an 'enterprise culture' centred on unfettered economic individualism that, according to the historian David Marquand, was abhorrent both to the Calvinist and Catholic traditions to be found there.[5]

In 1989, the Kirk's chief policy-advising body, the Church and Nation Committee, declared:

> It is our conclusion that it is not possible to resolve the question of the democratic control of Scottish affairs and the setting up of a Scottish assembly apart from a fundamental shift in our constitutional thinking away from the notion of the unlimited or the absolute sovereignty of the British Parliament towards the historic and reformed constitutional principle of limited or relative sovereignty. [6]

Devolution, with Scotland acquiring a parliament that would control most domestic policy, was accomplished in 1999. The Kirk went on to provide the General Assembly Hall near the top of the Royal Mile in Edinburgh for sittings of the Scottish Parliament from 1999 to 2004. A form of civic patriotism had been devised by figures drawn from the media, the churches, trade-unions and local government so as to give intellectual coherence to most of the nation's rejection of Thatcherite economic values. But the churches would not be among the interest groups which wielded influence in the new devolved order. Scotland would also be slow to witness any transformation of political ethics.[7]

Donald Dewar, the first person to head the devolved system of government, found it hard to conceal his distaste for organised religion.[8] There was a

---

[4] Andrew Marr, The Battle for Scotland, London: Penguin, 1992, p. 68.

[5] David Marquand, Britain Since 1918: The Strange Career of British Democracy, London: Weidenfeld & Nicholson, 2008, p. 336.

[6] Kenyon Wright, The People say Yes, Glendaruel: Argyll Publishing 1997, p. 121.

[7] See Tom Gallagher, The Illusion of Freedom: Scotland Under Nationalism, London: Hurst & co, 2009, from chapter 5 onwards.

[8] Stephen McGinty, The Turbulent Priest: The Life of Cardinal Winning, London: Harper-Collins, 2001, p. 389.

consensus among Labour and Liberal Democrat politicians in charge until 2007, and indeed their SNP successors from that period onwards that the policy agenda be drawn up by the bureaucracy and the third sector, one with the need for social and economic equality at its core.

In the new political era, few politicians now turned up to the debate of the Church and Nation Committee's report at the General Assembly to find out what the Kirk was thinking about wider national concerns.

Religious activists who felt that Christian perspectives were being excluded from policy-making would stand for the Scottish Parliament in 2010, but in two rival parties. They made little impact, which perhaps confirmed the view of most in the governing elite that bodies, even ones as central to national life as the Church of Scotland had been, could now be safely overlooked.

In the United States, the energies of conservative Christians had been channelled into politics for several decades. But in Scotland traditionalists, often with an evangelical perspective, operated mostly at the parish level. They were concerned with saving souls at home and sometimes also abroad, through missionary work.

Increasingly, it was liberal and left-leaning members of the Kirk who came forward to fill vacancies in the Church and Society Council, which emerged in 2005 from an amalgamation of Church and Nation and other committees. They were mostly dedicated and well-organised individuals, with the greatest appetite for attending committee meetings far from their parishes. Just as the Labour Party became dominated by a minority of zealous activists, as it retreated from being a body with a mass presence in the British working-class, so the same phenomenon became noticeable in the Kirk.

The body that expressed the Kirk's views on national issues asserted a range of concerns that often did not resonate with traditional working-class congregations. Climate change, zero tolerance on domestic abuse, and Palestine were issues of recurring concern for the Council. Scots in the over-fifty age-group were still an important mainstay for the Kirk in terms of regular attendance and donations. But, except for the question of assisted suicide, concerns that they might have had, such as crime or the performance of the National Health Service, rarely, if ever, figured in Church and Society business. Nor, surprisingly enough, did the plight of Christians in countries like Syria when the 'Arab Spring' descended into sometimes horrific violence.

In inner city areas, parishes declining in size, received a sometimes much-needed boost from people who had arrived in Scotland as refugees or asylum seekers from the Middle East and further afield. Understandably, some of the global concerns taken up by the Kirk resonated with them. But others were attracted by the evangelical flavour of some churches where the ardour of heeding Christ's calling fulfilled a real spiritual and emotional need. The appeal of Protestant evangelicanism was strong enough for some to convert from other religions so as to give them the spiritual resources for coping with the challenges in a new adopted homeland.

From 2012, the head of the Church and Society Council has been a new Scot, originally from Seneca, in South Carolina. Sally Foster-Fulton is an energetic and articulate church minister, not yet 40, with a mission of passionate engagement with a host of global concerns. She visited Israel and the occupied West Bank during her first year as convener and expressed her shock "at the dangerous inhumanity of the checkpoint" constructed by Israel in order to thwart suicide bombings.[9] A report entitled 'The Inheritance of Israel: A Report on the Promised Land' followed three months later. It brought the Kirk an unusual amount of attention beyond Scotland. This sprung from its claim that promises made to the Israelites in the Old Testament of the Bible were never intended to be taken literally, and that "Christians should not be supporting any claims by Jewish or any other people to an exclusive or even privileged divine right to possess particular territory."[10]

The 2012 General Assembly had agreed that the Church of Scotland would no longer consider the Israeli perspective when campaigning on the Israeli-Palestinian conflict.[11] This was the culmination of a shift in the Kirk's position on this polarising issue. Until the 1980s, there had been more sympathy than hostility for Israel within its ranks. Until the previous decade, theological students preparing for the ministry had been required to read the original texts in Hebrew and Greek in order to obtain divinity degrees from the major Scottish universities. Later, it became sufficient just to study interpretations in other languages. Perhaps this prior learning experience had helped foster a Christian Zionist outlook among generations of ministers. Certainly, many in the past would have identified with the statement made in 1917 by the British foreign Secretary, Lord Arthur Balfour (a Scottish Tory) that "His Majesty's government view with favour the establishment in Palestine of a national home for the Jewish people."[12]

But British Zionism, a perspective hugely influential within much of the political left until the late 1970s, went into an inexorable retreat. A generation emerged no longer influenced by the traumatic events of 1933-1945. The visibility of decolonisation struggles in the 1960s led much of the global left to favour the Palestinian cause. It is therefore not surprising that, as the Kirk itself swung leftwards, the British Zionist outlook became the preserve of ageing church ministers.

In the face of strong criticism from the Israeli government, the Kirk retreated somewhat on the eve of the General Assembly. On 9 May, a joint

---

[9] Sally Foster-Fulton, 'Fences make good neighbours? I don't think so', 21 February 2013, <www.churchsociety.blogspot.co.uk>.

[10] *Haaretz*, (Israeli daily newspaper), 3 May 2013.

[11] *Jewish Chronicle* (London), 31 May 2012.

[12] See Robert Carr, 'From Balfour to Suez: Britain's Zionist Misadventure', *History Today*, 2004, <www.historytoday.com/robert-carr/balfour-suez-britains-zionist-misadventure>.

statement was issued with the Scottish Council of Jewish Communities that said:

> We agreed that the drafting of the report has given cause for concern and misunderstanding of [the Church's] position and requires a new introduction to give clarity about some of the language used. There is no change in the Church of Scotland's long-held position of the rights of Israel to exist; the Church condemns all violence and acts of terrorism; the Church condemns all things that create a culture of anti-Semitism.[13]

But calls in the Assembly for further dialogue with the Jewish community were rejected, and a revised version was passed on 21 May. Ephraim Borowski, the director of the Scottish Council of Jewish Communities, stated that "the Church of Scotland has deliberately and knowingly burned bridges with the Jewish Community in Scotland." He claimed that it contributed to a climate "in which Jewish people in Scotland tell us they feel uncomfortable, alienated and unsafe."[14]

The SNP politician George Kerevan chided the Church of Scotland for having "blundered into the Israel-Palestine issue with great big muddy boots."[15] But the Scottish political classes retained a terse silence during this controversy, as most have done when the anti-Zionist activities of the Scottish Palestine Solidarity campaign have spilled over into disrupting cultural events in Edinburgh involving Israeli citizens.[16]

Perhaps it was necessary to go back to the 1930s to find another time in the normally placid life of Scotland's capital when public disturbances possessed such an obvious ethno-religious dimension. The anti-Catholic agitation of the Protestant Action movement shook up the city in 1935-36. Arguably, a sympathetic atmosphere had been provided by the Kirk's Church and Nation committee. Founded in 1919, under the aegis of the Rev John White, anti-Irish Catholic reports and lobbying at government level had often dominated its agenda of work into the 1930s.[17]

In 2002, a report of the Church and Nation committee was approved by the General Assembly (part of which read):

---

[13] Craig Brown, 'Israel blasts Kirk amid allegations of anti-Semitism', *The Scotsman*, 10 May 2013.

[14] Letter to the Editor, *The Herald*, 25 May 2013.

[15] George Kerevan, 'No solution in boycotting Israel', *The Scotsman*, 10 May 2013.

[16] See *The Scotsman*, 30 August 2008; and also 31 August 2012 for the disruption of public events involving Israeli performers that resulted in arrests.

[17] See S.J. Brown, 'The Scottish Presbyterian Churches and Irish Immigration, 1922-1938', *Innes Review*, vl. 42, 1991, pp.21-45.

Sectarianism is not someone else's problem. In the years around the Great Depression of the early thirties of last century, the Church and Nation Committee campaigned intemperately against Irish immigration into Scotland. From a current perspective it is a matter of regret that the Committee and the Church should have taken such a position.[18]

Liberal voices had asserted themselves in the Church of Scotland by the early 1940s. The theologian John Baillie proved influential in steering the church towards acceptance of the social reforms associated with the post-1945 Labour government. Thereafter, the Kirk never lost having a preference for the poor and, by the 1960s, was also publicly opposed to nuclear weapons and their siting at a military base on the Firth of Clyde.

The Church and Society Commission championed an engaged ministry, offering theological and ethical perspectives on major political concerns at home and abroad. (It already had the example of the Iona Community to draw upon in this respect). Its convenor Sally Foster-Fulton in 2013 is comfortable in such a role. She probably anticipated dissent after she claimed that, on Palm Sunday, Jesus's entry into Jerusalem, riding a donkey was one directed "against the power and might of the Roman Empire."[19]

Indeed, traditionalists quickly protested over what was seen as a politicisation of the Gospel story. One wrote:

Are you honestly suggesting that Jesus was leading a demo against the might of the Roman Empire? Jesus's entry into Jerusalem was the preparation for his death and resurrection, his death for our sins so that we might be put right with God and receive salvation rather than the death we deserve.[20]

Such arguments about the boundaries of moral Christian activism have always occurred. But perhaps the spectrum of thought on how to preach Christ's ministry may today be wider than it has ever been in the history of the Kirk. Church liberals may not have lost much sleep when the Orange Order passed a resolution in 2012 on 'Our Protestant Heritage'. Part of it read:

it is a sad reflection that in today's society, many Protestants consider that the Orange Order is more in harmony with their values and aspirations than the Kirk. We as an institution never

---

[18] Elinor Kelly, 'Challenging Sectarianism in Scotland: the prism of racism', *Scottish Affairs*, no 42, winter 2003, p. 7.

[19] Sally Foster-Fulton, 'Easter witness for peace at Faslane', 22 March 2013, <www.churchsociety.blogspot.co.uk>.

[20] *ibid.* (Comments), Gordon, 'Easter witness for peace at Faslane'.

envisaged nor aspired to such a position, and it is an appalling indication of how far the Kirk has deteriorated...[21]

The Rev.Foster-Fulton hit back. "The idea that the Orange Order speaks for anyone except its own members is laughable. . . They stand for an unjust world and the Church of Scotland rejects their beliefs as outdated, outmoded and just plain wrong."[22]

Harry Reid, arguably one of the few prominent journalists in Scotland with a strong understanding of religious matters, gave cautious backing to the Order on this issue, remarking: "The Kirk doesn't seem to be able to speak for Scotland, and it hasn't for a generation. The Orange Order are probably quite right about that."[23]

Distrust of Roman Catholicism and its educational dimension, merging with the need to defend Reformation principles and the Union, have been the official justification for the Orange Order's existence. But its colourful processions were the antithesis of Reformation austerity, and it brought colour into plain lives. These public affirmations of faith and patriotism were seen as increasingly archaic and also offensive not just to Catholics but to secular liberals uncomfortable with overt quasi-religious displays. However divisive some of its features are, Orangeism remains an expression of communitarian values at a time when working-class lifestyles are becoming increasingly privatised and centred around the home with its consumer goods and myriad forms of entertainment.[24]

The Orange Order is distinctive, due to assert a male working-class and Protestant presence. From the 1980s, the decline of heavy industry has thrown into sharp relief the absence of any meaningful role in life for a huge proportion of Scotland's men. Men without a purpose had contributed to a series of ferocious wars occurring in the Balkans during the 1990s after the collapse of communism led to a chronic shortage of jobs. The Irish demographer and social forecaster Gerard O'Neill argues that "no civilised society can survive without the engagement and commitment and support of its young men."[25]

Women appeared to benefit from the greater individualism in British life from the 1980s onwards, a trend that was reinforced by state efforts to narrow the gender wage differential. But it was middle-class and better-educated women who were really best-placed to seize the new opportunities.

---

[21] Gerry Braiden, '"Failures" of Kirk attacked by Orange Order', *The Herald*, 3 July 2012.

[22] 'Order's attack on the Kirk draws blood', *Orange Torch*, September 2012.

[23] *Ibid.*

[24] See Graham Walker, *Intimate Strangers*, Edinburgh: John Donald 1994, chapter 6.

[25] Gerard O'Neill, 'The Future of Marriage', *Turbulence Ahead*, 4 March 2012, <www.turbulenceahead.com>.

At conferences and fringe meetings on the future priorities of a devolved Scotland, it was usually young professional women (rarely men from any class) who boldly insisted that the process would be a sham unless it allowed Scottish womanhood to fulfill itself. Such advocacy led to the Labour party ensuring that half of its MSPs (members of the Scottish Parliament) would be women. They were nominated for eligible positions on the candidate lists by small caucuses, and many came from the state bureaucracy and quangos. Arguably, the limited amount of political talent to be found among women recruited through such a narrow selection process did not advance the feminist cause in Scotland.

But at the same time, with social restraints vanishing, and still facing educational and other disadvantages, growing numbers of girls from lower-income families made bad life choices.

Perhaps surprisingly, there were very few leading voices in the Kirk who spotted the dangers for social cohesion, and indeed Christian belief, of undiluted lifestyle liberalism. In the past, messages from the media and market forces that young people should go out and fulfill their material and emotional wants, would have been challenged from within the Kirk by those who argued that education, marriage and a Christian form of living would be the casualties of such hedonism. But in working-class communities, it was rare to find voices urging restraint and a longer-term perspective.

Poverty might no longer stalk the new communities hastily erected by urban planners to ease inner-city overcrowding, but they were often soulless places. Unless the priest or minister possessed remarkable dedication like the Rev John Miller (who worked for many years in Glasgow's Castlemilk from the start of the 1970s), the Christian clergy found it hard for their voices to count.[26] Their influence over young people, who often lacked any secure anchor in family, education, or faith, was increasingly tenuous. They asserted their ego, sometimes in distinctly edgy and destructive ways. This increased the already worrying level of inter-personal violence, with knives being reinforced by guns as weapons that were in increasing use.[27] By 2011, the murder rate per 100,000 people for Scotland was 2.34, compared to a figure in England and Wales of 1.35. Ten of America's 50 states actually had a lower murder rate than Scotland, despite the wide availability of firearms in the USA.[28]

While the traditional wing of the Kirk was often inclined to ascribe the scourge of violent crime to the failure to make Christian ethics a guide for living, liberals often preferred to single out economic inequalities as a primary reason for such strife. The Church and Society Commission has worked

---

[26] See 'The poor look after each other', The Herald, 21 February 2007; also Cate Devine, 'A man of God and the people', The Herald, 7 July 2007.

[27] See Carol Craig, The Tears That Made the Clyde, Glendaruel: Argyll Publishing, 2011, especially chapter 14.

[28] Richard Carey, Libertarian Home, 22 December 2012.

closely with a political elite which, in Scotland, is inspired by the desire to place equality at the centre of policy-making for a wide range of issues. The convenor pays an annual visit to Westminster, and the Rev Foster-Fulton declared after two days of engagements with Scottish MPs in 2012 that "the politicians that represent us in London work hard, care passionately and love the people they have been asked to serve."[29] This brave claim runs counter to numerous polling surveys which show a deepening disconnect between those in the political world and ordinary citizens in every corner of Britain.

Nearly seventy years since the end of the Second World War, politics in Britain has gradually evolved from upholding a culture of authority, where duties are emphasised as much as rights, to the championing of a compassion culture. The latter involves identifying with oppressed and overlooked groups both at home and abroad, whose current disadvantage may stem in part from past British state behaviour. Church figures have usually carried off the role of showing a preference for the poor and victimised with more conviction than politicians. It can sometimes appear as fake sincerity on their part and perhaps even backfire badly, as seems to have happened in the case of Prime Minister David Cameron's readiness to re-define marriage so as to place gay couples on an equal footing with heterosexual ones.

The compassion culture has been at the heart of the struggle within the Catholic Church in Scotland to cope with the revelations about its highest-ranking member, Cardinal Keith O'Brien in 2013. On 3 March he left Scotland after releasing a statement admitting that "there have been times that my sexual conduct had fallen below the standards expected of me as a priest, archbishop and cardinal."[30] But he returned unexpectedly, to the consternation of fellow bishops, several months later. Back in Scotland, he stated that "If Christianity is about anything at all, it's about forgiveness" and expressed the hope that his Church would help him to put the scandal behind him.[31] This brought a rebuke from some readers of the Catholic weekly carrying his remarks, one writing: "Forgiveness is a gift of God to those WHO REPENT. In order to repent, you first need to examine and fully understand the sin."[32]

This is a defence of 'the authority' culture' which had previously animated the Catholic church and, arguably, most other Christian denominations in Scotland. Clerical authority was legitimised by dedication and service. It is a conception of the church ministry which the new head of the church, Pope Francis, sought to reaffirm in May 2013, when he said: "...authority is always

---

[29] Sally Foster-Fulton, 'A Westminster Visit', 12 December 2012, <www.churchsociety.blogspot.co.uk>.

[30] Quoted in Severin Carrell, 'Cardinal Keith O'Brien admits and apologises for sexual misconduct', The Guardian, 4 March 2013.

[31] Elena Kurti, 'Does Cardinal O'Brien deserve banishment or pardon?', Tablet, (blog by the deputy-editor), 10 April 2013.

[32] Ibid.

synonymous with service, humility, love. It means to enter into Jesus' logic, who bends down to wash the feet of the Apostles." He then condemned the opposite:

> We think of the harm inflicted on the People of God by men and women of the Church who are careerists, social climbers, who "use" the people, the Church, brothers and sisters – those they should serve – as trampolines for their own personal interests and ambitions. But these do great harm to the Church.[33]

On 15 May, Rome announced that O'Brien was leaving Scotland to undertake a period of spiritual renewal, prayer and penance, and that any return would have to be agreed with the Vatican.[34]

A Church struggling to apply its own doctrine to a leading figure who admits defying them, will find it hard to avoid sliding into crisis. It is a gift for politicians who wish to be left alone to devise a public morality that will make their plans easier to accomplish. Some who openly embrace a secular world view are likely to welcome the sharp decline in membership for the main Christian denominations in Scotland, which is likely to be confirmed with the release of detailed data for the 2011 census.

But if radical secularism is asserting its strength over bedraggled Christian forces, it may be a hollow victory. Atheism lacks a mobilising vision and has been unable to find a substitute for the social energy that often drove forward Christianity. It is hard to envisage Irish emigrants facing a brutal struggle in Glasgow in the early nineteenth century, or else today's refugees fleeing to Scotland from Third World conflicts, embracing atheism rather than Christianity in order to provide a spiritual ark of survival. Occasionally, there have been individuals inspired by socialism, and unattached to religion,who have rightfully claimed a place in history thanks to their practical commitment to social justice. Jimmy Reid is one such individual, and lesser names associated with the Communist Party, especially in the areas where it enjoyed some municipal influence, deserve not to be overlooked.[35]

But an achieving atheism capable of improving living communities, arguably, has still to emerge. What it usually entails in a twenty-first century where the Scottish left is increasingly dominated by middle-class voices with often highly abstract perspectives, is scepticism and a posture of disengagement from the problems of society. There is no readiness to explore whether developments such as the collapse of traditional marriage may have played a role, along with industrial decline, in exacerbating social

---

[33] Jeff Mirus, 'Christ Loved the Church: Francis Throws Down the Gauntlet to Religious', *Catholic Culture*, 9 May 2013, <www.catholicculture.org>.

[34] Stephen McGinty, 'Cardinal Keith O'Brien to leave Scotland', *The Scotsman*, 16 May 2013.

[35] See Jimmy Reid, *As I Please*, Edinburgh: Mainstream, 1984.

problems among lower-income citizens. Re-writing the meaning of marriage so as to enable gay and lesbian Scots, already in receipt of civil partnerships, to be included in its provisions, is an indication of the firmly middle-class priorities of much of the Scottish political elite. In May 2013, it was announced that the Scottish government's consultation on gay marriage elicited over 50,000 responses, 67 per cent of them opposed.[36] Yet, at the end of that month, plans were announced for a bill to go ahead, with the revamping of marriage on the basis perhaps that the government was for the people despite the people.

A Christian ethical foundation may have retreated in a lot of once recognisably devout Scottish communities, but a new moral order shorn of the need for religious belief is still hardly in sight.[37] At least at community level, Individual Protestant churches may still be more effective in offering a moral vision for coping with some of the acute challenges in Scottish society – drug dependency and other addictions, youngsters unable to find a place in the labour market, children and young people growing up in dysfunctional families and without role models enabling them to avoid harm.

Christopher Lasch believed that a stagnant society could only renew itself from within through utilising "the traditions of localism, self-help and community action." In this way people build their own 'communities of competence', often enabling them to stand up to powerful interests ready to take them down harmful paths.[38] Chris Harvie's own dedication to such meaningful grassroots autonomy is one of the most consistent strands in his scholarship. In 1999, he drew attention to the 'people's church' phenomenon in several central European countries, seeking to be a focus of grassroots Catholic renewal.[39] His knowledge of, and empathy with, community movements seeking to defend the human and natural environment from predatory forces, will ensure that he is a reference-point for communities that seek to resist mighty corporations and uninspired state action long into the future.

It is perhaps through such loosely structured grassroots initiatives that Christians stand the best chance of influencing the direction of society. Denominational boundaries are already in retreat in Scotland as local initiatives with a Christian perspective get going. They may retreat even

[36] Euan McColm, 'Political consequences of gay marriage', Scotland on Sunday, 26 May 2013.

[37] For the advance of secularism, see the later chapters of Callum Brown, Religion and Scotland Since 1707, Edinburgh: Edinburgh University Press, 1997.

[38] Jeremy Beer, 'The Radical Lasch', American Conservative, 27 March 2007; see also Norman Birnbaum, 'Gratitude and Forbearance: on Christoper Lasch', The Nation, 13 September 2011.

[39] Christopher Harvie, 'A Costly but Noble State of Tension', in Andrew Morton and Jim Francis (ed.), A Europe of Neighbours: Religious Social Thought and Reshaping a Pluralist Europe, Edinburgh: Centre for Theology and Public Issues, 1999, p. 15.

further, given internal divisions in the Kirk and the so far uninspired response of the Catholic church to the abuse of power in its senior ranks, one not merely confined to sexual impropriety. There is room for innovative forms of Christianity in Scotland which could yet undermine the claims of some that modernity can only make dramatic strides in this country through the eclipse of religion.

Accelerating History:
The 1979, 1997 and 2011 Referendums in Wales

John Osmond

Accelerating history

Referendums are often regarded as conservative devices designed to frustrate progressive initiatives, especially where constitutional change is concerned. In the case of Wales, however, the three referendums of 1979, 1997 and 2011 had the opposite effect. The experience of living through them had a galvanising impact on the Welsh people. It changed their view of themselves and their country. It made them more Welsh in outlook and identity and more willing to contemplate radical constitutional options. In short, the referendums accelerated Welsh progress towards autonomy.

Of course, the 1979 referendum was instigated by those opposed to devolution, and it resulted in a heavy four-to-one defeat for the Welsh Assembly proposed at that time. Yet the overall outcome was to precipitate events and unleash forces that radically changed Welsh society. In the decade following 1979 these events and political and economic forces came together to underpin the emergence of a Welsh political nation. In turn, and within less than two decades this provided the basis for a constitutional advance.

Again, the 1997 referendum in Wales was certainly not sought by those advocating constitutional change. Instead, it was a by-product of a decision made in 1996 by Labour's Opposition leader Tony Blair in response to a problem he had in Scotland. The promise of a referendum was needed there to remove from the agenda of the forthcoming British general election the tax varying powers being proposed for the Scottish Parliament. And if a referendum was necessary for Scottish devolution, it followed that one had to be held in Wales as well.

Although the referendum was not sought in Wales, its impact in September 1997 was profound. It ensured, for instance, that when the National Assembly for Wales was established in 1999 it was elected using a partial form of proportional representation, sufficient to prevent overweening Labour dominance and to ensure a new fluidity in Welsh politics.

More immediately, the narrowness of the result – with its tiny 6,721 vote majority, out of a million votes cast – made the affair into something of a melodrama. This had the effect of concentrating the minds of the people of Wales. There is no doubt that their attitudes to possible constitutional futures for their country underwent profound changes as a direct result of living through the 1997 referendum.

By the time the 2011 referendum approached it was the pro-devolution forces that were seeking it, in order to secure further powers for the National Assembly. A referendum was the central feature of the One Wales coalition agreement negotiated between Labour and Plaid Cymru in the wake of the 2007 Assembly election.[1] The prospect of a referendum was contained in the 2006 Wales Act. This stated that one would be needed to give the National Assembly direct legislative powers over the functions for which it was responsible, from education and health to economic development, the environment and rural affairs.

The 2006 Act was Labour's response to the recommendations of the cross-party Richard Commission which, in the Spring of 2004 had recommended a fully legislative Assembly, with 80 members elected by the STV system of proportional representation. Labour, or at least most of the Welsh Labour MPs at Westminster, balked at these recommendations, which the Commission had insisted were interconnected and should be implemented as a whole, and especially the STV proportional system. Instead, the 2006 Act accepted that the Assembly could become a fully-fledged legislature, but only following a referendum. Further, the referendum could only be put into effect following a two-thirds majority vote by Assembly Members and subsequent approval by the Westminster Parliament.

These hurdles were obstacles placed in the path of the Assembly's development to mollify Welsh MPs hostile to the devolution process.[2] In the event they had the opposite effect. The holding of the referendum, and the experience of the campaign in the early months of 2011, only served to whet the electorate's appetite for even more powers. Once again, the experience of a constitutional referendum proved an accelerator in Welsh political history.

The political nation

In this discussion a key question will be: what it is that constitutes a political nation? The distinctive cultural identity of Wales is not in doubt. However, do constitutional politics necessarily flow from the presence of a cultural community? What requirement is there for the cultural identity of Wales to be accompanied by political institutions?

---

[1] See John Osmond, Crossing the Rubicon: coalition politics Welsh style, Cardiff: IWA, August 2007.

[2] In July 2009 Peter Hain who, as Secretary of State for Wales, promoted the 2006 Act, warned, "I have no doubt that if a referendum were held today, it would be lost. Indeed, I cannot see a successful one happening until well into the next decade" ('Devolution's Next Step', IWA, Agenda, Summer 2009).

Of course, Plaid Cymru has always been convinced of the necessity. This is its *raison d'être*. Saunders Lewis, one of the party's founders and also a poet and playwright of international repute, made the essential case as far back as 1930. As he put it:

> If a nation that has lost its political machinery becomes content to express its nationality thenceforward only in the sphere of literature and the arts, then that literature and those arts will very quickly become provincial and unimportant, mere echoes of the ideas and artistic movements of the neighbouring and dominant nation. If they (the Welsh people) decide that the literary revival shall not broaden out into political and economic life and the whole of Welsh life, then inevitably Welsh literature in our generation will cease to be living and viable.[3]

However, such ideas were held by a small minority for much of twentieth-century Wales. Even after Plaid Cymru began to make political advances in the 1960s, its support was confined to around 10 per cent of the electorate. The argument of this paper is that it took the referendums experienced in the late twentieth-century to persuade a significant proportion of the population, beyond the core Plaid Cymru support, to embrace the idea of Wales as a political nation.

The best short definition of a political nation that I have come across was provided by the Dutch theorist Herman Dooyeweerd, half way through the twentieth century. As he asserted: "A nation is a people ... which has become conscious of its internal political solidarity."[4] Even as late as the 1970s, as I will argue, Wales could not be regarded in this light. Disputes around the position and status of the Welsh language were only the most salient illustration of a lack of Dooyeweerd's "internal political solidarity". In itself this was a major reason, I would argue the major reason, why at that time a referendum could not succeed, and, indeed, why the 1979 referendum was lost so heavily.

This was in contrast with Scotland where a majority was achieved, though not sufficiently high to overcome the infamous hurdle of at least 40 per cent of the electorate assenting.[5] Nevertheless, the experience of building Welsh

---

[3] Saunders Lewis, *The banned wireless talk on Welsh Nationalism*, 1930. See Dafydd Glyn Jones's essay on 'The Politics' of Saunders Lewis in Alun R. Jones and Gwyn Thomas (eds), *Presenting Saunders Lewis*, Cardiff: University of Wales Press, 1973, for an extensive discussion.

[4] Herman Dooyeweerd, *A New Critique of Political Thought*, Amsterdam, 1957, p.470. It is quoted in R. Tudor Jones, *The Desire of Nations*, Swansea: Christopher Davies, 1974.

[5] The inclusion of this requirement in the legislation was testimony to the referendum's undoubted role as a device to prevent devolution going ahead. Since World War II no

politics to such a position that legislation for a Welsh Assembly went through the Houses of the Westminster Parliament in all their tortuous stages during the 1970s was a boost to Welsh political life.

Living through the resultant referendum and then its aftermath provided an immediate acceleration to Welsh political history, radically altering the outlook of many key political players and eventually the wider Welsh people.

Another way of thinking about this process is to compare Wales with Scotland. In Scotland the new Parliament that re-assembled in 1999 took charge of a pre-existing array of civic institutions that had survived and flourished beyond the 1707 parliamentary union with England. These included a distinctive legal system, a separate structure for education, and the Scottish Kirk. Later were added Scottish financial institutions, a system of administration in the form of the Scottish Office from the 1880s, and a highly developed press and media. To a great extent Scottish identity revolved around these institutions. They provided Scots with a civic, and because of that a unified sense of their nationality. Consequently, when the Scottish Parliament met in 1999 it was as though a keystone was placed in the arch of an already-existing structure.

In Wales the position could not have been more different. Apart from a much shorter experience of separate administration, by the Welsh Office from 1964, the idea of a civic identity embracing the whole of Wales was foreign to the Welsh. Instead, their identity relied upon a much more fractious sense of locality, language and culture. This was one reason why, in contrast to the Scots, the idea of a National Assembly was so controversial and when it came in 1997, only narrowly achieved. Moreover, when it came, far from completing an institutional structure, the Assembly had to set about building one. Before it could become the keystone it had, so to speak, to construct the arch.

The 1979 referendum

The modern era of Welsh politics can be said to begin in June 1966 when Gwynfor Evans won his by-election victory for Plaid Cymru in Carmarthen. Together with the Scottish Nationalists' success in the Hamilton by-election the following year, this thrust the constitutional position of Wales and Scotland seriously on to the political stage for the first time since the end of the nineteenth century.

The Government response was to establish the Kilbrandon Commission on the Constitution in 1969 to undertake a wide-ranging survey of the potential for devolution to Scotland and Wales. However, by the time the Commission reported in late 1973, the issue appeared to have gone off the boil, and in any event had been overtaken by more pressing concerns such

---

political party forming a government in Britain has won more than 40 per cent of the electorate. It was an impossible hurdle to mount and was quietly dropped as a requirement in the 1997 referendum.

as the oil crisis. There was a cursory debate in the House of Commons, but the Kilbrandon report was sidelined. No mention was made of devolution in the manifestos of either Labour or Conservatives in the February 1974 'Who governs?' general election, called amidst a miner's strike.

However, the narrowness of the Labour victory, and the gains made by both Plaid Cymru and the SNP, brought devolution swiftly back on to the agenda. With many of its Scottish seats threatened by the SNP, Labour hurriedly dusted off the Kilbrandon report and produced plans for Scottish and Welsh Assemblies. These were duly contained in its manifesto for the October 1974 election. The legislation that followed was to preoccupy Westminster and dominate Welsh and Scottish politics for the rest of the decade.

Bills to establish Welsh and Scottish Assemblies were eventually passed, but subject, to the referendums that were held on 1 March 1979. However, what the campaign leading up to the referendum in Wales demonstrated was that the country had not yet sufficiently developed a sense of nationality in that sense of Herman Dooyeweerd's "internal political solidarity".

Of course, the campaign was conducted in the worst of possible circumstances, in the middle of the so-called Winter of Discontent. James Callaghan's Labour government was beset by strikes in the public services. Piles of rubbish were left uncollected amidst ice and snow on the streets. Even the dead went unburied in some areas. This dramatised the general unpopularity of government, any government at the time. 'Get the Government off your back', was a slogan being promulgated by the leader of the Opposition, one Margaret Thatcher. Pro-devolutionists were shouting in the wind, trying to make the case for what the anti-devolutionists dubbed 'more government'.

But underlying these generally superficial arguments, was what opponents of the Assembly in Wales accurately identified as a distrust that existed between Welsh communities at that time. Undoubtedly, this was the major cause of the scale of the referendum defeat, compared with Scotland. No-one was more cunning in this respect than the architect of the referendum, Leo Abse, MP for Pontypool. As he argued:

> It is clear, isn't it, that in the Assembly people are going to exercise their undoubted right to speak Welsh. And, indeed, how could you deny it? Once they speak Welsh it means that you have to have interpreters for them, who have in the nature of things, to speak Welsh. Then all the top civil servants would have to speak Welsh because the same members who would speak Welsh in the Assembly would speak Welsh in committees and select committees. So it can't be disputed that, once there is an insistence on the part of those who are going to the Assembly that they have the right to use the language,

once that is established, you get the pattern for a huge and influential bureaucracy and it is one which will not be open to my people in Gwent.[6]

From the other side the view was often expressed that, contrary to the Welsh language gaining an advantage, it could be threatened by Welsh democracy. This is how the Carmarthen-born academic lawyer David Williams (later Vice Chancellor of Cambridge University) put it in 1975:

> The current policy of official benevolence, under a system of government from London combined with administrative decentralisation, may well be the most effective guarantee which supporters of the Welsh language can hope for in the immediate future. Simple democracy has its perils.[7]

In February 1979 the 'Labour No Assembly campaign' published a wide-ranging manifesto which tellingly took head on the notion that Wales should have its own political institutions simply because it was a nation. Drafted by Bedwellty MP Neil Kinnock and his constituency secretary, the late Barry Moore, the document accepted the nationality of Wales but rejected the idea that this should entail taking on the responsibilities of what it described as nationhood:

> The view is put forward, of course, that Wales has a special identity and urgent needs which make Devolution necessary. The Nationalists and Devolutionists say 'We are a nation, that makes a difference', 'We have a Welsh Office, that makes a difference', 'We have a Wales TUC, that makes a difference'. But none of that takes account of the realities. We are a nation, proud of our nationality. BUT there is little or no desire for the costs, responsibilities of nationhood as the puny voting support for the Nationalists shows. We do not need an Assembly to prove our nationality or our pride. This is a matter of hearts and minds, not bricks, committees and bureaucrats.[8]

The extent to which such arguments gained purchase in 1979 demonstrated that Wales had not matured as a political nation. As the main political party

---

[6] Gwyn Erfyl, *Talking about devolution: interview with Leo Abse*, Planet 47, 1979.

[7] D.G.T. Williams, 'Wales and Legislative Devolution', in Harry Calvert (ed.), *Devolution*, London: Professional Books, 1975, p.77.

[8] Labour No Assembly Campaign Wales, *Facts to Beat Fantasies*, February 1979, p.6. This important 50-page document can be seen at the Welsh Political Archive in the National Library.

in Wales, Labour was itself divided. The only political party convinced about devolution was Plaid Cymru, but it was a marginal force in Welsh life, winning around 10 per cent of the vote in general elections. There was only a vestigial notion of a Welsh civil society involving other groupings, and especially business. In short, there was very little "internal political solidarity".

The 1980s

Nonetheless, and albeit that it inflicted an undoubted defeat on devolution at the time, the 1979 referendum set in train a series of events that, with extraordinary rapidity, changed these realities fundamentally. The immediate effect was a vote of no-confidence in James Callaghan's Labour government, and the inauguration of eighteen years of Conservative rule. This was to have profound consequences. Oddly enough, so far as Wales was concerned, the first related to the language. Mrs Thatcher's incoming government soon reneged on a commitment to establish a Welsh language television channel, saying that Welsh language broadcasts should continue to be spread across the existing BBC and commercial channels.

This served to unite Welsh and English speaking Wales, the former because they wanted their own channel, the latter because they wanted the Welsh language removed from the English language channels they watched. In May 1980 Gwynfor Evans announced that he would fast to death unless a Welsh channel was established, as originally promised. This prompted a wave of activity and meetings across Wales, with thousands refusing to pay their television licence. But in September, a few weeks before Evans's fast was due to begin, the Government capitulated.

I recall attending the Press conference where the Conservative Secretary of State for Wales, Nicholas Edwards announced the decision. "We have lost the middle ground of opinion in Wales," he explained.[9] This was an extraordinary moment in the history of Welsh politics coming so soon after the referendum. There was now a middle ground of opinion on the Welsh language which was identified with Plaid Cymru.

Shortly before the referendum Saunders Lewis published the following letter in the *Western Mail*:

> We are asked to tell the Government on St David's Day whether we want a Welsh Assembly or not. The implied question is: 'Are you a nation or not?' May I point out the probable consequences of a 'No' majority. There will follow a general election. There may be a change of government. The first task of a new Westminster Parliament will be to reduce and master inflation. In Wales there are coal mines that work at a loss; there are steelworks that are judged superfluous; there are still

---

[9] Press conference, 17 September 1980.

valleys that are convenient for submersion. And there will be
no Welsh defence.[10]

Lewis's message was prescient. Within a few years Welsh steel mills and
coalmines were being closed on a large scale and unemployment rose steeply.
The 1984-85 miners strike was a seminal event that prompted collective
action in support from across Wales, orchestrated by a new organisation
known as the Wales Congress in Support of Mining Communities. Hywel
Francis, Chairman of the Congress, wrote at the time that the strike was
creating a sense of Welsh identity that transcended language and regional
differences:

> We brought together all these disparate elements across
> Wales and outside Wales which were supporting the miners.
> What we were trying to say was that Wales was united and
> they were embracing the miners and so we were creating a
> sense, a perception, that the miners, as the Cymdeithas yr Iaith
> slogan said, are fighting for Wales.[11]

One of the leaders of the miners, Kim Howells, now Labour MP for
Pontypridd, reflected at the time that the strike had led himself and others
to discover, as he put it,

> ... that we are part of a real nation which extends northwards
> beyond the coalfield, into the mountains of Powys, Dyfed and
> Gwynedd. For the first time since the industrial revolution in
> Wales, the two halves of the nation came together in mutual
> support.[12]

This judgement was confirmed a quarter of a century later by Hywel Francis
himself by then Labour MP for Aberavon, who said the strike paved the way
for 1997. He added that it "created a Welsh unity and identity, overcoming
language and geographical differences, which failed to materialise in 1979".[13]

Other elements came together in these years. A diverse range of new
organisations emerged, from the Welsh Union of Writers to the Institute of
Welsh Affairs and the St David's Forum, all dedicated to promoting Welsh
preoccupations. New publications were launched, including Rebecca,
Arcade, Radical Wales, Planet (re-launched in 1985), and New Welsh Review.

---

[10] Western Mail, 26 February 1979.

[11] Quoted in Leighton Andrews, Wales Says Yes, Seren Books, 1999, p.48.

[12] Kim Howells, 'Stopping Out' in Huw Beynon (Ed.) Digging Deeper, Verso, 1985, p.147.

[13] Hywel Francis, History on our Side – Wales and the 1984-85 Miners' Strike, Ferryside:
Iconau, 2009, p.69.

The rise of the women's movement found political outlets in the miners' strike and perhaps most notably, in the march to Greenham Common that originated in west Wales to protest against Cruise Missiles.

There were intellectual undercurrents, too, in particular a discovery of Welsh history, with television programmes and publications stimulating a good deal of popular interest.[14] Their impact was to solidify the connections between the Wales of the present with the past, an essential dimension in developing the "internal solidarity" of the people. A leading Welsh intellectual during this period was Raymond Williams, Professor of Drama at Cambridge. In a review of several new volumes of Welsh history he observed that they were an example of, as he put it, "industrial South Wales recovering its actual history":

> Every reader of this new history will find, at some point, a moment when his own memory stirs and becomes that new thing, an historical memory, a new sense of identity and relationships. I can record my own moment. I have always remembered my father, a railwayman, growing potatoes along the edge of a neighbouring farmers field, and then helping his farmer friend with the harvest. But what I just did not know was the complex history of potato setting, and its formal and informal labour obligations… The personal memory, local and specific, is then suddenly connected with the history of thousands of people, through several generations. As the particular and general, the personal and the social, are at last brought together, each kind of memory and sense of identity is clarified and strengthened. The relations between people and 'a people' begin to move in the mind.[15]

Above all, attitudes to the Welsh language palpably shifted. Welsh-medium education continued to flourish, especially in the anglicised areas of south-east Wales. A burst of energy surrounded a Welsh youth music culture, with the creation and impact of S4C (the Welsh television channel) in 1982 spreading its influence. The Welsh language came to be seen as a vehicle for modernity and renewal rather than being associated with the past, nonconformity, and decline.

---

[14] Most notable was the 1984 HTV series *The Dragon Has Two Tongues*, in which presenters Wynford Vaughan Thomas and Gwyn Alf Williams argued their way through two millennia of Welsh identity politics. Williams's associated volume *When Was Wales* was published by Penguin in 1984.

[15] Raymond Williams, 'Remaking Welsh history', *Arcade*, December 1980. He was reviewing David Smith (ed.), *A People and a Proletariat: Essays in the History of Wales*, London: Pluto Press, 1980; and Hywel Francis and David Smith, *The Fed: A History of the South Wales Miners*, London: Lawrence and Wishart, 1980.

The 1990s

In his analysis of these years the political scientist Vernon Bogdanor remarked on the paradox that following the 1979 referendum defeat Labour's commitment to devolution intensified. As he said, far from destroying what seemed a merely tenuous political commitment, the defeat served to intensify it. The explanation, he concluded, was not hard to find:

> Devolution had been pressed by its advocates as a means by which the distinctive voice of Scotland and Wales could be expressed through government. But it seemed unnecessary during the 1974-79 period because the voices of Scotland and Wales were already being heard by a government so dependent on Scotland and Wales for its majority. When, however, in 1979, 1983, 1987 and 1992 England voted for Conservatives, Scotland and Wales remained loyal to Labour.[16]

Bogdanor further remarks that previously in twentieth-century Britain there had never been so prolonged a period of geographically one-sided government. However, the reaction was far more profound than merely an intensification of a commitment to devolution. Additionally, and crucially, there was a rejection of the political framework that allowed the one-sided government to occur. In Scotland, this was explicitly stated through the Claim of Right, produced by the Scottish Convention and signed by every Scottish Labour and Liberal Democrat MP in 1988. It declared sovereignty to lie with the Scottish people rather than the Westminster Parliament.

In Wales the expression came later, was more implicit but nonetheless had the same effect. The key figure was Ron Davies who became Shadow Secretary of State for Wales in 1992 and began a process of leading Welsh Labour towards a clear devolution commitment. He began with a series of radical speeches that sounded so nationalistic to many of his colleagues that he was accused of "going native". In an address to the 1994 UK Labour conference in Blackpool, for instance, he declared:

> Like the Scots we are a nation. We have our own country. We have our own language, our own history, traditions, ethics, values and pride … We now in Wales demand the right to decide through our own democratic institutions the procedures and the structures and the priorities of our own civic life.[17]

---

[16] Vernon Bogdanor, *Devolution in the United Kingdom*, Oxford: Oxford University Press, 1999, pp.193-4.

[17] Quoted in John Osmond, *Welsh Europeans*, Bridgend: Seren, 1995, pp.79-80.

In the 1979 referendum Ron Davies had voted No. Why had he changed his position so radically? As he explained himself, it was the experience of living through successive defeats at the hands of the Conservatives through the 1980s. But the main point was that in Wales Labour had won. Ron Davies and many others in Labour in the late 1980s crossed a Rubicon when they began to reject the United Kingdom basis on which general elections are held. Instead they demanded a Welsh jurisdiction. This is how Ron Davies explained how he felt following the 1987 general election:

> I vividly recall the anguish expressed by an eloquent graffiti artist who painted on a prominent bridge in my constituency, overnight after the 1987 defeat, the slogan 'We voted Labour, we got Thatcher!' I felt the future was bleak. Despite commanding just 29.5 per cent of the Welsh popular vote and majorities in only eight of the 38 Parliamentary constituencies, the Conservatives had won a third consecutive General Election. The Labour Party had performed well in Wales, achieving a 7.5 per cent swing compared with a 2.6 per cent swing in England, and gaining 15 per cent more of the share of the vote in Wales than in the United Kingdom as a whole. If the party had performed as well in England we would have been elected. For me, this represented a crisis of representation. Wales was being denied a voice.[18]

Once this 'crisis of representation' – as Ron Davies put it – was on the agenda, it was but a short step to start thinking about how a Welsh perspective could be mobilised and channelled. This was entirely new in Labour thinking in Wales.

The cross-party Campaign for a Welsh Assembly was re-launched in 1987, after lying moribund since 1979, and held meetings around the country. By the early 1990s devolution was creeping back on the agenda of Welsh Labour conferences. However, there was no mood in the party for the kind of cross-party collaboration that was taking place in Scotland, with the launch of the Scottish Constitutional Convention. I well remember a trade union representative on Labour's Welsh Executive remarking bitterly at the time about the decision of the Scottish Labour Party to collaborate in the Scottish Convention. "They've contracted out their policy," he told me.

It would take another referendum to open the door to this kind of cross-party discussion in Wales. During the early 1990s Ron Davies was a minority voice in the Welsh Labour Party arguing for greater collaboration and the building of the "internal political solidarity" that would be required before a constitutional advance could be achieved. In response to calls for a Welsh

[18] Ron Davies, *Devolution: A Process Not an Event*, The Gregynog Papers, Vol. 2 No 2, Cardiff: Institute of Welsh Affairs, February 1999, p. 4.

constitutional convention the Labour Party established its own Commission to explore its devolution policy in 1992. As Shadow Secretary of State, Ron Davies had great difficulty in engaging with this Commission. This was how he described his problems in an interview some years later:

> I started working with the Commission and it became clearer that what I had in mind about devolution was not what the Labour Party had in mind ... I had two issues: trying to win public support, and how to manage the Party. We talked to people on the industrial side, and in the quangos, and there was no conceptualising; there was no nation building; there was no desire to enter the debate at all. It was all: what's in it for us? How can we protect our position?
>
> So what do I do? It was really about trying to do some nation building, identifying the strengths of Wales, building up its own identity and that meant dealing with issues like the language, for example, like the culture, like having the strength to say that we wanted to develop our own tourism, our own industry, that we would have to look at issues about the environment, and we would have to look at it from a Welsh perspective. That was all for me part of nation building ... The other signpost was: what are going to be the views of the other parties? The other parties, for me, were the critical issue.[19]

These references to 'nation building' and the need to take the views of other parties into account represented a profound shift in Welsh Labour thinking, albeit one that still had a long way to go to convince a majority in the party. However, Ron Davies was right to identify relations with other parties as a critical issue for the future of devolution. Indeed, cross-party collaboration in pursuit of a constitutional objective is a sure sign of Herman Dooyeweerd's "internal political solidarity".

In this particular context, Ron Davies saw a need for Labour to commit to proportional representation for electing an Assembly to get the Liberal Democrats and Plaid Cymru on board. However, this proved an impossible hurdle for Welsh Labour. It was a sticking point in Scotland as well, but eventually the Scottish Labour Party reached a deal on PR with the Liberal Democrats as part of the Convention process. In Wales, however, it took a referendum to force the issue.

In the Autumn of 1994 Ron Davies prepared a submission on behalf of Wales Labour MPs to the party's Policy Commission. This called for a 100 member Assembly elected by PR, with primary legislation and tax raising powers. It represented a maximalist position within Welsh Labour thinking

---

[19] Ron Davies, interviewed in Stephen Prosser et al., 'Making it Happen': Public Service: Devolution in Wales as a Case Study, Exeter: Imprint Academic, 2006, pp. 151-2.

and over the next year was considerably watered down. By the Autumn of 1995 the Welsh Labour Party voted in its conference for an Assembly with executive powers only, no tax raising powers, and crucially with its members elected by first past the post, with two members for each of the 40 parliamentary constituencies.

There is little doubt that if Labour had stuck with this policy the referendum that was held in 1999 would have been lost, since neither the Liberal Democrats nor Plaid Cymru could have been persuaded to support the package. However, the way the referendum came about enabled the policy to be changed.

In July 1996 Tony Blair visited Scotland. Still uncertain of his victory in the forthcoming general election, and exhibiting extreme caution over tax and spending commitments, Blair was determined to remove Labour's promise of tax varying powers for the proposed Scottish Parliament from the British election agenda. The mechanism was to be a referendum in which the people of Scotland would be asked two questions, one on whether they supported a Parliament and, crucially, a second on whether they agreed that it should have the power to vary income tax by 3p in the £ up or down.

By placing the tax decision directly in the hands of the Scottish people, the referendum would remove it from the immediate British general election debate. The commitment to a Scottish referendum was therefore driven entirely by the exigencies of Scottish politics and the impact it was feared they might have on Labour's electoral prospects in the United Kingdom as a whole. However, the most immediate effect was on Wales.

For it was soon appreciated that it would be impossible to have a referendum in Scotland without also having one in Wales as well. Tony Blair's referendum ploy had came out of the blue. The Shadow Secretary of State for Scotland, George Robertson, was informed shortly beforehand, but the Shadow Secretary of State for Wales, Ron Davies, was left in the dark. In fact, on the eve of the announcement he was taking part in a BBC Wales television programme on the forthcoming election and, under persistent questioning, insisted Labour had no plans for a referendum to endorse devolution.

Yet within days Ron Davies was locked in negotiations with Blair on the help he would need if he were to lead the Welsh Labour Party through the forthcoming general election and into a referendum. There was one pivotal requirement. Blair would have to lean on the party in Wales to reverse its conference decision a year before in favour of first past the post for a Welsh Assembly, and opt instead for some variation of proportional representation. Davies argued that without a commitment to PR it would be very difficult for Labour to win a referendum in Wales.

Ron Davies won his concession and went on to lead the Yes campaign to a wafer thin majority in the referendum that was held a little over a year later, in September 1997. There is little doubt, given the closeness of the result, that without the PR commitment the referendum would have been lost.

The 1997 referendum

In 1997 the *Wales Says Yes* campaign was relatively well organised, certainly in comparison with the *Yes for Wales* campaign in 1979. The sight of Labour, Plaid Cymru and the Liberal Democrats acting in unison across much of Wales was undoubtedly influential and did much to promote a sense of consensus around the change. It also emphasised the fact that by 1997 Wales had experienced 18 years of Conservative government.

Successive Conservative administrations had intensified and dramatised what became known as the democratic deficit. As we have seen, the main influence had been to change the mood in the Labour Party, with mainstream Labour leaders beginning to acknowledge the nationality of Wales in political terms.

Underpinning these changes was a more fundamental, in many ways psychological, shift between generations that took place during the period. In 1979 society was still governed by a generation whose formative experience had been the Second World War, the fight against fascism, the creation of the Welfare State after 1945, and the consciousness and then loss of Empire. By 1997 this generation had largely passed on. In its place were 600,000 people who in 1979 had been too young to vote. For them the Second World War was as much history as the Napoleonic Wars. This new generation were no less Welsh than their forbears but they regarded their Welshness in a different light. For example, as far as they were concerned language disputes were a thing of the past. Giving Wales a political voice seemed a natural thing to do.

This shift in generations was arguably the single most important explanation for the four-to-one majority against the Assembly in 1979 being overturned into a narrow majority in 1997. Table 1 gives the results of a survey of 700 people throughout Wales within three weeks of the 1997 referendum. It demonstrates that age was a key factor in determining the way people had voted. In summary, those under 45 were likely to vote Yes by a margin of 3:2, while those over 45 were likely to vote No by a similar margin.

Table 1: The Generation Divide and the 1997 Referendum Vote

Age	Yes	No
18-24	57%	43%
25-34	60%	40%
35-44	59%	41%
45-54	42%	58%
55-64	49%	51%
65+	45%	55%

Source: *1997 Welsh Referendum Survey, University of Wales, Aberystwyth.*

Equally as striking was the impact of the referendum itself on attitudes towards Wales's future constitutional relationship with the rest of the United Kingdom. In the years leading up to the referendum, polling (by BBC Wales and others) showed a consistent 40 per cent of the electorate that were against any change. The remaining 60 per cent were split between about 25 per cent that supported Labour's Assembly proposals, 25 per cent that favoured a Scottish-style Parliament, with the remaining 10 per cent or so opting for independence.

Following the 1997 referendum this pattern shifted fundamentally and has remained more or less constant ever since. Now fewer than 20 per cent are opposed to some degree of democratic self-government for Wales. About 25 per cent support the current Assembly. Around 12 per cent support independence. But approaching 40 per cent, depending on the fluctuating support for independence, now favour moving ahead to achieve a Scottish-style parliament. Table 2 shows how this new realignment solidified in the years immediately following 1997. The change occurred entirely as a consequence of the experience of living through the 1997 referendum, and was a powerful demonstration of the dynamic influence plebiscites can have.

Table 2: Constitutional Preferences (%) Wales, 1997-2011

Constitutional Preference	1997	1999	2001	2003	2006	2007	2009	2011
Independence	13.2	9.6	11.8	13.4	11.0	11.5	14.7	12.9
Parliament	18.3	28.3	36.8	35.9	40.2	41.5	34.3	34.0
Assembly	25.1	32.9	24.5	25.3	23.9	26.1	27.4	27.5
No elected body	36.9	24.3	23.1	20.3	20.4	15.7	17.1	18.0
Don't Know	6.5	5.0	3.7	5.2	4.6	5.3	6.4	7.6
Number of respondents	686	1,256	1,085	988	1,000	884	1,078	2,359

Sources: 1997 Welsh Referendum Study; 1999 Welsh Election Study; 2001 Wales Life and Times Survey; 2003 Wales Life and Times Survey; 2006 Survey by NOP for the Electoral Commission; 2007 Welsh Election Study; 2009 YouGov poll for Aberystwyth and Cardiff Universities; 2011 Welsh Election Study.

The extremely narrow result in the referendum was regarded by many in Westminster and Whitehall as indicating an under-whelming lack of enthusiasm for change in Wales. In fact, it represented a remarkable 30 per cent increase in votes for the Yes side, or a 15 per cent swing, compared with 1979. The more emphatic two-to-one majority in the Scottish referendum, held a week earlier, actually produced a smaller swing of 11.5 per cent. And as Vernon Bogdanor concluded:

> The referendum was won through an alliance between Welsh-speaking Wales, the heartland of the north-west, and the industrial Wales of the valleys, the former coalfield areas. It seemed by comparison with the 1979 result, to show that Welsh identity was becoming less divisive and that a sense of Welshness was growing irrespective of language, a sense of Welshness which may be more deep-seated than social analysts have noted.[20]

The 2011 referendum

Proportional representation ensured that the first elections to the Assembly in 1999 produced a minority Labour administration, one that within a year was forced to come to terms with coalition politics in the form of an alliance with the Liberal Democrats. Part of the coalition agreement between the parties, insisted on by the Liberal Democrats, was the establishment of a cross-party Commission to examine the powers and electoral arrangements of the Assembly. Under the chairmanship of Lord Richard this began work in September 2002 and duly reported in the Spring of 2004.

The creation and work of the Commission was a late Welsh substitute for the Constitutional Convention which had proved so influential in Scottish politics a decade earlier. It recommended that the Assembly should become a legislative Parliament along Scottish lines with a clear separation of powers between the executive and legislature. The membership should increase from 60 to 80, and be elected by the single transferable vote proportional system. Given the history of Welsh devolution going back nearly 50 years, it was remarkable that such a consensus could be achieved. The unanimous recommendation in favour of greater powers was widely commented upon as reflecting a maturing of civic society. As the First Minister Rhodri Morgan, said at the time: "All of us involved in political life in Wales know just how contentious the remit provided to the Commission was capable of becoming."[21]

In itself, this was an indication of a maturing political culture. Not only that, the report was well put together, logical and closely argued. Despite this it was too big a pill to swallow for the anti-devolution forces that still held the upper hand within the Welsh Labour Party, including most of its Welsh

---

[20] Vernon Bogdanor, op.cit. p. 200.

[21] Assembly Record, 31 March 2004.

MPs at Westminster. A special conference in September 2004 rejected the Richard proposals, and left it to the Secretary of State for Wales, Peter Hain, to come up with some compromise solution. This eventually surfaced in for the form of the 2006 Wales Act. The only specific Richard recommendation this accepted was the separation of powers between the Assembly itself and the Welsh Government which, de facto, was happening already.

However, Hain came up with a two-pronged initiative which opened the door towards greater legislative powers for the Assembly. Under the 2006 Act the Assembly could seek a Legislative Competence Order from Westminster to pass laws on specifically defined policy areas. The Act also allowed for the Assembly to gain more autonomous law-making powers following a referendum, which in order to be held would need the approval of a two-thirds majority in the National Assembly. Such a majority (in fact, unanimous) was achieved in early 2010 and the referendum was held on 3 March 2011.

The result was an emphatic two to one majority Yes vote, with 63.5 per cent voting Yes and 36.5 per cent No. This reflected the 'settled will' in favour of more powers that had been revealed to pollsters in the years following the 1997 referendum, shown in the constitutional preferences table on Table 2. The turn-out, at 35.6 per cent, was relatively low but polling at the time indicated that a higher turn-out would have produced much the same result, and probably an increase for the Yes side.

In striking contrast to the 1997 referendum, all the parties in the Assembly were now united in campaigning for a Yes vote. In particular, the Conservative leader Nick Bourne, who had led the No campaign in 1997, now lined up with the Labour, Plaid Cymru, and Liberal Democrat leaders in the Assembly in declaring that full legislative powers were necessary to give the Assembly the tools it needed to carry out its work.

Meanwhile, the so-called 'True Wales' No campaign, based in Newbridge in Caerphilly, was a tiny grouping that could not even afford to register with the Electoral Commission as a lead campaigning group. Following the campaign the Commission revealed that the registered Yes campaigns had between them raised a little over £140,000. However, the registered No campaigns raised less than £4,000.

Most importantly, compared with 1997, the campaign showed that Wales was no longer sharply divided over devolution. As Map 1 shows on the following page shows, all the counties voted Yes, bar Monmouthshire, and even there only a few hundred votes separated the two sides. There was a margin of greater than 60 per cent in all the Yes voting counties of 1997, now joined by the counties in north-east Wales and Cardiff. Indeed, the latter recorded the highest vote swings compared with 1997. All the statistics pointed to a much greater homogeneity of view across Wales compared with 1997. For instance, in 2011 the gap between the highest and lowest counties voting Yes was 26.6 per cent, compared with 34.5 per cent in 1997. The eight highest swings to the Yes side in 2011 were all in counties that had voted No in 1997.

Table 3: Constitutional preferences of those voting Yes in referendum

Constitutional Preference	% of those voting Yes
No devolution	3.0
Assembly with fewer powers	0.4
Leave things as now	12.7
Assembly with more powers	64.6
Independent Wales	14.6
Don't know	4.8

Source: Yougov poll for Wales Governance Centre and Institute of Welsh Politics, March 2011.

Significantly, too, extensive polling shortly after the referendum vote showed that a large majority of people who voted Yes, 75 per cent, either wanted even more powers or independence for Wales, as shown in Table 3. Other polling, shown in Table 4, revealed that majorities now support devolving criminal justice and tax varying powers to Wales.

Table 4: Attitudes to more powers for the Assembly

	Yes	No	Don't know
Police and criminal justice	56.2%	30.9%	17.3%
Raising and lowering taxes	54.1%	34%	11.9%

Source: The poll of 1,005 telephone interviewees, was carried by rmgclarity for the Western Mail between 2-5 April 2011.

More generally, the clear and emphatic nature of the result, together with the National Assembly becoming a fully-fledged legislative body, will have far reaching consequences for the development of Welsh institutions, for the future of Welsh politics, and for the wider constitutional development of the UK. An immediate consequence has been to add new weight to the arguments for a separate Welsh legal jurisdiction, to mirror those already existing in Northern Ireland and Scotland. This would mean Wales gaining its own Lord Chief Justice, High Court, and Court of Appeal. As early as 2007 the present First Minister Carwyn Jones drew attention to the potential anomaly of a fully legislative Assembly operating alongside the Westminster Parliament within a single jurisdiction. As he put it:

> If you've got two parliaments that have primary powers, I think
> it makes it very difficult to have one jurisdiction. I'm not aware
> of anywhere in the word where you have that.[22]

In June 2011 Professor R. Gwynedd Parry, director of Swansea University's
Hywel Dda Institute for Legal Research, declared:

> The referendum in March in which the people of Wales called
> for greater law-making powers was a significant step. Yet at
> the moment Wales is the odd man out with Northern Ireland,
> Scotland and the Isle of Man having their own legal system.
> Why should Wales be treated differently? At the moment laws
> created in Wales could be declared illegal by higher courts in
> England. What we don't want is laws made in Wales being
> scrutinised by the courts in London. That undermines the
> purpose of devolution. The absence of a Welsh jurisdiction
> therefore makes the current constitutional settlement
> incomplete.[23]

Broader political implications could flow from the Yes vote as well. Writing
in the IWA's journal *Agenda* in the aftermath of the referendum, Professor
Richard Wyn Jones, Director of the Wales Governance Centre at Cardiff
University, drew attention to five ways in which the result will have major
consequences:

> (1) It demonstrates a 'settled will' by the Welsh electorate. The
> legitimacy not provided by the 1997 result is now bestowed on
> the National Assembly, enhancing the self-confidence of those
> working in it.
>
> (2) The emergence of the Assembly as a legislative parliament
> means that it is now, without doubt, the main forum for Welsh
> democratic debate. Welsh political horizons have moved
> irrevocably to Cardiff.
>
> (3) The transfer of extensive legislative powers to the
> Assembly across a raft of domestic policy areas means that the
> 'West Lothian Question' – the problem arising because English
> MPs cannot vote on Welsh domestic matters, while Welsh MPs
> continue to vote on English matters - will now apply in its full
> effect in Wales. It is highly unlikely that a Welsh MP will ever

---

[22] *Western Mail*, 14 September 2007.

[23] *Western Mail*, 22 June, 2011.

Map 1: 2011 referendum (courtesy of the 2011 *Wales Yearbook*)

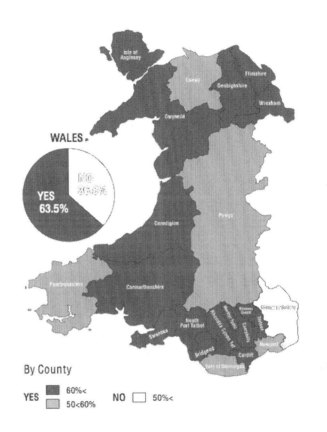

again hold a ministerial role in one of the major UK government departments whose responsibilities have been devolved, let alone become Prime Minister of Britain. Not only will there be fewer MPs but their role and status will also be diminished.

(4) The result changes the relationship between Wales and the UK state and, indeed, the nature of the State. Since the Acts of Union of the sixteenth century, Wales has been an integral part of the core of the State. Henceforth, however, Wales' relationship with the rest of the UK is destined to be inter-governmental in character.

(5) The Yes vote will now trigger a Welsh 'Calman' process with the creation of a Commission to re-examine how the Assembly is working – in fiscal and political terms. This signals a return to the Richard Commission agenda.[24]

Map 2: 1997 referendum Yes (white) and No (grey) counties

On the last point, establishment of a Commission was confirmed by Prime Minister David Cameron when he addressed the National Assembly in mid-July 2011, although he was vague on its remit and timing. A few days later, however, all the party leaders joined in signing a letter to the Secretary of State for Wales, Cheryl Gillan, demanding that the Commission have a wider remit than purely finance. The terms of reference they suggested, shown in the panel below, was closely followed by the Secretary of State in an announcement the following week.

This was yet another example of "internal political solidarity", of consensus working across the Welsh parties where constitutional advance was concerned. It demonstrated that when the party leaders in the Assembly acted in unison they could get their way with the London government.

Both Labour and Conservatives made concessions in the statement. First Minister Carwyn Jones accepted that fiscal devolution meant that

---

[24] Richard Wyn Jones, *Nation takes another historic step*, IWA Agenda, Spring 2011.

the National Assembly must have a tax varying role if its is to be financially accountable. This is how Cheryl Gillan put it:

> It is only right that the Welsh Government is accountable for the money it spends. We are only at the beginning of the process, but I believe that by working together across parties, between governments and institutions, we can reach agreement that will deliver fiscal accountability to the Assembly.[25]

For their part, the Conservative-led coalition in London accepted that fairer funding, which meant reform of the Barnett formula so that it reflects need rather than a crude population count, had to be on the table as well.

Terms of Reference for the new Welsh Fiscal and Constitutional Commission proposed by the four party leaders in the Assembly on 21 July 2011

The Commission is asked to undertake its work in two parts. In the **first part**, the Commission should consider options for **fiscal devolution**, taking into account the work already done by the Holtham Commission. This work would include identifying the practical and legal issues to be resolved before any agreed proposals could be implemented.

The Commission should commence its work in **September 2011** and report, with recommendations, no later than **September 2012**.

Secondly, and after **Part One** of the Commission has reported, **Part Two** of the Commission should look at the current **constitutional settlement** in the light of experience and recommend changes that would enable the National Assembly for Wales, and Welsh Government, to better serve the people of Wales.

The Commission is asked to report on this aspect of its remit, with recommendations as it considers appropriate, **by March 2013**.

The Commission should aim to reflect a consensual view. The Chair should have the confidence of the main Welsh political parties and both the Welsh and UK Governments.

Note: The signatories to the letter that accompanied this statement were Labour's First Minister Carwyn Jones, Plaid Cymru's leader Ieuan Wyn Jones, the Liberal Democrat leader Kirsty Williams, and the Conservatives' Paul Davies who at the time was still standing in as leader prior to the election of Andrew R.T. Davie.

---

[25] *Western Mail*, 15 July 2011.

Both Labour and the Conservatives ceded to demands from Plaid Cymru and
the Liberal Democrats that, over and above this, the whole constitutional
settlement had to be reviewed. This means returning to the 2004 Richard
Commission, signed off by all four parties at the time. This said that as well
as full legislative powers:

> (1) Wales should follow the Scottish model in which all powers
> are devolved except those explicitly reserved to Westminster
> – rather than the present arrangement in which nothing is
> devolved except those specifically conferred, which constrains
> the Welsh Government's scope for legislating effectively.

> (2) The National Assembly's membership should be expanded
> from 60 to 80 and all should be elected by the STV system of
> proportional representation.

The first opens up devolving criminal justice powers and creating a distinctive
legal jurisdiction for Wales. The second holds out the prospect for a
completely different political dynamic in Welsh politics and new relationships
between the parties. Both will be regarded as opening a Pandora's box by
many in the Labour and Conservative parties. But as Ron Davies famously
put it at the start of the devolution process in 1999: "Let no-one think that
now the devolution genie is out of his bottle he can be forced back in or that
he won't want to stretch his muscles."[26]

The devolution journey

Constitutional referendums represent a convulsion in a political system. If
politics more generally represent 'jaw jaw' in preference to 'war war', then
constitutional referendums represent a civil war conducted by other, more
civilised means. Whatever their results, their impact is to speed up the
political process.

Their announcement, usually about a year before the event, immediately
launches the political system into a new gear, with the creation of new
formations, often with a cross-party character needed to fight the campaigns,
bringing a heightened engagement in politics.

Cross-party campaigns also promote Herman Dooyeweerd's "internal
political solidarity". They send a message that the parties involved are
setting aside their own particular priorities in the interests of the nation as a
whole. This was most clearly seen in the 2011 referendum in Wales when first,
the Assembly voted unanimously for a referendum, and then the leaders of
all four parties joined together in campaigning for a Yes vote.

[26] Ron Davies, *Devolution - A Process Not an Event*, IWA, 1999, p.9.

Living through the referendums of the past thirty years has certainly hastened the maturing of politics in Wales. They have resulted in an historical acceleration in the development of the country's constitution. During referendum campaigns the political system is pulled backwards and forwards in polarising debates. In the Welsh experience referendums can be likened to an athlete preparing to throw a discus, leaping from one foot to another, gathering momentum to hurl the object as far as possible.

Where will the devolution journey take us? There can be no definitive answer to that question. Don, now Lord Anderson, the former Labour MP for Swansea East and a late convert to devolution, once described it as a mystery tour:

> I recall the fine story of a bus tour from Cwmrhydyceirw in my constituency. There was a sweep about where the tour would end, and it is said the driver won. The people of Wales are driving this mystery tour. They will decide the pace and direction.[27]

Although the destination of Welsh devolution remains uncertain, more than a decade into the experiment two things are clear. The pace is accelerating and the direction is in favour of more powers.

---

[27] House of Commons debates (Hansard), vol. 924, col. 458, 25 July 1997.

Northern Ireland and Scotland: Uncertain Destinations

Ian S Wood

Northern Ireland at the time of writing once again faces what may be a turbulent summer as the Loyalist marching season gets under way. Most of the parades held all over its six counties to mark the battle of the Boyne in 1690 will not pose any public order threat any more than they do in Scotland. It is, however, the ones that do that matter politically and in terms of the face that, fifteen years after the Belfast Agreement, Northern Ireland presents to the world's media.

The fear within the Police Service of Northern Ireland, whose officers in June 2013 have the huge task of protecting world leaders at the G8 summit in County Fermanagh, is that within the Loyal orders a hardline element will seek to by-pass or even ignore the authority of the Parades Commission. This body, set up by Tony Blair's government in 1998 to regulate and, if necessary, to re-route contentious Loyalist parades, has suffered a serious loss of credibility as a result of the protests over what was seen as the right to fly the Union flag all the year round on Belfast City Hall and the erosion of this right by nationalist and Alliance party councillors voting together on the issue on 3 December 2012.

These protests lasted for over three months and, at their height, involved attacks on the police, serious street violence in East Belfast and the regular disruption and closure of major roads. Much of this was clearly coordinated by the illegal Ulster Volunteer Force, especially in the East of the city. Its leadership, based in the Loyalist heartland of the Shankill, was not over-keen to take part, while the Ulster Defence Association's response was an ambivalent one. Its most senior figure, Jackie McDonald, was clearly worried about where the protests might lead, though some of the organisation's activists in North Belfast and in towns like Larne and Carrickfergus openly joined in.

At the time, the police were much criticised in the press for their low-key response, but since the protests died down some of its leaders have been arrested and charged. Published CCTV footage is also being used to start the process of identifying and charging alleged law-breakers. This will inevitably take time and has inflammatory potential if prosecutions start to overlap with the marching season when communal tensions always rise.

The PSNI's Chief Constable, Mark Baggott, whose officers are under regular attack from republican dissidents, has offered a robust defence of the way he has handled the flag protests. He points out that 186 cases arising from them are being prepared, with more on the way.[1] "We do not forget about it," he has told the press, "We go looking for justice afterwards."[2] This has not convinced his critics and, even as he spoke, the UVF was allowed to deck out large areas of East Belfast with flags commemorating the formation of the force in its original form in 1913. They did this without reference to the police or the city council, claiming that the flags were historical rather than paramilitary, though many of the men seen putting them up wore balaclavas while doing so.

The police cannot speak for the Parades Commission though, once they have received notice of any intended parade, they must pass it on to the Commission. It has no power to ban parades, but it can lay down requirements relating to the behaviour of participants, insignia carried and the type of music played at specific points along the route to be marched. It can also re-route parades, as it famously did at Drumcree in 1998. This decision prompted a violent Loyalist reaction, leading to serious disorder and several deaths. Since then the Orange Order in Portadown has been unable to exercise what it sees as its right to 'walk' form Drumcree down Garvaghy Road and back into the town centre.

Violence over this issue has now died down but, given the enduring potency of the Loyalist parade culture, trouble can always start elsewhere. The fiercely republican Ardoyne district in North Belfast invariably sees violence in July, as Orange lodges and bands pass the edge of it, never through it, on their way to and from their home areas. What happens there has been called 'recreational rioting', but it is more than that. It is now visibly well organised by republican dissidents who seem able to turn it on and off like a tap, though sometimes openly clashing with local Sinn Féin activists who support the Belfast Agreement and their party's participation in the power-sharing structures which it created.

In recent months, however, an ominous flashpoint has opened up close to Belfast city centre at St Patrick's church in Donnegall Street. For many years, bands and lodges passed it on the 12 July parade without incident, but during a halt in the 2012 'Twelfth', one band from the Shankill played and behaved in a highly provocative way right outside the church. This incensed the Catholic population of the nearby Carrick Hill estate, whose church it is.[3] Subsequent, though in fact smaller parades led to major disorder, and since then the Parades Commission has struggled to achieve compliance with its rulings on how parades past St Patrick's should be conducted.

The Commission's authority gained nothing when Peter Robinson, Northern Ireland's First Minister, added his name to a list of almost all of

[1] David McKittrick, 'Northern Ireland's top policeman gives wake-up call on paramilitaries', The Independent, 14 May 2013.

[2] Ibid.

[3] The Irish News, 17 and 19 July 2012.

Belfast's unionist councillors who condemned the Commission's handling of this issue. At this point he was very clearly wearing his Paisleyite and Democratic Unionist Party hat, as he also seemed to be when he declined to condemn a Loyalist drummer who was pictured in the press urinating at the gates of another Catholic church in East Belfast during the mammoth 30 September parade through the city to mark the 1912 Ulster Covenant.[4]

Brian Feeney, the always pugnacious *Irish News* columnist, has regularly derided the Commission for what he claims has been its self-imposed impotence during the flag protests. Many of these were indeed so close to parades as to make little difference to drivers, shoppers and pedestrians caught up in them. "Useless and gutless" was how he described the Commission in one of his articles.[5] Peter Osborne, the Commission's chairman, has argued that unnotified parades, which is how he classifies the flag protests, are not his direct responsibility but a police matter, depending on what offences are committed during them.[6] Early in May 2013, he could still see a role for the Commission in regulating the summer's parades, but he also appealed to the Loyal orders to talk to representatives of nationalist communities ahead of any parades that might cause trouble. There are now some signs of this happening, with the Orange Order in County Antrim agreeing with a residents' group in the mainly nationalist village of Rasharkin that the 12 July parade there should be re-located away from the centre of the village to minimise disruption or possible provocation.[7]

The Orange Order is in relative decline in terms of membership, but any moves by it to hold parades without reference to the commission can still have serious consequences. They have already announced what they describe as a 'mini-Twelfth' in Portadown on 8 June, and this is alarming Catholics in housing estates on either side of a public park where lodges and bands plan to gather marching off.[8]

The reality for Northern Ireland and for all who are concerned with communal relations there is that bands are recruiting much better than the Orange Order. Their membership is young, working-class and mainly male and they embody a raucous and exuberant plebeian Loyalism, as they do across West and Central Scotland. When fuelled by alcohol and sometimes drugs, they have always posed potential public order problems, something often very apparent during the years of the Troubles. Some of them, too, have always had paramilitary links, though the Parades Commission has the power to stop them wearing uniforms or displaying the insignia of illegal organisations.

---

[4] *Ibid*, 4 October 2012.

[5] *Ibid*.

[6] *Ibid*., April 2013.

[7] *Ibid*., 15 May 2013.

[8] *Ibid*., 9 May 2013.

Not all their energies are destructive, as Darach MacDonald, a Catholic journalist, has shown in his recent book on the bands.[9] "Many of them," he stresses "are content to parade in their own areas and invest huge effort in fund raising for uniforms and good quality instruments, as well as in practice, drill and good turnout." He sees them as an important non-violent assertion of an identity and of a shared history at a time when many of their community's old certainties have been turned upside down. As an other writer on these bands has put it,

> Sometimes the most aggressive displays are intended for home consumption and are not specifically directed at anyone else. They are a ritualistic, internal definition of identity, territory, and tribe, a rehearsal of mythic personality. They are a confidence-building, chest-beating rooster's crow, meant for their community's own ears.[10]

They are not going away any time soon, either in Northern Ireland or in Scotland, and they are likely to remain unloved and misunderstood by most of the politically correct intelligentsia on both sides of the water. They receive little attention in A Shared Future, a cliché-ridden and anodyne document recently issued by the First Minister and his deputy, Martin McGuinness,[11] yet they will have to be part of any future that there is for Northern Ireland.

Rather more creative thinking on that future is on offer in a new collection of essays on the situation there, edited by Professor Elizabeth Meehan and Dr Cillian McGrattan.[12] Policing and parades get some mention but, arguably, would merit a full chapter in their own right. One contributor, Professor Duncan Morrow, is close to the truth when he describes Northern Ireland as a society living within the framework of a truce rather than any transformation, where the realistic goal is one of "managed antagonism".[13] Some of last summer's parades and the Union flag protests certainly made it feel like that.

Other contributors to this important book explore how employment brings people together in areas like schooling, church-going and workplace relations in terms of how and if these have developed since 1998. Drs Neil Jarman and John Bell show us that, where employment brings Catholics and

---

[9] Darach MacDonald, Blood and Thunder: Inside an Ulster Protestant Band, Cork: Mercier Press, 2010.

[10] Gary Hastings, With Fife and Drum: Music Memories and Customs of an Irish Tradition, Belfast: Blackstaff, 2003, pp.14-15.

[11] The Irish News, 10 May 2013.

[12] Elizabeth Meehan and Cillian McGrattan (eds), Everyday Life After the Irish Conflict: The Impact of Devolution and Cross-border Co-operation, Manchester: Manchester University Press, 2012.

[13] Ibid., p.30.

Protestants together, people's interaction with each other is defined by a culture of avoidance where any issues of ethnic or political identity arise. Just how quickly workplace relations can come under strain became clear in August 2012 when Billy Hunter, an employee of Asda on Belfast's Shore Road, burned himself to death on a busy public road. He was a convicted UVF killer who had already caused some problems for the store's managers yet, in response to feelings within a predominantly Protestant workforce in a Loyalist locality, Asda allowed a book of condolence to be opened on its premises and floral tributes to be tied to the store's railings.[14]

Human rights and equality were core values of the Belfast Agreement. It had much to say about them and said it eloquently. Their achievement, however, remains a long and hard road, harder now thanks to rising unemployment and Westminster-driven cuts to essential benefits. Its transformational potential, where ordinary people's rights are concerned, remain mired in neglect.

Also neglected under its terms is the need for real truth-telling about the Troubles. In 2008, the author and journalist Henry McDonald, originally from Belfast but now based in Dublin, brought out his deliberately neglected book *Gunsmoke and Mirrors: How Sinn Féin Dressed Up Defeat as Victory*.[15] In it, he methodically unpicked the republican movement's calculated falsification of the history of the Troubles and its responsibility for unleashing a squalid, brutal, sectarian and futile war which it had lost long before the IRA's August 1994 ceasefire. This was no heroic struggle to secure civil rights and an 'equality agenda', but a failed attempt to impose Irish unification by naked force.

The Belfast Agreement is an ingenious document, which performed the vital feat of securing a framework for political power sharing but, where recent history is concerned, there is still a structured dishonesty built into it. It hardly mentions terrorism, settling instead for the pain-free phrase 'the tragedies of the past'. More work like Henry McDonald's is needed to puncture the queasy concensus that the discourse on the Troubles now seems to require, as people who should know better talk and write of the late Pat Finucane as if he had been some sort of martyr to the cause of human rights in Northern Ireland.

The IRA's war had failed long before 1994, because most of the nationalist community wanted no part of it and because the security forces defeated it with a great deal of help from within the organisation, reaching up to its senior command level. For it, after decades of promising victory at countless rallies, commemorations and funerals, not winning was defeat; but an always mendacious leadership has been allowed to mask this reality in the contrived discourse of a 'peace process' in which paramilitary republicanism has made huge gains at the expense of constitutional nationalism. But then, as Tony

---

[14] *The Irish News*, 12 September 2012.

[15] Dublin: Gill and Macmillan, 2008.

Blair is charmingly quoted as saying to the Social and Democratic Labour Party's leader Mark Durkan after the Belfast Agreement, "the problem with you guys is that you don't have any guns."[16]

Guns are still around in Northern Ireland, despite elaborately orchestrated exercises in paramilitary decommissioning, though it is mostly IRA dissidents who are using them at the moment. They might just have used them at the height of the flag protests at the start of this year when marchers tried to attack the strongly republican Short enclave in East Belfast. Gunmen there, during and since the Troubles, have never been hesitant in showing their hand, but it did not come to that.

It could easily have done so. Northern Ireland now is a more democratic and inclusive place than it was in 1968, with equality legislation and power-sharing structures securely in place, even if they have not delivered all that was hoped for back in 1998.Yet for some, especially the young with poor education and skills and even poorer work prospects, the concept of shared citizenship, as Professor Shirlow has shown,[17] is only acceptable if 'their' side wins, or at least is not seen to lose, over issues like flags, emblems, language rights or the re-naming of a children's playpark after a dead IRA hunger striker, as happened quite recently in Newry.[18]

In the midst of all its preoccupations with parades, paramilitarism and political structures, Northern Ireland's political class is increasingly watchful of events in Scotland, as our constitutional referendum draws slowly closer. Unionists are listening with care to the pronouncements of those in Scotland they regard as kindred spirits. That includes those who wear 'the sash across the sea'. Scottish Orangemen and flute bands have always had a strong presence during the Ulster marching season, proudly carrying the Saltire with the Union flag, as they do in hundreds of parades every year in Scotland.

The Grand Orange Lodge of Ireland was always going to support its Scottish counterpart in opposing a 'yes' vote in the 2014 referendum.[19] Ian Wilson, former grand master of the Order in Scotland and a skillful and articulate polemicist, now edits its monthly paper the *Orange Torch*. He loses no chance in its pages to flay and ridicule what he sees as the many twists and turns in Alex Salmond's presentation of the 'Yes' case, though he may end up playing the man too often, rather than the ball. In recent issues, however, he made space for a Catholic commentator, Professor Tom Gallagher, to reflect on the downfall of cardinal Keith O'Brien.[20] He also published this writer's

[16] Patrick J Roche and Brian Barton (eds), *The Northern Ireland Question: The Peace Process and the Belfast Agreement*, London: Palgrave Macmillan, 2008, p.263.

[17] Peter Shirlow, *The End of Ulster Loyalism?*, Manchester: Manchester University Press, 2012.

[18] Fionola Meredith, 'It's easy to demonise and ridicule loyalists in new NI', *The Irish Times*, 7 December 2012.

[19] Gerry Braiden, 'Orange Order in No vote campaign', *The Herald*, 23 April 2013.

[20] *Orange Torch*, April 2013.

thoughts on how the Union has evolved over time and how, before the First World War, there was wide support for replacing it with a decentralised form of federalism, 'Home Rule all round', as Churchill and Lloyd George called it.[21]

Chris Harvie, proponent of a confederal future for these isles, has of course contributed substantially to this debate and did so recently on one of Scotland's best online discussion forums. There, he reminded us that he had argued, back in 1983, that Northern Ireland's self-government should be anchored by a "state treaty between Dublin and the Scottish government, guaranteeing community rights: Ulster being our problem, not London's."[22]

Addressing the Scottish Conservatives at their March 2012 conference Lord Trimble, as he now is, stressed to delegates that in his homeland the Union was safe not just because the security forces had defeated the IRA but because "we won the political argument."[23] For the SNP, his message was an uncompromising one: "In saying that you want to take Scotland out (i.e. of the Union) and take the Scottish identity out into a separate place, you are doing violence to part of the identity of every Scotsman."[24] His confidence has not been enough to allay the fears of other Ulster Unionists. Proof of this seems to lie in their growing attacks on the 'Yes' campaign here. One former Ulster Unionist Party leader, Lord Reg Empey, has argued that a Scottish secession from the Union could push Northern Ireland back into conflict. His successor Tom Elliot thought much the same, but the party's present leader, Mike Nesbitt, has tried to talk down the dangers to the *Scotsman*.[25] Loyalists, in his view, though they support Rangers and welcome Scottish marchers on the Twelfth, do not have a particular view on our referendum.

This could change nearer the time for voting. After all, Dr Ian Paisley, at the height of his alienation from and distrust of what he saw as the duplicity and infirmity of purpose of British policy, flirted with the idea of Ulster independence. The Ulster Defence Association did more than that, bringing out in 1978 a substantial document called *Beyond the Religious Divide*. This made a thoughtful case for independence in a form which, they argued, could appeal to the minority community. Some of their leaders, like Glen Barr and John McMichael, drew upon the advice and good offices of the late Professor Bernard Crick.[26] In a second document, *Common Sense*, published

---

[21] *Ibid.*, February 2013.

[22] Christopher Harvie, 'There could still be life in a federal UK', *Scottish Review*, 21 February 2013 <www.scottishreview.net/ChristopherHarvie61.shtml?utm_source=Sign-Up.to&utm_medium=email&utm_campaign=8427-288708-The+jury%27s+out%3A+lessons+from+the+Vicky+Pryce+shambles>.

[23] *The Irish News*, 24 March 2012.

[24] *Ibid.*

[25] *The Scotsman*, 21 February 2013.

[26] Ian S Wood, *Crimes of Loyalty: A History of the UDA*, Edinburgh: Edinburgh University Pres, 2006, pp. 71-75 and 91-97; also Peter Shirlow, *The End of Ulster Loyalism, op. cit.*, pp. 89-97.

in 1987, not long before John McMichael was murdered by the IRA, with some likely help from friends within the UDA, they backtracked from full independence, but in some important respects signposted the way to the Belfast Agreement.

Some Irish republicans already sense new possibilities. One of them, Barry McElduff, Sinn Féin Assembly Member for West Tyrone, has told the Scottish journalist David Maxwell that in his view Scottish independence would leave Northern Ireland and Wales as poor relations in a supposedly multinational partnership defined by the interests of an England where the reactionary right would have a secure hold on power.[27] "If Scotland breaks away from the Union," McElduff has said, "then the Union is no longer what it was. Will we be in a union with London? Even for Unionists that's not a very attractive proposition because in any partnership with London your needs will always be peripheral."[28] The Scottish debate, in his view, can only provoke a new crisis for Ulster Unionism, as all its old certainties slip away alongside Scotland's journey to an uncertain destination.

If that destination is indeed to be the break-up of the Anglo-Scottish union, it is not guaranteed to bring any nearer Sinn Féin's goal of an all-Ireland republic. A brutal twenty-five year war failed to do that and, with Sinn Féin the largest nationalist party in Stormont, support in opinion polls for a united Ireland remains strikingly low, despite the shifting religious composition of the electorate revealed in the recent census. Hardcore republican dissidents will not let that stop their attacks, which are part of a calculated strategy to provoke the Loyalist community in the way that it was back in 1970 and 1971. They are more than likely to fail, just as paramilitary nationalism failed in Scotland. It has shown its face here over the years and caused the British state some real alarm in the nineteen-seventies and early eighties,[29] but it has had no part to bringing us to where we are, with an independence referendum in the offing.

The SNP does have some skeletons in its cupboard and prefers to keep quiet about them. Dr Gavin Bowd's book *Fascist Scotland* has reminded us that from 1960 to 1970 its chairman was Arthur Donaldson, a man who in 1940 and 1941 was at the very least a defeatist, who used the name 'Quisling' for fellow-Scots who went public to dispute his view that self-government should take priority over destroying the barbarism of Hitler's New Order. By 1940, he had already been expelled by the SNP and few within its small membership shared his views, though they continued to find some toxic expression in the party's publications.[30]

---

[27] *The Scotsman*, 21 February 2013.

[28] *Ibid.*

[29] Andrew Murray Scott and Iain MacLeay, *Britain's Secret War: Tartan Terrorism and the Anglo-American State*, Edinburgh, Mainstream,1990.

[30] Gavin Bowd, *Fascist Scotland: Caledonia and the Far Right*, Edinburgh: Birlinn, 2013

Today's SNP has its faults, like any other party, and its leader often looks and sounds like a populist fixer who gives too many hostages to fortune with the frequency of his often ill-considered and conflicting promises and policy commitments ahead of the referendum vote. Yet, his party remains one with a reasonable claim to a civic and inclusive nationalism that, in words used by Hamish Henderson in one of his great war poems, is without "villainy of hatred."[31]

---

[31] Hamish Henderson, 'First Elegy', *Elegies for the Dead in Cyrenaica*, in Hamish Henderson, *Collected Poems and Songs*, edited by Raymond Ross, Edinburgh: Curly Snake Publishing, 2000, p.53.

Regional Socialism – Socialist Regions: Labour Scotland, Britain, and the Hopelessness of the Bavarian Social Democrats

Thomas Leuerer

"Ja, wenn es sich um die eine rote Republik handelte".[1]

In his enlightening study on the socialist traditions in Northern England, Paul Salveson describes regional socialism not only as deeply rooted in the fabric of regions, but also as an answer to the challenge of a socialism for the twenty-first century.[2] Different socialist cultures emerged from different experiences, John Prescott writes in the foreword for the study, and Paul Salveson concludes:

> Wales and Scotland currently enjoy more of the democratic foundations to take the twin pillars of freedom and equality forward – though both Welsh and Scottish socialists would say there was still a long way to go. In the North, we haven't even got to the starting line, and are moving towards an ever-increasing dependence on a centralised Whitehall and Westminster government. Creating a values-led socialism which is democratic, ethical and rooted in its communities is necessary if Labour is to become a credible force for change, and an electable political party.[3]

Much has been said concerning the crisis of European Social Democrats and their defeat at the ballots over recent years. Franz Walter and others traced this crisis back to what Salveson calls value-led, democratic and ethical socialism. From Blair's New Labour to the SPD of Gerhard Schröder and the French *Parti*

---

[1] Hugo Lindemann, 'Zentralismus und Föderalismus in der Sozialdemokratie', *Sozialistische Monatshefte* 11 (1905): 767-773, p.771; electronic ed.: Bonn: FES Library, 2006. [Yes, if it were the one red republic!]

[2] Paul Salveson, *Socialism with a Northern Accent: Radical Traditions for modern times*, London: Lawrence & Wishart, 2012.

[3] *Ibid.*, p.202.

Socialiste, Walter found in a comparative study patterns of neo-liberal politics in all European socialist parties with similar and disastrous consequences.[4] This paper aims at the last of Salveson's elements of modern socialism: a socialism rooted in its communities – or, in our case: regions. Salveson's conclusion for Northern England gives a still positive account for the desperate situation of Bavarian socialists, whose position has been correctly described as hopeless.[5] I will argue that one of the reasons for the failure of the Bavarian SPD to be the force for change and an electable political party is not being rooted in the region and communities. Quite contrary, the public regards the SPD as a non-Bavarian party. A survey taken in 2003, asking how strong those polled would link the parties to Bavaria, produced 90 per cent for the conservative Christian Social Union (CSU), still 43 per cent for the Green Party, and a mere 36 per cent for the Social Democrats.[6] The result at the last Landtagswahl (regional election) in 2008 produced a historic low for the SPD, with 19.1 per cent oft he vote. The question arising is: do Bavarian Social Democrats have any chance at all to become an electable party again? British experiences suggest that this might be the case.

The first question is one basically answered long ago: the (in-)compatibility of class and territory for socialist parties. The second question aims at conditions for the success of regionalist parties. Territory and class have always been difficult to deal with for the left. Especially the German SPD has been caught up in disputes between those favouring federalism and those insisting on the one (and in that case: red) republic. In the wake of the SPD Convention of Jena 1905, the party centralised its organisation, causing fierce disputes between Southern and Northern members.[7] As soon as Social Democrats had a chance to shape the character of the German Republic, a debate between the options of a unitary state, a decentral unitary state or a federal state erupted. In the wake of the Constitutional Assembly at Weimar in 1919 and after, the left-wing monthly *Sozialistische Monatshefte* documented a strong discussion within the socialist movement, with a notion to prevent a Unitary state and towards a moderate federalism, or

---

[4] See Felix Butzlaff, Matthias Micus and Franz Walter (eds), *Genossen in der Krise? Europas Sozialdemokratie auf dem Prüfstand*, Göttingen: Vandenhoeck & Ruprecht, 2011.

[5] Alf Mintzel, 'Regionale politische Traditionen und CSU-Hegemonie in Bayern', in: Dieter Oberndörfer and Karl Schmitt (eds), *Parteien und regionale politische Traditionen in der Bundesrepublik Deutschland (Ordo Politicus 28)*, Berlin: Duncker & Humblot, 1991, pp.125-180, p.

[6] Andreas Kießling, 'Das Parteiensystem Bayerns', in: Uwe Jun, Melanie Haas and Oskar Niedermayer (eds), *Parteien und Parteiensysteme in den deutschen Ländern*, Wiesbaden: VS Verlag, 2008, p.141.

[7] Julius Bruhns, 'Zur Neuorganisation der Partei', *Sozialistische Monatshefte* 11 (1905): pp.481-485, p.482; electronic ed.: Bonn: FES Library, 2006.

decentralisation with space for strong regionalisms.[8] This debate was never-ending, be it in favour of a decentralised Unitary state,[9] be it in favour of a central state.[10]

The British Labour Party, on the other hand, has a far longer experience to balance territorial identities.[11] It would lead us too far astray to relate at this point the entire story of Home Rule and Devolution.[12] Britain rests upon a long tradition of, and experience in, balancing territory and power.[13] Within this balance, a federal solution never seemed to be attractive.[14] Devolution, introduced by the UK Labour government in 1997, offered the latest but, given the pending referendum on Scottish independence, potentially not the lasting solution. The Labour Party, however, acted by no means as a unified and strong supporter of regionalism. Time and again, Labour beat the Unionist drum.[15] Yet, Labour adapted to Devolution quite successfully within the constraints of ideology, party organisation and multiple intra-party understandings.[16] These 'understandings' have, however, been differently spelt in London and Edinburgh, and Labour has to pay a price.

Peter Mair proved more than thirty years ago that the territorial and the class cleavage are not incompatible for socialist parties, especially not for

---

[8] Especially Heinrich Peus (1862-1937), a social democrat politician from Dessau, produced numerous contributions in favour of a socialist regionalism: 'Das Grossdeutsche Reich.' *Sozialistische Monatshefte* 24 (1918), pp.1113-1115; electronic ed.: Bonn: FES Library, 2006; 'Zum Aufbau des Reichs', *Sozialistische Monatshefte* 25 (1919), pp.436-440; electronic ed.: Bonn: FES Library, 2006; 'Das Reich und die Länder', *Sozialistische Monatshefte* 29 (1923), pp. 329-333, electronic ed.: Bonn: FES Library, 2006; 'Für einen deutschen Regionalismus', *Sozialistische Monatshefte* 33 (1927), pp.878-882; electronic ed.: Bonn: FES Library, 2006; Bruno Jacob, 'Partikularismus und Föderalismus in Deutschland', *Sozialistische Monatshefte* 28 (1922), pp.981-985; electronic ed.: Bonn: FES Library, 2006.

[9] Manfred Turlach, 'Föderalismus oder Selbstverwaltung?' *Neue Gesellschaft: Frankfurter Hefte* 9 (1962), pp.38-43.

[10] Klaus von Dohnanyi, 'Ein gut geführter Zentralstaat ist besser als ein unentschiedener Föderalismus', *Neue Gesellschaft: Frankfurter Hefte* 51 (2004), pp.40-44.

[11] See, for example, Barry Jones and Michael Keating, *Labour and the British State*, Oxford: Clarendon, 1985.

[12] For the history of Scottish Devolution, see Christopher Harvie and Peter Jones, *The Road to Home Rule: Images of Scottish Nationalism*, Edinburgh: Polygon, 2000.

[13] Jim Bulpitt, *Territory and Power in the United Kingdom: An interpretation*, Manchester: Manchester University Press, 1983.

[14] John Kendle, *Federal Britain: A History*. London, New York: Routledge, 1997.

[15] Peter Jones, 'Scotland: The Nationalist Phoenix', in: Alan Trench (ed.), *The State of the Nations 2008*, Exter: Imprint Academic, 2008, pp.23-55, p.31.

[16] Martin Laffin and Eric Shaw, 'British Devolution and the Labour Party: How a National Party Adapts to Devolution', *British Journal of Politics and International Relations (BJPIR)* 9 (2007), pp.55-72.

national parties.[17] Michael Keating once identified a specific socialist/social democratic type of regionalism, mainly in the Labour Party, the SPD, in France and Italy.[18] This is why the case of the Bavarian SPD, in contrast to Scottish Labour (or Welsh Labour) and the Labour Party in Northern England, is interesting. Both party organisations are but regional arms of an otherwise mainly centralised national party organisation. This rests on the presumption that there still is a British Labour Party, and that the federal organisation of the SPD is, nevertheless, largely centralised.

Mair had identified four dichotomies to analyse the conflicting appeals of territory and class:[19]

> (a) The timing of the territorial dimension sets a dichotomy between the younger and more regionalist (nationalist) parties, clearly identified with the territorial question, and the older regional branches of national parties, where the central party normally keeps a close watch so that territorial appeals do not trump those of class and ideology.

> (b) The second dichotomy is the policy response of the party: all peripheric and national parties had endorsed territorial appeals in their programmes – never, however, to a point where it would become a dominating point.

> (c) The third dichotomy is the source of pressure – external or internal. While nationalist parties bear the pressure for territorial questions somehow genetically, Labour in particular adopted the devolution issue, driven mainly by an external electorate (e.g. post 1974). Mair could not know in 1982 that Blair's new Labour would answer Scotland's call for autonomy with a promise for constitutional change and a new referendum in 1997.

> (d) The last dichotomy is the organisational response of the parties. None of the parties in 1982 suffered major difficulties in incorporating the territorial dimension, except for minor schisms in the then LPSC (Labour Party Scottish Council). In 2013, however, the situation is different.

---

[17] Peter Mair and Ian McAllister, 'A Territorial *versus* a Class Appeal?: the Labour Parties of the British Isles' Periphery', *European Journal of Political Research*, 10 (1982), pp.17-34.

[18] Michael Keating, *The New Regionalism in Western Europe: Territorial Restructuring and Political Change*, Cheltenham: Edward Elgar, 1998. p.105.

[19] Peter Mair and Ian McAllister, pp.29-31.

In a contribution to Gerry Hassan's history of the Scottish Labour Party, Michael Keating places socialist territorial thinking in a wider perspective of the history of ideas. Class, ideology and territorial demands pose a considerable challenge for all socialist movements and parties in Western Europe, which they meet with various solutions depending on time and region.[20] As for the second half of the twentieth century, he shows various examples from the British Isles, Spain, France and Flanders – but without any reference to Bavaria. Here we return to the starting point in Paul Salveson's Northern England. How can a party meet the standards of ethical socialism, democracy and, at the same time, be regionally rooted? Even in Bavaria?

Keating was right not to mention the Bavarian Social Democrats in the same breath with other successful regional socialists, because successful they are not. It is well worth noting, though, that the founding fathers of both the first Bavarian republic in 1918, and of the re-constitution under the auspices of the American Military Government in 1946, were socialists: Kurt Eisner (USPD) and Wilhelm Hoegner (SPD), respectively. The ballot box, though, shows a different picture. The Social Democrats had their best result, winning 35.8 per cent of the vote, in 1966, and suffered the worst defeat in 2008, with just 18.6 per cent. The actual trend for the 2013 elections in Bavaria[21] does not give much hope, with support lingering at an average of 20 per cent.[22]

(Regional) milieux and (political) ideologies are manifestations of political culture, which in turn account to a good part for electoral choice and therefore have to match if a party aims for success at the ballot box.[23] Following Keating, Jörg Kammerzell in his study on regionalist parties points out the specific importance of institutional settings, in addition to the economic and cultural macro-levels.[24] At the same time, though, he ignores intra-party and organisational resources. Combining Mair and more recent studies, the following is an attempt at outlining a short comparison between regional socialism in Scotland, Northern England and Bavaria.

---

[20] Michael Keating, 'Socialism, Territory and the National Question', in: Gerry Hassan (ed.), *The Scottish Labour Party: History, institutions and Ideas*, Edinburgh: Edinburgh University Press, 2004, pp.233-244.

[21] The Bavarian *Landtag* is to be elected on 15 September 2013, a week before the German federal elections.

[22] Sonja Kowarschick and Stefan Plöchinger, 'Wahlumfragen-Trendmonitor: So wollen Deutschland, Bayern und Hessen wählen', *Süddeutsche Zeitung*, 24 April 2013.

[23] Karl Rohe, Regionale (politische) Kultur: Ein sinnvolles Konzept für die Wahl- und Parteienforschung?, in: Dieter Oberndörfer and Karl Schmitt (eds), *Parteien und regionale politische Traditionen in der Bundesrepublik Deutschland*, (Ordo Politicus 28), Berlin: Duncker & Humblot, 1991, pp.17-37.

[24] Jörg Kammerzell, *Entstehungs- und Erfolgsbedingungen regionalistischer Parteien: Eine Analyse des politisch-institutionellen Kontextes*, Baden-Baden: Nomos, 2008, p.258.

(1) The institutional and cultural context

While both Scotland and Northern England share a deeply rooted socialist culture, and Labour is still, at least in Westminster elections, Scotland's leading party,[25] the Bavarian tradition and political culture is a much more hostile environment. Modern Bavaria started as a kingdom installed by Napoleon Bonaparte and bearing in its institutional design, to the present day, the French heritage, imported by Montgelas, in the form of a stout centralism with Munich as the overwhelming centre. Bavaria, however, never developed a unified political culture, due to the annexation of the greater part of Franconia and Swabia. These cultural subregions developed their own political culture, with a far stronger socialist element in the Franconian-Protestant regions around Nuremberg and the Franconian North-East. Post-war Bavaria then saw the hegemony of the conservative cross-confessional Christian Social Union (CSU). The different subcultures gradually lost their political-structural meaning and have now been downgraded to regional subcultures without the capability to challenge the official hegemonic culture of the Bavarian state.[26]

The first vaguely socialist organisations in Bavaria date back to 1866 in Nuremberg, the Bavarian branch of the SPD enters the stage not until 1892. Twenty years later, in 1912, an account of the 11th Party Conference still paints a bleak picture of a party desperately attempting to enter the state parliament, finding that hard to achieve, faced with a voting system designed by Catholic centrists and Liberals with a view to keep the socialists out.[27] In general, the Bavarian Social Democrats always took the side of the reformist wings of the SPD, rather than following radical or revolutionary notions. Especially during a period prior to the First World War and in the days of the Weimar Republic, this strategy proved to be rather successful. Following the defeat of Nazi Germany in 1945, the SPD led several governments, under Prime Minister Wilhelm Hoegner, until 1957 when they lost potential coalition partners and consequently were submerged in an asymmetric party system and a dominant conservative culture.[28]

(2) The territorial dichotomy

It seems to be common sense that the German party system does not know any relevant regional party – except for the CSU. Political Parties in Germany

---

[25] At the 2010 UK General Election, Labour won 41 out of the 59 Westminster seats in Scotland, taking back two the party had lost in by-elections.

[26] Alf Mintzel, p.176.

[27] Kaspar Schmidt, 'Die Sozialdemokratie und die Politik in Bayern', *Sozialistische Monatshefte* 18 (1912), pp.1052-1055; electronic ed.: Bonn: FES Library, 2006.

[28] Rainer Ostermann (ed.), *Freiheit für den Freistaat: Kleine Geschichte der bayerischen SPD*. Essen: Klartext-Verlag, 1994.

have been, and still are being, perceived as motors of national integration and social cohesion.[29] Heidrun Abromeit once criticised this correctly as a deformation of the German federal state. Neither the political parties nor the intermediate system are pillars of federal thinking. Though formally federal in their organisational structure, they think and act nationally.[30] Consequently, she characterised Germany as a centralised state in disguise (*Der verkappte Einheitsstaat*). Interestingly, Eve Hepburn regards the CSU, due to the party's distinctiveness, as a regionalist party, and Bavaria, with its unique post-war party system, as a special case of 'Autonomist Regionalism'.[31] She argues that the CSU constructs Bavaria as a nation (Heimat) in its own right. This, however, is at best only partly true. Admittedly, Bavarian conservatism always had separatist notions, and recently Karl Scharnagl, a senior CSU party journalist and political thinker, published a book stating Bavaria would be better off on its own, like Scotland or Catalonia.[32] Bavaria is, most definitely, a strong region, but most certainly not a nation. Bavarian separatism has always been answered from the Franconian side with the demand to remain with the (German) nation and to secede from Bavaria.[33]

Similar to the CSU, Hepburn and Hough also regard the post-communist PDS as a party of 'Protectionist Regionalism'.[34] The PDS grew out of the East German SED (*Sozialistische Einheitspartei Deutschlands*), a product of the enforced merging of the SPD und the Communist KPD in the Soviet Zone of Occupation in 1946. The PDS has since merged with the West German WASG (*Wählerinnen- und Wählerinitiative Arbeit und soziale Gerechtigkeit*), made up mainly of left-wing dissidents from the SPD, and become the Left Party (*Die Linke*). Accepting the dominant role the PDS played during the 1990s in some of the East German *Länder* and the protectionist policies the party pursued in order to aid the economically neglected regions of the former GDR, calling its outlook 'Protectionist Regionalism' – in the sense of Michael Hechter's 'internal colonialism' – (Hechter 1975) seems acceptable.[35] However, the dichotomy of class and territory remains unresolved, as neither the SED nor the PDS nor *Die Linke* ever voluntarily retreated to a certain region. Their socialist ideology was at least national, if not internationalist.

---

[29] Eve Hepburn and Dan Hough, 'Regionalist Parties and the Mobilisation of Territorial Difference in Germany,' *Government and Opposition* 47 (2012), pp.74-96, p.74.

[30] Heidrun Abromeit, *Der verkappte Einheitsstaat*, Opladen: Leske und Budrich, 1992, p.130.

[31] Hepburn and Hough, p.82.

[32] Wilfried Scharnagl, *Bayern kann es auch alleine: Plädoyer für den eigenen Staat*, Berlin: Quadriga-Verlag, 2012.

[33] Hanns Meinhart, *Franken in Bayern – ein Problem!*, Nuremberg: Lorenz Spindler Verlag, 1949.

[34] Hepburn and Hough, p.86.

[35] See Michael Hechter, *Internal Colonialism: The Celtic fringe in British national development*, London: Routledge, 1975.

(3) Party Programme

While it was no problem to embed the territorial demands in the programme of the Scottish Labour Party, the Bavarian SPD in 2013 retreats to classic social issues. Justice (*Gerechtigkeit*) is the keyword for the SPD campaign, at the regional as well as the national level:

> "We are the Bavarian Social Democrats – and here is our home" – this statement from our leader, Christian Ude, sums up our understanding of ourselves and the message of our programme for government. Bavaria – this *Land*, which in other parts of Germany is much admired but sometimes not fully understood, is our home. Our Free State is, moreover, an invention of our political ancestor Kurt Eisner, who proclaimed it 94 years ago. The renowned Bavarian Social Democrat Wilhelm Hoegner designed Bavaria's progressive constitution. For over 120 years, we have supported and shaped our home, politically and socially. And from September this year, we will also assume government responsibility in the Free State.
>
> Our guiding principle is justice. Bavaria is, economically, the most successful German federal state. The many New Bavarians, who come from all over Germany and Europe to us to live and work here, bear witness to the great appeal of our home. Of this we can all be proud. But it is obvious that our country is out of balance. We challenge, with Christian Ude leading us, to change that.[36]

(4) The Electorate

Again, Mair suggested that Labour reacted to serious electoral pressure concerning the territorial question. The Scottish voters pushed Labour toward devolution. The nationalist challenge, the electoral success of the SNP, certainly does not make things easier for Labour. Moreover, Scottish Labour and the SNP are rivals tilling the same field, and it could be argued that there are in fact two social democratic parties in Scotland.[37]

In order to be an electable party for larger groups of the electorate, the Bavarian SPD would have to solve the contradictions of class and territory. Bavarian nationalism resides in the CSU. Standing alone and always capable of risking disputes with its sister party, the CDU, this party has learned to play the territorial game without impairing conservative core values. The

---

[36] *Regierungsprogramm der BayernSPD*, 2013 – Manifesto of the Bavarian SPD.

[37] Carla Grund, *Zwei sozialdemokratische Parteien in Schottland: Labour und SNP im Spannungsfeld zwischen Devolution und Britishness*, Würzburg: unpublished Thesis, University of Würzburg, 2012.

SPD, however, would have to act openly against 'Berlin', the national centre, and also to attack Willy-Brandt-House, the party headquarters, potentially violating socialist core values such as solidarity, justice and national unity.

An unpublished survey by the research group on voting behaviour at the Institute of Political Science and Sociology at the University of Würzburg suggested that the BayernSPD has to be very careful not to move too far to the right. Voters who associate themselves more with the conservative end oft he political spectrum reject the SPD harshly and categorically, so the party has very little to gain on the centre-right. On the other hand, leftist voters can easily be lost tot he Greens or *Die Linke* – as the result of the 2009 German general elections proved.[38] Electorally, the SPD seems to be caught in a painful quandary.

(5) Organisation

The organisation and institutions of Scottish Labour experienced under devolution far reaching changes and damages. We will get to that in a moment. In terms of being rooted in the communities, the Bavarian Social Democrats may have made a decisive mistake in 1991. Traditionally, the Bavarian SPD did not have a unified organisation. Bavarian Social Democrats had been organised in three traditionally independent districts: Franconia, Southern Bavaria and Lower Bavaria/Upper Palatinate. Attempts to unify these districts into one homogenous Bavarian SPD organisation were numerous (1949, 1966, 1977, 1985) but failed, due to the deep roots these regional structures had. In 1991, following a disastrous electoral defeat, the Party Conference accepted a reorganisation of the party following the political districts – and following the organisational structure of the CSU.[39]

There is little academic knowledge about interdependences between the way a party is organised and reactions in the electorate. Be that as it may, the electoral results of the BayernSPD did not improve. The party has, ever since, suffered from a deadly downward spiral. Fewer votes mean fewer financial resources; fewer resources mean fewer personnel. More and more, the party disappears from many constituencies. The centre at Berlin seems to be of little to no help.

(6) The British/Scottish experience and Bavarian Social Democracy

So, is Scottish Labour the shining example of a successful regional branch of the British, perhaps even international, Labour movement? Gary Hassan and Eric Shaw recently shattered that impression: their study, *The Strange Death of Labour Scotland*, paints a grim picture of contemporary Scottish Labour.

---

[38] The SPD ended on disappointing 23 per cent (its worst result ever in a federal election); The Left got 11.9, and the Greens 10.7 per cent.

[39] Rainer Ostermann, p.179.

According to their analysis, the myth of 'Labour Scotland' is now completely over.[40]

The authors' analysis covers all points that have been discussed here, primarily with a view to Bavarian Social Democracy, and their findings are, in a way, not that different, even if Scottish Labour is undoubtedly much more successful than its Southern German counterparts. Ideology, Institutions and programmatic trajectory bring as much stress on Scottish Labour as on Bavarian Social Democrats, and the dynamics of devolution – concerning voting behaviour, internal politics and, last but not least, the territorial dimension – are well known: constitutional de-centralisation; territorial party competition; party management; institutional inheritance; party discipline. They are at the very heart of the debate about a Scottish Social Democracy.

Conclusion

If we accept that European Social Democracy is caught in a crisis, which poses a threat of 'Losing Labour's Soul?',[41] there are at least hints that one way out of this crisis is to take Social Democracy back to where it once began. Initially, socialist ideas were local, work place-centred, and the general attitude of socialists towards the state was suspicion. For Northern England[42] and for Scotland, scholars like Paul Salveson, Eric Shaw and Gerry Hassan suggest a return to local and regional roots and traditions. This has nothing to do with mystifying Red Clydeside or the Spartacist *Räterepublik* in Bavaria 1919. Social Democracy in the twenty-first century has to be local as well as global. Winning regional votes, however, means offering regional policies, maybe the search for a radical Scotland,[43] a radical Bavaria – or even a radical Franconia?

---

[40] Gerry Hassan, with Eric Shaw, *The Strange Death of Labour Scotland,* Edinburgh: Edinburgh University Press, 2012, p.17.

[41] Eric Shaw, *Losing Labour's Soul? New Labour and the Blair Government 1997-2007.* London: Routledge, 2007.

[42] See Thomas Leuerer, 'Re-thinking Northern Politics? Northern England and Devolution', in: Christoph Ehland (ed.), *Thinking Northern: Textures of Identity in the North of England*, Amsterdam: Rodopi, 2007, pp.33-72.

[43] Gerry Hassan, with Rosie Ilett, *Radical Scotland: Arguments for Self-Determination,* Edinburgh: Luath Press, 2011, p.9.

Where the Wild Onions Grow
Scotland's Local Democracy Deficit

Eberhard Bort

"Free communes are indispensable for a living democracy."[1]

Winooski

A few years ago, I missed by a whisker the town hall meeting in Winooski, Vermont. But friends (and the internet) filled me in on how the assembled citizens of this small town of 7,300 souls just outside Burlington had elected their mayor, their councillors and their police chief. How they discussed and, eventually, approved the annual budget of over $6m, and taxes to the tune of $4.7m (over 77 per cent property taxes). Winooski, the town's name, comes from the language of the Abenaki tribe. It means "the place where the wild onions grow."

From 1980 to 1995, I served on the town council of Ilsfeld in Baden-Württemberg, as one of 22 councillors in that 8,500 strong community. The annual budget then was rising from about DM 15m to over 30m – in 2012 it was in excess of €28m. Our mayor was also directly elected, and we voted on the budget, including a ream of local taxes.

Now, Oban has a population just over 8,000 people. It prides itself to be Scotland's seafood capital, and the gateway to the islands. There may even be wild onions growing there. But council it has none. And neither has it an elected mayor. It is part of the council area of Argyll and Bute – which takes in Cowal, Dunoon, Helensburgh and Lomond South, the Isle of Bute, Kintyre, Islay, Argyll, Oban, and the Isle of Mull. 11 wards, with a total of 36 councillors. Five of them represent Oban.

That snapshot is instructive. While Baden-Württemberg, with roughly double the population of Scotland, has nearly 20,000 councillors with considerable local powers, Oban *sans* its own local government is only a random example of the local democracy deficit in Scotland – unbelievably, for many outside observers, even municipalities like Chris Harve's birthplace Motherwell (population: 30,000), the constituency he contested, Kirkcaldy (50,000), or East Kilbride (75,000) have no self-governance structures.

In addition to its 20,000 councillors in 1101 municipalities (each also with an elected mayor), Baden-Württemberg elects some 2000 borough councillors. Chris Harvie stood in Kreis Tübingen (one of the 35 Baden Württemberg

---

[1] Godesberger Programm der SPD, 1959, in: Fritz Sänger, *Soziale Demokratie: Bemerkungen zum Grundsatzprogramm der SPD*, Hannover: J.H.W. Dietz, 1960, p.138.

boroughs) at the local elections of 2004. He was placed on position 12 (of 31 SPD candidates). Alas, unlike three years later in Fife, that time he was not elected, but he polled a very respectable 3,903 votes and ended on position eight on the SPD list.

The contrast is striking: there, in Baden-Württemberg, some 22,000 councillors at municipal and borough level; here, the Scots in 2012 had to elect a grand total of 1223 councillors.

Appalling Turnout

Those elections, on 3 May 2012, were the first stand-alone local elections in Scotland for 17 years. After a lackluster campaign, widely "met with apathy,"[2] a mere 39.8 per cent of the Scottish electorate could be bothered to vote, "the lowest turnout in Scottish local elections since the wholesale revision of the structure of local government in 1974."[3] Despite the much publicised battle for Glasgow between the SNP and Labour, and despite having the largest number of candidates, Glasgow took the wooden spoon, with a turnout of 32.4 per cent – and in Aberdeen, where the controversial Union Street Gardens scheme was supposed to add a bit of pizzazz to the competition, the turnout was a likewise disappointing 33.2 per cent. Only the island councils exceeded a 50 per cent turnout. In the 1980s and '90s, the turnout ranged between 40 and 45 per cent. Table 1 shows that the UK's – and Scotland's – participation rates in local elections are way behind other European states.

Table 1 Voter Turnout at Local Elections[4]

Denmark	(2009)	60 per cent
Finland	(2008)	61 per cent
France	(2011)	64 per cent
Germany	(2008)	60 per cent
Italy	(2013)	62 per cent
Spain	(2011)	66 per cent
England	(2013)	31 per cent
Scotland	(2012)	40 per cent

[2] Tom Peterkin, 'We don't need Ken or Boris, but Scottish council elections are in dire need of some charisma', *The Scotsman*, 11 April 2012.

[3] David Denver, Hugh Bochel and Martin Steven, 'Mixed Messages for (some) Parties: The Scottish Council Elections of 2012', *Scottish Affairs*, no.80 (Summer 2012), pp,1-19; p.6.

[4] adapted from David Wilson and Chris Game, Local Government in the United Kingdom, Basingstoke: Palgrave Macmillan, fifth edition, 2011, Exhibit 14.3, p.252.

SCOTLAND'S LOCAL DEMOCRACY DEFICIT

It is noteworthy that voter turnout across Europe is declining – only Spain saw an increase after 1995. In Germany, over the past few years, voter turnout has also declined, in 2011 it ranged between 47 per cent in Mecklenburg-Vorpommern and 59 per cent in Bavaria. Two decades earlier the turnout in local elections had averaged at over 75 per cent.[5] The recent Italian local elections had a turnout of 62.3 per cent – 14.7 per cent less than five years before.[6]

Loss of Power

This low turnout, still declining, is a reflection of the loss of power local government in the UK and in Scotland has suffered in recent decades. "The powers and functions of UK local government have been steadily eroded over the past fifty years," wrote John Loughlin, citing the welfare state and its centralisation of policy-making, and the Conservatives' "antagonism towards local government", which led to reforms he classifies as "Agentization": the transfer of functions to agencies of central government; local government as "enabling" authorities, i.e. transferring service provision to private operators, and reduced autonomy over spending.[7]

That process of transferring power from local government to statutory agencies has continued largely unabated into recent times. This concerns the steady loss of powers, functions and budgets relating to public health, hospitals, water and sewerage, environment, countryside, countryside recreation, tourism, public transport, airports, economic development, police, childrens' panels, and housing.

Furthermore, local government in the UK occupies an ambivalent position in the democratic arena, since local authorities are creatures of central government, and answerable to them, as well as being locally elected. For Scottish local government, Devolution did not change that relationship: "local councils have the same constitutional, statutory and legal limitations on the extent of their independent activities as before devolution. They are constitutionally just as subordinate to Scotland's devolved institutions as they were to the Scottish Office and the UK parliament."[8]

---

[5] Manfred Güllner, 'Eine vergessene Ebene der Politik', *Cicero*, 15 September 2011, <www.cicero.de/berliner-republik/eine-vergessene-ebene-der-politik/43034>.

[6] 'Regionalwahl in Italien: Rückenwind für Letta, Verluste für Grillo', *Der Standard*, 28 May 2013.

[7] John Loughlin, 'The United Kingdom: From Hypercentralization to Devolution', in: John Loughlin, *Subnational Democracy in the European Union*, Oxford: Oxford University Press, 2004, pp.40-41.

[8] Neil McGarvey, 'Centre and Locality in Scottish Politics: From Bi- to Tri-partite Relations', in Charlie Jeffery and James Mitchell (eds), *The Scottish Parliament 1999-2009: The First Decade*, Edinburgh: Luath Press (in association with Hansard Society), 2009, pp.125-131, p.125.

Local Services *and* Local Democracy

Local government is both a manifestation of local democracy and a provider of public services. The second function – the 'local administration' – is concerned with efficiency and economies of scale, and a tendency towards top-down centralisation; the first function, local democracy, acts as a focus of civic engagement and participation, a source of civic identity and pride, and as a bulwark against central government domination, and is dependent on the structures and powers of local government. While the second aspect, it may be argued, does work reasonably well in Scotland, both the reduction of local government to acting as an executive extension of central government in delivering outcomes and the remoteness of local government (particularly outside the four main cities) have thrown Scottish local democracy into crisis.

James Kellas observed:

> What has changed considerably since 1980 has been the power of central government to control local expenditure and to intervene in the setting of the level of rates. This direct intervention into local budgeting has led many to complain that local government has lost its independence and has become the mere agent of central government.[9]

That this tendency has not abated is indicated by Michael Heseltine who commented much more recently on the English situation, calling local authorities "the branch offices of the London spending departments."[10] And Gerry Stoker, while conceding that "local government is better managed, more strategic and more joined up than ever," also contended: "The trouble is that citizens have been largely left behind in this managerial revolution."[11]

Yet, even that second aspect is under mounting pressure, caused by the cuts at Westminster and at Holyrood, and the continuing council tax freeze which robs Scottish councils of one of the few powers they had: to set the council tax rate for their council area. When the SNP minority government took office in 2007, it promised to liberate and empower local communities by removing ring-fencing. The 'concordat' between the councils and the SNP government

> was supposed to set councils free again after decades of servitude to the central government. They were to be allowed

---

[9] James G. Kellas, *The Scottish Political System*, Cambridge: Cambridge University Press (third edition), 1984, p.172.

[10] Michael Heseltine on *The Daily Politics*, BBC Two, 17 April 2012.

[11] Gerry Stoker, 'Foreword', in: Catherine Durose, Stephen Greasley and Liz Richardson (eds), *Changing local governance, changing citizens*, Bristol: The Policy Press, 2009, p.xvii.

to spend more of their allotted funds as they saw fit, not have it ring-fenced around the government's priorities. But instead we have them tied into 'single outcome agreements' covering all sorts of central government targets, including a council tax freeze. The result is that councils are left paring away at their services, not able to make one bold cut – like closing under-utilised schools, or pulling out of nursery provision or care homes. Nor are they able to go the other way and increase taxes.[12]

Indeed, when Alex Salmond introduced the Scottish government's legislative programme for 2012-13, the expected Community Empowerment and Renewal Bill was conspicuous by its absence.[13] Alan Alexander vented his anger at the SNP government's handling of local democracy in a piece for Kenneth Roy's *Scottish Review*. He argued that local government in Scotland

- has been emasculated by successive governments but most seriously by the SNP government, through the freeze on council tax, single outcome agreements and aggressive intervention in significant policy areas;

- that the refusal of the Scottish Government to permit even discussion of reorganisation/structural change is indefensible and a further instrument of centralisation;

- that local government without a power to tax is not local government at all, but a particularly inefficient form of local administration;

- that the current Scottish Government regards local authorities as instruments for imposing its own policies rather than as institutions with the autonomy to determine, within legal limits, how their communities are to be governed;

- that while it may be argued that local government has been complicit in its own decline, in particular by signing

---

[12] John Knox, 'Analysis: mayors the way to combat cuts?', *Caledonian Mercury*, 22 February 2010, <http://politics.caledonianmercury.com/2010/02/22/mayors-the-way-to-combat-cuts/>.

[13] 'Referendum and same-sex marriage bills announced in SNP plans', *BBC News Scotland*, 4 September 2012, <www.bbc.co.uk/news/uk-scotland-scotland-politics-19469440>.

up to the concordat and the council tax freeze, the penalties that it would have suffered by not agreeing were such as to make its assent less than freely given.[14]

The latest examples have been the establishment of a single Scottish police force and fire service, which robbed local councillors of their role in formulating policy. There may still be local policing, but it rest within the police organisation – policy is now made centrally at Holyrood. In June 2011, a slim majority of MSPs (five votes to four) backed plans to shut ten sheriff courts and seven justice of the peace courts – Dornoch, Duns, Kirkcudbright, Peebles, Rothesay, Cupar, Dingwall, Arbroath, Haddington and Stonehaven – despite local protests. Lewis Macdonald, a Labour MSP for North East Scotland, voiced the opposition's concern about the closures:

> It is surely a matter of principle to this committee that local communities the length and breadth of Scotland should have access to justice, and that those accused of serious offences should, where possible, be tried by a jury from their local area, and should certainly stand trial as close as possible to their local community.[15]

But there is a wider context. Politicians and business leaders also fear local economies will be affected. "Some of these towns are already struggling economically," a *Herald* editorial reasoned, "and courts provide both employment and income for local businesses. There seems to be an inability to consider such issues in the round. For many communities, this decision means the end of local justice."[16] For Haddington, the closure decision means that it will face having, from 2015, "a large empty court building and a large empty fiscal's office in the town centre and, according to council calculations, a £360,000 hole in its economy."[17] There is little doubt that the absence of local government in all of these places weakens any resistance against further centralisation.

The Passing of the Burghs

How did we arrive at this situation? Local Government has a long history in Scotland, originating in the 'sheriffdoms' created by King Malcolm III in the

---

[14] Alan Alexander, 'Say anything you like, except the thing you really want to say', *Scottish Review*, No.560, 12 June 2012 < www.scottishreview.net/AlanAlexander283.shtml>.

[15] 'Scottish court closures: Justice committee backs plans', *BBC News Scotland*, 11 June 2013, < www.bbc.co.uk/news/uk-scotland-south-scotland-22859425>.

[16] 'A sad day for Scottish justice', *The Herald* (editorial), 12 June 2013.

[17] Ian Swanson, 'No justice in voting to back closures of courts', *Edinburgh Evening News*, 13 June 2013.

eleventh century AD. These were the basis for shires, which became known only much later as Counties. His son, David I, founder of the Border Abbeys and Holyrood, created the first royal burghs in the twelfth century.

The Reform Acts of 1832 and 1833 changed the way Scotland was governed "quite fundamentally", although the effects of the legislation took decades to sink in.[18] The number of shires, burghs and parishes gradually expanded, 33 shires being named in the Local Government (Scotland) Act of 1889, which also tidied up boundaries and definitions.[19] This became the pattern for the local government system in the twentieth century.[20] According to the *Wheatley Report*, up to 1929 there were, in terms of local government structure in Scotland:

> 4 Counties of Cities
> 21 Large Burghs
> 176 Small Burghs
> 33 Counties
> some 878 Parishes[21]

The parish councils, elected every three years by taxpayers (including single and married women), though "preoccupied with parochial affairs [which] laid them open to a charge of indulging in parish-pump politics," according to C. W. Hill

> provided, with the burgh and county councils, a network of democratic government at grass roots level throuhghout Scotland. The councillor, whether skilled craftsman, retired army or naval officer, dominie, tradesman or manufacturer, was able to make a significant contribution to the life of the community in which he lived.[22]

We note that this was not exactly inclusive 'local democracy' – rather, it was rule by local elites, the landowners, the manufacturers. And yet, it was an improvement on the earlier 'top-down' running of Scottish parishes.

The Parishes were abolished as local government entities in 1929, and 196 county or landward districts were introduced in the same year. The functions

---

[18] John F. McCaffrey, *Scotland in the Nineteenth Century*, Basingstoke: Macmillan, 1998, pp.28, 35.

[19] See Hay Shennan, *Boundaries of Counties and Parishes in Scotland*, Edinburgh: William Green & Sons, 1892.

[20] See Arthur Midwinter, *Local Government in Scotland: Reform or Decline?*, Basingstoke: Macmillan, 1995, p.11.

[21] Wheatley Report, Royal Commission on Local Government in Scotland 1966-1969. (Chairman: The Rt. Hon. Lord Wheatley), Edinburgh: HMSO, 1969. Cmnd. 4150, p.143.

[22] C. W. Hill, *Edwardian Scotland*, Edinburgh: Scottish Academic Press, 1976, p.40.

of the Parishes were transferred to the remaining 430 local government entities, while the smaller burghs lost some power to the counties. The Reform of 1929 "swept away many small units of local government and transferred their responsibilities to county and burgh councils" which "had a dramatic impact in professionalising the system."[23] A pattern evolved: "While many, mostly Liberals and Labour, deplored the elimination of small local democratic institutions, the government stressed the gains in efficiency and professionalism that would ensue."[24]

As Chris Harvie argued, under the sub-heading of 'The Passing of the Burghs' in *Scotland and Nationalism*, "the abolition of parish councils in 1929 boosted the National Party, as local government was assumed to be guaranteed by the Act of Union." He continued: "The year 1929 probably accelerated the loss of community Edwin Muir mourned; it certainly heralded forty years of indifference to local democracy."[25]

This then is a brief overview of the situation up to the time of the 'Wheatley Commission' of Local Government in Scotland, which sat from 1966 to 1969 and, after much debate, led to the 1974 reform of local government in Scotland:

> Wheatley recommended the creation of seven new regional authorities, with responsibility for strategic services, the major local government functions of police, fire, water and sewerage, roads and transport, education, social work, housing and planning; and 37 district councils responsible for environmental and amenity services of a local nature. Recommendations were also made for a system of community councils with consultative powers to act as a voice for local communities.[26]

Following the Wheatley reforms of 1974, Scottish local government had two tiers consisting of 9 Regional Councils, 53 District Councils and 3 all-purpose Island councils serving Orkney, Shetland and the Western Isles, having the functions of both Regions and Districts elsewhere. Regional councils were responsible for major functions such as education, transport and strategic planning, while more localised functions such as urban recreation, housing, libraries, development control and local planning, were the responsibility of District Councils.

---

[23] Iain G C Hutchison, 'Government', in: T M Devine and R J Finlay (eds), *Scotland in the 20th Century*, Edinburgh: Edinburgh University Press, 1996, p. 60

[24] I G C Hutchison, *Scottish Politics in the Twentieth Century*, Basingstoke: Palgrave Macmillan, 2001, p.52.

[25] Christopher Harvie, *Scotland and Nationalism: Scottish Society and Politics 1707 to the Present*, London: Routledge (fourth edition), 2004, p.137.

[26] Midwinter, p.16.

The present Scottish local government structure has resulted from the 1996 reorganisation as a result of The Local Government (Scotland) Act 1994. This led to the abolition of the 9 regions and 53 districts and their replacement by 29 single tier bodies, with the 3 unitary island councils remaining unchanged. The argument was that single tier authorities would result in a more economic, cohesive, accountable and effective system. These 32 councils are responsible for all the local government services formerly administered by their predecessors with two main exceptions: water and sewerage (passed to Scottish Water, a centralised and unelected 'non-departmental public body', and the reporters to Children's Panels, also re-centralised). Chris Harvie summed up the effect: "Since councillors were fewer, and as many formerly regional functions were now carried out by joint boards or the new water authorities, government was even more remote."[27]

While it was maybe understandable that the Scottish Parliament in its early years refrained from fundamentally reorganising local government (the system was still reeling from the Tory reform of 1994/96), it established the McIntosh Commission,[28] followed by the Kerley Commission, and in the second session passed the Local Government Bill, introducing proportional representation (single transferable vote) – with "large repercussions on the balance of influence within the Scottish body politic, since," as Michael Keating predicted, "it will destroy the one-party municipalities which are the power base of the Labour machine."[29]

Indeed, in 2007 Labour was returned in overall control of just two councils – rather than 13, as in 2003,[30] and a majority of voters gave preferences to candidates from more than one party.[31] Apart from introducing Single Transferable Voting for local government elections from 2007, the Local Governance (Scotland) Act made the following provisions:

- Lower the age at which people can stand as a councillor from 21 to 18;

- Remove unnecessary political restrictions on council employees standing for local authority elections;

---

[27] Christopher Harvie, No Gods and Precious Few Heroes: Twentieth-Century Scotland (third edition), Edinburgh: Edinburgh University Press, 1998, p. 178.

[28] Peter Lynch, Scottish Government and Politics: An Introduction, Edinburgh: Edinburgh University Press, 2001, pp.221-25.

[29] Michael Keating, The Government of Scotland: Public Policy Making after Devolution, Edinburgh: Edinburgh University Press, 2005, p.46.

[30] John Curtice, David McCrone, Nicola McEwen, Michael Marsh and Rachel Ormston, Revolution or Evolution? The 2007 Scottish Elections, Edinburgh: Edinburgh University Press, 2009, p.11.

[31] Ibid., p.174.

- Establish an independent remuneration committee for councillors;

- The reduction to three months of the period during which most former councillors are unable to take up employment with the council after their period of service as a councillor comes to an end;

- The introduction of a new system of remuneration;

- A one-off severance payment to councillors who decide not to stand at the next local government election;

- Powers to introduce a pension scheme for councillors to allow future service to count for pension purposes.

The reform was an important step, with regard to the electoral system, the status of councillors and the composition of councils, but did not change the structure of local government, and it did not herald any bold change in the power relations concerning local government.

Size Matters[32]

Fewer councils (and fewer councillors) in Scotland than any comparable European country (or devolved or federal sub-state) make Scottish local government remote:

> Take Highland Council, which covers an area the size of Belgium with a population the size of Belfast. Councillors drive hundreds of thousands of miles a year to create a sense of connection through meetings, surgeries and local events. Despite such superhuman efforts, many remote communities feel largely negative, reduced to questioning, suspecting and vetoing whatever emanates from Inverness.[33]

"Local Government in the Highlands has grown distant, and in doing so is damaging democracy and economic development in Scotland," according to Rob Gibson MSP and his 'Small Works' consultation paper:

[32] See Eberhard Bort and Lesley Riddoch, 'Size Matters', *Scottish Left Review*, 68, (January/February 2012), pp.6-8.

[33] Lesley Riddoch, 'Mini-councils will energise Scotland's communities', *The Scotsman*, 28 June 2010.

> We have a situation in my constituency where councillors can decide planning applications for projects hundreds of miles away and where spending decisions are made by officials with little or no knowledge of the places they are affecting. Ordinary folk in the Far North feel disconnected from their council, and many businesses and voluntary groups feel frustrated by the lack of local involvement in Council matter. This must be addressed.[34]

"Treated in isolation, a crude ratio of representative to electorate is an unreliable indicator of democratic quality"[35] – as there are other factors that are important – first and foremost the powers and responsibilities that come with the job of councillor, the qualifications councillors bring to the job, the funding of local councils, and the way representative democracy is augmented by ways of direct democracy and e-democracy to make it more participative, i.e. how councils share their power with the community. All these factors are important, but 'comparative research, on Denmark, the Netherlands, Norway and the UK has shown that the amount of trust is related to the size of local government.'[36] In that respect, clearly, "the number of elected representatives is a key aspect of local democracy."[37]

As Clarke and Stewart have argued, "the primary role of local authorities is local government and not local administration;" they also state that this role "must have its basis in citizenship". Therefore, its structure should be based "not on the alleged efficiencies of administration but on the perceived and felt community of place."[38]

The Bigger Picture: Some European Comparisons

There is a lot of talk about 'localism' and 'empowering' of local communities. Yet, Scotland has 'the largest average population per basic unit of local government of any developed country.[39] And there is talk of further

---

[34] Rob Gibson, 'Small Works', August 2011, ww.robgibson.org/2011/02/21/welcome/

[35] Kingsley Purdam, Peter John, Stephen Greasley and Paul Norman, *How many elected representatives does local government need? A review of evidence from Europe*, University of Manchester: Cathie Marsh Centre for Census and Survey Research (CCSR) Working Paper No.6 (2008), p.4; <www.ccsr.ac.uk/publication/working/2008-06.pdf>.

[36] *Ibid.*, p.15.

[37] *Ibid.*, p.19.

[38] Michael Clarke and John Stewart, *The Choices for Local Government – for the 1990s and Beyond*, London: Longman, 1991, pp.76, 74.

[39] Michael Keating, *The Government of Scotland: Public Policy Making after Devolution*, Edinburgh: Edinburgh University Press, 2005, p.12.

centralisation![40] Some European comparisons[41] will show how out of kilter Scotland really is when it comes to local democracy. Seven indicators will be compared:

- Geographical size of local authority area (→ Table 2)

- Numbers of local and regional tiers of governance (→ Table 3)

- Number of electors per local elected official (→ Table 4)

- Turnout (as a proxy for the interest in local democracy from local people) (→ Table 1)

- Number of candidates as a proportion of the population (indicating public interest in getting involved in politics)

- Number of candidates contesting each seat (as a measure of how plural 'competitive' local democracy is)

- A rough estimate of the costs of local democracy

The EU average municipality size is 5,630, and the average municipality area covers 49 sqkm. Here a selection of European countries:

---

[40] Following the merger of Scotland's eight police forces into one, David O'Connor, Association of Scottish Police Superintendents president, said similar cost-saving measures should be considered for councils, health boards and sheriffdoms. See 'Police chief in council merger call', *BBC News Scotland*, 22 May 2013, <www.bbc.co.uk/news/uk-scotland-22622306>.

[41] For a comprehensive review of the situation based on 2007 figures, see Council of Europe, *The relationship between central and local authorities: Report of the European Committee on Local and Regional Democracy (CDLR)*, prepared with the collaboration of Alba Nogueira López, Santiago de Compostela University, Spain, Strasbourg, 2007 <https://wcd.coe.int/ViewDoc.jsp?id=1364497&Site=COE>.

Table 2 Average Size of Municipality[42]

Country	population	area (sq km)
Austria	3,560	36
Denmark	56,590	440
Finland	15,960	1,006
France	1,770	17
Germany	7,080	31
Italy	7,470	37
Spain	5,680	62
UK	152,680	601
Scotland [43]	163,200	2,461

Another way of looking at it is to compare the number of local and regional tiers of governance in a selection of European countries:

Table 3 Number of Sub-National Governments[44]

	Local tier	Borough/County	Regional tier
Federal States			
Austria	2,357	99	9
Germany	11,553	301	16
Unitary States			
Denmark	98	5	
Finland	336	2	
France	36,697	101	27
Italy	8,094	110	20
Spain	8,116	52	17
UK	406	28	3
Scotland	32		

[42] The Council of European Municipalities and Regions (CEMR)/Dexia, EU sub-national governments: 2010 figures (2011/2012 edition), <www.ccre.org/docs/Nuancier2011Web.EN.pdf>.

[43] <www.gro-scotland.gov.uk/statistics/theme/population/estimates/mid-year/2010/index.html>.

[44] The Council of European Municipalities and Regions (CEMR)/Dexia, EU sub-national governments: 2010 figures (2011/2012 edition), <www.ccre.org/docs/Nuancier2011Web.EN.pdf>.

When we apply these figures to gauge the ratio between elected members of local government and the number of citizens they represent, we find – again – that Scotland sticks out.

Table 4 Ratio Elected Councillors – Citizens Represented[45]

Austria	1 : 200
Denmark	1 : 2,000
Finland	1 : 500
France	1 : 125
Germany	1 : 400
Italy	1 : 600
Spain	1 : 700
UK	1 : 2,860
Scotland	1 : 4,270

It should also be mentioned that nearly all European countries have, over the past decades, reduced their numbers of municipalities in an effort to maximise efficiency – and most are are still in the process of further centralising local democracy. But, as the above comparisons show, they are still in a different league when compared with the situation in Scotland.

Table 5 Contraction of Local Authorities

Country	1950	2001	average population
Austria	4,065	2,359	3,437
Denmark	1,303	276	19,381
France	37,997	36,585	1,615
Germany	33,932	13,854	5,931
Italy	7.802	8,100	7,141
Switzerland	3,097	2,867	2,488
Norway	744	435	10,295

Fusions and mergers are continuing. Switzerland, for example, reduced its number of municipalities to 2,551 by 2010, and to 2,495 at the beginning of 2012.[46] With its 2,495 municipalities in 26 cantons, Switzerland has 98,000 people with a popular mandate at the municipal level. That equals 38 people per municipality. Given its population of 7.9 m people – this gives a ratio of 1 : 800 of elected representatives and the people they represent. In Finland (5.2 m people, just like Scotland), and its 448 municipalities (Scotland: 32!), 10,412 councillors were elected in 2008 – a ratio of 1 : 500. The turnout was 61.3 per

---

[45] adapted from David Wilson and Chris Game, *Local Government in the United Kingdom*, Basingstoke: Palgrave Macmillan (fifth edition), 2011, Exhibit 14.3, p.275.

[46] Schweizerische Bundeskanzlei, *Der Bund kurz erklärt*, Bern, 2012.

cent. In Scotland, as we have seen, the ratio is 1 : 4,270! Overall, we have seen that there is a huge gap in the ratio of councillors and population between the rest of Europe and Scotland (the only exception being Denmark, which still has double the representation density of Scotland).

Case Study 1: Norway

Norway – with 4.7 m of a comparable population size as Scotland's 5.2 m – currently (as of 1 January 2012) has 429 municipalities. There are also 21 county councils in Norway's 21 counties, with 787 county councillors overall.[47] The average Scottish council serves, as we have seen, over 163,00 people; the average Norwegian municipality has 11,000.

Municipal councils, elected for a period of four years, are the foundation of Norwegian democracy. For decades, the devolution of central powers to local governments aimed to focus as much as possible on the municipal level. The philosophy behind this was that decentralisation is an expression of applied democracy, that it brings decision-making closer to those who are affected and promotes popular participation in local political affairs. In Norway's three-tiered structure of governance, "elected regional governments (regional councils) are very weak … and have few administrative tasks. It is the central state and the 435 municipalities that are important."[48]

Voters in Norway elect representatives to the municipal councils and county councils (according to the Representation of the People Act (Act No. 57 of 28 June 2002)) on a proportional list electoral system. Lists must contain a minimum of 7 candidates, they may contain a maximum of six names more than councillors to be elected in the municipality. The Local Government Act specifies the minimum number of representatives to be elected:

> A municipality with a population under 5,000 is to have at least 11 members in its council – with a population from 5,000 to 10,000 at least 19 representatives are required. An equivalent system determines the size of the county council. But it is then up to the municipal council and the county council to determine whether to increase the respective number of their representatives beyond the legal minimum. Quite often, they opt to do so.[49]

---

[47] <http://welections.wordpress.com/2011/09/15/norway-locals-2011/>.

[48] Einar Overbye, Signy Vabo and Knut Wedde, *Rescaling Social Welfare Policies in Norway*, Oslo: Oslo University College, 2006, p.13.

[49] Norwegian Ministry of Local Government and Regional Development, *Local Government in Norway*, Oslo, 2008; p.13. <www.regjeringen.no/upload/KRD/Vedlegg/KOMM/internasjonalt/H-2224.pdf>.

The capital Oslo is the largest municipality with 599,230 residents, while Utsira in Rogaland is the smallest with 216 residents. The average size of municipalities in Norway is just under 11,500 residents. More than half the municipalities have fewer than 5,000 residents. Kautokeino in Finnmark is the largest municipality in area at 9,704 sqkm, while Kvitsøy and Utsira in Rogaland are the smallest at 6 sqkm.[50]

The municipalities are a fundamental part of the infrastructure of the Norwegian welfare state and they have a wide ranging responsibility for public welfare services. What lies behind this is the principle that tasks shall be performed as close as possible to the residents.

> The Government bases its policy on the principle that, as a system of government, democracy means influence and power being spread as widely as possible. A vibrant and decentralised democracy based on broad participation is crucial if we are to address the challenges facing society.[51]

Variations in size, both geographically and in number of residents, give the municipalities different conditions in which to exercise their role as service provider, social developer, local authority and arena for local democracy.

The municipal sector is constantly facing challenges connected with the need to coordinate municipal activities across administrative boundaries for the benefit of residents. One challenge the municipalities face is covering the lack of specialist expertise and keeping people in key positions. This applies in particular to the smaller municipalities. The lack of expertise and manpower can be challenge for all the municipality's roles. Intermunicipal collaboration or the merging of municipalities could be a solution to these challenges.[52] But overall, as the Norwegian Minister for Local Government and Regional development recently again emphasised,

> The government wants municipalities and counties with room to manoeuvre. Good and effective social welfare services and vibrant local communities require a strong municipal sector with plenty of freedom. (...) The variations between municipalities and regions are substantial, and this is often the case for the challenges as well. It is therefore important to

---

[50] Norwegian Ministry of Local Government and Regional Development, Government. No: *Information from the Government and the Ministries*; <www.regjeringen.no/en/topics/Municipalities-and-regions.html?id=921>.

[51] *Ibid.*

[52] Norwegian Ministry of Local Government and Regional Development 'Municipal Structure', <www.regjeringen.no/en/dep/krd/Subjects/municipal-law-and-municipal-organisation/municipal-structure.html?id=540087>.

> ensure that it is the local democratically elected representatives who make the decisions for the individual citizen, as they know the local conditions best.[53]

As a result, "civic participation and support for local government still is high in Norway." Although, here too, there have been changes:

> Support for local government as a political institution has declined, whereas people now tend to stress the service delivery function of local authorities. This development also signifies a change in people's role orientations towards local government, from the role of citizen to the role of user or consumer. People's participation turns from broad civic involvement in local affairs to greater single issue orientation.[54]

In the local elections in Norway in September 2011, 10,7812 councillors and 787 county councillors were elected – Scotland – just to recap – has 1223. In Norway, one out of 800 citizens is an elected member of local or regional government – in Scotland the ratio is in excess of 1 : 4,000. Norwegian local councils raise 40 per cent of their revenue, Scottish councils 20 per cent – and they are further curtailed in their power by the ongoing council tax freeze. Turnout in Norway in 2011 was 63.6 per cent – Scotland's in 2012 did not reach the 40 per cent threshold.

Case Study 2: Baden-Württemberg

Baden-Württemberg in the south-west of Germany is one of the 16 Länder of the Federal Republic, with a population of 10.7 m people. Below the Landtag (the Baden-Württemberg Parliament in Stuttgart with currently with 138 MPs[55]), there are 35 boroughs and 9 city districts, and below that 1101 municipalities – each with n elected town council (and an elected mayor). In addition, the Greater Stuttgart region elects – since 1994 – the *Regionalversammlung Stuttgart*, 84 councillors representing over 2 million residents.[56]

---

[53] Norwegian Ministry of Local Government and Regional Development, 'State and municipality – governance and interaction: 'Municipalities need freedom' (Press Release), 9 March 2012, <www.regjeringen.no/en/dep/krd/press/press-releases/2012/state-and-municipality--governance-and-i.html?id=672115>.

[54] Jacob Aars and Audun Offerdal, 'Local Political Recruitment in Crisis? A Comparison of Finland and Norway', *Scandinavian Political Studies*, Bind 21 (New Series) (1998) 3, pp.207-228, p.208; <http://tidsskrift.dk/visning.jsp?markup=&print=no&id=99281>.

[55] <www.landtag-bw.de/abgeordnete/index.asp>.

[56] See Helmut Doka, 'A Region is a Region is a Regon – is it? Planning in the Stuttgart Region', in: Eberhard Bort and Neil Evans (eds), *Networking Europe: Essays on Regionalism and Social Democracy*, Liverpool: Liverpool University Press, 2000, pp.463-71; also: Bernard Jouve and Christian Lefèvre, 'Metropolitan Governance and

At the latest local elections, in 2009, the total number of elected town councillors was 19,006; 2,273 councillors were elected to the *Kreistage* (borough/county councils). The number of candidates for the local elections was 60,182[57] – on lists, with the possibility for voters to cumulate votes (up to three per candidate) and transfer candidates from one list to another, or put new names on the lists – all up to the number of councillors to be elected.[58]

Councils consist of 8 to 60 elected members, depending on the size of the municipality:[59]

Table 6 Ratio Population – Size of Council in Baden-Württemberg

Municipalities	council members
under 1,000 people	8
1,001 – 2,000	10
2,001 – 3,000	12
3 001 – 5 000	14
5,001 – 10,000	18
10,001 – 20,000	22
20,001 – 30,000	26
30,001 – 50,000	32
50,001 – 150,000	40
150,000 – 400,000	48
over 400,000	60

Two-thirds of Baden-Württemberg's municipalities have a population of less than 20,000; 100 have more than 20,000 people; 23 have over 50,000 people.[60]

Let us look more closely at some examples. Stuttgart, the capital, with just

Institutional Dynamics', in: Robin Hambleton, Hank V. Savitch and Murray Stewart (eds), *Globalism and Local Democracy: Challenge and Change in Europe and North America*, Basingstoke: Palgrave Macmillan, 2003, pp.197-98.

[57] Monika Hin and Dirk Eisenreich, 'Nach den Kommunalwahlen 2009: Präsenz von Frauen in der Kommunalpolitik Baden-Württembergs', Landesamt für Statistik Baden-Württemberg, *Statistisches Monatsheft Baden-Württemberg*, 9/2009; <www.statistik-bw.de/Veroeffentl/Monatshefte/PDF/Beitrag09_09_09.pdf>

[58] For greater detail, see Udo Bullmann, 'Germany: Federalism under Strain', in John Loughlin, *Subnational Democracy in the European Union*, Oxford: Oxford University Press, 2004, pp.83-116, pp.93, 110.

[59] <www.landesrecht-bw.de/jportal/?quelle=jlink&query=GemO+BW&psml=bsbawu eprod.psml&max=true&aiz=true#jlr-GemOBWpP25>.

[60] Paul Witt, Christina Krause and Adrian Ritter, *Wer sind die Gemeinderäte in Baden-Württemberg?*, Kehl: Hochschule für öffentliche Verwaltung, 2009, p.7; <www.hs-kehl.de/DE/Hochschule/Forschung/Forschungsergebnisse/Forschungsarbeiten/Studie_Gemeinderatsbefragung.pdf>

over 600,000 residents, has 60 councillors. At the last elections, nine lists competed, with a total of 420 candidates. In addition, Stuttgart has 23 sub-districts (*Stadtbezirke*), with a total of 322 *Bezirksräte* (roughly equivalent with Scottish community councillors). In bigger towns they could be elected, but no town in Baden-Württemberg has availed itself of that right yet. They are proposed by the groups and parties represented in the council, and then installed by the lord mayor (who is directly elected). Their role is to advise and make recommendations to council and administration. Turnout in Stuttgart for the council elections in recent times have fallen from 57.5 and 64.3 per cent in 1989 and 1994 respectively to 47.7 per cent (1999), 48.7 per cent (2004) and 48.7 per cent (2009). Overall, the turnout in 2009 was 50.7 per cent (a record low, down from 52 per cent in 2004.[61]

Freiburg (230,000) had eleven lists, with 528 candidates competing for the 48 seats on the council. (Freiburg also has 41 districts). Heidelberg (147,000) has 40 councillors, elected from 10 lists (400 candidates), and registered a turnout of 48,8 per cent. Heilbronn, a town of 120,000, has 40 councillors, elected in 2009 on eight lists, with 320 candidates. The turnout was 42.9 per cent. Öhringen, a smaller town with 23,000, has 38 councillors. At the last election, there were five lists with 139 candidates – the turnout was 38 per cent.

Lauffen (Neckar), with 11,000 residents, has 22 councillors, elected from five lists with 110 candidates – the turnout in 2009 was 53 per cent. Ilsfeld (8,500) has 20 councillors, elected on two lists (40 candidates), on a turnout of 59.2 per cent. Abstatt, a small town with 4,500 residents, has 14 councillors, elected from four lists (56 candidates) – the turnout here was 57 per cent. Mundelsheim, just 3,150 residents, has 12 councillors, elected from four lists (48 candidates) – the turnout was 62,6 per cent.

The smaller the municipality, the higher tends to be the turnout; Conversely, the bigger the municipality, the greater the percentage of women councillors. 28.8 per cent of all candidates were women; 22 per cent of the elected councillors in Baden-Württemberg are women. In 1984, the female percentage had been 9 per cent.[62] In Scotland, the number of female councillors improved from 2007 to 2012 from to 297 (out of 1223) – or 24.3 per cent (up from 21.8 per cent).[63]

---

[61] Monika Hin and Dirk Eisenreich, 'Baden-Württemberg hat gewählt: Vorläufige Ergebnisse der Kommunalwahlen 2009', Stuttgart: Statistisches Landesamt Baden-Württemberg, *Statistisches Monatsheft Baden-Württemberg*, <www.statistik-bw.de/Veroeffentl/Monatshefte/essay.asp?xYear=2009&xMonth=09&eNr=08>.

[62] Monika Hin and Dirk Eisenreich, 'Nach den Kommunalwahlen 2009: Präsenz von Frauen in der Kommunalpolitik Baden-Württembergs', Landesamt für Statistik Baden-Württemberg, *Statistisches Monatsheft Baden-Württemberg*, 9/2009; <www.statistik-bw.de/Veroeffentl/Monatshefte/PDF/Beitrag09_09_09.pdf>.

[63] Meryl Kenny and Fiona Mackay, 'Less Male, Pale and Stale? Women and the 2012 Scottish Local Government Elections', *Scottish Affairs*, No.80 (Summer 2012), pp.20-32; p.21.

Table 7 Ratio Elected Councillors – Population

Stuttgart (600,000)	1 : 10,000
Freiburg (230,000)	1 : 4,800
Heidelberg (147,000)	1 : 3,675
Heilbronn (120,000)	1 : 3,000
Öhringen (23,000)	1 : 605
Lauffen am Neckar (11,000)	1 : 480
Ilsfeld (8,500)	1 : 425
Abstatt (4,500)	1 : 320
Baden-Württemberg (10.5m)	1 : 560

What Price Local Democracy?

All this representation must cost a penny? Let us pick out Öhringen, and build it from there. The 38 councillors receive a monthly basic amount of recompensation of €50 (£42), plus €30 (£25) for every council or committee meeting. There are ten to twelve meetings of the council, and roughly the same number of committee meetings – which gives us a total of just over €70,000 per year.[64]

The monthly allowance for councillors varies slightly, from a basic rate of €20 per month in Sigmaringen to the top rate in Stuttgart of €1,200. On top of that, there are payments per council or committee meeting, of €20 to €120.[65]

Bearing in mind that of the 1101 Baden-Württemberg municipalities nearly 1,000 are below 20,000 residents, this gives us a grand total of c€50 mill for the all municipal councillors; we may add another €3,5 mill for the county councillors, and another (generous) €300,000 for the Greater Stuttgart regional assembly. That would make it, say, €55 m for 21,363 councillors.

There are, of course, also 1101 directly elected mayors and lord mayors in Baden-Württemberg. Their period of office is eight years. In municipalities with a population of under 2,000, the mayoralty can be an honorary position, if the council does not decide to make it a full-time salaried post. As from municipalities of 20,000 residents and above, the post is that of a lord mayor. The pay scale looks like this:

---

[64] <www.oehringen.de/main/stadt-info/gemeinderat.html> (2009).

[65] Wolf von Dewitz, 'Neben Aufwandsentschädigung nur wenig Extras für Gemeinderäte', *Schwäbisches Tagblatt*, 17 August 2010.

Table 8 Pay Scale for Elected Mayors ad Lord Mayors in Baden-Württemberg[66]

Size of municipality	Pay per month (first period of office)	Pay per month (second period of office)
Up to 2,000	€3,120	€4,130
Up to 10,000	€4130	€4,560
Up to 20,000	€6,040	€6,400
Up to 30,000	€6,400	€6,780
Up to 50,000	€7,210	€7,620
Up to 100,000	€7,620	€8,020
Up to 200,000	€8,430	€8,940
Up to 500, 000	€8,940	€10,540
Over 500,000	€10,540	€10,950

On top of that, mayors in Baden-Württemberg receive a tax-free expense allowance of 13.5 per cent of their gross salary and a family allowance.[67]

In Baden-Württemberg, the directly elected mayors have a strong position – not only as chair of the council and all council committees, but also as head of the administration.[68] They are also the legal representatives of the municipality they serve. Thus, if we want to compare costs of local representatives, there is a case of excluding mayors, as they are full-time and part of the executive. Anyway – their cost, bearing in mind the structure of municipalities and the pay scale, amounts to c€60 million (c£50 m).

Scotland's councillors – all 1222 of them – earned a total £22.8 m in 2011.[69] In March 2011, the Scottish Local Authority Remuneration Committee 2010 Review had suggested that backbench councillors should see their pay rise from £16,234 to £18,916. But in December, the Minister for Local Government, Derek Mackay, decided not to implement these recommendations, which meant that Scotland's councillors had their pay frozen for a third year running.[70]

---

[66] Wolfgang Müller, 'Bürgermeister wollen mehr Geld', Heilbronner Stimme, 22 October 2008.

[67] 'So viel verdienen Bürgermeister in Baden-Württemberg', Südkurier, 12 February 2009, <www.suedkurier.de/region/bodenseekreis-oberschwaben/langenargen/So-viel-verdienen-Buergermeister-in-Baden-Wuerttemberg;art372483,3634290>.

[68] See Udo Bullmann, 'Germany: Federalism under Strain', p.93.

[69] Simon Johnson, 'Scottish councillors "should receive 24 per cent pay rise"', The Daily Telegraph, 11 March 2011; <www.telegraph.co.uk/news/uknews/scotland/8376053/Scottish-councillors-should-receive-24-per-cent-pay-rise.html>.

[70] David Maddox, 'Councillors' pay to be frozen after minister blocks rises of almost 20 per cent', The Scotsman, 30 December 2011.

Gordon Matheson, the leader of Scotland's biggest council – Glasgow – currently receives about £45,000. But, as recent figures show, councillors also claim more than £3m a year between them on top of their taxpayer-funded wages.[71] The difference between Baden-Württemberg and Scotland is, of course that, in Germany as in most parts of Europe (and in England, for that matter), councillors are unsalaried, only receiving expense allowances, while being a Scottish councilor is a full-time occupation.

As importantly, there are, in other European countries, many more candidates than in Scotland. In Norway, there were 59,505 candidates competing for 10,785 seats on local councils. In Baden Württemberg 60,182 candidates competed for 19,006 local council seats, and 15,544 for the county councils.[72] In Scotland, the 1,222 seats (1223 in 2012) were contested

- in 1999, by 3,934 candidates
- in 2003, by 4,195 candidates
- in 2007, after the introduction of STV, by 2,607 candidates[73]
- in 2012, 2,496 candidates.[74]

In other words, in Scotland nearly every second candidate is elected. In the 2012 election, Edinburgh (460,000 pop.; 58 councillors) was fielding 127 candidates; Glasgow (592,000 pop; 79 councillors) had 225 candidates; Aberdeenshire (245,000 pop; 68 councillors) had 129 candidates – needless to say that, to take Aberdeenshire, none of the bigger municipalities like Peterhead (pop. 17,500); Fraserburgh (pop. 12,500), Inverurie (pop. 11,000), etc. have a council of their own.

---

[71] Dean Herbert, 'Scottish councillors hit by pay freeze as salary rise put on ice', *The Daily Express*, 30 December 2011.

[72] <www.statistik-bw.de/Veroeffentl/Monatshefte/essay.asp?xYear=2009&xMonth=09&eNr=09>.

[73] David Denver and Hugh Bochel, 'A Quiet Revolution: STV and the Scottish Council Elections of 2007', *Scottish Affairs*, no.61 (Autumn 2007), pp.1-17; p.4.

[74] David Denver, Hugh Bochel and Martin Steven, 'Mixed Messages for (some) Parties: The Scottish Council Elections of 2012', *Scottish Affairs*, no.80 (Summer 2012), pp,1-19; p.4.

Table 9 Proportion of the Population Standing in Local Elections[75]

Country	Population (million people)	Candidates in all local elections	Proportion of population standing as candidate
Finland	5.4	38,509	1 in 140
Norway	4.8	59,505	1 in 81
Baden-Württemberg	10.7	75,726	1 in 141
Sweden	9.4	64,810	1 in 145
Scotland	5.2	2,607	1 in 2,071

That means, many more people are locally engaged in policy- and decision-making. If we just concentrate on Baden-Württemberg and Scotland, we find that Baden-Württemberg, with

- roughly, double the population of Scotland (10.7 v. 5.2 m people)
- has c.18 times more elected councillors at local and county level
- at roughly 3 times the cost
- and about 30 times as many candidates for the electorate to choose from, in a very personalised electoral system.

"Representative democracies depend on a supply of persons who are willing to work with matters which are defined as being of common concern to the citizens."[76] But first, the structures must be there that allow people to engage. In Scotland, these are missing in large parts of the country.

Table 10 Number of Candidates Contesting each Seat[77]

Country	Candidates in all local elections	Number of seats	Number of candidates contesting each seat
Finland	38,509	14,412	3.7
Norway	59,505	10,785	5.5
Baden-Württemberg	75,726	21.279	3.6
Sweden	64,810	14,631	4.4
Scotland	2,607	1, 223	2.1

[75] References for Norway and Baden-Württemberg as case studies above. Sweden Statistiska Centralbyrån 2012, Finland: Statistics Finland, 2012.

[76] Jacob Aars and Audun Offerdal, 1998, p.210.

[77] References for Norway and Baden-Württemberg as case studies above. Sweden Statistiska Centralbyrån 2012, Finland: Statistics Finland, 2012.

The fundamental distinction is between full-time councillors being paid a wage, and honorary councillors paid expenses and allowances. Across Europe, the second model is being followed, with, as we have already seen, different ratios of councillors and represented population.

> Clearly a greater number of councillors is likely to increase the administration support costs, however this may lead to savings in the longer term as a result of more effective policymaking and use of resources as councillors are more likely to be in close contact with residents and have a greater understanding of their views and concerns.[78]

Against the Tide

Recently, Local Government Minister Derek Mackay made clear the Scottish Government was happy with progress on making public services "simpler, better co-ordinated". He said: "We have made clear, that there will be no reorganisation of local government in the foreseeable future."[79] Content with small mercies, we have to take that as a positive statement. It was a response to demands for further concentration and centralisation. Arguing for a revival of local democracy is like swimming against the tide. Much of the local government reform discourse tends towards further centralisation, often with a populist slant: Scotland being 'too heavily' governed, decentralisation would only mean more politicians, more bureaucracy, more expenditure. No one expressed that kind of populism better than Edinburgh SNP councillor Martin Hannan in one of his columns for the *Edinburgh Evening News*:

> Let's halve the number of MPs, MSPs and MEPs, and cut the number of Edinburgh council seats to, say, around 25. We should also quadruple the deposits to stop crank candidates standing, and generally make the whole process simpler so that people can cast their votes in a few minutes every five years. Because frankly, that is all the attention most of our politicians deserve.[80]

The self-government of Scotland's capital city reduced to the size of a Scandinavian oder German village?

---

[78] Kingsley Purdam et al, 2008, p.15.

[79] Robbie Dinwoodie, 'Government rules out further reorganisation of local councils', *The Herald*, 23 May 2013.

[80] Martin Hannan, 'I vote for one day of elections', *Edinburgh Evening News*, 22 February 2011.

When John Knox – the Calvinist preacher ultimately responsible for the introduction of universal education and the high levels of literacy found in Scotland in the seventeenth and eighteenth centuries – formed the Scottish Kirk in the sixteenth century, he built it from the ground up. A present-day namesake, the political journalist John Knox, seems to endorse this principle for local government, pleading for a return to municipal councils:

> A return to municipal government would be one way of restoring faith in democracy. Local people could really decide how they want to live, how much they want to pay in taxes for what services. It would also, in my view at least, reinvigorate the economy by breaking it up into smaller units which could satisfy many of their citizens needs locally: such as energy, water, food, education, health services, transport, and, dare I mention it, banking.[81]

Kenneth Roy lamented the demise of "human-shaped" local government units, and linked it to the sad decline of small-town Scotland:

> The towns remain, of course, but shorn of all responsibility for their own affairs. Is it any coincidence that many, if not most, are sadly diminished communities? It will be argued that the decline of the small town owes more to economic forces than to the deprivation of self-governing status brought about by local government reorganisation. But the malaise has deeper roots. When human beings lose the capacity to exercise a degree of immediate control over their own conditions, when intimacy of scale is sacrificed, the result is Newport-on-Tay; or, from my own experience, the derelict small towns of Ayrshire, sullen places from which all vibrancy and hope seems to have been sucked. The former system had many imperfections, but it was essentially human-shaped. What we have now suits the executive. It is convenient because it is a long way from the people.[82]

Roy is right in pointing out that painting a rosy past is not entirely helpful. Too often was true what Wood referred to in his response to demands for the re-instating of the 'wee burghs': "Small town politics, including in the

---

[81] John Knox, 'Analysis: mayors the way to combat cuts?', *Caledonian Mercury*, 22 February 2010, <http://politics.caledonianmercury.com/2010/02/22/mayors-the-way-to-combat-cuts/>.

[82] Kenneth Roy, 'Are we best suited to live in "wee burghs"?', *Scottish Review*, 17 February 2010, <www.senscot.net/view_art.php?viewid=9199>.

Labour heartlands, meant small-minded politics." Checks and balances are needed. Wood advocates the return to regional governance:

> The regions were too large for any local faction to dominate. A degree of fairness across schools was the result. The regions were also efficient, using economies of scale to keep the centre relatively small but to push expenditure to the chalk-face. Perhaps most impressive was the fact that councillors set the authority's strategy but left daily management to the schools. The division between the political and the professional was clear. Some public services, both for reasons of efficiency and reasons of fairness and impartiality, are far better managed on a large scale.[83]

Dare we say that the one does not have to preclude the other, that a Scotland in which local communities had their locally elected councils and where regions took responsibility for spatial and infrastructure planning might be a more democratic and, ultimately, a better Scotland?

In the run-up to the referendum, Scotland's three island councils – Shetland, Orkney and Comhairle nan Eilean Siar (Western Isles) – have outlined demands for greater control over their own resources. Western Isles leader Angus Campbell said:

> The constitutional debate offers the opportunity for the three island councils to secure increased powers for our communities to take decisions which will benefit the economies and the lives of those who live in the islands.[84]

They want talks with the Scottish and the UK governments about

- control of the sea bed around the islands, allowing revenues currently paid to the Crown Estate to be channelled locally;
- new grid connections to the Scottish mainland for wave, tidal and wind energy resources;
- new fiscal arrangements to allow the islands to benefit more directly from the harvesting of local resources, including renewable energy and fisheries;

---

[83] Alex Wood, 'Better big', *Scottish Review*, 3 June 2010, <www.scottishreview.net/AWood213.html>.

[84] 'Orkney, Shetland and Western Isles councils lobby for more powers', *BBC News Scotland*, 17 June 2013, <www.bbc.co.uk/news/uk-scotland-scotland-politics-22934024>.

- and recognition of the status of the three island groups in a new Scottish Constitutional Settlement.

Shetland MSP Tavish Scott said both the Scottish and UK governments "must react positively" to the case for more powers: "Centralisation in Edinburgh has to stop and be reversed."

Conclusions

Local government is about more than the provision of specific services. Following Daniel R. Grant and Lloyd B. Omdahl,[85] we can list a "variety of reasons" for local government. Although coming from an American analysis, their 'top ten' is of nigh universal relevance:

1. Self-determination: "Locally elected means locally responsive; it also means applications of the state laws in conformance with local desires, traditions, and customs, within legal parameters."

2. Provide services: "Local discretion in the provision of certain services will vary with the type of local government," but local governments have options which make them "able to respond to the particular interests and desires of their respective constituencies."

3. Resolve local conflicts: "Local governments mediate and resolve conflicts on a local level."

4. Enable some to keep advantages: "Local governments are strongly supported because they provide political, economic, or social advantages."

5. Laboratories of government: "Local governments serve as laboratories of government. Municipalities and counties with home rule powers have opportunities to create new responses to old service problems."

6. Train officials: "Local governments are training schools for higher governments. Many state legislators and executives, not to mention large numbers of federal officials, began their political careers by serving as members of school

---

[85] Daniel R. Grant and Lloyd B. Omdahl, *State and Local Government in America*, Madison, Wisconsin: Brown & Benchmark, (sixth edition), 1993, pp.297-99.

boards, county commissions, city councils, or local executive agencies. (...) If state service is the prep school for the federal government, then local government is certainly the grammar school for all levels."

7. Intergovernmental representation: "Local governments are intergovernmental representatives of local interests."

8. Provides base for parties: "Local governments provide a base for the political party system."

9. Convenient for state: "Local governments are an administrative convenience for the state (...) state governments look to cities, counties, towns, townships, and special districts to bring state programs to the people."

10. Tradition: "Some local governments exist merely as the result of tradition." Also not viable, they continue to exist. "Perhaps, it is more than tradition. It may simply be the need of human beings for identification with a geographic place."

Coming back across the Big Pond, the smaller scale of local government in all other European countries[86] adds to the legitimacy of local government in those countries. There, it is constitutionally based,

> As part of that constitutional status, the concept of general competence is important at least symbolically but also as a statement of local government's wider community responsibility, if not always of wide spending functions.[87]

Bearing in mind that 'practices cannot be simply transferred and, in any case, there should be no suggestion that the Holy Grail can be found in any of the other countries studied,'[88] comparisons have clearly shown that local government involves more people in the rest of Europe, keeps elected representatives and represented population at a much closer distance, and gives voters greater choice – contributing to 'create a healthy relationship between elector and political representative.'[89]

---

[86] Richard Batley, 'Comparisons and Lessons', in Richard Batley and Gerry Stoker (eds), *Local Government in Europe: Trends and Developments*, Basingstoke: Macmillan, 1991, pp.210-229; p.226.

[87] *Ibid.*

[88] *Ibid.*, p.225.

[89] Gerry Stoker, *Why Politics Matters: Making Democracy Work*, Basingstoke: Palgrave

Many of the above comparative statistics found their way into a Report the Jimmy Reid Foundation published just before the May 2012 local elections. It suggested complementing the existing council structure by introducing an elected and accountable local level of governance at community level.[90] Reform Scotland also produced a Report on local government in Scotland, also advocating empowerment of community councils. Unfortunately, their proposal anent reducing the number of existing councils caught the headlines, and fuelled demands for even more centralisation.[91]

The Common Weal[92] has among its blueprint for a fairer and more just Scotland the demand for more local democracy, "to bring decision-making closer to people."[93] And Lesley Riddoch's Nordic Horizons project raises the issue of local democracy regularly. But, unfortunately, voices like Andy Wightman's are still in a minority:

> My own view for a long time has been that all of Scotland's 196 burghs should get back their town councils. Only in Scotland do we not have a real level of local representative government. Compare with kommunes, municipalities, even parish councils in England. Bring back parish councils too I say – we had them in Scotland till 1929. I grew up in Kinross and the spirit of the place was much greater than now with elected councillors remote from the affairs of the town and officials even less so. Go to Kinross and look at the state of the town hall and library where Aly Bain used to play at the Kinross folk festival and where the local community council have been fighting hard to secure its future. It is strange that there is so little political support for the resurrection of town councils. I think this is a reflection of the growing divide between the political classes and the people.[94]

Macmillan, 2006, p.170.

[90] Eberhard Bort, Robin McAlpine and Gordon Morgan, *The Silent Crisis: Failure and Revival in Local Democracy in Scotland*, Biggar: The Jimmy Reid Foundation, 2012 <http://reidfoundation.org/portfolio/the-silent-crisis-failure-and-revival-in-local-democracy-in-scotland/>.

[91] Reform Scotland, *Renewing Local Government*, Edinburgh, May 2012, <http://reformscotland.com/public/publications/Renewing_Local_Government.pdf>; BBC News Scotland, 'Reform Scotland proposal to cut Scottish councils', 22 May 2012 < www.bbc.co.uk/news/uk-scotland-scotland-politics-18150399>.

[92] See Robin McAlpine's chapter in this volume.

[93] See Tom Gordon, 'A new blueprint for an independent Scotland', *Sunday Herald*, 5 May 2013.

[94] Andy Wightman, 'Kinross', *Scottish Review*, 27 April 2010, <www.scottishreview.net/Kinross'Burghs209.html>.

True, as mentioned above, other European countries have reformed and centralised their local and regional government structures over the past decades. Denmark went from 25 counties in 1970 to the present 14, and from 1,400 local authorities to 275. Iceland had 204 municipalities in 1990 and cut them down to 101 in 2005, and then to 79 in 2006. And Finland is deliberating a reduction of the number of local authorities from presently 348 to about 90, augmented by 20 to 25 regional councils. But when these countries debate 'centralisation', they are still maintaining a level of local representation way beyond the Scottish system.

> North or south, Baltic or Mediterranean, most European states are micro-sized at their local tier. That means more councillors and more cost. It also means more connection, traction, trust, effective service delivery and involvement than our disempowering and distant 'local' government.[95]

Having so few people involved in the only level of governance below the Scottish Parliament deprives the Scottish polity of the 'natural training ground' for political talent. Local communities are important as "schools of democracy" and "centres of legitimisation", wrote Angelika Vetter, and they encourage democratic development in political systems.[96]

Many MSPs were councillors – but there are not that many councillors to choose from. And there are no elected mayors either.[97] But the most dangerous deficit – and we can see it in many Scottish towns and communities – is the lack of a political identity and structure which would allow for an input into communal or municipal development, a source of local spirit and civic pride. Scottish local government does not provide a sufficient and inviting framework for active citizenship. In a smaller-scale local democracy, 'mini polities,

> each with its own identity, political life, fiscal resources, priorities and concerns, and each under its own local democratic leadership, would not merely provide public services. They

---

[95] Lesley Riddoch, 'Mini-councils will energise Scotland's communities', *The Scotsman*, 28 June 2010.

[96] Angelika Vetter, *Lokale Politik als Ressource der Demokratie in Europa? Lokale Autonomie, lokale Strukturen und die Einstellungen der Bürger zur Politik*, Opladen: Leske + Budrich, 2002, p.16.

[97] The embryonic debate about elected mayors in Scotland is hampered by the fact that there are only four city councils (Glasgow, Edinburgh, Aberdeen, Dundee) for whom this would be an option. Elected mayors could be part of a solution to the 'silent crisis', but only in combination with strong councils. See Institute for Government, 'Elected mayors', London, May 2012, <www.instituteforgovernment.org.uk/our-work/new-models-governance-and-public-services/elected-mayors>.

would also be sites of civic education and popular participation, empowering people and helping communities to articulate their own needs and priorities. They would teach us to relate to public authorities not as passive, individualistic consumers but as mutually responsible citizens.[98]

The remedy for the *malaise* of Scottish local government could be, as the Greens suggest, the empowerment of hitherto toothless community councils: "An administration inspired by Green policies," Robin Harper wrote, "would devolve much more responsibility to community councils, give them proper budgets within which they could decide their own expenditure, and we would bequeath to them a sound electoral process."[99]

The present omens are no good. In July 2011, the Association of Scottish Community Councils (ASCC) announced its demise, after a drastic funding cut from the Scottish Government. As they are constituted, the 9,000 or so community councillors, now left without a guiding and coordinating body, are part of the problem rather than the solution. One might apply Robin Harper's dictum on most school councils – "All the kids learn is that democracy does not work."[100]

According to Vincent Waters, the last ASCC president, community councils 'are dying off', characterised by ageing and dwindling membership.[101] They are toothless, bereft of real powers; they cannot legally own an asset. A BBC survey in November 2011 found that a fifth of community councils were suspended due to lack of interest.[102] The exception are a few cases where the windfall from windfarms has given them real cash, and with it real responsibility, and thus real power.

> Powerless community councils are so toothless they can't legally own an asset. So development trusts have been set up to handle community orchards, lochs, pubs, libraries, bridges and wind turbines – and in the process a very practical, capable and focused set of people have been gathered together and let rip.[103]

---

[98] W Elliot Bulmer, *A Model Constitution for Scotland: Making Democracy Work in an independent State*, Edinburgh: Luath Press, 2011, p.92.

[99] Robin Harper (with Fred Bridgland), *Dear Mr Harper: Britain's First Green Parliamentarian*, Edinburgh: Birlinn, 2011, p.190.

[100] *Ibid.*, p.85.

[101] Kate Shannon, 'Heart of the community: Vincent Waters interview', *Holyrood*, 28 November 2011.

[102] *BBC News Scotland*, 'Reform Scotland calls for more powers for community councils', 20 May 2012, <www.bbc.co.uk/news/uk-scotland-scotland-politics-18122993>

[103] Lesley Riddoch, art.cit.

But do development trusts compensate for democratically elected and accountable councils?

Accountable, accessible and transparent local government is necessary to foster 'trust, empathy and social capital' – enabling and supporting 'a wide range of local institutions of governance.'[104] More scope for local communities to make their own decisions needs to be balanced, particularly in Scotland, with the need to address inequalities, recognizing 'both diversity in communities and a concern with equity issues.'[105] Empowered and truly local government would mean seeing citizens not just as customers, but as actively shaping – and sharing ownership in – their local communities and local services. Let us be guided by the late Campbell Christie's demand that 'reforms must aim to empower individuals and communities receiving public services by involving them in the design and delivery of the services they use.'[106]

> In a time of limited budgets and difficult spending decisions, surely local communities should take responsibility for delivering local savings in a manner that best suits that community. And in a time of fierce competitiveness for resources, surely local communities will argue for investment more fiercely than a centralised body.[107]

The 2011 Scottish Household Survey (SHS), published by the Scottish Government, showed that only 23 per cent of adult respondents agree that their council is good at listening to local people's views before it takes decisions.[108] Back in 1998, Gerry Stoker warned that "local government and democracy is running the risk of becoming irrelevant" – yet, he argued:

> The case for effective local democracy in a globalised and changing world is greater than ever. People need an element in the governmental system that they can gain easy access to and participate in. They need a local political system that enables them to understand problems and make choices in a complex world. They should have their interests and concerns given expression in wider national and international stages.

---

[104] Gerry Stoker, 2006, p.176

[105] Ibid., p.177.

[106] Campbell Christie, 'Foreword', Report on the Future Delivery of Public Services by the Commission chaired by Dr Campbell Christie, Edinburgh, 2011, <www.scotland.gov.uk/Publications/2011/06/27154527/1>.

[107] Rob Gibson, art.cit.

[108] See Scott MacNab, 'Scots families are becoming happier and more content', The Scotsman, 18 August 2011.

They want local services that are responsive and tuned to their needs. For all these reasons effective local democracy and government is required.[109]

Iain Macwhirter summed Scotland's local democracy deficit up best, when he came to the sad conclusion that "local government is dying in Scotland, as turnout falls and central government increasingly diverts the local revenue and tells councils what to do. The only thing that will keep local government alive is democratic engagement – the active support of the people."[110] And without such a revival, as Leslie Riddoch remarked *vis-à-vis* the looming independence referendum, "It's hard to see how people deemed incapable of running their towns and villages – uniquely in Europe – will confidently vote to run their own country."[111]

Will we, whichever way the referendum pans out, ever see a mayor or a council leader in Oban, in Kircaldy or in Motherwell echo Michael O'Brian, the mayor of Winooski, who addressed his fellow citizens in the town's *Annual Report*:

> This is our City and I ask all citizens to get involved in the community. We are fortunate to have so many individuals who give their time and effort to making our city great. We are grateful to all the folks who serve on the varied boards and who put in their time to help throughout the city. But we need more folks to get involved. I again ask you to look at this Annual Report to see what volunteer positions are open and where you might be able to help. I encourage you to attend City Council meetings, the dates are posted in this report. Make your voice heard. Everyone is welcome at Council meetings. And finally, please feel free to call City Hall, or call members of the City Council if you have any questions, want to find out about an issue the Council is discussing, or to talk about an issue that you think should be discussed.[112]

That is the place where the wild onions grow. Let us have some of that in Scotland, not just in Edinburgh, Glasgow, Aberdeen and Dundee, but in

---

[109] Gerry Stoker, 'Foreword', in Andrew Adonis, *Voting in proportion: Electoral reform for Scotland's councils*, Edinburgh: Scottish Council Foundation, 1998, p.2.

[110] Iain Macwhirter, 'Let's bring councils into line with elected mayors', *The Herald*, 1 September 2011.

[111] Lesley Riddoch, 'Foreword', *The Silent Crisis*, 2012, p.i.

[112] Michael O'Brian, Mayor of Winooski, in the Ninetieth Annual Report (2011-12), <https://docs.google.com/file/d/0B4mBI8xioET6TlJHQ2xwaVZmcFU/edit?pli=1>.

every municipality, and regardless of the outcome of the Referendum. Local government is devolved – reform is within the remit of Holyrood. Local democracy should be a vital part of the constitutional debate.

"If citizenship is going to be a living practice rather than a spectator sport for most citizens, we need to create a far wider set of opportunities for real decisions to be made at the local level that people care about."[113] That is the message MSPs should take to heart if they are serious about mending Scotland's local democracy deficit.

---

[113] Gerry Stoker, 'Foreword', p.xvii.

More Direct Democracy: *Ja, bitte!*

Peter Conradi and Helmut Doka[1]

A spectre is haunting Germany – the spectre of direct democracy. Other federally-organised states like Switzerland, Austria and the United States of America have, at local and state level, elaborate ways of involving citizens in deliberating and making decisions. But in Germany these are exotic. At the Federal level, the Parliamentary Council of 1949 expressly excluded them (except for a possible restructuring of the federal territory); at Land and local levels stipulations vary but usually have prohibitively high hurdles for any initiator. At he *Land* level, Baden-Württemberg has not had a single successful referendum 'from below' for 60 years, as 33 per cent of all registered voters (!) need to assent. Even after all these years of stable democracy, the Federal Republic cannot grant its citizens the direct participation in decision-making that is the rule in many neighbouring countries. The events surrounding 'Stuttgart 21' have re-ignited the debate.

The Present Debate

"More citizen participation": that call now seems omnipresent. Prompt and better information, transparency in planning decisions and permissions, round tables, info-bureaux ... Following the planning disaster of 'Stuttgart 21', mayors and councillors, regional managers, ministers all now insist that nothing like it must ever happen again, and that in future they want to involve citizens more.

But what, we hear you ask, was/is Stuttgart 21?

This rail project started its planning stages more than 20 years ago as part of the High-Speed Train Project from Paris to Bratislava. It involves putting Stuttgart Station underground, as part of a 60 km tunnel system. Doubts about the good sense of the project, benefiting builders more than travellers, its technical feasibility and its effectiveness, an explosion in cost (from €4.5bn to €6.8bn and probably more) and, above all, a blundering authoritarian political management, led to a popular counter-movement. This culminated in huge demonstrations of up to 60,000 people in 2011-12.[2] In a widely televised one-week mediation process in 2010, well-informed opponents had *Deutsche Bahn* professionals on the ropes on many points, visible to everybody watching the process, though the findings of the

---

[1] Translated into English by Eberhard Bort and Christopher Harvie.

[2] See Volker Lösch, Gangolf Stocker, Sabine Leidig and Winfried Wolf (eds), *Stuttgart 21 – oder: Wem gehört die Stadt?*, Cologne: Papyrossa, 2010; Wolfgang Schorlau (ed.), *Stuttgart 21: Die Argumente*, Cologne: Kiepenhauer & Witsch, 2010;

mediator Heiner Geissler (a Tübingen philosophy graduate and prominent CDU polician) did not reflect this. Continuing gatherings of thousands of demonstrators every week contributed to the ousting of the CDU/FDP *Land* government in the May 2011 *Land* elections (after 59 years of uninterrupted CDU dominance in Baden-Württemberg). Although a *Land*-wide referendum on 27 November 2011 decided that the *Land* continue to fund S21 (58.8 per cent of the votes cast were against withdrawal), Fritz Kuhn was elected as the first Green Governing Mayor of Stuttgart in October 2012.

The S21 crisis became a nationwide synonym for squandering public money, trying to bulldoze critics, deploying dodgy information and outright deceit – all this by public or governmental institutions. It has now become a call for citizens' participation in future public planning processes. Time will tell how serious these promises are. In the past, it was often the league of investors, builders and power providers, auto-industry and banks who decided what was to be built and where. Mayors, local and regional councils, *Landtage* and *Bundestag* nodded through what they were presented with. But there is now a growing unease about the way big projects are planned. Information has been absent, late, simply wrong. Planners' promises turn out to be false, in a top-down culture that rules out alternatives, stifles communication and any efforts to reconcile different interests.

'Direct democracy' has become a hot topic, particularly as it would not only mean *information* for citizens about pending projects and legislative proposals, but also their direct participation in *making decisions*. Representative democracy – where policies are made by political parties and elected representatives, i.e. in local and regional councils, in the *Landtag* and the *Bundestag* – has in recent years lost approval, for several reasons:

- National parliaments are losing relevance, as national governments also negotiate and decide in international negotiations, at EU, UN, world summits and G-8, G-20 meetings.

- Political parties are less distinctive than in the past, and party alignments are weakening – as with churches, trade unions and local ties.

- Many people are no longer content with going to the polls every four or five years; demands for direct participation *between* elections is growing, particularly when voters/ members of a particular party want to take a different line on a policy from head office. Impossible in a representative democracy – direct democracy gives such a chance.

- The level of education among the population has risen, thanks to forty years of reform. As with the movement against nuclear power, people have become experts on the subject; consciousness and knowledge of related issues has also grown – just as in the Stuttgart 21 mediation, when opponents showed up *Deutsche Bahn*.

- The people who in their youth carried the peace, women's and environment banners now channel their campaign experience, knowledge and engagement into present-day conflicts.

- The digital age and information technology open new possibilities for fast information, communication and organisation.

More Direct Democracy –
The first stages in the decision-making process

Discussing direct democracy does not mean wanting it to replace representative systems, but to strengthen them by adding elements of direct democracy: trying for a sensible partnership of parliamentary and plebiscitary decisions. Not easy, as parliamentarians, who have to make the decisions on such arrangements, are – through past experience – reluctant to share with the people the power granted *temporarily* to them by the people.

The first steps to build up the influence of citizens on the actions of the state relate to information and surveying opinion. Both are important, but do not legally bind decision-makers. A people's petition carries greater weight: a demand that representatives in parliament pass a law, or a project. But this instrument of direct democracy does not yet exist at the federal level in Germany. If a majority of their voters supports such an initiative, the local or regional council, *Landtag* or the *Bundestag* and their governments must address the issue within a given time-frame. But the sole decision-making competence still lies with the parliament or council.

A Question of Power

At the second stage – the referendum – it really becomes a question of power. An initiative can get down to business: through a successful people's petition or through a parliamentary vote. At stake could be a new law or project, or the alteration or cancellation of a law or project already passed by parliament. In the latter case, a time limit within which a law can be challenged by a petition is necessary. In Switzerland, that time limit is a hundred days; if in this time 50,000 signatures can be collected, then a referendum on changing or rejecting a law or project is triggered. If there are no complaints, the law comes into force.

Plebiscites obviously change the political decision-making process. If an administration knows that its decisions are subject to a potential referendum, and push comes to shove, it has to concede. No longer can projects be rushed through parliament or council, brushing aside reservations, pleading factual or time constraints, *rien ne va plus*, etc. Opposition will now have to be identified early, readiness to talk and negotiate signalled, costs realistically listed, and alternatives offered to gain a new consensus. More work in the early phase of a project? Yes but, according to experienced city planners, saving much time later on – and the possibility of integrating people's expertise, which can substantially improve planning and acceptability, and therefore an outcome that lasts.

These positive effects have, hitherto, been hardly acknowledged. If the consequences of a referendum prove negative, the electorate must assume responsibility. If needs be, the decision must be corrected in another referendum, or parliament can overturn it with a very high (two-thirds) majority. This would clearly strengthen civic responsibility.

Needless to say that the rules and regulations of referenda – how to trigger them and how they are conducted – have to be weighed carefully and thought through. In Germany, again and again, horror scenarios and reservations are conjured up about plebiscites, instead of drawing on the rich practical experiences of many countries, analysing good and bad with best practice in mind, as to their application in Germany. The United States, Switzerland or Austria have yet to perish through their constitutional element of direct democracy. Though we may criticise particular decisions there, we have causes for unease, plenty of them, at home.

The Role of Elected Members of Parliament

In the exercise of power, direct democracy is partly in competition with elected members in a representative democracy. Hence they growl about their profound dislike of it, insisting that being elected by the people gives them the final say. Normal enough among conservatives – but why does this line also come from *progressives*? More information for citizens and citizens' surveys may be OK, but plebiscites? Too deep an intrusion into the monopolistic domain of MPs and interest groups, their power of negotiating outcomes in committees and among power elites? A demand too far that they extend their political role towards mediating in civic processes?

So, will elected representatives from all parties put their collective foot down on expanding participatory citizens' rights, plebiscites and the rules guiding them? The red-green government of Baden-Württemberg agreed in its coalition agreement on a new form of citizens' participation, following Stuttgart 21. It is assumed that a first draft of the bill will be presented by the autumn of 2013 – two-and-a-half years after the government took office. It will be interesting to see the rules respecting referenda; how easy or difficult it will be for people to make policy decisions in the future.

Direct Democracy –
The Role of Government and the Courts

The administration, i.e. the executive, has come to see itself as opposed by parliament or council and the judiciary. If there were better instruments of direct democracy, then administrations would have to reckon with referenda about their planning and projects, with new actors and a different administrative culture, characterised less by authority than by weighing options and balancing different interests, for example through mediation.

Decisions made by direct democracy are, of course, subject to control by the courts, as are those of governments and parliaments. But does this privilege the wealthy and corporate, if citizens as a group have no way to intervene? Are states based *only* on law, and reliant on it, more unequal? Other countries, such as Switzerland, put more trust in the people, with instruments of direct democracy, without limiting the powers of the courts.

Direct Democracy
... at the Federal Level

Article 20, paragraph 2 of the Basic Law states: "All state authority emanates from the people. It is exercised ... through elections and votes." This is followed by a lot about representative democracy, but little is said about direct democracy. Was it feared through its abuse in the Weimar Republic, with referenda manipulated by populist campaigns? There are, apart from restructuring the *Länder*, no provisions for referenda at the federal level in the Basic Law, and a constitutional amendment to enhance such polls is long overdue, especially as other Europeans can vote on important issues, such as the development of the EU. Such a change, however, will affect the constitutionally-protected participation of the *Länder* in legislative matters. The position of the second chamber, the *Bundesrat*, will have to be addressed and clarified.

... in Municipal, County, and *Länder* politics

The local level is particularly well suited to instruments of direct democracy. Its issues directly affect citizens; they can judge from between their own experience, the representative body or council, or the magistrate. Some *Länder*, like Bavaria and Baden-Württemberg, have had positive experiences with public decisions at the local level.[3]

---

[3] In Tübingen, for example, the controversial *Nordtangente* – a municipal motorway – was prevented by a plebiscite in 1979, when 84 per cent voted against it. See Eckhard

... at the European Level

New, and in the face of rising dissatisfaction with policies from Brussels even explosive, is the extension of direct-democratic influence of citizens at the European level, following the European Citizens' Initiative of 2012. Part of the Lisbon Treaty of 2007, this opens the door to citizens' initiatives, despite the Commission's rather restrictive style.[4] Conflicts about participation seem inevitable, but this could go hand in hand with a strengthening of the supine European Parliament *vis à vis* the Commission. 'Politically Disadvantaged of All Levels, Unite?'

... and Social-political Exclusion

At parliamentary elections, usually the more affluent middle and upper classes participate in greater numbers than 'the gentlefolk of no property': the latter are less integrated, less informed, and therefore less interested and less likely to be mobilised. This social exclusion can also occur in referenda. In Hamburg, voting results in the referendum on the school reform passed by the legislators showed that the better-off and the privileged prevailed over the socially disadvantaged, whose children were what the reform was all about. Specific voting arrangements can counter this tendency but, in the long term, the situation will only improve if the socially disadvantaged are empowered through civic processes (e.g. community politics) to participate fully in the decisions.

... and the Question of Responsibility

Direct democracy is no guarantee against bad decisions. The people can be just as wrong as the Parliament they have elected. Populist demagogues play their role in elections as well as in plebiscites, and the power of interests, especially economic interests, will try to influence elections as well as referenda.

A deficiency in referenda is that, at the end, no one is personally responsible for the result. Should a plebiscite produce what later emerges as the wrong decision, the people cannot recall themselves. It is conceivable to give Parliament the opportunity to repeal the result of a referendum with a

Ströbel, 'Der erste Bürgerentscheid in der Stadt', *Schwäbisches Tagblatt*, 8 July 2004. In Munich, a third runway for the airport was stopped by a citizens' petition in June 2012. In Bavaria, in 2010 a 61 per cent majority enforced a strict smoking ban in public places. 'Volksentscheid: Strikte Rauchgegner siegen in Bayern', *Spiegel Online*, 4 July 2010. For the increased use of plebiscites, see 'Direkte Demokratie: Zahl der Bürgerbegehren ist deutlich gestiegen', *Spiegel Online*, 5 September 2012, <www.spiegel.de/politik/deutschland/direkte-demokratie-mehr-buergerscheide-in-deutschland-a-854154.html>.

[4] <www.citizens-initiative.eu>.

large (say, two-thirds) majority. Or, perhaps better, the people could correct their decision in a second vote – indeed, a government or a council, too, could initiate a referendum.

For every issue, consensual procedures need to be found so that polemical or grossly misleading formulations of the issues at stake do not, from the outset, make a fair debate and vote impossible. Laws may be amended or repealed; that is not possible with regard to projects like roads, concert halls or railway stations once they are built. All the more necessary is an open, transparent planning process.

Conclusion

Improved citizen participation makes sense only if it embraces the instruments of direct democracy. Like judicial review, these would influence the actors in politics, administration and the economy. Without the ability to question draft legislation, building projects, roads and rail routes, through plebiscites, a citizens' participation that is only about improved information, remains a blunt sword.

Priority lies with opening local government to citizens' initiatives by amending its constitution regarding topics and quorums for local referenda. The growing disenchantment with political parties in Germany doesn't reflect the importance accorded politics, which direct democracy can revitalise and strengthen. Serious discussion can enable a balance between representative and direct democracy. Both can inspire one another.

Joachim Gauck, the first President of Germany drawn from the civil rights movement, not the legislature, talked in his inaugural speech about representative democracy as "a system capable of learning" making it possible for citizens to "exercise responsibility" through contributing and participating:

> Alongside the political parties and other democratic institutions … there is a second pillar of our democracy: active civil society. Through their commitment, but also through protests, civic initiatives, ad hoc movements and elements of the digital community, they complement parliamentary democracy and compensate for its shortcomings.[5]

New elements of direct democracy would expand the ability of citizens to play a role in the shaping of their country beyond mere participation in elections, proclaimed the President, and that would strengthen the "culture of freedom".

---

[5] Joachim Gauck, 'Inaugural Speech' (23 March 2012), <www.bundespraesident.de/ SharedDocs/Reden/EN/JoachimGauck/Reden/2012/03/120323-Swearing-In-Ceremony. html>.

Regional Politics and Policies

The Motley Crew that Made the Open University

Henry Cowper

I first met Chris Harvie in 1962 when he came straight from the Royal High School to the University of Edinburgh. My journey to the Old Quad was a bit more ponderous via various jobs and a stint in the Army. We were both active in the University Labour Club, of which I was the Treasurer for a while. I seem to recall we almost depleted the Club's funds by entertaining Hugh MacDiarmid and Norman MacCaig at Milne's Bar prior to a talk by MacDiarmid in the Students' Union.

My first recollection of Chris was how much he knew about Scottish politics and Scottish poetry. Some seven years older, I stood in awe of his intellectual brilliance. He lived up the road from me in the posher part of Morningside with his parents. Later on we became colleagues at the Open University. He joined the central academic staff at Milton Keynes in 1969. I was appointed to what was then called 'the Regional Staff' in 1970.

Roger Carus, the first Scottish Director, made sure that the organisation bore the title *The Open University in Scotland*. Today it has over 100 full-time staff and around 500 part-time tutors, catering for some 16,000 students. Multiply this by 10 and add on 50,000 foreign students and you can see why the OU is Britain's biggest single institution of higher education.

It could have been strangled at birth

The Open University was very much the brain-child of Harold Wilson, but it was Jennie Lee who, as Minister for the Arts, fought hard to get the 'University of the Air' transformed into the Open University. Professor Walter Perry, a Scot, was appointed in May 1969 as the University's first Vice-Chancellor, and he started to recruit staff immediately. By September 1969, 80 people had been appointed.

Where the OU was unique was in its radical admissions policy – it did not insist on any prior educational qualifications. In 1970 there were still a large proportion of adults who had missed out on higher education for a wide variety of reasons, not least the Second World War.

Students were required to take two foundation courses before moving on to higher level study, building up credits towards a degree. By August 1970, when applications for prospective students closed, 42,000 applications for 25,000 places had been received. Women made up only 25 per cent of applicants at this stage.   Students started studying in January 1971. Over

30 per cent lacked the qualification for entry to other British universities. Around 40 per cent were three-year non-graduate teachers, which meant that they could fast-track a degree.

From its inception, the University was determined to maintain high academic standards, since there was opposition to the entire project from a variety of quarters. Jennie Lee was later to write of these early days:

> I knew it had to be a university with no concessions, right from the very beginning – I knew the conservatism and vested interests of the academic world. I did not believe we could get it through if we lowered our standards.[1]

Walter Perry, the Open University's first Vice-Chancellor and a distinguished Professor of Pharmacology at the University of Edinburgh, had similar thoughts:

> I came to the Open University from a wholly traditional background – it wasn't that I had any deep-seated urge to mitigate the miseries of the depressed adult, it was that I was persuaded that the standard of teaching in conventional universities was pretty deplorable. It suddenly struck me that if you could use the media and devise course materials that would work for students all by themselves, then inevitably you were bound to affect – for good – the standard of teaching in conventional universities.[2]

To service its four faculties – Arts, Social Sciences, Mathematics and Science – the University appointed around 2000 part-time staff. These people came from the traditional universities and from other sectors of further and higher education. The vast majority were committed to the idea of the Open University; a few were curious about how the organisation actually worked.

The first teaching year in 1971 got off to a bad start when British postal workers went on strike for eight weeks on 20 January. However, course materials and other written texts were distributed through regional offices and local study centres. Information was given out on BBC Radio and on Television about the collection of this material. By March, things got back to normal, but it was a testing time for the new University. That year also saw the first summer schools taking place at various conventional universities throughout Britain. They gave students the opportunity to meet with staff, both full-time and part-time. Also, distinguished academics from the

---

[1] 'History of the OU', <www.open.ac.uk/about/main/the-ou-explained/history-the-ou>.

[2] *Ibid.*

traditional universities wrote material for Open University courses and lectured at the summer schools.

Local tutorial services ensured that, in addition to summer schools, there were opportunities for students to have face-to-face teaching on a weekly basis. This was relatively easy to provide in urban areas, but proved difficult in out-lying rural areas. Nevertheless, the University had a strong following in the Highlands and Islands, especially in Orkney and Shetland.

As Secretary of State for Education and Science, Margaret Thatcher was at first wary about the concept of the Open University, but she was to change her mind. In her memoirs she wrote:

> I was hailed in a modest way as the saviour of the Open University. In Opposition both Iain Macleod and Edward Boyle, who thought that there were educational priorities more deserving of Government help, had committed themselves in public against it. And although its abolition was not in the manifesto, many people expected it to perish.
>
> But I was genuinely attracted to the concept of a 'University of the Airwaves', as it was often called, because I thought that it was an inexpensive way of giving wider access to higher education, because I thought that trainee teachers in particular would benefit from it, because I was alert to the opportunities offered by technology to bring the best teaching to schoolchildren and students, and above all because it gave people a second chance in life.
>
> In any case, the university was due to take its first students that autumn, and cancellation would have been both expensive and a blow to many hopes. On condition that I agreed to reduce the immediate intake of students and find other savings, my Cabinet colleagues allowed the Open University to go ahead.[3]

Clearly, the Open University could have been strangled at birth, but its survival owed a lot to Mrs Thatcher. Her initial antagonism gave way to approval of what the University hoped to achieve.

The early days of the OU

In the early days, the Open University, like any other intellectual establishment, had its share of Marxists. The three outstanding ones were Arnold Kettle, Mike Pentz and Stuart Hall, and there is no doubt that many staff were left of centre. But, although there was criticism about the content of some social science courses, it was hard to prove that there was outright Marxist bias. OU teaching by its very nature was *public*, since course materials and course texts were generally available. Indeed, a great deal of

[3] Margaret Thatcher, *The Path to Power*, London: HarperCollins, 1995, p.179.

Open University courses were greedily seized on by academics in all areas of higher education for use in their own teaching.

As early as 1972, there was a keen interest in OU teaching methods throughout the English speaking world, and the University set up a North American Office in Washington DC – I worked there for six weeks in 1975. Many American universities, including MIT, bought OU course material for use in their undergraduate classes. The same was true for Canada, Australia, New Zealand and India.

Looking back from a distance of 40 years, it strikes me what a motley crew we were. Many of the central academics came from prestigious institutions, most of the regional staff were from the world of adult education, and there were those with a colonial or military background represented in the Administration. For many, it was their first real job on leaving university.

Arthur Marwick (1936-2006) had previously taught at Aberdeen and Edinburgh when he was appointed to the Chair of History at the OU. He had established his reputation with *The Deluge: British Society and the First World War* (1965) and *Britain in the Century of Total War* (1968). Marwick was dismissive of 'patriotic polemic' in historical writing and was equally critical of both Marxist and post-modern theories. He had firm views on how history should be taught. To him, history was the systematic study of the human past through the close scrutiny of primary sources. He also placed emphasis on 'witting' and 'unwitting testimony'. Years before he wrote these words he was urging students to write clear and explicit essays devoid of cliché or other forms of sloppy writing:

> Texts, or as we should prefer to say 'Primary Sources', are certainly not transparent. But provided we have a precise topic in mind, have sufficient contextual knowledge, and can practise the quite complicated technical skills of source analysis, we will be able to extract firm information relevant to our topic.[4]

In many ways, Marwick was a traditionalist. He particularly liked the structure of the Honours history course in Scottish universities and sought to establish something of the same at the OU. As well as recruiting Chris Harvie, he took with him from Edinburgh Neil Wynn, a recent graduate who went on to become a distinguished Professor of American History. Neil was first employed as a research assistant and gained his PH.D from the Open University in 1973 – one of the first recipients of the degree. His work on African Americans in the US armed forces in World War II was ground-breaking.

Television and radio were certainly important for OU students, but its role tended to be over-emphasised. What mattered was the *unit* or course

---

[4] Arthur Marwick, *A History of the Modern British Isles, 1914-1999*, Oxford: Wiley-Blackwell, 2000, p.396.

booklet, together with prescribed books and document collections. Methods varied across faculties but, as far as history was concerned, Marwick placed great emphasis on *primary sources* – especially written records.

Here is a typical example of the advice given to history students at the OU:

> During the first eight weeks of this course we want you to look at these 'Revolutions' from a historian's point of view. This does not mean we are simply going to give you a list of political events and economic facts which will serve as the background to the literature, music, art, science and philosophy units which are to follow in the course. Remember history is not just a collection of undisputed facts and figures, it is a matter of interpreting and communicating such fats as we have. Certainly we want you to have some idea of what contemporaries saw in these events and how historians have understood and interpreted them so that you can go some way towards drawing your own conclusions.[5]

War and Society (A301) comprised of 12 blocks of 32 units and covered periods starting with Thucydides, the Hundred Years War, the Napoleonic Wars, War and Technology in the Nineteenth Century, World War I and its Aftermath, World War II, and War in Our Own Day. As always, the course was inter-disciplinary, but reflected Marwick's deep concern that all aspects of social history were studied. It was not concerned solely with economic and political history – in 1971, Chris wrote a fine piece on 'Rudyard Kipling: War and the Imperial Mind' as a unit for A301.

1976 saw the introduction of *The Revolutions of 1848*, a course which embraced that revolutionary year in all its aspects. Flaubert's *Sentimental Education* was a set text, and many students were introduced to the music of Verdi for the first time. Jane Rendall from the University of York contributed an exceptional essay on 'Feminism in 1848', pointing out that many of the history books of the period had scant reference to women: "Half the population of Europe has somehow escaped the historian's notice." Chris Harvie, as prolific as ever, wrote extensively on 'European Diplomacy from Revolution to the Crimean War'. There were also detailed interpretations of the writings of Karl Marx and Alexis de Tocqueville.

An aura of missionary zeal

The work-load on both central academic staff and on regional staff was considerable. Academic staff at Milton Keynes had to produce *written* lectures and tutorials, and at the same time engage in research on their subject. They produced the bulk of the course material, but often regional

---

[5] *The Revolutions of 1848* (A321), 1974.

staff made special contributions, and also specialists from the traditional universities.

Regional staff, particularly in Scotland, had a more gruelling task in that they had to travel regularly down to Milton Keynes and to far-flung areas of Scotland. I recollect that in the first few years there was a real aura of dedicated missionary zeal which embraced all staff, whether full-time or part-time. Travel by train, air, bus or car were just taken for granted by regional staff. In the space of a week, I remember, Allan Macartney, our staff tutor in social sciences, was in Barcelona, Milton Keynes and Shetland.

We all got used to this routine of going up and down to Milton Keynes: sleeper to King's Cross, then train to Milton Keynes (the old station at Bletchley) and a bus to the campus. Often arriving there about 8.30 am; then back to London in the late afternoon after a variety of meetings, in time to catch the 6 pm train to Edinburgh. November could be the cruellest month, with exam meetings held at various times throughout the month. Angus Calder once chalked up six trips to Milton Keynes in three weeks!

If the staff worked hard, the students worked even harder. Having put in a day's work, they had to find time to put in an evening or week-end of studying. Some, inevitably, dropped by the wayside, but the survival rate was high. As Peter Clarke has written:

> Mature students, women students, disadvantaged students – for many people with thwarted educational aspirations the Open University became a lifeline. It was given broadcasting facilities on BBC networks at unsocial hours, which initially served to test the devotion of its students, until the advent of cassettes and videos eased this particular rigour.[6]

By the mid-1970s, the OU was firmly established. The first degrees were awarded in 1973, and the University's expansion continued throughout the rest of the decade. By the time Chris left to go to Tübingen in 1980, its future was secure.

As Dominic Sandbrook writes in his history of the 1960s:

> Although, like Milton Keynes itself, the Open University was easily mocked, its success was indisputable. Since lectures were broadcast on television, usually late at night or early in the morning, its students were very different from the middle-class youngsters who attended other universities: there were more women, far more mature students, and more students from poor backgrounds. By the 1980s it was awarding more degrees than Oxford and Cambridge combined, and by the end of the century it was admitting more than 100,000 students a

[6] Peter Clarke, *Hope and Glory: Britain 1900-1990*, London: Allen Lane, 1996, p.290.

year and had one of the highest research ratings in the country.
It was not merely Wilson's proudest achievement; it was one of
the most popular and successful legacies of the sixties.[7]

As one of the 'pioneers' or '69ers', Chris Harvie made an impressive
contribution to the teaching of history, and all his colleagues were sorry to
see him go. He could take some pride in the fact that many of his fellow Scots
had also made the University a success – from Walter Perry, Arthur Marwick,
Neil Wynn, Ian Donnachie, Angus Calder, Gordon Brown, John P Mackintosh,
and even the arch-Tory Michael Fry!

---

[7] Dominic Sandbrook, *White Heat: A History of Britain in the Swinging Sixties*, London:
Little, Brown, 2006, p.313.

Why Scotland Matters: The Governance of Scotland's Universities

Terry Brotherstone

> [Scotland's] advantage lies not just in having ... a tradition to appeal to, but in the fact that it is a tradition with built-in democratic purchase...
>
> *Stefan Collini*[1]

I

As I write in mid-2013, there is just over a year and a quarter until the Scottish electorate will be asked to vote on whether it wants Scotland to be a 'independent country'. On the one hand, it seems to me, much of the debate so far has really been about extending devolution to a logical conclusion; and, on the other, too little of it is focused on the implications of the decision for the United Kingdom as a whole. The full-bloodied establishment of a new nation – with its own head of state, currency and other key features – is not on offer. And, in many ways, Scotland already is an independent country, having retained key social institutions – legal, religious, educational and cultural – at the Union of 1707; and having had its own domestic parliament and government since 1999. 'Independence' offers for some Scots a vision of development into a Scandinavian type social democracy; but the more the details of the transition are discussed (and the more the small northern European nations themselves change), the more complex the practicalities of such a future seem. What is certain, however, is that a 'Yes' vote in September 2014 would change the relationships amongst the four territorial units of the UK and bring greater attention to the question of how, in the world as it now is, a new political entity can act differently, free from the constraints its previous constitutional arrangements imposed.

I make these initial observations only as background to an essay that focuses on one aspect of Scotland's relationship with the rest of the UK (rUK): higher education. The system is at present highly integrated at the UK level, but also diverse both in terms of the institutions and national sub-systems it already embraces. I want to argue that the discussion currently

[1] Stefan Collini, 'The English Problem and "the Scottish Solution"', unpublished paper delivered at a conference on 'The Future he of Scottish Higher Education', organised by UCU Scotland and the University Lecturers Association of the Educational Institute of Scotland, Scottish Storytelling Centre, Edinburgh, 22 February 2011.

taking place about reforming the governance of Scotland's universities is more significant for the independence debate than is generally recognised; and also that it should be seen as part of a broader discourse about the future of universities in the UK as a whole, in which the dominant country, England, is embarked on what has been variously called (to quote only the more moderate comments) a "leap in the dark" and "the great university gamble."[2]

The essay's origins can be traced back to a talk I gave at Freudenstadt XXI in July 2011,[3] when I was anticipating my role as the Scottish Trades Union Congress (STUC)-nominated member of an advisory panel the Scottish Government had set up to review university governance and to propose reforms. The panel was chaired by Professor Ferdinand von Prondzynski, Principal of The Robert Gordon University in Aberdeen. It reported early in 2012, and its creator, Cabinet Secretary for Education and Lifelong Learning Michael Russell, presented its Report to the Holyrood parliament in the February of that year. The experience of working as part of von Prondzynski's group proved far more stimulating than I had expected. The chair – relatively new to a leading management role in a Scottish university (he had come from Dublin City University) – was interested in ideas, eager to familiarise himself with the Scottish political, cultural and intellectual scene and open to a wide range of campus opinion, not only that of his fellow senior university managers.[4] The Cabinet Secretary had provided him – certainly by recent Westminster standards, which seem based on the idea that advice about education policy is best entrusted to members of the business and financial elite – with a surprisingly representative group of colleagues (although some will very properly call in question the representativeness of five white males). Each had experience of various aspects of higher education, whether in governance, management, student affairs or staff trade unionism.

Along with von Prondzynski himself, the panel comprised Alan Simpson, then chair of the Scottish Committee of the Chairs of University Courts (governing bodies) and himself chair of court at Stirling University; Iain

---

[2] Ibid.; Andrew McGettigan, The Great University Gamble: Money, Markets and the Future of Higher Education, London, Pluto Press, 2013.

[3] My other reflections on the importance of the von Prondzynski Report have appeared as 'Why Scotland Matters: devolution, neoliberalism and the fight for the future of the public university in the UK', accessible at <andreasbieler.net/wp-content/files/Brotherstone.pdf>; 'Why History Matters: an academic trade unionist's contribution to the von Prondzynski debate', accessible at <wearenotrats.co.uk/why-history-matters-an-academic-trade-unionists-contribution-to-the-von-Prondzynski-debate>; 'Good Governance: "an idea whose time has come"', Agora: the newsletter of the Aberdeen University and College Union, 18,1 (March 2013); and 'University Governance' in the 2013 Annual Report of Aberdeen TUC.

[4] Press reports all too often imply that university opinion is synonymous with what individual principals, their collective body Universities Scotland or governing bodies think.

Macwhirter, a distinguished political commentator and (Glasgow) *Herald* columnist, at the time still the student-and-staff-elected Rector of Edinburgh University; Robin Parker, president of the National Union of Students Scotland; and a sometime president of the University and College Union Scotland and former member of the general council of the STUC – me. At the outset, I found it hard to imagine how such a group would reach agreement: in the event, however, Simpson was the only dissident, explicitly in respect of three key recommendations but also, I think, with regard to the group's approach more generally.[5]

I shall return to the recommendations, the political fate of which at the time of writing remains to be determined, and the cause for minority dissent. But if the von Prondzynski Report is to find its way, as I believe it should, into the annals of Scottish (and I would further argue, UK) intellectual and administrative affairs, its practical outcome should not be its only call on historical memory. At a recent 'think tank' introducing the work of an important Economic and Social Research Council (ESRC) Fellowship Project on 'Higher Education, the Devolution Settlement and the Referendum on Independence', it was suggested by one of the research team that higher education (HE) will not only inevitably be affected by constitutional change, but also that it is a lens through which the broader issues involved in such change can usefully be viewed.[6] That is also my standpoint, one which I think affords Scotland's universities a central role in national affairs, in line with their history, but at odds with the historically ignorant, policy-led methods of evidence-gathering that have dominated recent UK decision-making, particularly since the arrival of Thatcherite neoliberalism in the 1980s. Debate about Scottish universities must take into account the history of Scotland's distinctive educational system and their role in it: it should not be confined to the demands of global competition as defined by the various metrics that inform the increasingly baroque jargon of HE senior managers. And this debate should be a *public* debate, part of a discussion about what sort of society Scots – as they approach the independence referendum – want.

At the same ESRC Fellowship Project think tank, one educational sociologist opined that the 'no tuition fees for Scottish-domiciled students' policy, steadfastly adhered to by Scotland's First Minister Alex Salmond

---

[5] The report can be accessed at: <http://www.scotland.gov.uk/Resource/0038/00386780.pdf>. It was published on 1 February 2012. Simpson's dissenting letter is at <http://www.scotland.gov.uk/Topics/Education/UniversitiesColleges/16640/ReviewHEGovernance/RecommendationsLetter>. We were also well supported by two civil servants who played an active part in the discussions.

[6] The seminar was held at the University of Edinburgh on Tuesday 21 May: ESRC Fellowship Project, 'Higher Education, the Devolution Settlement and the Referendum on Independence', Think Tank I: 'The funding of higher education in Scotland, the UK and internationally'.

since before the 2007 Holyrood election that first brought him to office, had been reiterated in 2011 purely as a populist election slogan; and that 'globalisation', and the determination of the university employers' body, Universities Scotland, to see its member institutions remain competitors fully integrated into UK HE,[7] dictates that there will soon be 'no alternative' to students in Scotland paying for tuition as they do in England. 'No fees' in Scotland, he suggested, was a policy that had become embedded purely as a result of the 'accident' of the electoral cycle.

In 2010, it is true, Cabinet Secretary Russell was under pressure from university vice-chancellors and their allies to reinstate some form of student fee-payment. The HE bosses were campaigning to re-introduce the idea that fees were inevitable into the core assumptions underpinning Scottish political discourse. Whether or not it was regrettable, the argument went, there was no other way that universities north of the border could be financed adequately to 'compete' with HE institutions elsewhere in the UK and internationally. Russell was actively discussing the possible acceptability of a fee regime of some sort with the then Scottish president of the National Union of Students and was probably minded to go down that route.[8] It then became clear, however, that this would not be acceptable to the Scottish National Party rank-and-file, which had sensed the mood of the Scottish electorate, or to First Minister Salmond, who, in a spirit of bardic reverence, declared at the opening of a new Burns Centre in Ayrshire early in 2011 that not until "the rocks melt wi' the sun"[9] would he allow Scottish students to pay for education.

Within this 'accident' of electoral timing, therefore, a far from accidental view of social priorities was contained and, in a nowadays rare moment of progressive democratic assertion, this is what found its way into the policy process. To dismiss this as *simple* accident – and proclaim as essential truth that 'there is no alternative' to a view derived from the neoliberal doctrine that higher education is merely a positional good which should be paid for by the consumer like any other commodity – would in effect be to declare the entire independence referendum process a waste of time. If the policies that will make an independent Scotland a better or worse place to live in are allowed to be pre-determined by a neoliberal elite convinced it is in tune with

---

[7] See <http://www.universities-scotland.ac.uk/uploads/ConstitutionPaper2012final. pdf> for Universities Scotland's view of the implications of the independence referendum for HE.

[8] The radical-right views Russell expressed before he was in government – in Dennis Macleod and Michael Russell, *Grasping the Thistle: how Scotland must react to the three key challenges of the twenty first century* (Glenadaruel, Argyll Publishing, 2006) – while he clearly no longer adheres to them at least for practical purposes, suggest that he might not have seen insuperable ideological barriers to imposing individual charges for HE on students.

[9] A reference to Robert Burns's poem 'My Love is like a Red Red Rose'.

the inexorable demands of capitalist globalisation, what is the point of going to the trouble of changing the constitutional arrangements that currently underpin the process of political decision-making? The widespread idea that politics itself – as a process by which a democracy actually decides, or even influences, policy – is no longer effective would simply be transferred from one constitutional entity to another. If the independence debate is to grip the people whom it affects, it must be seen to be about real decisions about policies and institutions that matter to them. It was striking in the Scottish election of 2011 that opinion polls showed that higher education was one such institution and 'no tuition fees' one such policy. While the Scottish Government is expected to reach some conclusions about the von Prondzynski proposals at some point in the relatively near future, the Report itself has the wider potential of informing a public debate about higher education more generally.

II

Finance was not part of the von Prondzynski panel's remit: it was asked to address issues of governance.[10] The chair and the majority of his group, however, were clear that how an institution is governed is inextricably linked with how people understand the nature of that institution, its internal purposes and its role in society. A review of governance could not be simply a technical exercise – deliberating on (albeit important) matters such as the ideal size of senates (academic boards) and governing bodies. And it was the fee issue that had re-emphasised that the Scottish HE system is on a divergent course from the rUK. Since von Prondzynski reported, this has been valuably spelt out in a Higher Education Policy Institute (HEPI) report by Tony Bruce.[11] Bruce's Report, *Universities and Constitutional Change in the UK: the impact of devolution on the higher education sector*, indicates that there are four separate HE systems in the UK, with Wales and Northern Ireland as well as Scotland demonstrating different characteristics, but that Scotland is most strikingly different. As reported in the *THE Higher* – and the HEPI Report itself, though primarily a descriptive exercise, does afford justification for this – England, although its new HE policies stand out from the rest of Europe,

---

[10] The panel did conduct a snap survey on how different university governing bodies arrived at their decisions on what level of rUK fees (to be paid to their particular universities by students domiciled in the rest of the UK) to impose.

[11] Higher Education Policy Institute (HEPI), *Universities and constitutional change in the UK: the impact of devolution on the higher education sector* (2012) at <http://www.hepi.ac.uk/455-2053/Universities-and-constitutional-change-in-the-UK--the-impact-of-devolution-on-the-higher-education-sector.html>. The report, by Tony Bruce, draws attention for the first time in the official documentation to the increasing diversity of policy and experience in the component nations of the UK, with particular emphasis on the England-Scotland contrast.

is following the path of 'freedom', realism and internationally-measured 'excellence', whereas Scotland appears ready to sacrifice these priorities in the cause of social inclusion promoted through a controlling state.[12]

Putting the issue like that has the virtue of indicating that there are choices to be made about what sort of university system the Scottish (and rUK) people want, but that is not the way the von Prondzynski Report poses the choice. Universities are centres of both education and research – and essentially concerned with the relationship between the two. Affordability in a small nation will always be a factor in determining the balance to be struck, but a worthwhile university system has to fulfil both functions. And Scotland's universities, the Report asserts, are, in important ways, very successful in doing so. By the criteria university managers and governments like – league tables, ability to attract research grants, student satisfaction surveys and other such metrics – they do well and bring international prestige as well as both economic and social benefit to the nation.

But their continuing success depends on their being run in a way that sustains the morale of the academic and support staff, whose efforts are at the heart of this success. And they have to retain the confidence of Scottish taxpayers, who must fund them adequately if they are to remain, as the Report is clear they should, 'autonomous public institutions', which admit students on the basis of the Robbins principle of ability to benefit intellectually, not ability to pay, and which carry out internationally important research.[13] There cannot be a rational debate about their future that does not take this into account, and the danger of a governance regime lacking in transparency and democratic accountability is that it will be unable, over time, to continue to command either internal respect or broader democratic assent. The von Prondzynski Report therefore attempts to deal with what the majority of the panel recognised as a widely perceived 'dual democratic deficit' in university governance – its lack of fully participative internal decision-making and the opaqueness of its relationship to wider society.

It has been said that there are 'two narratives' about Scotland's universities, and the evidence submitted to the von Prondzynski panel (all available on the Scottish Government website) bears this out. There is the institutional, senior management narrative, one of success, dynamic change, distinguished institutions helping a small nation to 'punch above it weight'.

---

[12] David Matthews, 'Price of Avoiding the Market: your freedom', THE Higher, 19 April 2012, accessible at <http://www.timeshighereducation.co.uk/419670.article>.

[13] The von Prondzynski Report points out that there has been no comparable review of UK (including Scottish) HE since Lionel Robbins's historic report of 1963 and that society and access to HE has changed hugely since then. But subsequent UK inquiries have been largely pragmatic and made little effort to consider, and invite public debate on, the principles that should inform an HE system. It should also be said that, compared with the brief heyday of the Robbins era, talk of 'free' university today ignores the huge debts students are also incurring for maintenance costs.

And there is the campus staff narrative, one of overwork made more stressful by endless, and often seemingly arbitrary, 'restructuring' plans; exponentially growing salary differentials; and a sense of disenfranchisement from the decision-making process. This last development has occurred as collegial forms of governance – informed by, and informing, necessary *management* – have been replaced by regimes of more or less unaccountable *managerialism*, staffed by a growing, relatively highly-paid managerial caste, for the most part arising out of the academic community but now claiming exclusive ownership of the institutional interest.

An aside. I first heard the phrase 'two narratives' used in this context at a seminar in Aberdeen addressed by the educationalist research professor, Walter Humes. He was responding to a vice-principal who thought Humes' initial presentation had defamed university managers in a manner amounting to 'group slander'. This event entered history when it informed a subsequent edition of *The Poppletonian*, Laurie Taylor's satirical weekly contribution to *THE Higher*. "No one could possibly say that about Poppleton", Taylor had his "thrusting Director of Corporate Affairs," Jamie Targett, declare when he asked for a comment "on the recent assertion by Walter Humes ... that the new corporate culture of universities had led to the 'replacement of truth by loyalty as the prime institutional value'." Rather, Taylor's Targett explained, what had happened at Poppleton was that academics now recognised "different domains of truth" and understood

> the need to confine notions of truth to their own disciplinary domain and to leave matters of institutional truth to our highly paid managerial teams of fabricators and redactors. It would [Targett] contended, be no more appropriate for an academic to comment on the brand value of their institution "than for a meat-processing operative to comment on the nutritional value of a Big Mac."[14]

Putting satire to one side, reading through the submissions to the von Prondzynski panel from, on the one hand, governing bodies and managements, and, on the other, staff unions and individuals, it is sometimes difficult to believe they refer to the same institutions.[15] No one suggests that universities – as they faced the challenge of the belated (and largely unfunded) move in

---

[14] Laurie Taylor's *The Poppletonian* column, 'Hamburger Truths', *THE Higher*, 18 November 2010.

[15] When I spoke about the Review to the UCU Scotland Congress in Edinburgh in March, the newsletter of Glasgow Caledonian UCU reported that: "The debate on [the] current misgovernance of Scotland's universities set the tone for the rest of the congress." It underpinned delegates' anger with a system, "which, some felt, [is] not fit for purpose." As one speaker proclaimed: "Good governance is an idea whose time [has] surely come ..."

the UK to a mass HE system in the 1980s and 1990s did not need to change from forms of collegialism that sometimes seemed rooted in what for some of them was a centuries-long history, and the von Prondzynski Report is certainly not recommending putting the clock back to some mythical 'golden age'. Its proposals do, however, point to the need to re-examine critically the way university governance has been transformed over the last two or three decades without serious attention to, and debate about, what has been happening. It is striking that the transition from collegialism to managerialism is usually justified by generalised assertions about the supposed realities of the world of global capital and neoliberal political economy rather than by seriously researched argument about what is the best way of running unique institutions with a history of many centuries of contribution to knowledge and human civilisation behind them.

III

An earlier version of this essay was written specifically for an English readership and argued that more attention should be paid south of the border to the von Prondzynski Report proposals and the direction of Scottish HE policy. The Westminster government's 'gamble', in effectively privatising the bulk of university teaching by funding it through a loan-financed system of competitively determined fees, has been so dangerous to the values most academics working south of border value that their fight to defend the concept of the public university and the Robbins principle of democratic access has inevitably been all-absorbing on its own terms. But it is important that the existence within official public discourse within the UK of a policy-oriented document on HE that reflects a different trajectory from the course being followed at Westminster should be part of the wider debate. I turn therefore to how the von Prondzynski panel was formed; what its Report's main recommendations were; what the reaction to them has been; and what opportunities the Report may have created.

Behind the Scottish Government's decision to establish the von Prondzynski panel lay a number of factors. These included political and public disquiet about disputes involving university principals' relations with their governing bodies, or with academic staff and students, in a number of Scottish universities – notably but far from exclusively Glasgow and Abertay; questions being asked by more than one government minister about the performance and remuneration of some HE senior managers, with Cabinet Secretary Russell amongst those raising the question of whether principals should be paid so much more than democratically elected and responsible cabinet ministers; about Universities Scotland's demonstration of its members' remoteness from Scottish opinion in lobbying unsuccessfully for student tuition payments; and about a sustained campaign by the University and College Union (UCU) Scotland to put education unions in the forefront of public debate about the future of Scotland's universities.[16]

It is difficult to say how influential this last factor was; but the union clearly did have an impact. Ever since the devolution of higher education policy in the early 1990s (well before the referendum of 1997 that brought about political devolution), UCU Scotland, while continuing to prioritise its strictly trade-union functions, had sought a public profile in policy discussion. This process reached a new level with the 2007 Holyrood elections that resulted in the first (minority) SNP government. Rather than give in to the general labour-movement bewilderment at having lost office to 'the Nats' in 'social-democratic Scotland', UCU sought to engage the new government in discourse about what the particularly Scottish concept of 'the democratic intellect' might mean in practical terms today. Excluded from a so-called 'Task Force' – comprising only principals, the Scottish Funding Council and the Government – set by the then education minister, Fiona Hyslop, to report on the future of the universities in the light of the SNP decision to abolish graduate payments (deferred tuition fees), the Westminster move to increasing fees and the SNP Government's first (unfavourable) HE funding settlement – the union embarked on its own policy process. In addition to some effective lobbying, this included three important meetings: two Edinburgh conferences – 'Intellect and Democracy' in 2008 and 'The Future of Scottish Higher Education' in 2011 – and an open meeting with The Cabinet Secretary, now Michael Russell, in late 2010, at which a copy of the edited transcript of the 'Intellect and Democracy' conference was presented. (It was at this meeting that it became clear that Russell was at least actively considering a return to some form of individual fee-payments.)

This work bore fruit after the SNP overthrew all expectations in the May 2011 election and, benefitting from disillusion with Labour both at the UK and Scottish level and fear of the coming to office of a new aggressively neoliberal government in London, won an absolute majority. The Nationalists did this despite the proportional electoral system devised in the 1990s with the intention of ensuring that no single party (least of all the SNP) could govern alone in what was to be a single-chamber parliament. Russell – retaining his post at Education and Lifelong Learning – had now to deal, without the constraints of enforced compromise, with his party's potentially contradictory pledges not to charge students for tuition and to ensure that Scottish universities were not at a competitive disadvantage financially with institutions in the rUK; and to do so when he was clearly at odds with at least some leading principals. He made three key decisions: to take money from other areas of public spending, notably further education (which he

---

[16] For an account of the latter conference and a link to video coverage, see the UCU Scotland website at <http://www.ucu.org.uk/index.cfm?articleid=5240>, where there is also a link to the published version of the first conference ('Intellect and Democracy') submitted to the Cabinet Secretary in 2010 and to some of the papers delivered at the second ('The Future of Scottish Higher Education').

was also subjecting to a process of structural reform) to give the universities a remarkably generous financial settlement; to allow individual institutions to charge rUK students and retain maximum fees (up to £9,000 a year – making a four-year degree at the top-charging Edinburgh and St Andrews for example, at £36,000, the most expensive in the UK for non-Scottish or EU students)[17]; and, in the early weeks of the new government, to set up the von Prondzynski review panel.

Von Prondzynski, as I have indicated, interpreted his remit broadly and sought to produce a report that would invite critical debate. As far as possible within the constraints of time and resource – and also the desirability, if its recommendations were to gain Governmental assent, of achieving the greatest possible degree of consensus amongst a disparate group – the panel was invited to discuss the nature of the institutions whose governance was under review.[18] The majority of its members were clear that, however successful domestically and in terms of international reputation, Scottish universities are,[19] there is ample room for much greater 'transparency' and 'democratic' accountability, both internally within campus communities and externally with regard to the university's role in wider society.[20] A 'dual democratic deficit' needs to be addressed. My own priority in contributing to the panel's discussions was modest: to argue for changes to the decision-making process in higher education that would see a significant move away from a growing culture of *dismissive superiority* ('we note your view but we decide'!) towards one of *meaningful consultation*. In this way there could be a small, but potentially decisive, shift in the direction of travel from aggressive *managerialism* towards an understanding of *management* as the necessary facilitator of efficient collegial governance.

The Government's remit to the von Prondzynski group called on it to take evidence about current institutional governance arrangements in Scottish higher education, and report on whether they provide appropriate democratic accountability, given the level of public funding institutions

---

[17] This comes about as a result of the increasingly resented anomaly that EU students have to be treated on the same terms as their Scottish-domiciled colleagues; but that, because the relationship between Scotland and the rUK, as far as EU regulations are concerned, is an internal one *within* a single member state, it is not subject to EU rules. Should Scotland become an independent EU member, rUK fees, and the income 'elite' universities will get from them, would probably disappear.

[18] Appointed in the early summer 2011, the panel first met in late August, was scheduled to report by Christmas, and actually did so in January 2012.

[19] 'Scotland, with a population of only five million, has eight universities in the world's top 400 and five in the top 200,' is an oft-repeated mantra, dependent of course on international league-table scores. Scottish universities have also recently won disproportionately levels of funding from the UK research councils.

[20] Alan Simpson was the dissenting panel member about this as about some other matters.

received; to identify and examine proposals for change which observe the benefits of an autonomous sector while considering the importance of full transparency; to examine the effectiveness of management and governance, the clarity of strategic purpose and its efficient implementation; and to explore any other key areas thought relevant.

Amongst the Report's recommendations are:

(i)   academic freedom and institutional autonomy should be protected as core principles. It has to be recognised, however, that while in the past the two things were very closely connected, this is no longer necessarily the case: the way autonomy is managerially exercised today can actually threaten academic freedom;[21]

(ii) there should be two nominees of both staff and student unions on governing bodies and proper representation on committees;

(iii) there should be greater transparency in appointments and remuneration of senior management; and in how senior management salaries are determined, with top salary increases limited to the level of the annual rise for all staff until reform has taken place. The practicality of determining *all* salaries through the national pay framework should be seriously examined);

(iv) the chairs of governing bodies should be elected in the way that rectors, who are student (and in one case, also staff) representatives on courts, already are in five Scottish universities; they should also be modestly remunerated to help widening the social profile of those likely to be able to undertake this role

(v)   there should be a broadening of the experience of governing body members and greater transparency in appointment procedures;

(vi) there should be a serious move towards gender equality and other changes in the practice of governing bodies

---

[21] The von Prondzynski Report contains as an appendix – and as a proposed template for local negotiation in Scottish universities – a Trinity College Dublin document on academic freedom, which spells out the ways in which this core value can nowadays be threatened by institutional planning as much as by government interference.

to make their operation much more transparent and less intimidating for academic staff, student and lay members;

(vii)   senates should be more genuinely representative of staff *as a whole* and of students, and should be of a manageable size;

(viii) there should be a Scottish supervisory forum representing the university community as a whole at which general policy ideas can be exchanged amongst managements, academic team representatives, all campus unions, the Scottish Funding Council and the Government;

(ix)   a permanently updated and accessible evidence-base about the way higher education in Scotland works is needed to inform further reform;

(x)   the process of amending university regulations should be transferred from the Privy Council in London to a committee of Scottish ministers and legal figures and subjected to parliamentary scrutiny at Holyrood; and

(xi)   there should be a new Scottish higher education act, defining universities as 'autonomous public bodies' and spelling out their rights and responsibilities.

These recommendations attracted widespread staff and student support and have been adopted as policy by the Scottish TUC. "[I]f implemented in full," UCU Scotland stated, the Report "... will go some way to addressing our concerns about the breakdown of governance and the lack of accountability in decision-making in universities."[22] Cabinet Secretary Russell's statements accepting the Report and its main recommendations have been broadly positive, but not free from ambiguity, particularly with regard to some of the changes known to be unpopular with many senior managers and governors. And one recommendation – that the Scottish Funding Council should draw up a new Scottish Code of Conduct for members of university governing bodies – was diverted when the offer of the Scottish Committee of Chairs of Court to undertake this task was accepted. When their draft Code was published – with a great fanfare celebrating its supposed embrace of transparency and accountability – in April 2013, widespread disquiet was expressed at the lack of consultation with staff unions and students that had been undertaken,

---

[22] See <http://www.ucu.org.uk/index.cfm?articleid=5894> for UCU Scotland comment on the von Prondzynski Report.

and opposition to its general tenor which many thought calculated to undermine rather than fulfil the aspirations of the von Prondzynski Report.[23]

Some of the von Prondzynski recommendations (on greater pay equalisation for example) are not within the remit of the Government to implement, although legislation and Government policy could set a new framework for negotiation. (Strikingly, one of the moments annually when universities impact on the public consciousness in a negative way is when the salaries of principals are announced, and it is clear that they are now valued by university governing bodies as company CEOs rather than as senior colleagues – *primus inter pares* – amongst academic staff; and their remuneration and pension packages substantially exceed those of even the First Minister). And amongst the recommendations provoking the greatest argument are three that panel member Alan Simpson (representing the chairs of court) publicly rejected. These are: that chairs should be elected, primarily by staff and students; that there should be a modest level of remuneration and adequate administrative back-up for chairs to enable them to be drawn from any social background and to act effectively in ensuring governing bodies are well-informed and encouraged to exercise critical scrutiny over senior management; and that trade unions should be directly represented on governing bodies and thereby on key bodies such as remuneration committees.

In reality, these would be very modest reforms. The three Scottish 'ancients' (St Andrews, Glasgow and Aberdeen) and the late-sixteenth-century foundation, Edinburgh, already have student-elected 'rectors' (in the case of Edinburgh, staff also elect), who have the right to chair their courts and usually do. (Dundee – a 1960s offshoot of St Andrews – also has a rector, but without the chairing role.) The idea is simply that all universities should have such a responsible and committed figure (not necessarily called 'rector') to ensure campus confidence in how governing bodies are operating. An election every three or four years would also, in an orderly way, bring democratic attention to how universities are acting to fulfil their academic, educational and social goals.

The presence of trade unionists on governing bodies would merely be a minor modernising measure reflecting the way in which university staff are increasingly treated as employees rather than members of a collegial community. Even if that trend can be slowed or halted, developments in employment law, amongst other things, mean that it is unlikely to be entirely reversed. Most courts already have trade union members, and, although they are usually not on court as union nominees, the argument (which Simpson made) that a trade unionist is incapable of distinguishing between his or her role as a responsible court member, subject to rules of confidentiality when it is genuinely necessary for commercial, legal or data-protection reasons –

---

[23] On the draft Code of Conduct, see < http://www.scottishuniversitygovernance. ac.uk/. For the UCU critique, see, for example, <http://www.ucu.org.uk/6577>.

whereas other categories of court member are – is scarcely tenable. But the exaggeratedly hostile reaction to these minor reforms by some managements and governors is significant as it indicates a different perspective from that of most university staff on the *trajectory* of change. For the latter, it should be towards collegial accountability and meaningful consultation; for the former, it seems, towards increasing management control and the ongoing dominance of business models.

Criticism of the proposal to elect chairs has also come from an opposite direction. It is held by some to be far too limited, a mere sop to still demands for more radical, democratic reform. Why not elect principals? All court members?[24] As to the former, this was considered by the panel and put on one side, *pending further research*. It was felt that we neither had the time nor the resources to reach an evidence-based recommendation that would command sufficient consensus. It was also argued on the panel that the example of Trinity College Dublin suggests that the modern history of elections to its Provostship reveals a bias towards internal candidates, and it can be argued that this *may* not always be a good thing; and that to elect principals without also electing courts would actually enhance the authority of senior managements over governors. But further reform to develop the practice of electing senior university figures much more widely is certainly not ruled out by the von Prondzynski Report – and, in my view certainly, this should be a matter of ongoing debate, to which the Scottish Government should pay attention.

IV

A striking aspect of negative responses to the Report is that they largely ignore its historically-informed introduction. This is important if the von Prondzynski process in Scotland is to help facilitate a more serious public debate about the future of UK universities than the way the changes driven through by the current Westminster Coalition has permitted.[25] Von Prondzynski draws attention to aspects of Scottish history and tradition, which provide the

---

[24] The latter was recommended by a former employee of Universities Scotland, now of the left-leaning think-tank, the Jimmy Reid Foundation, in a striking opinion piece, Robin McAlpine, 'Our universities cannot be run like banks', *The Scotsman*, 12 July 2012. For my letter proposing that this discussion should take the von Prondzynski Report as its starting point, see the same paper on 14 July 2012.

[25] Key texts in this ongoing discourse include a number of articles by Stefan Collini, Howard Hotson and others in the *London Review of Books* (see *LRB* website, <www.lrb.co.uk>) and, of course, *The Alternative White Paper* on English Higher Education (2011), which can be accessed at <http://www.guardian.co.uk/education/interactive/2011/sep/27/higher-education-alternative-white-paper>. See, too, the work of the Council for the Defence of British Universities: <http://cdbu.org.uk/>; and the Campaign for the Public University: <http://publicuniversity.org.uk/>.

rest of the Report with an underlying rationale – a contrast to the general assumption in recent UK documents on university policy that the only context within which higher education systems should be discussed are the demands of the system of global capital and of international competition. Opponents of the general drift of the von Prondzynski Report show little sign of wanting to engage with alternative visions. They prefer to pick and choose particular proposals for de-contextualised criticism. For them, the idea that there is a 'Scottish university system' with its own history and important traditions, as opposed to a group of discrete institutions open for operation on business lines as competitive corporations, is something either to be ignored or dismissed as of no practical relevance. And this approach is very much in line with the ahistorical nihilism on which neoliberal ideology depends.

Scottish education is one of the social institutions that has been, since the Treaty of Union between England and Scotland in 1707, a key element in preserving a sense of separate identity which has survived decades of the integrative pressures of modernisation within the UK. The Union was accomplished by treaty not conquest, and Scots law, the Scottish church and the then-linked educational system and traditions of local government remained independent. At the end of the nineteenth century, the development of state education was central to the UK government's need to set up a separate Scottish department of state with a Secretary of State for Scotland, which, with the evolution of the Welfare State, became a major multi-functional administration doing most of its executive work in Edinburgh. This meant that political devolution, when it came in 1999, was a relatively simple matter of transferring democratic policy direction and scrutiny of social administration already being carried out in Scotland from Westminster to an elected parliament at Holyrood.

The Scottish universities' distinctiveness *as a system*, moreover, is not simply a matter of administration. The growth of Scottish nationalist politics in the second half of the twentieth century had, as an important element in its intellectual rationale (as opposed to its pragmatic justification and emotional appeal), the notion that the national outlook is characterised by the myth (but it is an operative myth) of 'democratic intellectualism'. First advanced by the Tory politician, Walter Elliot, in the 1930s, this idea was famously developed by the philosopher-historian George Elder Davie in the 1960s. In his *The Democratic Intellect*,[26] Davie made this the core of a study of nineteenth-century university reform that was flawed as empirical history but proved powerful as intellectual critique. The Scottish education tradition, he in effect argued, centres on relatively democratic access and

---

[26] G. E. Davie, *The Democratic Intellect: Scotland and her universities in the nineteenth century*, Edinburgh: The University Press, 1961, and *The Crisis of the Democratic Intellect*, Edinburgh: Polygon, 1986.

providing specialist scientific and professional training that is founded in basic philosophical understanding.

Actually the 'lad o' pairts' – the poor boy advancing through the system to university and the professions – though a real phenomenon, has been much exaggerated. But the idea that a university system should promote social mobility and the production of professionals with a sense both of the interconnectedness of different areas of specialist knowledge and the social purpose of acquiring higher education (and not simply employment-oriented training) remains powerful. All this helps to explain why the Scottish *National* Party's recent electoral success has depended on the support of many non- or even anti-nationalists who see its values as more effectively *social-democratic* than those of neoliberalism whether it presents itself under the banner of Thatcherism, New Labour or Coalition deficit-reduction. And, moreover, why, in the 2011 Scottish election campaign, some surveys suggested that the SNP's pledge to retain a no-fees policy in higher education was ranked the third most important issue by voters.

My point is not to examine the realities behind the 'democratic intellect', but to stress the potential significance of the existence of such a 'myth' for advancing a serious campus-wide and public resistance to neoliberalism and the demands it makes on universities. In 2011, at one of the union-sponsored conferences mentioned above – on 'The Future of Scottish Higher Education' – the intellectual historian Stefan Collini put it like this:

> South of the border the intellectual and educational case for the distinctive value of universities is poorly articulated, and as a result it is not a political force with which the government has to reckon. Instead, we get third-hand clichés about promoting economic competitiveness and training an adaptable workforce. Of course, we get a lot of that in Scotland as well, and it is obviously easy to fall into a cheap romanticisation of the 'lad o'pairts' tradition and all that. Nonetheless, [Scotland's] advantage lies not just in having such a tradition to appeal to, but in the fact that it is a tradition with built-in democratic purchase and appeal. It is very cheering – and, for an Englishman these days, all too rare – to come across a sentence in an official document that declares as roundly as the Green Paper does when discussing where the main burden of funding higher education should lie: 'The Scottish government believes that the prime responsibility should lie with the state'. I wish my Scottish colleagues every success in translating that admirable sentiment into a workable system that shows up the narrow-minded philistinism of the 'English solution' for what it is.[27]

---

[27] See Colllini, 'The English Problem and "the Scottish Solution".

I would add only that we should not wait to see if a 'workable system' does in fact emerge in Scotland. The incorporation of the reform discourse in Scotland into the campaign for the public university throughout the UK needs to take place now.

Tony Bruce's HEPI report on devolution and HE is helpful for this discussion.[28] Bruce suggests that the decision not to place the responsibility of paying tuition fees on students north of the border represents a sacrifice of 'freedom' and that the choice is between 'autonomy', dependent on making students pay, and state control. But this is not the real issue.[29] As the sociologist John Holmwood of the Campaign for the Public University has argued, in defending 'autonomy' it is nowadays important to interrogate just *how* it is exercised.[30] The important choice is not between 'freedom' dependent on market economics on the one hand and state control on the other. It is rather between, on the one hand, an autonomy that is protected by a democratic state in order to defend academic freedom and, on the other, an autonomy exercised as the means to growing commercialism, promoted by a neoliberal state and often actively destructive of academic freedom. The terms of public debate need to be reframed along these lines. It is the future of the university as a space for independent research and intellectual criticism in a democratic society that is at stake. It is in that context, above all, that the discursive space created by what Collini called a "tradition with built-in democratic purchase and appeal" – into which, in its own limited but important way, the von Prondzynski report has located itself – should be used.

V

The von Prondzynski Report, then, in my view represents one important starting point both for those who want to defend the public university and the critical values of academic freedom throughout the UK; and for everyone, whether HE is a main concern for them or not, who wants to see the independence debate become a serious discourse about what sort of society,

---

[28] See footnote 11 above.

[29] "Time was," I wrote in response to the THE *Higher* report, "when the concepts 'university autonomy' and 'academic freedom' were interchangeable: the former was necessary to protect the latter. What [the] von Prondzynski Report recognises – as do the key UNESCO statements on these matters – is that that is no longer self-evidently or unambiguously true... [For] those who sustain what is excellent about UK higher education – lecturers, researchers and support staff ... academic freedom (underpinning *critical* autonomy) is the core value of a university and they feel increasingly excluded from how the institutional autonomy that once protected it is now exercised." THE *Higher*, 26 April 2012.

[30] John Holmwood, 'With managers in charge, autonomy isn't what it used to be,' THE *Higher*, 17 May 2012.

with what sort of key institutions, is desirable, whether in an independent Scotland or in the UK as a whole. It is important, too, for those who want to see trade unions, and the education unions particularly, move beyond their defensive role to exercise influence in the discourse of higher-education policy-making. It makes immediate proposals which, if fully implemented, could at least begin to shift a trajectory that has recently proceeded in an apparently inexorable neoliberal and managerialist direction.

The Report puts into the public domain in the UK some proposals that rest on the need for universities to be public institutions, open on grounds of talent and ability, not privilege and private wealth. It defends academic freedom but, in the manner of the UNESCO statements the Report references, makes a distinction between the core principle of responsibly-exercised academic freedom and the important desideratum of institutional autonomy, which can only be justified if it is used to defend academic freedom and contribute to the democracy of society at large. It seeks, at a minimum, to restore the balance between the necessary management of complex institutions and collegial values: it is *for* good management but *against* corporate-style *managerialism*. It is in favour of replacing an encroaching culture of 'dismissive superiority' with one of 'meaningful consultation'. It proposes that future higher education policy should be informed by objective, publicly-accessible research. Above all, the Report is there to be publicly debated, in the UK, not only in Scotland, and critiqued, from the left as well as from the right. I claim no more for it than that it represents, to adapt Portia, a Scottish 'good deed' in the 'naughty world' of Thatcherite neoliberalism that has set the tone of UK political debate since the 1980s. It is far from perfect but its analysis and proposals deserve serious debate within a context in which university reform can indeed be a 'lens' through which the more general questions surrounding the UK's constitutional and political future can be instructively viewed.

'A lot done, more to do': The Impact of European Union Membership on Women in Ireland

Patricia Conlan

Introduction

1993 was the twentieth anniversary of Ireland's accession to the European Communities (ECs). It was also the year of the Freudenstadt III conference, which carried the umbrella title of 'Women's Work and Life'. Specifically, the question raised and addressed under this umbrella title was whether a regional Europe was something for women to embrace and to look forward to. Work,[1] finances,[2] female emigration[3] and making towns 'fit' for women[4] were among the sub-themes discussed under the broader title.

The early years of EC membership had been a period of change for Ireland as a whole,[5] and very much so for women in relation to their participation in economic life. Change has continued apace, and twenty years later it seems timely to address a variation on that 1993 Freudenstadt theme, namely the impact of European Community (now Union) (EU) membership on women (in Ireland), especially in relation to economic activity, specifically equal pay, with some reference to equal access to economic activity. This is a vast, multi-faceted topic, and length constraints will curtail treatment. This contribution will address five areas: first, an historical overview of European Union developments in relation to sex discrimination/gender equality; second, a brief outline of Ireland pre-accession; third, some potential influences on our subject matter; fourth, setting out some salient aspects of the interaction between EU provisions and application in Ireland, and finally, addressing the question in the title and offering a view. Official publications and a selection of secondary literature will be drawn on.

---

[1] Jane Aaron, 'Women in a Wales Without Miners', in: Eberhard Bort and Neil Evans (eds), *Networking Europe: Essays on Regionalism and Social Democracy,* Liverpool: Liverpool University Press, 2000, pp.111-128.

[2] Gotlind Braun, 'Female, Old and Poor? German Unification and the Financial Situation of Older Women: A Short Survey in 15 Figures', in: Bort and Evans (eds), pp.155-173.

[3] Patricia Conlan, 'Female Emigration from Ireland', in: Bort and Evans (eds), pp. 175-192.

[4] Beate Weber, 'Towns Fit for Women, Towns Fit for People' ,in: Bort and Evans, (eds), pp.141-154.

[5] See, *inter alia,* National Economic and Social Council (NESC), *Ireland in the European Community: performance, prospect and strategy,* No. 88: Dublin: NESC, (1989).

European (Communities, now) Union: gender equality – an overview

The European Economic Community Treaty (EECT) entered into force in 1958, just over a decade after the end of World War II. It was not surprising that it reflected the period of its birth, not least in relation to its focus and its contents. Gender equality was not a particularly prominent preoccupation at that time, nor was it shown to be in the drafting of the EECT, which built on the *Spaak Report*.[6] Examining the Preamble to the EECT gives a sense of its general purpose, *inter alia*, of "laying the foundations of an ever closer union (sic) among the peoples of Europe" and "to ensure the *economic* and *social* progress of [the] countries by common action to eliminate the barriers which [divided] Europe." The task of the Community established by the EECT was to establish a Common Market – a term used in Ireland and the UK in the early days, to refer to what is now legally the European Union. The task of the Community was also to contribute to economic development and related improvements.[7] In pursuit of the task of the Community, there was a list of activities,[8] of which only one had a stated social basis, namely the creation of a European Social Fund (ESF).[9] To find specific Treaty reference to a Social Policy, including equal pay for men and women, one has to look in the body of the EECT.[10] Of the six provisions under the heading 'Social Provisions' only one, EECT article 119 (equal pay for men and women), was mandatory in language.[11]

There was no *Treaty* reference to equal opportunities or equal treatment of men and women in matters of employment and occupation until the Treaty of Amsterdam, which amended the European Community Treaty (ECT).[12] By then, several relevant Directives had been adopted, mainly but not exclusively based on general harmonising EECT articles. A major change post Treaty of Amsterdam is the specific Treaty base for secondary legislation,

---

[6] See, *inter alia*, <http://europa.eu/about-eu/eu-history/1945-1959/1956/index_en.htm>, accessed 30 May 2013.

[7] EECT article 2.

[8] EECT article 3.

[9] EECT article 3(i). The contribution of the ESF to improving employment prospects of disadvantaged groups, including women, is acknowledged. This continues to be the case, and TFEU article 164 is the legal basis for adopting secondary legislation.

[10] EECT articles 117-122. Articles 123-128 deal with the ESF.

[11] Case 43/75 *Defrenne v Sabena* [1976] ECR 455 (*Defrenne II*), para 32, "The very wording of article 119 shows that it imposes on states a duty to bring about a specific result to be mandatorily achieved within a fixed period." Note: in some instances versions of ECR cases accessed had page numbers only, and some had paragraph numbering, hence some differences of location style used.

[12] Originally EECT article 119, subsequently ECT article 141(3) now TFEU article 157(3) – Treaty basis for adoption of secondary legislation.

now Treaty on the Functioning of the European Union (TFEU), article 157(3). The adoption of the early Directives dealing with sex discrimination, in the absence of a specific Treaty base, is an example of the political willingness to use the (general) legal means available to do so; this in itself underlines the difference in thinking and response to gender issues in the intervening period since the foundation of the European Communities. The portfolio of secondary legislation in relation to gender equality (originally referred to as sex discrimination), building on, and including specific Treaty provisions, is now considerable.[13] Of particular relevance for our topic is Directive 2006/54/EC, which repealed and replaced four earlier Directives, including those dealing with equal pay and equal treatment in all aspects of employment. These have played an enormous part in allowing women to achieve the rights conferred on them. The unique nature of the European (Communities, now) Union legal system is well established.[14] This unique legal order includes the primacy – or supremacy – of European law in those areas transferred from the national sphere to the European level, in the event of a conflict with national provisions. The Irish courts have confirmed their acceptance of this, as is well documented by Hogan and Whyte.[15] An important example of Irish judicial acceptance of the primacy of European law can be seen in a case very relevant to our topic, *Murphy v Bord Telecom Éireann*[16] – as we shall see presently.

As has been mentioned, EECT article 119 was the only mandatory article of the Treaty in the area of Social Policy. It provided for the introduction and maintenance (by the Member States) of the principle of equal pay for equal work, for men and women, within a stated period. However, its origins did not lie in a concern for gender equality, but rather in the desire to avoid competitive disadvantage. The Opinion of Advocate General Dutheillet de Lamothe, in the first of the trilogy of cases taken by Madame Gabrielle Defrenne, contributes to our understanding of the obligation on Member States, by discussing the negotiation period, prior to the drafting of the EECT.[17] EECT article 119 necessitated very lengthy negotiations.

---

[13] See <http://europa.eu/legislation_summaries/employment_and_social_policy/equality_between_men_and_women/c10161_en.htm>.

[14] Case 26/62 *NV Algemene Transport- en Expeditie Onderneming van Gend & Loos v Netherlands Inland Revenue Administration* [1963] ECR 1.

[15] For an overview of the judicial acceptance of the principle of supremacy (primacy), as well as some qualified views of the application of the principle in Ireland, see G.W. Hogan and G.F. Whyte (eds), *J.M.Kelly The Irish Constitution Fourth Edition,* Dublin: LexisNexis Butterworths (2003), p.513 et seq, pp.533-536.

[16] It is interesting to compare Case 157/86 *Murphy v Bord Telecom Éireann* [1988] ECR 673, *Murphy v Bord Telecom Éireann* (No 1) [1986] ILRM 483, and *Murphy v Bord Telecom Éireann* [1989] ILRM 53, and to see the acknowledged change in (Irish) judicial thinking, on receipt of the CJEU's ruling. See, too, Hogan and Whyte, pp.533-534.

[17] Case 80/70 *Defrenne v Belgium* [1971] ECR 445, p.455 (*Defrenne I*).

According to the Advocate General, there were few difficulties for those three (future) Member States which had ratified ILO Convention No. 100 on Equal Remuneration, as it was seen as having very much the same scope, and on certain points, the same wording as the draft (article 119). However, it must be noted that there were differences in the material scope between the ILO Convention and EECT article 119. As Landau points out,[18] article 119 spoke of "equal pay for equal work," whereas the ILO Convention refers to "remuneration for work of equal value." This important gap in material scope of the *Treaty* was subsequently addressed. It would appear that the remaining three founding Member States had not ratified the ILO Convention, due to the fact that its application risked creating very serious difficulties for them in internal law. According to the Advocate General, it was possible to reach agreement on article 119 by virtue of the double objective – namely social and economic – pursued by it. The social objective reflected the principle raised by the ILO Convention, and the economic objective was directed at deterring 'social dumping', by means of using cheaper female labour. However, it is also worth noting that the impact of equal pay on the economic viability of businesses was a long-running theme, forming very much part of the 'debate' in Ireland, as we shall see. Regarding the initial reason for the inclusion in the EECT, some commentators emphasise the economic arguments, referring to French concerns at being at a competitive disadvantage if France were to maintain equal pay for men and women, arising from its ratification of the ILO Convention, and other Member States did not adopt the same approach.[19] The Advocate General also pointed out that the economic objective allowed the achievement of one of the fundamental objectives of the Common Market, namely the establishment of a system ensuring that competition was not distorted.[20] Thus we see the economic argument for this obligation on Member States.

The first deadline indicated in EECT article 119, the end of the first stage (of the transitional period), expired on 31 December 1961. The logic of this explicit time limit was that the founding Member States were under an obligation to ensure the application of the principle of equal pay for equal work for men and women from that date. However, implementation of the obligation was delayed. Coinciding with the implementation date originally

[18] Eve C. Landau, *The rights of working women in the European Community*, Office for Official Publications of the European Communities, 1985, p.18.

[19] See, *inter alia*, Laurence W. Gormley (ed.), *P.J. Kapteyn and P. Verloren Van Themaat, Introduction to the Law of the European Communities after the coming into force of the Single European Act (second edition)*, Deventer: Kluwer, 1990, p.632. See also Olivier de Schutter, 'Anchoring the EU to the ESC: the Case for Accession', in: Gráinne de Búrca and Bruno de Witte (eds, with the assistance of Larissa Ogertschnig), *Social Rights in Europe*, Oxford, Oxford University Press, 2005, pp.111-152, p.112.

[20] Compare the focus in EECT article 3(f) (*Common Market*) with TFEU article 3(1)(b) (*Internal Market*).

indicated (from 1 January 1962), the Member States adopted a Resolution (on 30 December 1961) concerning the harmonisation of rates of pay for men and women, which was intended to provide further information concerning certain aspects of the material content of equal pay, while delaying its implementation according to a plan spread over a period of time. Interestingly, under the terms of that Resolution all discrimination, both direct and *indirect*, was to be completely eliminated by 31 December 1964.[21] Tackling indirect discrimination – which is extremely difficult to challenge successfully – has been a major contribution of the Court of Justice, not least by providing an initial definition. There is now a legislative definition of the concept,[22] which is also the definition used in the two non-gender Directives from 2000,[23] thus providing for symmetry in all areas where indirect discrimination is prohibited. The two 2000 Directives expand the personal scope of European anti-discrimination provisions beyond 'sex discrimination'. There are several views on this extension: does it weaken gender equality, or does it mainstream it? Does it recognise the 'blot' that all forms of discrimination are? At the very least, it marks a stage in the development of EU anti-discrimination protection which started in 1958. This concept has been central for Irish cases, both at national level and at European level, in areas of relevance to this topic.[24]

Despite the Resolution, when the opportunity arose, the Court of Justice made clear that the original Treaty time-limit held, as it was a Treaty obligation, and amendments to the Treaty could only be made by following the procedure laid down (in the Treaty).[25] Unfortunately, implementation continued to be delayed, despite the Commission issuing many reports and even indicating its intention to initiate proceedings (under EECT article 169, now TFEU article 258). This was not followed through.[26] What did happen, apart from Madame Defrenne's three brave actions, was that the Council adopted Directive 75/117/EEC (on equal pay), in order, it was said, to hasten the full implementation of article 119.[27]

There was a coincidence of timing between *Defrenne (II)* being received by the Court Registry, the (eventual) adoption of Directive 75/117/EEC and,

---

[21] See the Opinion of the Advocate General in *Defrenne (I)*, p.456, as well as in Case 43/75 *Defrenne v Sabena*, [1976] ECR 455 (*Defrenne (II)* paras 47-48).

[22] See, *inter alia*, Directive 2006/54/EC, article 2(2)(b).

[23] Directive 2000/43/EC (... race or ethnic origin), article 2(b) and Directive 2000/78/EC (... general framework on equal treatment ... employment/occupation –religion or belief, disability, age or sexual orientation), article 2(b).

[24] *Nathan v Bailey Gibson* ([1998] 2 IR 262 and Case C-243/95 *Hill and Stapleton v Revenue Commissioners* [1998] ECR I-3739.

[25] *Defrenne (II)* paras 57-58.

[26] *Defrenne (II)* para 51.

[27] *Defrenne (II)* para 53.

the following year, the Court's judgment in *Defrenne (II)*. The relationship between ILO Convention No. 100 and EECT article 119 was (again) confirmed by the Advocate General in *Defrenne (II)*, by which time it had been ratified by all Member States (as well as the three which acceded on 1 January 1973, including Ireland). The 1973 acceding Member States' obligation regarding equal pay was addressed in the Accession Treaty, and applicable/effective from 1 January 1973.[28] As we shall see, this generated a robust intervention in *Defrenne (II)* by the UK and Irish Governments.

The Advocate General noted that the different ratification dates of the ILO Convention resulted in differing dates from which it was applicable in the Member States, and also noted that this had no bearing on the interpretation in 'Community' law of EECT article 119.[29] It is worth bearing in mind the Advocates' General (and CJEU's) views on the obligation contained in EECT article 119 when considering the subsequent attempts by the Irish Government to seek derogations from the application of the principle of equal pay, due to fears of loss of employment. Later acceding Member States' obligation regarding equal pay is also addressed in the relevant Accession Treaties.

TFEU article 157 continues the obligation of its predecessor[30] on Member States, in relation to ensuring equal pay, but with some amendments. The subsequent amendments include the application of the principle (of equal pay) to "male and female workers" (not men and women), and not just for equal work, but also for "work of equal value". This latter wording is derived from Directive 75/117/EEC, although the Directive's additional reference to "the same work" is omitted. The original definitions of "pay" and "equal pay without discrimination" remain.

To complete the picture of gender equality measures, reference must be made to the measures adopted in the area of equal treatment in employment, including access, training and promotion, plus protection against victimisation and for the self-employed. Case law led to the legislative development of concepts such as the burden of proof in equality (gender and non-gender) claims. Changes in societal expectations as well as economic developments led to measures facilitating better work/life balance, as well as the (mainly female) 'atypical' work pattern (part-time work, for example), and protective measures for expectant and new mothers. Parental leave – albeit unpaid – is also provided for, which facilitates parental and not just maternal family commitments – an indication of changing patterns of family and work balancing of commitments.

---

[28] *Defrenne (II)* para 59. Directive 75/117/EEC is one of four Directives which have been repealed and replaced by Directive 2006/54/EC.

[29] *Defrenne (II)*, p.484.

[30] EECT article 119, which had become EC T article 141 after the entry into force of the Treaty of Amsterdam, now TFEU article 157.

Historical context – Ireland: pre-accession

General political/economic situation

The period between 1922 and 1972 (when the first Irish referendum on accession to the European Communities was held) has been described as not conducive to a change in the status of women. This view was influenced by the fact that this was a period of Civil War political divisions and ensuing lack of political consensus, of protectionism on the economic front and, on the broader political front, a policy of neutrality (during World War II), and an all too familiar pattern of emigration.[31] This was the period when women could not serve on juries,[32] when married women were domiciled in law where their husband was domiciled, regardless of their own wishes or actual location, had limited freedom of contract, could not receive the State children's allowance, and birth control was subject to a legal framework dating from 1876 to 1935 – to mention just some issues indicative of the position of women in Irish society.[33] These issues were not addressed by the legal framework arising from membership of the European Communities (now Union), but are mentioned to provide some context for the overall position of women when Ireland acceded to the European Communities and for some years afterwards. Change came in some instances due to the legal challenges mounted by brave women.[34] The 1970s were years of social and legislative change for a variety of reasons, due to a range of actors, and coinciding with accession to the ECs.[35]

Access to economic activity– participation of women:

In the early years of the last century, the majority of women worked in agriculture or domestic service, if not solely in the home. This gradually changed, although women were less numerous in the labour force than in other countries. During the years between 1926 and 1966, women gradually moved

---

[31] Richard B. Finnegan and James L. Wiles, *Women and Public Policy in Ireland, A Documentary History 1922-1997*, Dublin: Irish Academic Press, 2006, p.9; Conlan, 2000.

[32] Until 1973, only three women had served on juries – see Yvonne Scannell, 'Changing Times for Women's Rights', in: Eiléan Ní Chuilleanáin, (ed.), *Irish Women, Image and Achievement*, Dublin: Arlen House, 1985, pp.61-72, pp.62-63. In relation to applications from nine citizens to be empanelled as jurors between 1963 and 1973, of whom five were called and two of whom were challenged in court, see Mary Robinson, 'Women and the New Irish State', in: Margaret MacCurtain and Donncha Ó'Corráin, *Women in Irish Societ: The Historical Dimension*, Dublin: Arlen House, 1978, pp.58-70, p.63.

[33] See, *inter alia,* Diarmaid Ferriter, *Ambiguous Republic: Ireland in the 1970s*, London: Profile Books, 2012, p.661.

[34] *McGee v Attorney General* [1974] IR 284 and *De Búrca v Attorney General* [1976] IR 38 are two examples of individual actions achieving far reaching change.

[35] See, *inter alia,* Ferriter, Scannell for commentary on the period as well as *Report of the Commission on the Status of Women 1972*, Dublin: Stationery Office, December 1972.

out of domestic service and agriculture, and into factory (manufacturing) work. For women, this was seen as more attractive (than domestic service), and as for employers – they saw the benefits of paying lower wages (than to men).[36] The attraction of female workers for employers – including new foreign firms, availing of the change in industrial policy – of lower pay for female workers has been documented.[37] Ann Wickham was of the view that, historically, commentators on the role of women in the labour market in Ireland have tended to concentrate on their overall participation rate (low), rather than on the changes in occupation, thereby allowing the importance of women in this regard to be underestimated.[38] Over time, women did participate in greater numbers in the nursing and teaching professions, forming the majority in fact. It is noticeable that these professions are often identified as 'caring' and 'vocations', thus matching the stereotypical role attributed to women, and attracting lower remuneration than many less challenging and responsible jobs. A key factor in low rates of pay is where the employment is segregated.

Changing employment opportunities also led to increased female membership of trade unions. Given the status of women (in general), it is interesting to note that three officials of the Irish Women Workers Union became presidents of the Irish Trade Union Congress.[39] Mary Daly records many of the achievements of the women trade unionists, affecting not just women, but workers in general.[40] However, the low participation of women in certain occupations did continue even over time, and several reasons were advanced to explain this phenomenon. These included denial of access to certain skilled occupations and professions and fewer women pursuing third level education, in particular in the science and technology areas.[41] It also has to be remembered that trade unions – including the Irish Women Workers Union – were not supportive of women working outside the home, or even to their employment at all, given the impact on male employment (or male unemployment). In fact, there was actual hostility to the employment of women, who were seen as taking male jobs. Daly tells us that a (woman) member of the Tailors and Garment Workers Union wanted to request the Minister for Industry and Commerce (in 1942) to bar women

---

[36] Ann Wickham, 'Women, Industrial Transition and Training Policy in the Republic of Ireland', in: Mary Kelly, Liam O'Dowd and James Wickham (eds), Power, Conflict and Inequality: Studies in Irish Society, Dublin: Turoe Press, 1982, pp.147-158, pp.148-149.

[37] Wickham, pp.151-152, in referring to studies carried out.

[38] Wickham, p.147.

[39] Mary E. Daly, 'Women, Work and Trade Unionism', in: Margaret MacCurtain and Ó'Corráin (eds), pp.71-81, pp.72-73.

[40] Daly, pp.74-75.

[41] John Blackwell,'Government, Economy and Society', in: Frank Litton (ed.), Unequal Achievement: The Irish Experience, 1957-1982, Dublin: Institute of Public Administration, 1982, pp.43-60, p.49.

from major areas of the tailoring trade. The Minister declined, but there were several subsequent similar resolutions proposed at Congress sessions. Daly comments further – with some diffidence – that it is difficult to pinpoint many instances where the trade union movement contributed to removing discrimination against women workers. She emphasises that this assessment has to be understood in the context of the period.[42] However, the attitude to women workers in what was seen as 'male employment' lingered for quite some time, as case law shows.[43]

Writing in the early 1980s, some commentators noted the change in the role of women over the previous twenty-five years as being one of the striking features of that period, and, equally so, the resistance to that change. Up to the early 1970s, there was wide acceptance that the prime role of women was in the home, we are told.[44] Bearing in mind Wickham's exhortation not to overlook those sectors where women were actually active in the labour market, while looking to the labour force in general, we see that this increased by 1.6 per cent a year in the period 1971-1979, including an increase in the female labour force of 2.2 per cent a year.[45] More specifically, two years *before* the 1973 accession to the European Communities, that is, in 1971, the participation rate of married women was 7.5 per cent, and within four years of accession this had almost doubled to 14.4 per cent.[46] The reason for the low participation rate of married women in the labour force has been linked to the marriage bar, which has been referred to above. This was a clear barrier to equal access to economic activity, and would have been contrary to the provisions of Directive 76/207/EEC on equal treatment in employment (access, conditions, promotion etc.) when eventually it entered into force.

The 'marriage bar' or 'marriage ban' was a well developed phenomenon in the years prior to Ireland's accession to the European Communities. We have already referred to the wide acceptance up to the early 1970s that the prime role of women was in the home. The existence and application of the 'marriage bar' has been described as exemplifying this attitude.[47] While, from a legislative point of view, this was a public sector regulation, the *practical* effects were that in many private sector employment women were at the very least 'expected' to leave on marriage, if indeed not required to do so. This would have been particularly the case for major employers. This is one of the most striking changes in the 40 years of membership, providing as it did for the wasted potential of women to contribute to society.

---

[42] Daly, p.75.

[43] See, *inter alia*, *Murtagh Properties v Cleary* [1972] IR 330 and *Nathan v Bailey Gibson* ([1998] 2 IR 262.

[44] Blackwell, pp.49-50.

[45] Blackwell, p.48.

[46] *Ibid.*

[47] Blackwell, p.49.

Historically, not only had there not been trade union support for the removal of the marriage bar, but there had been active opposition to its removal – including from the Irish Women Workers Union; it was seen as a blight on society, affecting men's employment. Until the 1960s, restrictions increased on married women working outside the home. The Irish National Teachers Organisation (INTO), a trade union traditionally with a majority of women members, having opposed a marriage bar, accepted it, on condition that existing teachers were exempted.[48] This reflected what is now called a lack of inter-generational solidarity. The marriage bar was removed for teachers in 1958, and within the wider public sector on 31 July 1973, *seven months after accession* to the European Communities. According to Eunice McCarthy, many large (private sector) organisations followed this example and removed the *practice* of having women resign on marriage.[49]

Pay levels

We have seen that women tended to be found in segregated employment, with low pay. This phenomenon is recognised as a major barrier to women's economic advancement – world-wide. The EC approach, by providing for equal pay for equal work, work of equal value, facilitates acknowledgement of the value of women's work, and appropriate levels.[50] The first equal pay resolutions were proposed at the 1917 Conference of the Irish Trade Union Congress, but Daly is of the view that, until the 1960s, the commitment to this was questionable.[51] The reasons for this may be found in the general Irish public – as well as official – opinion to these issues, and the emphasis on the 'family income', that is: the income of the married man. An example of the thinking of the time can be seen in the support of the Irish Women Workers Union for an equal pay resolution at the 1953 Congress, but at the same time, the wish was expressed to debar young married women and single girls from equal pay.[52]

Against this background of the lack of support for equal pay, even among women, and more specifically among women trade unionists, it is hardly surprising that equal pay for men and women has had a long journey. As regards some examples of actual pay levels in the period prior to accession to the European Communities, there is considerable literature addressing the unequal pay levels between men and women workers from the early

---

[48] Daly, pp.75-77.

[49] Eunice McCarthy, 'Women and Work in Ireland: the Present, and Preparing for the Future', in: MacCurtain and Ó'Corráin (eds), pp.103-117, pp.104-105.

[50] As an example of the contribution of the CJEU to ensuring the principle of equal pay (also for work of higher value) see, *inter alia*, Case 157/86 *Murphy v Bord Telecom Éireann* [1988] ECR 673.

[51] Daly, p.76.

[52] Daly, pp.76-77.

years of the new State.[53] As one example, drawing on the First Report of the Commission on the Status of Women,[54] Finnegan and Wiles tell us that the Commission was not supplied with comprehensive data on income levels for men and women. However, quarterly data for the industrial sector and other sources, such as from parts of the 'distributive trades', services and the public sector, did give an insight into pay levels. For example, in September 1970, 90 per cent of women industrial workers earned less than IR£16, while 90 per cent of men earned more that this. In March 1972 (a couple of months *before* the referendum on accession to the European Communities) women industrial workers had hourly earnings averaging 57 per cent of men's earnings. In the distributive trades and in the civil service, women's earnings were about 75-85 per cent of men's wages.

Daly does point out that the most significant change during the 1960s was the growing concern on the part of the trade union movement with concrete issues of women's pay and conditions, rather than generalities. Resulting from this, a degree of equal pay was achieved in certain areas of the public sector (semi-state companies).[55] This has to be seen against the background of actual hostility to female employment and the concept of equal pay – even from women, and indeed from women trade unionists, as we have noted.

According to Finnegan and Wiles, when the Commission on the Status of Women looked at the causes of unequal pay, a mix of reasons was cited. On the one hand, the narrow range of occupations where women were employed, matched by lower levels of skill and responsibility – which we have already identified as being the case – seemed to be an obvious reason. However, even where women were engaged in work which was the same or similar to that being performed by men, there were also instances of unequal pay. At a remove of 40 years, the explanations considered by the Commission for this pay inequality give a strong impression of how far attitudes have changed in the interim. These included:

- Tradition and social attitudes;
- Age (women being generally younger) and consequently less experienced than men;
- Greater cost for the employer due to higher turnover and absentee rates;
- Legal restrictions on the employment of women, rendering them less useful to the employer;
- Women's lesser physical strength and, consequently, women

---

[53] See, *inter alia*, Finnegan and Wiles, McCarthy, Daly.

[54] *Report of the Commission on the Status of Women 1972*, Dublin: Stationery Office, December 1972.

[55] Daly, p.79.

unable to carry out the heavier tasks;
*   The position of women in trade union organisation leaving them open to exploitation.[56]

The hostility to equal pay, which has been touched on above, must also be taken into account. In other words, it was a big task to change the mindset as well as the economic impact of the introduction of gender equality in the workplace.

Impetus for change – potential?

International

The adoption of the International Labour Organisation's Convention No. 100 on Equal Remuneration was an important world-wide landmark for tackling the issue of equal pay for men and women. As we have seen, this Convention was important for the development of the *principle* of equal pay as expressed, initially in EECT article 119, and subsequently in Directive 75/117/EEC, now TFEU article 157 and Directive 2006/54/EC. Ireland was the last of the first nine Member States to ratify it, on 18 December, 1974.[57] Belgium had ratified it in 1952, Denmark in 1960, and the UK had done so in June 1971 – prior to accession but, interestingly, at the same time as the Netherlands, which was one of the founding Member States. The other four founding member states had ratified prior to the entry into force of the EEC Treaty. We can see from this scattered pattern of ratification that the Convention caused some Member States some concern, as the Advocate General in *Defrenne (I)* had indicated.

Article 1(a) defines the term **remuneration** as including the ordinary, basic or minimum wage or salary and any additional emoluments whatsoever payable directly or indirectly, whether in cash or in kind, by the employer to the worker and arising out of the worker's employment. Article 1 (b) clarifies the term **equal remuneration for men and women workers for work of equal value** as referring to rates of remuneration established without discrimination based on sex. Extending the material scope to 'work of equal value' rather than confining it to 'equal work' allows for the monolith of segregated employment to be breached.

Taking the delayed ratification by Ireland, until post accession, it cannot be said that the ILO Convention represented a direct impetus for change in Ireland, but it clearly was, indirectly, given its relevance for EECT article 119.

At the regional (Council of Europe) level, the European Social Charter (ESC61) of 18 October 1961 provided for signatories to be bound by a range of

---

[56] Finnegan and Wiles, pp.10-25.

[57] <http://www.ilo.org/dyn/normlex/en/f?p=1000:11200:0::NO::P11200_COUNTRY_ID:102901>, accessed 17 April 2013.

rights for individuals including, *inter alia,* equal pay. Ireland ratified the ESC61 on 7 October 1964, and it came into force on 26 February 1965. The revised European Social Charter (RESC) was ratified by Ireland on 4 November 2000. It is worth remembering that Ireland was one of the founding members of the Council of Europe.

Among the (ESC61) provisions not accepted by Ireland was the provision on equal pay.[58] When the Department of Labour, which was the then responsible Department, was asked to clarify why this provision had not been among the list of obligations accepted, the response was to the effect "that the right of men and women to equal pay for equal work was not a recognised concept in Ireland."[59] Ireland subsequently accepted this provision, as now included in RESC.[60] This acceptance, of course, was post-accession to the European Communities.

An assessment of the impact of the ESC61 on Irish labour law, including equal pay and equal access to economic activity, concluded that its impact had been slight – if at all.[61]

National: Trade Union

The issue of equal pay was raised in a number of fora over a period of years, prior to accession to the European Communities. We have touched on some of the developments within the trade union movement, over the years, and the change to be discerned in its support at the end of the 1960s. According to Daly, there was what she described as an 'initial flurry' of Equal Pay Resolutions (in Congress) inspired by the ILO Convention, but this lapsed – due in no small part to emigration and general economic stagnation. It could not be said to have been a welcoming atmosphere in which to pursue gender equality. The period to the end of the 1960s did see some activity within the Trades Union movement in relation to equal pay. However, eventually the output from the Committee on Equal Pay which had been established, was

---

[58] Article 4 paragraph 3, *"With a view to ensuring the effective exercise of the right to a fair remuneration, the Contracting Parties undertake to recognise the right of men and women workers to equal pay for equal work; exercise of these rights shall be achieved by freely concluded collective agreements, by statutory wage-fixing machinery, or by other means appropriate to national conditions."* The 1961 wording is repeated in the 1996 revised version of the European Social Charter.

[59] Culled in brief from the files of the Department of Industry and Commerce then responsible for labour matters, see Patricia Conlan, 'Ireland', in A.Ph.C.M. Jaspers and L. Betten (eds), *25 Years European Social Charter,* Deventer: Kluwer, 1988, pp.53-80, p.64. See, too, Patricia Conlan, *The European Social Charter – Implementation of international economic and social rights: Ireland,* unpublished LL.M dissertation, NUI Galway, 1985, pp.105-108.

[60] <http://www.coe.int/t/dghl/monitoring/socialcharter/CountryFactsheets/Ireland_en.pdf>, accessed 21 May 2013.

[61] Conlan, 1985 and 1988.

merged into the Congress submission to the Commission on the Status of Women. It was, one might say, a missed opportunity for the Trade Union movement to show leadership in this area. However, given the views of the general population on the subject of gender equality, it was perhaps a leap too far to expect.

According to von Prondzynski and McCarthy, it would not be true to say that all the impetus (for change) came from abroad. They instanced the submission of a memorandum prepared by the Public Services Industrial Committee of the Irish Congress, following which the Executive Council decided to set up an Equal Pay Committee to prepare a report on the matter. They say that this marked a fairly intensive campaign by the ICTU to secure equal pay for women. [62] However, as we have seen, Daly sounds a less positive note on the ICTU development. She points out that the Equal Pay Committee never actually reported to Congress. There would appear to have been a delay, for a variety of reasons, which in her opinion indicated that it had been given a relatively low priority.[63] Daly does concede that, despite the non-appearance of a report, it did considerably increase interest in women's issues, and in 1969 Congress requested the Minister for Labour to set up a permanent consultative body to consider the problems of women at work.[64]

Political initiatives of a sort

An early proposal for addressing the question of equal pay had been included in the Interim Report of the Committee on the Constitution. This informal Committee had been set up in August 1966, following agreement between the three political parties in the Dáil.[65] An interesting aspect of this informal agreement was that the Committee functioned in a non-prescriptive manner. For example, participation in the Committee did not automatically indicate acceptance (by the parties) of whatever recommendations emerged. In the event, the Report, published in 1967, recommended that *Bunreacht na hÉireann*, Article 45, *Directive of Public Policy*,[66] in setting out the directive principles of social policy should include a provision establishing the principle of equal pay for men and women for work of equal value.

There was a further development of relevance to our topic, a short while

---

[62] Ferdinand von Prondzynski and Charles McCarthy, *Employment Law*, London: Sweet and Maxwell, 1984, p.83.

[63] Daly, pp.78-79.

[64] Daly, p.79.

[65] Finnegan and Wiles, p.21.

[66] For a discussion on *Bunreacht na hÉireann*, Article 45 and its judicial interpretation as well as reports of the Constitutional Review Groups 1966 and 1996, see Hogan and Whyte, pp.2077-2086.

later, in September 1966. Jack Lynch, T.D., Minister for Finance, established a group to examine and report on the organisation of the Departments (of State = ministries) at the higher levels. This group, known formally as the Public Services Organisation Review Group, reported in 1969 to the then Minister for Finance, Charles J. Haughey, T.D. The Report (known informally as the Devlin Report, drawing on the name of its Chairman, Liam St. John Devlin), made reference to the practices of pay differentiation – sex and civil status based – in the civil service. The question was raised as to what might happen if Ireland were to join the European Communities, as such practices – or at least sex discrimination – would be contrary to the EEC Treaty. The recommendation was that a full examination of the problems should be made, "in the *hope* that a solution, possibly on a *phased basis*, might be found."[67] The tentativeness of the recommendation raises the question as to how deeply sex (and civil status) equality in the workplace was seen as an ill to be addressed by the authorities. It should be remembered that civil status and not just gender differences, was a factor in unequal pay (and access to economic activity) in Ireland in the period under review. The Group did see that a solution to this 'problem' could be helpful in attracting and retaining highly qualified staff. Given the paucity of women at the higher levels,[68] could one infer that that hope related to attracting and retaining highly qualified 'female' staff?

The Minister for Labour commissioned the Economic and Social Research Institute (ESRI) in 1968 to carry out a survey of views on income differentials and income increases. This was meant to provide material for an assessment of prevailing attitudes to questions of pay and their bearing on the development of an incomes policy. The results were published in August 1970. All those surveyed were male. The survey questions were nuanced and, due to length constraints, will not be elaborated here,[69] but for our purposes it is sufficient to point out that the overwhelming majority felt that married men should have a higher pay rate than a married woman, and that a single man should have a higher rate than a single woman. Only 5.4 per cent considered that each of the categories should have the same minimum rate.

Civil Society

The role of civil society, especially women's organisations such as the long established Irish Housewives' Association, the Association of Business and Professional Women, the National Association of Widows (to mention just a few), as well as the newer Irish Women's Liberation Movement and similar

---

[67] Finnegan and Wiles, p.21.

[68] See, *inter alia*, Joy Rudd, 'On the margins of the Power Élite; Women in the Upper Echelons" in: Kelly, O'Dowd and Wickham, pp.159-170, p.162 (Table 2).

[69] See para 63 of the First Report. Finnegan and Wiles, pp.22-25.

groups, was unquestionably important in raising the issue of sex equality, in general and in the workplace. Some groups had come together to form an *ad hoc* committee to press for women's rights in 1968, and in 1969 Taoiseach Jack Lynch announced the establishment of the Commission on the Status of Women.[70]

As set out earlier, the position of women in Irish society in the years post Independence, up to and including accession to the European Communities, was one of inequality in many areas of life, especially that of married women. Robinson comments on other forces which were accelerating the change in Irish society in the period under review. She refers to voluntary organisations such as AIM, ADAPT and Cherish, which were seeking reform in various social areas.[71] In other words, equal pay and equal access to economic activity were just two of the myriad of social inequalities which were tackled thanks to voluntary engagement at that time.

Commission on the Status of Women, 1970

The Commission on the Status of Women was established by the Government on 31 March 1970. Its terms of reference gave it a wide brief, with some aspects of specific relevance to our topic.[72] Robinson tells us that "so great was the pressure on the specific issue of equal pay that the Commission brought in an Interim Report on Equal Pay, published in October 1971".[73] The First Report of the Commission was presented in 1972 to the Minister for Finance, and published in 1973, and it included a list of recommendations for the Government. A key recommendation in the First Report was that a policy of equal pay be followed. This was further qualified by setting out, *inter alia,* the circumstances in which equal pay should apply, how disputes should be settled, how equality of treatment between men and women should apply in a given situation, and that legislation should be enacted to ensure effective implementation of equal pay. The Second Report of the Commission on the Status of Women, presented in January 1993, reviewed this list of recommendations and came to the view that they had, to all intents and purposes, been implemented.[74] Perhaps more appropriately to note a 'lot done, more to do'.

[70] Ferriter, p.659. For a wider analysis of the period and the contributions of individuals and organisations, see further pp.656-679.

[71] Robinson, p.67.

[72] "To examine and report on the status of women in Irish society, to make recommendations on the steps necessary to ensure the participation of women on equal terms and conditions with men in the political, social, cultural and economic life of the country and to indicate the implications generally – including the estimated cost – of such recommendations."

[73] Robinson, p.65. See Commission on the Status of Women, Interim Report on Equal Pay, presented to the Minister for Finance August 1972 (Prl. 1959).

[74] Second Report, p.365.

Pre-accession: Political comment and proposed action

Given, not least, the setting up of the Commission on the Status of Women, it is clear that political attention had been drawn to the need for change in relation to women. In his Budget speech for 1972, the then Minister for Finance, George Colley T.D., had included reference to two areas of particular relevance to our topic.[75] He had characterised these as 'important'. The first of these was equal pay for women, which the Government accepted in principle and which it affirmed as a national aim. The language could be described as nuanced (accepted 'in principle'); on the other hand, to refer to equal pay as a 'national aim' raised it above a mere platitude. The second area raised related to efficiency in the public service. This would be a consequence of the introduction of equal pay, as extra costs for the public service would ensue. The Minister made reference to the First Report of the Commission on the Status of Women from 1972, and its recommendations on the subject. The setting up of a new Department of the Public Sector was meant to play a role in bringing about efficiencies. Interestingly, the Minister went on in his speech to make reference to the Report of the Public Services Organisation Review Group, which emphasised the great responsibility of the Government to select the right *men* for the top posts in the new Department. The Government had recognised this by the exceptional arrangement whereby two of the three posts of Deputy Secretary in the new Department were filled by a competition 'open to all comers'. Given the gender imbalance in the public service, and particularly at the highest level,[76] this reference to 'all comers' must be understood as 'all interested men'. He noted that the Employer-Labour Conference had arranged that the working party established to negotiate on pay, with a view to reaching a new National Agreement, would take the recommendations of the Commission into account in these negotiations. Legislation to provide for the phasing in of what emerged was to be enacted. This *seemed* to knit all efforts towards equal pay seamlessly together.

It was also intended to consider the question of the ending of restrictions on the employment of women which, by excluding them from equal work with men, were an automatic barrier to equal pay. Restrictions on married women, the so-called 'marriage bar' in the public service, both statutory and non-statutory, were to be examined, and removed/repealed as appropriate. As we have noted, the 'marriage bar' operated 'in practice' in the private sector.[77]

The Budget speech was on 17 April 1972, and the referendum on accession to the European Communities took place on 10 May 1972. Was there perhaps a coincidence of timing with this expression of the importance of the topic?

[75] *Dáil Debates* Vol. 260 No. 4 Col. 577-578, 19 April 1972.

[76] See, *inter alia*, Rudd, p.162, Table 2.

[77] McCarthy, p.104.

Early judicial interpretation of constitutional right to livelihood

Bunreacht na hÉireann contains a number of Fundamental Rights which, over the course of time, through judicial interpretation, have confirmed and protected individual rights. These are to be found in articles 40-44. In addition, article 45 of the *Bunreacht*, entitled 'Directive Principles of Social Policy', although largely ignored in the early years of the Constitution, and in fact seen as being outside the range of judicial consideration, did in time come to be used as an 'aid' to interpretation.[78] Coincidentally, it would seem to have been influential in relation to the Constitutions of other former British colonies.[79] It is worth noting that the activist period of judicial interpretation of the 1937 *Bunreacht* was most marked when post-independence educated members of the Bench were nominated to the higher courts, especially the Supreme Court. This was especially the case in relation to those Fundamental Rights articles of the *Bunreacht*. In *Murtagh Properties v Cleary,*[80] by coincidence from 1972, trade union members objected to the employment of women bar tenders. This was at a time when women were not 'welcome' in bars, and societal norms would have reflected this. Scannell points out that while the court confirmed that "article 40.3 of the *Bunreacht* included the right of women to an adequate means of livelihood and that, consequently, a policy or general rule under which anyone seeks to prevent an employer from employing men or women on the ground of sex only is prohibited by the Constitution",[81] this was a limited interpretation. The court said that the guarantee in article 40.1 "had nothing to do with the trading activities of citizens or the conditions under which they are employed." She was of the view that the court in its judgment had virtually closed off the possibility of pursuing (successfully) a claim for equal pay for equal work through constitutional action.[82] This was because the court had specifically held that, concerning the right to earn an adequate means of livelihood, differences in salary would not be unconstitutional. Certainly, one can agree that it was a case of one step forward and two steps back, where one might have hoped to build on the confirmation of a constitutional right to earn an adequate living. What one can welcome in *Murtagh Properties v Cleary* is a clearer judicial attitude to article 45. It was held that, while the courts may have no jurisdiction to consider the application of the principles in the making of laws, this did not involve the conclusion that the courts may not take the article into consideration when deciding whether a claimed constitution right exists.[83]

[78] Hogan and Whyte, p.2079.

[79] Hogan and Whyte, pp.2078-2079.

[80] [1972] IR 330.

[81] Scannell, pp.61-72, p.62.

[82] Scannell, p.64.

[83] Hogan and Whyte, p.1425 – referring to Kenny J., at [1972] IR 330, 336.

Robinson[84] had noted the lack of litigation by women's organisations in pursuit of equality, being of the view that it usually plays an important part in any campaign for minority (sic) rights. Perhaps the financial aspect of such a step played a role? Or could it have had to do with the then predominantly male legal profession, including the Bench?[85] She welcomed the *Murtagh* case as an example of how potent a test case can be,[86] although, as we have seen, Scannell was less enthusiastic about the judicial views expressed in the *Murtagh*.[87]

European Union – impact of membership on women in Ireland?

Taking two of the institutions of the European Union which have had direct impact on (working) women in Ireland, we can offer some examples of the impact of membership of the European (Communities, now) Union on them. Looking first at the European Commission, there was an early intervention in relation to the planned Government derogation from the equal pay provisions. The Anti-Discrimination Pay Act, 1974 had been piloted through the *Oireachtas* by the Minister for Labour. At the same time, Ferriter tells us of the considerable lobbying against its provisions, because of the perceived impact on the economy and the financial viability of enterprises.[88] The Anti-Discrimination Pay (Amendment) Bill, 1975 was introduced with the purpose of amending the 1974 Act in this light. According to the Minister for Labour, the proposals addressed a situation where *employees* in an undertaking were convinced that job losses would be a consequence of the implementation of the 1974 Act. Arising from this assessment by employees, those employees could decide on their own phasing in of the relevant provisions, subject to a time limit of two years.[89] Relying on EECT 135, the Irish Government had sought what the Minister described as "limited derogation" from Directive 75/117/EEC. However, this request was rejected by the European Commission where, by an irony of fate, the relevant Commissioner was a former Government minister, a member the then Opposition Party. As a result, the Anti-Discrimination Pay (Amendment) Bill, 1975 fell, and the 1974 Act came into force.

The CJEU also had an early intervention in relation to equal pay, and one can see a thin line being followed in its judgment in *Defrenne (II)*. It will be noted that the 1974 Act of 1 July 1974 pre-dated the adoption of Directive 75/117/EEC

[84] Robinson, p.67.

[85] See Rudd, p.161, where she points out that, in 1981, of the 80 members of the judiciary, four were women. This imbalance has been addressed in the intervening years. In 2013, the four most senior lawyers in the State are women (Chief Justice, Attorney General, Director of Public Prosecutions and Chief State Solicitor).

[86] Robinson, p.67.

[87] Scannell, p.54.

[88] Ferriter, pp.669-670.

[89] *Dáil Debates*, Vol. 290 No. 5, Col. 688-693, 5 May 1976.

on 10 February 1975, and its transposition deadline (31 December 1975) came between the judgments in *Defrenne (I)* and *Defrenne (II)*. The United Kingdom and Irish Governments took the opportunity to intervene in *Defrenne (II)*. The timing of this action could be described as taking swift advantage to use the opportunities presented by accession to try to re-balance the 'burdens' arising from accession. More specifically, the realisation that the Accession Treaty provided for application of the principle of equal pay from 1 January 1973 prompted the Irish Government to set out counter arguments. These included not just financial burdens for Irish employers, which they might not be able to bear, but for the Irish State it would mean that according equal pay to State employees from that date would exceed the entire allocation to Ireland from the Community's Regional Fund for the period 1975-1977.[90] The Irish Government also took the opportunity to indicate that the Anti-Discrimination Act, 1974 came into force on 31 December 1975.[91] However, as we have seen, there had been an attempt to defer this, thwarted only by the reaction of the European Commission.

In its judgment, the CJEU took cognisance of the lack of enforcement action by the European Commission to ensure that the obligation inherent in EECT article 119 had been achieved by the founding Member States within the deadline set (in the EECT) and the ensuing lack of knowledge amongst employers and workers alike of the issues surrounding equal pay, led to a lack of legal certainty. In other words, employers had not been in a position to prepare for the obligations now to be imposed. The financial implications for employers arising from this obligation, if equal pay were to apply retrospectively to the EECT article 119 deadline for the six founding Member States (and for the UK and Ireland – and Denmark - from the date of accession), were emphasised to the CJEU. Put briefly, retrospective application would not apply, but prospective application of the principle of equal pay was confirmed, unless a claimant had initiated an action.

In a more direct way, the CJEU has contributed in no small way to ensuring equality for women in the workplace. Women have sought preliminary rulings from the CJEU, which has allowed them to pursue rights conferred by the European Communities' Treaties (and ensuing secondary legislation). By coincidence – or is it? – the State as employer has been the respondent in many of these cases. Some examples of referrals will be offered here. An early and important example of the benefits of the preliminary ruling procedure, and the teleological approach taken by the CJEU can be seen in *Murphy v Bord Telecom Éireann*,[92] which has been mentioned above. The different interpretative approaches taken by the High Court and by the CJEU were commented on by Keane.[93] Had Ms Murphy not had the possibility to

---

[90] *Defrenne (II)*, p.461.

[91] *Defrenne (II)*, p.462.

[92] Case 157/86 *Murphy v Bord Telecom Éireann* [1988] ECR 673.

[93] See Hogan and Whyte (eds), pp.533-534.

seek a preliminary ruling, she would have been doomed to receive lower pay for work of higher value, due to the different approaches to statutory interpretation between the national court and the CJEU.

Indirect discrimination is a particularly insidious practice and difficult to pursue successfully, due to lack of obvious proof. The CJEU developed this in the first instance, as we have indicated above, and there is now a legislative definition. This concept has allowed a number of preliminary rulings from Ireland to protect the rights of the women workers involved – usually arising in the public sector, and affecting considerable numbers of women. One case was that of Ms Hill and Ms Stapelton, who worked on job-sharing, and then returned to full time employment, but who were disadvantaged on the pay scale, as a result.[94] The overwhelming numbers of colleagues in their position were women. The CJEU held that the EECT article 119 and Directive 75/117/EEC precluded (national measures):

> where a much higher percentage of female workers than male workers are engaged in job-sharing, job-sharers who convert to full-time employment are given a point on the pay scale applicable to full-time staff which is lower than that which those workers previously occupied on the pay scale applicable to job-sharing staff due to the fact that the employer has applied the criterion of service calculated by the actual length of time worked in a post, unless such legislation can be justified by objective criteria unrelated to any discrimination on grounds of sex.

As the two women were in a predominantly female employment, their situation met the definition of indirect discrimination as set out by the CJEU.

A recent case again addressed the issue of indirect discrimination between civilian (mainly women) clerical workers and uniformed members of An Garda Síochána (mainly men) who undertook clerical tasks.[95] Interestingly, the CJEU was prepared to allow the "interests of good industrial relations" be taken into consideration by the national court as one factor among others, in its assessment of whether the burden of proof on the employer in relation to the grounds for the pay differences had been discharged. However, the CJEU also repeated the established steps in relation to providing objective justification for these differences. It remains to be seen how the national court will implement this interpretation from the CJEU.

It is well-established that women comprise the majority of workers falling into the 'atypical work' category, that is outside the 'regular' pattern

---

[94] Case C-243/95 Kathleen Hill and Ann Stapleton v The Revenue Commissioners and Department of Finance [1998] ECR I-3739.

[95] Case C-427/11 Margaret Kenny et al v Minister for Justice, Equality and Law Reform, Minister for Finance, Commissioner of An Garda Síochána, (28 February 2013 nyr).

of working time. This can be very suitable for both parties – workers with family responsibilities and employers with troughs and peaks. However, atypical work can be open to abuse, and to prevent abuse through the use of successive fixed-term contracts, Directive 1999/70/EC was adopted to set down a framework to apply to this form of work. In the case of *Impact v The Minister for Agriculture and Food and Others*,[96] the CJEU held, *inter alia*, that an authority of a Member State, acting in its capacity as a public employer, may not adopt measures contrary to the objective to be pursued by the Directive (essentially the prevention of abuse by the issuing of a succession of fixed-term contracts). This was an important development for women and their access to (atypical) employment, when trying to reconcile family and work demands.

Finally, in relation to equality in matters of social security, the cases of Ms McDermott and Ms Cotter addressed the issues arising because of the paternalistic nature of the Irish social welfare system.[97] Equality in social security matters does not reflect an automatic dependency position for women in the family. Unfortunately, because of 'inadequate' transposition of Directive 79/7/EEC, the two women had to take the road to Luxembourg twice.

Conclusion

If we reflect on the journey taken by women entering the workforce and compare their situation prior to Irish accession to the European Union and subsequently, we have to acknowledge the positive impact of membership on women in Ireland (and in all the Member States). If we reflect on specific actions by the two institutions used as examples in this contribution, the Commission and the Court, we can identify some of the impact on women in Ireland; this is not to ignore the contribution of other actors (such as the European Parliament and Council of Ministers of the EU) who contribute to the legislative process and thus to the legislative framework providing for gender equality.

The response of the Irish Government to the economic arguments advanced against the introduction of equal pay might have prevailed, but thanks to the response from the European Commission – led ironically by the Irish member of the Commission – this economic argument was overtaken by the rule of law (obligation undertaken on accession) with positive consequences for women workers – despite the current gender pay gap.[98]

---

[96] Case C-268/06 [2008] ECR I-3483.

[97] *Norah McDermott and Ann Cotter v Minister for Social Welfare and Attorney-General* [1987] ECR 1453 and Case C-377/89 *A. Cotter and N. McDermott v Minister for Social Welfare and Another (II)* [1991] ECR I-1155.

[98] <http://ec.europa.eu/justice/gender-equality/gender-pay-gap/situation-europe/index_en.htm>, accessed 2 June 2013. Ireland's pay gap was 13.9 per cent – according to the latest statistics for 2010.

The change in Ireland – both as relates to women in the labour force, in general, and married women in particular – in the years since accession can be seen in more recent statistics. In 2009, there was a participation rate of 54 per cent of all women, and the same participation percentage of married women, in the labour force.[99] The mainstreaming of gender equality into all the activities of the Union[100] when compared with EECT article 119 as a lone reference to equality between men and women gives some sense of the journey travelled. Despite this however, the years since accession could best be described as "A lot done, more to do."

---

[99] See, inter alia, Margaret Fine-Davis, *Attitudes to Family Formation in Ireland Preliminary Findings: Qualitative Study,* Dublin: Social Attitude and Policy Research Group, Trinity College and Family Support Agency, September 2009, p.13.

[100] TFEU article 8: "In all its activities, the Union shall aim to eliminate inequalities, and to promote equality, between men and women."

Next Stop for Community Rail?
The Sustainable Branch Line

Paul Salveson

I am not certain when I first met Chris Harvie, at least 20 years back, but I am sure it was something to do with railways. It was nice finding someone who was not only a rail crank but shared my own brand of left-wing politics. Whilst Chris is a left-leaning Scottish nationalist, I am a similarly inclined Northern English regionalist. I have spent some very pleasant hours on English, Welsh, Scottish and German rural railways with Chris, musing on how the rural railways of Europe could do so much better if, like the Swiss, they were locally-managed and owned. This article is a re-edited chunk of a book I am having published later this year called *Railpolitik – Bringing Railways Back to Communities*.[1] It is dedicated to another Scotsman, Jock Nicholson. Jock also had close German connections, having married a high-ranking DDR politician way back in the 1960s. Jock – alongside Chris – was one of the most interesting people I have ever met and a pleasure to be with. A communist throughout his life, he was brought up in poverty and spent most of his life doing hard, dangerous jobs in railway goods yards, interspersed by stints on his union's executive. I doubt that they ever met, but it would have been a lively encounter.

So here we go, the sustainable branch line. If my editor kindly agrees, I will dedicate this chapter of the book to Professor Harvie.

The Sustainable Branch Line

'Community rail development' has become an established part of the UK rail scene, supported by government – local, national and devolved – and industry. It is a peculiarly British success story and is about involving local communities in hundreds of different ways with their local railway: from looking after station gardens to involving children in arts projects, live music and beer on local trains and taking over unused station buildings. The approach has succeeded in generating new business for local railways and attracting external investment to traditionally-neglected routes. But can it go further? And could it be applied to the German context?

There is clear potential to develop a new approach to stations, in both the UK and Germany, bringing the dreary unstaffed halt back to life. But this needs to form part of a holistic vision for local lines, re-visiting the radical vision of *New Futures for Rural Rail*[2] – and seeing how a local railway can be

---

[1] Paul Salveson, *Railpolitik: Bringing Railways Back to Communities*, London: Lawrence & Wishart, 2013.

[2] Paul Salveson, *New Futures for Rural Rail: An Agenda for Action*, London: Transnet, 1993.

at the heart of local sustainable development, with people having a more direct stake in their local railway, which should form the core of a community transport network. The UK Government's *Community Rail Development Strategy* has been enormously helpful in raising awareness and ambition, but its potential to create a flourishing local rail network comparable to the Swiss, German and Swedish lines has yet to be fulfilled. In Germany, there are excellent models of locally-managed railways, such as the Hohenzollern Railway, but the UK has more examples of community involvement. Maybe it is partly cultural, with Germans seeing railways as a state (or 'local state') responsibility. But that is how we used to see them as well, and it is a perception that needs changing.

Community rail in the UK needs a refresh, with a combination of national and regional support (and political will) with grass-roots creativity and determination. It is about going beyond the narrow confines of 'the railway' or even transport, and looking at the relationship with the wider community, whilst ensuring the railway and its complementary transport modes operate in the most sustainable way. Enter the concept of 'the sustainable branch line'.

It should integrate with wider local development and act as a motor for growth. The sustainable branch line is an integrated vision of a railway, forming the core of a transport network fully integrated with the local economy and society – an energising spine based along the *rail corridor*, providing high quality, community-focused transport services which are safe, environmentally benign and socially responsible – supporting a diverse and complementary range of economic activities.

On the continent and in the United States we are seeing examples of development which is closely integrated with rail, using stations as community hubs. A new organisation called 'Smart Growth UK' aims to learn the lessons of this experience and apply it to the UK. It says:

> Smart Growth is a sustainable approach to planning that emphasises compact and accessible urban communities and which opposes urban sprawl and car dependency. It seeks 'traditional' ways of planning towns based around local services, ease of walking and cycling and good public transport, especially rail-based. It looks for ways to rebuild our lost sense of community.[3]

This fits perfectly with what 'the sustainable branch line' is about.

Whilst the optimum management solution may well be a 100% locally-owned and run community railway such as we see in Switzerland, the approach could be implemented more quickly through an existing train

---

[3] Smart Growth UK <www.smartgrowthuk.org>.

operator and Network Rail[4] working with a community-rail partnership, transformed into a more developmental body. This could be a 'local sustainable transport company' (LSTC) which manages or provides directly a range of commercial activities – but not the most safety critical roles which would be left to a licensed train operator and Network Rail.

So much boils down to having the right people on board, with enthusiasm and knowledge, working within a supportive framework, both local, regional and national. The community rail partnership should be the over-arching body, driving new ideas and approaches forward. It should ensure a form of governance which brings the railway right into the community, with a route manager working with a partnership board that includes employees, volunteers, local businesses, municipal and community representatives.

Some of this is not new. In the nineteenth century, some railways developed as genuinely community-owned businesses, such as the tiny 'Killin Railway', which operated in the Scottish Highlands. I am sure Chris will be familiar with this fascinating example of community enterprise. The company was funded and owned by the local community, which included not just the inevitable laird but local businesspeople and farmers. It was 'their' railway in every sense![5] I am not suggesting we go back to that degree of local independence; local railways need a sensitive balance between local focus and economies of scale, but we have tended to over-emphasise the latter and give insufficient weight to the former.

Achieving the vision of the sustainable branch line will require determination and leadership. It will be faced with the reality of an existing service pattern on many lines which is resource-led, rather than customer-led. Changing that can be initially expensive but the long-term growth in revenue through more people travelling, and savings through doing things differently, justify the initial investment. It will be important to focus on short-term improvements which can bring rapid results but have a longer-term vision that flows on from the short-term wins. Developing a virtuous spiral of modest improvements, better marketing and publicity and a real sense that the railway is part of the community is the way forward for many local lines or small network of lines. This will require start-up funding to establish a virtuous spiral of growth. Possible sources for a pilot project could include local and regional support, foundations and Government sources. Would it not be exciting if there could be a parallel scheme in Germany!

What follows should be seen as an evolutionary process rather than all happening in a single 'big bang'. In outline, the sustainable branch line should feature:

---

[4] In the UK, Network Rail owns and manages the railway infrastructure; most passenger services are provided by franchised train operators.
[5] See John Thomas, *The Callander and Oban Railway*, Newton Abbot: David & Charles, 1968.

- People: The 'sustainable branch line' should be founded on its staff and be an outstanding employer, offering salaries and conditions with high levels of employee involvement and direct participation in how the business is run. A demoralised workforce leads directly to a failing railway deserted by its customers. Train operator and Network Rail employees need to be brought into the partnership.

- Service: A train service which is run to meet the needs of the local communities along its route, as well as serving the needs of visitors – including evening services and all-year round Sunday operation. It should be accessible and affordable, with feeder buses and taxis, and easy access for walkers and cyclists.

- Stations: Station buildings which are built and operated on sustainable principles, are welcoming and full of life, with good passenger facilities at stations, including staff.

- Trains: Modern, technically standardised rolling stock which is high quality, light weight with low (or nil) emissions and plenty of space for luggage and cycles, which are serviced and maintained locally and internally/externally reflect the culture of the area.

- Information: Good quality information on transport facilities and all other local facilities and activities/attractions for visitors arriving at stations; similar information available online and by phone, and the rail service linked to a wide range of local business and tourism web sites.

- Management: A railway which is managed locally and based locally, and supports the local economy by providing employment and supporting other local businesses through local purchasing, with a high level of community governance, operated at least in part by a locally-based social enterprise which is an active player in the local economy.

- Local economy: Locally-produced goods for sale at stations and on trains, e.g. local food and drink, local crafts, guides, etc. Partnerships with local businesses, e.g. hotels and B&Bs, cycle hire, holiday packages and use of station buildings for small business development.

- Community: Active involvement of the local community through an enhanced 'community rail partnership' and individual 'station friends'; a railway at the heart of social and cultural life, playing an active part in festivals and events, from 'Britain in Bloom' to cultural events, schools projects and celebrations, food fairs and music.

- Value for money: A railway operation which offers good value to the community for the financial support it receives, including development of innovative low-cost forms of operation, from staffing to signalling, making the most of community-rail designation. Discounted fares to socially-excluded groups.

- Environment: A railway operation committed to sustainable principles, including energy use, recycling of materials, and making best use of its existing resources.

- Local planning: A railway which is linked into to local planning strategies and provides suitable locations for sustainable development, be it housing or employment-related. Station areas should be hubs of social and industrial activity, as they originally were. Communities should be encouraged to develop around station hubs, avoiding sprawl which encourages car use and promote walking and cycling access.

So let us look at each of these issues in turn, in more depth.

People

The success or failure of 'the sustainable branch line' will stand or fall on whether it has the right people involved. Above all, that means the staff, including front-line workers as much as managers, but also volunteers doing peripheral but important jobs.

Applying 'localism' to a local railway runs up against ingrained railway operating practice, not least the use of non-dedicated staff. Having conductors, drivers and station staff who feel that they have a stake in the community makes a huge difference. Customers and staff get to know each other, and conductors become familiar with the route and what's out there – and can act as real ambassadors for the service.

The pattern could vary from line to line. It may not at first be appropriate for a local company to take over employment of on-train staff, whether conductors or drivers owing to the complexities of today's railway and safety critical tasks of train crew. There are, however, very strong arguments for drivers and conductor to feel part of the local operation, rather than working through a complex link of other routes. The best option is for a dedicated team ('link' in railway speak) of drivers and conductors for that particular route, employed by the parent train operator and possibly based along the route itself, instead of a large central depot.

One of the exciting challenges of running local railways differently is looking at how people can best be deployed. Some jobs, such as the driver, seem to have a very specific remit, but there may be scope for drivers being multi-skilled in relevant areas, e.g. engineering. Many drivers are already adept at sorting out technical problems and, to an extent, this is already part of their training and competence. Conductors do much more than sell tickets – they can be ambassadors and guides.

However, where we have gone wrong in the past is to come up with top-down solutions to how employees' duties should be defined. The right way is to get employees based on a particular route together and get them to come up with the best solution for how current resources can be best deployed to ensure that their jobs are well-rewarded, fulfilling and creative. This will be challenging for management and also for the trades unions to whom most of the employees will belong. It may come up with solutions that are innovative and positive. Should there be a different approach to salaries and job descriptions? Yes there should, but taking that forward needs the direct involvement of the employees themselves, as well as their union representatives.

Finding appropriate mechanisms to involve staff at a local level should be an important part of the 'sustainable branch line'. It should not just be about having one or two 'representatives' sitting on some consultative body. Finding ways of involving all employees would, for a relatively small number of staff, not be a difficult task.

Running a railway is a highly professional job, whether it is a high-speed main line or a rural branch. Volunteers can contribute greatly on the margins, as we have already seen with station friends groups. Even for heritage railways, getting the right mix of professional staff and volunteers is an issue, with some railways opting for more paid staff for core tasks. The general principle should be that 'core' jobs, including bus driving, on-train conducting and track or station maintenance should be the responsibility of paid staff. Volunteers can provide important back-up through 'additionality' – looking after station gardens, acting as couriers on trains aimed at the tourist market and assisting with catering services. Volunteers must be trained to the appropriate standard, have a strong safety awareness, and be subject to the same discipline as paid staff.

An integrated local network

Currently, many services on local railways in the UK offer inadequate, infrequent, services which inhibit growth. Some routes have no Sunday service. The last train home from many large towns is often much too early to allow people to attend concerts, visit friends or just have an evening out. It is depressingly common that the train arrives at a station just as the bus is departing. If local railways are to get out of the double bind of poor services, lack of co-ordination with other transport and low demand, there needs to be a commitment to extending and enhancing services as part of either the franchise specification or a contract between the train operator and transport authority.

Ensuring high levels of integration between bus and rail is crucial, yet Britain is still way behind other European countries. Ensuring good connections to/from train and bus need to be written into contracts, with incentives on the part of rail and bus operators to co-operate, instead of hiding behind competition legislation, which is a paper tiger. It is ironic that very often train and bus operations are owned by the same parent company.

Having a local operator running both buses and trains could be a very attractive solution in many rural areas. This is the situation in some areas of Germany, Switzerland and the Netherlands, and there is no doubt that single ownership and unified local management does lead to very high standards of integration and quality. And, as a result, ridership increases. But it is a long road to get there, and a gradualist approach makes sense in the UK context. The current de-regulated bus environment is completely at odds with this approach and 'local integrated transport zones' would allow for a far better use of scarce resources.

Cycling and walking are important complementary modes for rail. Every station should have well-signed safe routes to and from town and villages centres, places of employment and education. A locally-based railway operator should be well placed to work with bodies like Sustrans and the highway authority to develop a range of initiatives, with safe storage for bikes at stations. Cycle hire at stations, for both leisure and irregular commuting journeys, could be developed as a subsidiary business for the LSTC.

Taxis are a vital community resource in many rural areas, and the railway should work with local taxi firms to develop good integration. Train-taxi schemes have particular relevance to rural areas where population densities are low. This is a relatively unexplored area, with scope for much more development, using the experience of train-taxis in the Netherlands. Integration is not just about integration between transport modes.

For many people, in both rural and outer urban areas, the car will continue to be an essential means of getting to the train. If stations do not have sufficient car parking there is a risk that people will drive the entire journey. But we should be looking at some innovative solutions such as community car clubs, car-sharing and lift-sharing to stations which avoid over-dependence. 'Commuter' lift-sharing has taken off in a big way in many countries and would be relatively easy to organise through a community rail partnership or the local sustainable transport company.

Access for all

Rail is the most accessible form of public transport, and most modern trains have reasonable standards of accessibility – though there is still much to do with older trains such as the 'Pacer' fleet whose derogation for disability legislation expires in 2019. The biggest problem is stations, and access to stations. Many local stations remain inaccessible, with footbridges often providing the only means of access to platforms. This is not just an issue for disabled people, but also a major problem for people with prams, and elderly people who may not see themselves as 'disabled' in the strict sense. The 'Harrington Hump' has been a simple and affordable solution to raising platform heights for a short part of the platform at many lightly-used stations.

Developing easily accessible links to stations – including footpaths and cycleways as well as accessible bus and taxi services – is a key issue which should be the concern of the railway company. Ensuring that the street environment is safe and accessible – pavements with dropped kerbs, good street lighting and safe crossing points – is essential.

Personal security is part of the 'accessibility' issue. People will not wait at stations which are dark, threatening and unwelcoming. The security problem can best be solved by changing stations into places of human activity with a people presence. The concept of the 'secure' station should be dumped and replaced by the idea of the 'sociable' station where security is not an issue.

A local railway company should secure grants to improve accessibility and provide a focus for management attention to develop practical solutions to access issues. This could include re-opening disused entrances, or looking at other alternatives to costly, fully-accessible ramped bridges which may be seldom used by anybody. In the case of low-speed lines with good sight-lines, traditional 'barrow crossings' offer a basically safe, low-cost means of accessing platforms providing they are subject to a full risk assessment.

Affordability remains one of the major disincentives to use rail, and Britain has the highest fares in Europe. It is the issue which comes up with monotonous regularity when people are asked what puts them off using trains. A local railway company could do more to develop special deals with job centres and local authorities, for example, aimed at people going to job interviews, and half-price travel for their first month of employment. Local residents' railcards, offering discounts of up to 50% on local rail fares, have been shown to bring in substantial new business and encourage train travel. These work well on a line of route or local network basis, and help generate new business for local lines. But they need strong local promotion which takes us back to having a local, not remote, management which knows the local scene in detail.

A sustainable station

Stations are the gateway to the railway, but also gateways from the railway into the wider community. The 'station partnership' approach, involving local volunteers in adopting their station, has been hugely successful and has reversed the decline of the unstaffed station. Why cannot more stations be warm, welcoming and convivial places that are operated along eco-friendly lines? We have to move away from lonely, unloved unstaffed stations that people only use as a last resort, and make them vibrant centres of community life, day and evening.

The aim of the sustainable branch line should be to have as many stations staffed as possible in some way – not necessarily by a railway employee, but by someone doing something which adds value to the railway service and fills a gap in the community, be it a shop, service or facility. The suggested local sustainable transport company could provide this service, or an individual small business. The alternative for very small stations is to use a local shop, pub or café as a source of information and sales point for selected tickets (e.g. rover tickets aimed at the leisure market).

Stations should, in appropriate locations, be developed as business centres with low-rent 'starter' units available for small businesses. A central, easily-accessible location where there is a cluster of enterprises would stimulate local economic development and provide quality, accessible jobs. A good example is Redcar where the former station buildings have been converted into a business centre. More recently, Moorthorpe in Yorkshire has been re-developed by the local town council to provide space for small businesses and an arts training centre. Millom, in Cumbria, is another outstanding example of integrated community enterprise. Bargoed (South Wales) was an early pioneer, where the train company got a local taxi company to relocate to the previously defunct station building, breathing life back into the station. Vandalism stopped overnight and passenger numbers grew.

An advantage of local authorities leasing the station is that they could locate a range of public services, e.g. libraries, nurseries and tourist information centres within them. Again, it happens in Sweden (e.g. Nassjo) and in other countries. It makes sense in transport terms but also in ensuring local services are protected in smaller communities. Bringing a mix of facilities under one roof, with easy access by train, bus and bike and car, would help sustain the local economy and services which may well disappear if they are seen as 'stand-alone' facilities.

In many locations, staffing smaller stations by a conventional train operator is unlikely to be commercially viable, because of high overheads. However, a community-run facility forming part of a greater whole (possibly through a route-based co-op or partnership) might have more chance of success, whilst still offering staff good salaries and conditions. Location is 99% of the battle, and some very small rural stations, miles from the nearest settlement, may never qualify for extra special treatment. But in many cases there is enormous scope for transforming some of the current unwelcoming, unstaffed, dismal places we call stations, into something much better.

A small 'sustainable' station should be just that, with solar-powered heating and lighting which reduces the initial setting-up costs as well as on-going charges. Water could be provided by rain-water harvesting, with chemical toilets or shared use of an adjoining facility. It should offer the benefits of a modern, welcoming facility with comfortable facilities. A combination of paid staff and volunteers would ensure that the station is staffed for at least a core period. The advantage of an 'independent' retailer running the station is that they can sell what people want to buy, not just rail tickets. So teas and coffee, newspapers and magazines, light snacks might be popular. Cycle hire and repair could be another side-line, again depending on location. There is considerable potential in business travel, if there is a large local employer in the area whose staff make frequent longer-distance journeys.

Convivial space at stations

An important part of the sustainable station concept is 'convivial space'. One fellow passenger at my local station told me: "I'd like comfy seats and tables inside where people can wait for their train during the long Pennine winter, with local art work displayed on the walls; and space outside for a tea garden in the summer!"[6] Utopian? It should not be. We have to reject the idea (enthusiastically adopted in Germany as well as the UK!) that local stations should be minimalist unstaffed halts.

One of many enemies of progress in the railway industry is often an understandable desire to be 'different'. If Network Rail could agree a simple design for what would basically be a well-insulated secure box with doors and a retractable window, costs could be kept down to a sensible level. Fitting-out would include retail space, an area to sit and read the paper whilst enjoying a cup of freshly-brewed coffee and chat with your fellow travellers, and a toilet. In the evening the space could be used for community meetings. The 'box' could be produced by Network Rail and either stay in their ownership, leased to the local group, or be sold outright. The best solution would probably be for Network Rail to retain ownership and offer the building at a low rent, but one which ensures their direct costs are covered.

The active support of the railway company (be it a local operator or a larger franchise), as well as Network Rail and the Office of Rail Regulation, would be essential. Modern ticket machines are expensive and need well-trained operators. A rail industry contribution could be staff training and leasing ticket machines at attractive rates (i.e. free). Ultimately, everyone benefits. The community gets a facility that it can be really proud of; the train operator and Network Rail get a well-managed safe and cared-for station. More people start using the trains. The role of the local transport authority would be equally important; being part of a regionally-managed ticketing system would be vital for the viability of the booking office side of the business.

---

[6] Conversation with a passenger at Slaithwaite station, April 2013.

Trains: light, accessible and spacious

Trains are – together with stations – the most important 'physical' element of the passenger's travel experience. Trains need to be clean, comfortable and accessible. The interiors should be welcoming and bright, with some local branding so that passengers feel they are travelling on *their* line and something special. People should be able to see out of the window – enjoying the view is an important part of train travel, which many rolling stock designers seem to have forgotten about. There should be adequate space for prams, bikes and luggage. The new fleet of light, accessible and spacious diesel railcars in Germany, such as the 'Talent' and slightly older 'RegioShuttle' have transformed the quality of local rail travel.

Getting suitable rolling stock for local rail services is becoming an increasingly difficult problem in the UK. There are two really big challenges: cost and availability of suitable designs. It is outrageous that we are still paying large sums of money to leasing companies, owned by major banks, for life-expired trains. The other big obstacle is the fact that suitable modern diesel designs for local railways are non-existent in the UK, and the situation is not helped by EU legislation on emissions which is becoming more stringent. We are at the early stages of the 'end of diesel', and there is an urgent need to think about replacements, though there may be scope for low emission diesel engines in the short to medium term. The option of electrification is an attractive and realistic one for some routes, but the sort of longer-distance, relatively lightly-used local railway that forms the typical 'sustainable branch line' need a different approach. The initial capital costs of electrification are high and the programme of electrification work facing Network Rail over the next 20 years is huge, so management resource will be in short supply.

The Parry People Mover (PPM) ultra-light rail vehicle has been operating successfully on the short branch from Stourbridge Junction to Stourbridge Town. It uses zero-emission flywheel technology and is suitable for very short distance lines and has potential for longer routes if a viable design with greater capacity can be developed. Network Rail has been in discussions with manufacturer Bombardier on alternative motive power for some time, and a battery-operated vehicle should be trialled sometime in the next year. The concept is that the batteries are charged from the overhead line equipment and it can then run over a non-electrified branch and back. Network Rail is looking at branch lines like Colne Valley in Essex or the Matlock line, which are relatively short distance and where there is difficulty in making the case for full electrification. The Railway Industry Association is doing its best to promote innovation, and a number of energy storage systems for trains are about to be trialled. There is potential for tram-train on some routes. However, it is not a cheap option and works best in more urban areas.

In Hungary, an independent narrow-gauge railway has designed a solar-powered train with a modest top speed of 25 km/h (the line's maximum speed in any case). The experimental train is called *Vili* (William) and will undergo more tests during 2013. The single carriage vehicle has 9.9 square metres of solar panels on the carriage roof which feed batteries underneath the seats. Regenerative braking also feeds the storage units.[7] I think Chris would love its quirkiness.

Developing designs for an eco-friendly train is an area where a partnership with a university or universities could bring great benefits. Is this an area for German-British collaboration?

Information: the wired-up branch line

Getting accurate and up to date information about a transport service is critical, and people have increasingly high expectations of their train or bus service. Several community rail partnerships have developed websites which include timetable information but also other news and information about what is happening in the area served by the train. An inclusive website which uses the railway as the main structure but has much wider business, tourist, cultural and social information would help bind the railway and the community together. Each community served by a specific station could have a click-on page which has very local information. Each sustainable branch line should have all the relevant social media infrastructure – twitter, facebook and other emergent means. At the same time, local railways must be fully integrated with the national rail enquiries website

A good transport service needs to have up to date paper-based information – timetables, line guides, posters which are available beyond just the railway station. Again, CRPs have been successful in getting transport information into guest houses, pubs, hotels and tourist information centres. Estate agents should be targeted, with proximity to a railway station seen as a major selling point. Public transport information should be available in publications from a wide range of local organisations, from local press to church newsletters, tourist guides and community magazines. It is easy to do if you have the resources to do it in the community.

Information at stations is crucial, and this should be a mix of 'display' information on poster boards, real-time electronic information and aural announcements, and staff with access to up to the minute information and deep knowledge to advise potential passengers on their journey. Staff at the sustainable information must be knowledgeable about their local community and be able to advise arriving passengers on places to eat, drink, visit and stay – with tourism information readily available at the station.

Information on trains is equally important and trains should have visual and aural information about destinations and the next stop. This is well-established technology. Even more traditional, but of vital importance, is announcements by the train crew when there is a problem or delay.

On the Far North Line in Scotland (Inverness to Wick/Thurso) several stations have customer information displays which are solar-powered. They

[7] See *Today's Railways Europe*, May 2013 p. 209.

have an automated speech facility for the visually impaired, and at some sites the displays are also fitted with a system which allows visually impaired passengers to trigger the system using a small personal radio fob. The screens use a combination of solar power, and large batteries storing excess summer energy will support the systems in leaner winter months.[8]

Infrastructure

Infrastructure is, by a very large margin, the biggest driver of costs on the railway, be it a high-speed main line or a rural branch. We're talking not just track but signalling, bridges, viaducts, tunnels and stations. Getting an appropriate level of infrastructure that can safely and efficiently handle the traffic expected is a critical issue for the sustainable branch line.

Most rural railways in the UK have been reduced to the bare minimum necessary for them to function with single line operation, removal of 'surplus' crossing loops, limited facilities at terminal stations. This often means that useful extra traffic, such as locomotive-hauled charter trains, find it difficult if not impossible to use some lines. The potential for enhancing frequencies is reduced because of lack of capacity – mainly lack of crossing loops along the line, and additional track capacity at the terminus. Costs of enhancing existing infrastructure are very high.

However, a locally-managed railway, if it had some degree of control over track maintenance and renewals, could ultimately undertake such trackwork to appropriate industry group standards, allowing the railway to be more responsive to needs. In the short term, a route or small networks of routes should have dedicated multi-skilled maintenance gangs employed by Network Rail.

This does not mean taking infrastructure ownership away from Network Rail, rather a re-structuring of responsibilities. In time, the 'local sustainable transport company' could become infrastructure controller, employing its own staff, or using qualified locally-based sub-contractors where appropriate. Track maintenance could be taken over by those local railway companies with access to the right skills, which might include a heritage railway based nearby. It has to be stressed that today's railway is both a very tightly regulated and increasingly specialised industry, and letting untrained workers, whether paid or volunteer, loose on even a low-speed and lightly-used railway is not recommended. Yet, if trained and fully skilled staff can be available locally, costs could be reduced and efficiency improved.

There are more innovative opportunities for rail re-openings where the track-bed is not owned by Network Rail. However, the experience of the 'Borders Railway' project (close to Chris's heart) where the Scottish Government attempted such an arrangement but eventually gave the project to Network Rail, suggests that caution is required. A regional version

---

[8] See Paul Salveson, 'The Far North Line', in *Today's Railways*, November 2011.

of the proposed 'not for dividend' company could be established, which takes ownership of the formation and acts as a developer for sites along the rail corridor. Most UK tram infrastructure is owned by public sector bodies such as passenger transport executives, so there are many precedents. This body would charge track access to either an established TOC, or to a local operator. Alternatively, it could run the trains itself, along the lines of several independent railways on the continent.[9]

Management

Whatever the company structure or ownership the management of the sustainable branch line should be locally-based, with – as a minimum – a manager who is based on the route and has responsibilities for all employees concerned with the line. Network Rail and train operators have already developed some innovative joint working arrangements known as 'alliancing' with some success. This approach should be taken forward for local lines or small networks, with one person having overall management responsibilities for operations and infrastructure. This could work under both the current structure as well as with a more integrated (and possibly publicly-owned) regional operation.

Currently, many local lines are resourced from a large central depot. This seems sensible in traditional (i.e. the last 40 years) railway terms but in fact is far from the right way to run a local railway. Most journeys on local lines start from the periphery and go into the centre, e.g. a large town or city, with people returning home in the evening. The logical place to have a train depot, with train crew, is at or towards the peripheral end of the line, not in the centre. Otherwise, you have trains running out from the main depot, empty, in the morning and returning back in the evening – again, carrying fresh air. Locating depots in peripheral locations makes operational and financial sense and gives a huge boost to local economies. It also nurtures a strong sense of local ownership and camaraderie by small teams of dedicated workers. Again, a balance is needed between 'big depot' and tiny sub-depot. What would work is a number of smallish depots at nodal points, doing overnight stabling for perhaps 7-12 trains and 15-20 crews. With modern rolling stock trains having extended intervals between servicing and examinations, this is increasingly possible, and a number of operators are already doing this.

A further advantage of 'remote' depots is the potential for local purchasing, discussed below. Managers should be freed up to make decisions within a specified budget to buy in local services and, where appropriate, expertise. Currently, there is huge wastage by calling out maintenance workers often based scores of miles away at 'central' depots for relatively small jobs which would be within the competence of, for example, a local electrician, painter or joiner.

---

[9] e.g. Hohenzollern Regional Railway, which I visited with Chris some years ago.

An enterprising railway supporting the local economy

A local railway operation, however managed or structured, could take on more and more 'peripheral' commercial activities and build up strong commercial expertise which provides a range of services to meet local needs. The suggested 'local sustainable transport company' could develop commercial activities alongside the 'parent' community rail partnership (see below 'Community'). These activities could include:

- rail-link bus services and other community transport
- on-train and station catering
- marketing
- station cleaning and maintenance
- tourism packages
- cycle and electric car/bike hire
- lift-sharing schemes

The initial focus should depend on location and what the demand is. The Settle-Carlisle Railway Development Co., a 'not for profit' company limited by guarantee, provides trolley services on trains and runs the station café at Skipton. Using this approach, a rail-based social enterprise could develop as a focus for rural enterprise with the railway at the heart of a range of commercial activities and stations as hubs of business activity.

Community-rail partnerships (CRPs) have been able to exert considerable influence with friendly operators. However, some have potential for doing more and becoming social enterprises undertaking the sort of duties suggested above. Some CRPs could go beyond the useful but peripheral mix of marketing and community development and provide direct services which complement the core railway service. Having a 'commercial' arm might be one way of safeguarding the important community activities whilst freeing up some entrepreneurial talent. Local railways bring visitors into the area who spend money – not just on the railway, but in shops, pubs, and visitor attractions. A community rail partnership with its own 'commercial manager' would be an exciting step forward in the short-term.

An economically sustainable railway is not just one that pays its bills, though that is important. Being able to win new passengers through offering improved, good quality services is an essential part of what the sustainable branch line should be aiming for. Additional business can also be won through peripheral – but important – business activities, outlined above. A locally managed railway could play a central role in economic regeneration, directly and indirectly. We should see the railway has providing the spine for economic and social regeneration with the community-rail partnership becoming more of a local development agency and less of a local marketing operation.

The railway could have a very direct economic impact, as an employer of local labour, with locally-based train crew, track maintenance staff, administration and management. At present, with centralised operation of local lines being the norm, the direct employment benefits of particularly the more rural railways are negligible. That should change, with more railway employment based along the route, bringing focus and commitment (see above under 'people').

The other principal economic benefit of a local railway operation is through its purchasing power. A locally-managed railway should purchase goods which are available locally, for catering, office services and equipment, and a wide range of other goods and services. This happens almost spontaneously through business networking and informal social contacts. It does not happen now because railway managers are often hundreds of miles away, not based in the local community. The local railway should be proud to offer local produce for sale at its stations and on its trains, rather than mass-produced, anonymously-sourced goods.

A local railway with a pro-active rail partnership can bring other benefits, e.g. ticket sales in local shops. On the Tarka Line in Devon, local businesses help drive up use of the smaller stations such as Morchard Road and Copplestone where local shops sell carnet tickets supplied by the Partnership. It gives discounted travel for rail users, and the local shop gets a percentage of the carnet ticket's price, so everyone benefits.

Getting under the skin of communities

Community rail partnerships have already achieved more than anyone might have dreamed when the first CRPs were formed in the 1990s. Stations have been transformed into lively and welcoming community centres, with art work, community facilities and attractive gardens. The sustainable branch line needs to find new ways of linking up with local communities. Developing on-going work with schools is a particularly important area, and several CRPs (e.g. Lancashire) already excel in this area. It is labour intensive work but immensely productive, by creating a new generation of public transport users. Ways in include art work, free days out on the train to visit other schools or places of interest; film-making, creative work on the train itself.

The most effective CRPs take their message out into the community rather than staying within their railway comfort zone. Having a presence at festivals, agricultural shows and community galas helps embed the idea that the railway is part of the community.

Community rail has a big role to play in social cohesion. The Northern Rail 'community ambassadors' programme has been highly successful in reaching out to communities who, for various reasons, do not make best use of local rail services. These include ethnic minority communities. In East Lancashire the community ambassador, Sultana Jamil, has worked with Asian women's groups to encourage group trips by train and build up confidence so that rail travel becomes the normal way to get about.

Effective use of the local media is crucial; the local media likes 'good news' stories about the local community, and it is not difficult to get press releases published, if they are deemed relevant and news-worthy. Local radio is another useful way of getting messages across. Most CRPs have up to date and easily accessible websites, are on facebook and twitter and other media (see above).

Each station along the sustainable branch line should have an active 'station friends' group of volunteers which develops gardens, vegetable beds, promotes public art and a whole range of activities that highlight the station as a special part of the community. Sundays are a good day to make use of lightly-used station car parks and organise farmers' markets, car boot sales and other events which raise the station's profile.

Value for Money and Funding: the Affordable Branch Line

The ideas behind the sustainable branch line require some initial investment, in rolling stock, infrastructure and stations. If the maximum benefits are to be extracted it will require some risk-taking which we are not good at doing. However, time after time, we have seen investment in local railways to be not only justified but way exceeding expectations, be it new lines (Ebbw Vale, Alloa) or enhancements to existing services (Chester – Shrewsbury).

A pilot 'sustainable branch line' ought to get funding, be it from Europe, Department for Transport, Transport Scotland, Welsh Government or English regional consortia. The idea of a really innovative EU-funded scheme, learning from experience across Europe, is a really exciting prospect. A half-hearted attempt was made at the time of community rail 'designation' in 2005, but little radical change ensued. Only through a well-funded pilot project, involving at least three lines with different characteristics, starting from a blank sheet of paper, can we really get out of the current impasse in how local railways are run.

To get out of the vicious circle of under-investment and stagnation, there is a need for a number of complementary investments, but the most important is rolling stock. Local services need more trains now and that, in many cases, will require old, inadequate stock. However, experience shows that increased frequencies, regardless of how poor the rolling stock is, generates big increases in passengers.[10] That lays the foundations for getting something better, and elsewhere in this chapter I have outlined what we need from new rolling stock. In the short-term, rolling stock leasing companies should be persuaded or compelled to offer their bottom-end products (e.g. 'Pacer' trains) as an initial contribution to the sustainable branch line concept. They, and colleagues in the railway industry, have the expertise to come up with something much better but we know that takes time.

---

[10] Cf. Matlock Line – a 25% increase in number of trains brought a 90% increase in number of passengers – not least because trains ran at times when people wanted to travel, and connections became much better.

The Department for Transport's *Community Rail Development Strategy* has an objective of bringing down costs. In reality, this has proved difficult to do. It is a myth that local lines have a lot of 'fat' which forces up costs. BR stripped out most of the remaining fat in the 1980s. The challenge is to look at cost-effective ways of running local lines efficiently and cost effectively, providing a springboard for further growth and investment. If the scope for conventional economies is very limited (and the option of closing booking offices, even where they exist, is totally the wrong direction to go) are there options for more unconventional approaches? Signalling is one of the biggest infrastructure costs, and conversion of some lines to tram-style 'on-sight' driving has been suggested. However, the down-side is reduced speeds (even with improved 'track' brakes) and public concern about safety. However, the technology exists to signal single-line branch lines with passing loops simply and relatively cheaply, once the initial investment is made. The entire Highland line network is controlled by two signallers based at Inverness.

Network Rail has track engineers who have a very clear understanding of infrastructure maintenance and argue, convincingly, that if you provide modern track used by lightweight trains, it will last a very long time, with minimal maintenance. The down-side is that you do not permit heavy, track-wearing locomotives. This means that the occasional charter special, or freight train, cannot operate on your line. But the gains in terms of cost savings and potential improved frequencies are vast.

Environment: The 'Green' Branch Line

Environmental sustainability has a number of dimensions in the local railway context. Rail is accepted as one of the more environment-friendly forms of transport, with substantially lower emissions than road traffic and having a less damaging impact on land. New railways are few and the land they take is generally less than that of a new road. Rail can provide a quality alternative to using the car, as well as taking freight off the roads. But it needs to be demonstrated and fought for, not simply asserted. People will rarely choose rail simply because it is more 'green' – they need to be convinced that it is a better quality product. And it has to be remembered that an empty train is far from 'green'.

Rail must not rest on its 'green' laurels, but should strive to maintain and improve its position. New trains are needed, and low or nil emission trains will be necessary (see above on rolling stock). Stations should be environmentally sustainable, using appropriate materials, minimising waste, being energy-efficient and, where possible, using alternative energy sources including solar and wind power. For a while, several stations on the Heart of Wales Line had their modest lighting requirements met by solar power. Ironically, Network Rail had these removed and replaced them with cable-supplied electricity from the National Grid in order to confirm to group standards. There needs to be more focus on getting appropriate standards, for a wide range of railway activities, which may involve getting derogations from standards which are designed more with a busy high-speed railway in mind. My understanding is that Germany has already achieved this.

Stations should aim to provide a high quality environment, whether the buildings be relatively new, or historic. In the case of our many historic station buildings, there is a need for much greater day-to-day care and attention, which can be achieved through having a small business located within the station. A new modular design for a small-scale 'eco station' needs development. Why not a national competition which invites architects to come up with a new design which combines sustainability, easiness of maintenance and passenger friendliness? The example of Accrington's new eco station shows the potential of stations serving medium-sized towns which meets all of those demands.

Thinking laterally

A local rail operation is well placed to make best use of resources and recycle and re-engineer equipment, where possible, using its local expertise. It can also profit from re-use or sale of surplus materials. One heritage railway earns around £10,000 each year from the sale of timber it fells along the lineside; others make money from hosting film crews wanting a 'railway' back-drop. On the 'commercial' main line railway, contractors often just leave cut timber to rot. Having a local focus means that you can spot business opportunities of a multitude of different kinds.

Many local railways, through CRPs, are linking up with community food projects which provide healthy and cheap food for the local community. In most cases these gardens are developed and maintained by the local community. The nationally-celebrated 'Incredible Edible Todmorden' scheme, in the Pennines of Northern England, began with some herbs being grown on the station platform; Accrington has the 'Accrington growers' project based at the station. There is great scope for developing food projects on stations, with station shops selling the produce.

Sustainable Local Planning

There is growing pressure to decentralise planning decisions as part of the UK Government's 'localism' agenda. Instead of seeing this as a threat, promoters of the sustainable branch line should see it as an opportunity and mould it in a democratic and inclusive direction. Neighbourhood plans should have the station as the core of local development, with housing and business located within easy reach of the station. Care needs to be exercised not to build on land that may be needed for railway use, including car and cycle parking. However, developing former railway land for sustainable and affordable housing makes planning sense and will be commercially attractive to developers.

Devon County Council's *Structure Plan* zones new housing development along rail corridors, bringing a major upsurge of use to small stations, for example along the Tarka Line. Copplestone, for example, has developed into one of the busier small stations along the line following some enlightened planning by the local authorities. The village has tripled in size, with quality housing development located around the station, offering an example of truly sustainable development.[11] Some of the growth in rail travel was driven by planning policy guidance which encouraged development around transport hubs.[12] That guidance has now been abolished but there remains a commitment, arguably weakened, to integrated transport and land use planning in the *National Planning Policy Framework*.

Where major development is planned, the local railway should benefit from planning agreements, and from the Community Infrastructure Levy, which has already been used to fund new station development. The same process could be used for enhancements of existing facilities. Too often, opportunities are missed because planners do not understand how the railway works, and the railway does not understand the planning framework. Every community rail partnership should have a planning and development specialist.

Directing development along rail corridors, with stations becoming hubs of transport, commercial and residential activity, is well-established in Germany and the Netherlands, and many US towns and cities. The 'Smart Growth' movement is looking at ways of applying those principles in the UK. Its core principles include promoting 'compact communities' which conserve open space and urban fringes, reducing dependence on the car. At the same time, intelligent planning "increases opportunities for walking, cycling and public transport. Towns, cities and villages should be pedestrian-friendly and rail-accessible".[13] For communities to successfully implement Smart Growth "they must ensure all three sectors of the economy – public, private and community – function successfully and sustainably."[14]

The route to the sustainable branch line

Most aspects of 'the sustainable branch line' can be seen in operation in many parts of Europe, including the UK, but there are few examples where everything is brought together in an existing sustainable branch line. As with 'community rail' in the 1990s, the concept brings together a range of disparate but potentially complementary activities and concepts into one whole.

---

[11] For a detailed overview of post-war railways and planning see Russell Haywood, *Railways, Urban Development and Town Planning in Britain 1948-2008*, Farnham: Ashgate, 2009.

[12] Planning Policy Guidance Note 13 Transportation. It was abolished in 2012.

[13] See <www.smartgrowthuk.org>.

[14] *Ibid.*

It needs champions at local, regional and national level. A well-resourced community rail partnership could, with the right people on board, be the driving force behind it, and the way forward should be through a combination of grassroots, bottom-up involvement with support from a national or regional agency – be it the Department for Transport, North of England consortia or Welsh/Scottish Governments. It needs to be tested out as a pilot project, in two or three parts of the country and perhaps other parts of Europe. It could form part of an existing or future franchise or management contract in which the parent train operating company devolves a significant part of its responsibilities to a local level, whilst retaining the most safety critical part of its responsibilities. Equally, if the 'radical alternatives' I suggest in my book *Railpolitik* are adopted, it could easily sit within a socially-owned parent company. We need more 'out of the box' thinking, and there is nobody better qualified to do that than Professor Harvie.

The importance of devolution

The idea of the 'sustainable branch line' should be an evolving one. It will not suddenly happen, and there is a continuum along which an existing or future 'community rail' route might go, possibly leading to completely locally-owned and managed railways on the Swiss model. There are advantages, but also some disadvantages, to this, and we do not have the form of devolved governance which the Swiss – and Germans – have. There is a lot we in the UK can learn from Germany and Switzerland, which goes way beyond railways. Above all, the importance of devolution. Scotland and Wales have benefitted from the transfer of powers from London, yet the English regions remain subject to the whims of London-based civil servants and politicians. For local railways, I believe that the UK's 'community rail' experience has relevance for other parts of Europe. We can learn much from the achievements of locally-managed railways in Germany and Switzerland.

I look forward to many more rural rides on German and British branch lines with my good friend Chris, and perhaps above all sharing a pint in Carlisle, having arrived on the first train on the re-opened Waverley Route from Edinburgh[15] – with steam traction, of course! Scotland and the North of England united in a cloud of steam and real ale – what could be better?

---

[15] See Eberhard Bort and Christopher Harvie (eds), *The Borders & The Waverley Route: Transport Problems and Solutions for an Excluded* Region, Edinburgh: International Social Sciences Institute, 1999; David Spaven, *Waverley Route: The Life, Death and Rebirth of the Borders Railway*, Glendaruel: Argyll Publishing, 2012.

Holding the Body Politic to Account?
A Beleaguered Fourth Estate

Douglas MacLeod

The 1987 General Election result was the moment the tectonic plates shifted in the UK. North of the border, the Conservatives found themselves reduced to holding only 10 of the 72 Scottish seats. This left the Secretary of State, Malcolm Rifkind, with the immediate problem of finding enough live bodies to run administrative and parliamentary business in Scotland, ensuring that these live bodies had a minimum level of ability necessary to understand and carry out their ministerial briefs, and find the necessary number of spokespersons to feed an ever hungrier media. The result also gave that media in Scotland, and the BBC in particular, their own set of editorial problems.

How do you cover this political landscape, where the governing party in Westminster is so clearly unpopular in Scotland, and where the main opposition party in Westminster, Labour – stuffed with talent and well organised by Donald Dewar – ran rings round the stretched Scottish Office ministerial team and came to dominate the news agenda North of the Border? With difficulty is the answer, particularly for BBC Scotland, charged with reflecting Scottish life and politics as it is, whilst the Corporation as a whole is legally charged with being politically even handed.

Political activists create amazing conspiracy theories about bias and the BBC. Depending on their hue, it is either a nest of Marxists, a Tory plot, or a London based conspiracy to deny Scotland freedom. None of this is true, and you hang up your own preconceptions at the newsroom door with your coat.

At the time, I was on the editorial staff of 'Good Morning Scotland', BBC Radio Scotland's morning news programme. Scottish Office Ministers had a plan. Press Officers were issued with stop watches and charged with timing the length of political interviews. When the programme came off air you dreaded the ringing phone as you returned to the production office lest you heard the words, "That's the Scottish Office for you." I am not making this up as a script for a satirical look at the era. Often the complaint was that the Tory spokesman got five minutes, whilst Labour got five minutes and thirty seconds. On more than one occasion they argued that if you had gone to all of the three main opposition parties on some issue, then the Conservative should have had a slot equal to the cumulative amount of time allocated to Labour, SNP and Liberal Democrat. Had they got away with this, it could have led to some memorably boring radio as a minister droned on for twenty minutes about fisheries policy. Sometimes the complaint was that nobody had appeared to represent the Government view, and you would have to remind them that you had made twenty requests for a spokesperson, but nobody had been available, so stretched were ministerial and party resources. This led to some awesomely awful interviews where the spokesperson they found was a backwoods Tory peer from the English shires as in touch with Scottish life and politics as a Morris dance troupe.

All of this reached a climax in 1989, the year the Poll Tax was introduced in Scotland as a pilot project, something which must rate highly in the league table of truly inept political decisions. Aside from generating the need for endless monitoring of the political output, a regular traffic of internal memos to staff and external memos to the Scottish Office, it being the BBC, it also generated meetings, where political balance was top of the agenda.

It was the habit of the then Head of Radio News, Jack Regan, to have an entirely informal gathering in his office on Friday evenings, where he would open a bottle of whisky and discuss the week's events. Jack was one of the finest radio journalists of his generation, astute and affable; he knew the Scottish scene inside out. In the spring of 1989, however, he made a mistake that cost him his job. On one of his Friday evening gatherings we were discussing the leaking of Scottish Office documents on the costs of a proposed joint rail and road bridge across the Dornoch Firth, which appeared to indicate that Ministers were being economical with the figures. Again, Labour had made the running with the story. Somebody came out with the phrase that it demonstrated that "the Scottish Political scene is out of kilter with the scene south of the border." Alas, Jack used the phrase in a memo to the Scottish Office. Michael Forsyth was Under Secretary of State and new chairman of the Scottish Tories. He seized on it as 'proof' that BBC Scotland was biased, and the ensuing row produced headlines of the 'Open warfare between BBC boss and Forsyth' type.[1] This farce is but one example of what became known as the 'democratic deficit'.

Meantime, in the print media, the main Scottish tabloid, the *Daily Record*, staunchly Labour, and the two great newspapers of record in Scotland, the (Glasgow) *Herald* and the *Scotsman*, were, broadly speaking, pro-active in their support of devolution. This had not always been the case with the broadsheets. When ideas for Home Rule re-emerged in the 1930s, the then *Glasgow Herald* took a very pro unionist stance, quoting a Chamber of Commerce Manifesto in a leader, claiming that

> the interests of England and Scotland are so interwoven, and the ramifications of trade so intricate, that home rule for Scotland would be altogether contrary to the interests of the country.[2]

[1] See Allan Laing, 'Forsyth and BBC clash on political bias claims', *The Glasgow Herald*, 16 December 1989.

[2] The *Glasgow Herald*, leader, September 1932. Full quote in Jack Brand, *The National Movement in Scotland*, London: Routledge & Kegan Paul, 1978, p.219.

The Scotsman was more emotional in support for devolution, claiming that

> Scotland would acquire a larger and freer life, that, less in the shadow of her dominating neighbour, she would experience a spiritual and possibly also an economic rebirth.[3]

Of course there were nay-sayers in the 1980s, notably Alan Cochrane in the *Daily Telegraph*, but in the main the concept of devolved power in general and of the blueprint for a Scottish Parliament drawn up by the Constitutional Convention formed to solve the 'democratic deficit' had a good press. Until that parliament became a reality and opened for business. The great beasts of Labour – the Gordon Browns, Alasdair Darlings and George Robertsons – stayed put in Westminster.

This has become a continuing problem for unionist parties in general and Labour in particular, aspiring politicians looking to Westminster rather than Edinburgh, whereas the reverse is obviously true for SNP hopefuls. The electoral list system ensured that party bosses could award sundry apparatchiks with a good crack at putting MSP after their names. In a piece for the *New Statesman* in 1999, the veteran political correspondent Tom Brown analysed the new intake of MSPs. Fourteen had been researchers, MPs' gophers and bag-carriers and "have never had a proper job," and there were 33 former councillors. The result was, particularly on the Labour back benches, a group of politicians who, to be kind, did not exactly represent the sharpest political intellects of our generation. An old Scots word was brought back into common usage, by broadsheets of record and tabloids alike, to describe our parliamentarians and their performance in the early debates: numpty. In 2007, it was voted Scotland's favourite word, according to a poll by BT Openreach.[4] The term implies general idiocy, accompanied by self-importance and a tendency to be a windbag. Brown found that "Politicos, local government functionaries, trade unionists, lecturers and lawyers make up four-fifths of the parliament."[5]

This was hardly the 'new politics' which had been promised, rather it re-enforced the growing notion of an out of touch professional political class. The public relations problem was exacerbated because they were being scrutinised by some of the sharpest political commentators around who had cut their journalistic teeth at Westminister and come home to cover the promised excitement of the 'new politics' in the Scottish Parliament. It led to an outburst from Tony Blair: "A bunch of unreconstructed wankers" was how he famously characterised the men and women of the Scottish press in a moment of irritation as those early bad reviews came in.[6] A little later, in March 2000,

---

[3] *The Scotsman*, leader, September 1932.

[4] Jenny Colgan, 'What is a numpty?', *The Guardian*, 4 September 2007.

[5] Tom Brown, 'A load of numpties and sweetie-wives', *New Statesman*, 5 July 1999.

[6] Alastair Campbell, *The Alastair Campbell Diaries*, Vol.1, *Prelude to Power, 1994-1997*, London: Hutchinson, 2010, p.584.

addressing the Scottish Parliament, then meeting in the Kirk's Assembly Rooms on the Mound, his language was more measured, but the sentiment was much the same. After accusing the hacks of doing what they could to knock over an edifice that they had been instrumental in erecting, the Prime Minister declared: "Scepticism is healthy. Cynicism is corrosive. And there is no cause for it."[7]

This was a classic case of trying to shoot the messenger. As Blair castigated the hacks. Executive Ministers were admitting (privately) that parliament did itself no good by setting as its first priorities the business of deciding on MSPs' holidays, wages and expenses. There was a barrage of bad publicity to be taken into account: political lobbyists and their high-level connections ('lobbygate'); the ever rising costs of the new parliament building, where again the new polity did itself no PR favours by selecting a celebrity panel which chose a daring design and a site bought from one of the Tory party's financial supporters; meantime ministers and MSPs demanded more and more space for themselves, the building programme dropped further behind schedule and costs soared to an eye watering ten times the original estimate. It is little wonder that public support dwindled. The referendum of 1997 would have been won even if the notorious 40 per cent rule that had stymied hopes of an assembly in 1979 had applied. The first election produced a more than sixty per cent turnout, high by modern standards. The second election produced a turnout of just over 49 per cent. The long hoped for Scottish parliament had become just another modern political institution inspiring, at best, nothing very much in the hearts of most Scots, at worst, the usual contempt of the modern voter for politicians. Subsequent electoral turnouts have hovered just above fifty per cent.

This is now compounded by the decline of the Scottish media. A fourth estate rightly scrutinising a parliament and an administration and holding them to account when necessary is the very stuff of an informed democracy. Surveying the current scene, it is no longer possible to write of 'two great newspapers of record' or a home-grown tabloid with a strong political presence. They are but pale shadows: as recently as 2000, industry figures showed, The Herald and The Scotsman both sold more than 90,000 copies a day, while the Daily Record sold more than 600,000. In 2012, the monthly sales figures over the year painted a sorry picture: the Daily Record fell from 307,000 to 276,000 – of which 248,000 were in Scotland. The Scotsman fell from 42,000 to 36,000, while Scotland on Sunday declined from 55,000 to 43,000. The Herald and Sunday Herald (the latter founded in 1999 at the dawn of Devolution) had given up on publishing monthly figures. Latest figures I have to hand, from the media magazine The Drum, for April 2013 show a further overall drop of eleven per cent in Scottish newspaper sales.[8]

---

[7] BBC Scotland, 'Blair denies union will break', 9 March 2000, <http://news.bbc.co.uk/1/hi/scotland/671774.stm>.

[8] Fiona Booth, 'Decline Continues for Scottish Newspapers', The Drum, 15 April 2013.

You could, of course, argue this is all part of the digital revolution, and the new journalism is emerging on line. I have no doubt that this is true, that we are, in terms of the internet, in an age which is an electronic version of the early days of printing where, along with much that was great and good, a confusion of dishonest pamphlets, scandal sheets, pornography and salacious satire spewed forth from the early presses. I have also no doubt something will emerge from the current chaos of online noise, but that is long term; here and now we have a problem.

It is not a problem confined to Scotland and the UK but a phenomenon of the increasingly digitized western world. There has been a vast expansion of the newspaper industry in Asia, particularly in India and China. Decline in the West is led by the United States. A survey by *The Economist* in 2011 showed that since the turn of the century the number of journalists employed in daily newspapers fell from 56,000 to 40,000. In the two years following the onset of recession in 2007 revenues fell by thirty per cent. In Western Europe it found what it described as 'managed decline'. In the same period in France revenues fell by just two per cent, and in the biggest market, Germany, by ten per cent. However, in European terms the UK led the field with a fall of a fifth.[9] It is clear that an historic process of change is underway in the way news is transmitted and political debate is conducted, and for Scotland, this state of media flux exists at the moment when a monumental and historic decision is to be made and the nation has to decide whether to opt for independence and break up a 300 year old union.

Whereas newspapers are suffering from competition from new media, radio audiences overall have grown, and not faced the fragmentation suffered by television come the digital revolution, which is good reason to deplore the present condition of BBC Radio Scotland. At a debate held by the Scottish Constitutional Commission in January 2013, one of Scotland's most respected academic historians fired a timely broadside. A well briefed Professor Tom Devine described how senior staff at Radio Scotland are so demoralised that many were regularly looking for opportunities to leave, and that they held the higher echelons of management at Pacific Quay – the neo-Stalinist bloc that is now headquarters – in contempt. He contrasted the former successes of the station with what one senior producer had told him was the "embarrassing, inept pap" of much of the current output. I can only nod in agreement. One senior member of the production staff and former colleague told me that BBC Scotland now 'resembled a failed state'.

Chris Harvie commented back in 2008:

> In order to afford the bonuses ladled out to Clarkson, Ross, Paxman, etc, and its Broadcasting House apparatchiks, the BBC – stingy as ever in its treatment of freelances – has cut back on serious journalism and features. Many of its best producers

---

[9] 'A Little Local Difficulty', *The Economist*, 7 July 2011.

have retired early or gone on to the PR payroll of worthy public concerns. Who can blame them?[10]

The stark fact is: somewhere between 100 and 120 jobs are planned to go by 2017 as part of a drive to cut the budget by 16 per cent, but this disguises just who are in the process of going and who have already departed. In the main, they are experienced and specialist journalists. A recent tranche of redundancies saw the departure of the Education Correspondent, at a time of major upheaval in the sector. And surely the age of austerity is not the time to axe the business correspondent on 'Good Morning Scotland'?

As for the loss of experience, not to mention flair, gone is the voice of the Highlands for his generation, Iain Macdonald, together with a small clutch of the talented Highlanders from the Glasgow newsroom. And that is in just one month. It has been going on for a decade of sundry redundancy and early retirement 'deals'. The finest editor I worked with on GMS left in his early 40s and is now a press officer at a University. An award winning Aberdeen reporter joined the happy ranks of the early retired in his early 50s. When I retired in 2006, I was the only editorial retiree that year who had reached the requisite age. Pacific Quay has destroyed corporate memory, a huge loss in a news organisation.

How will it cope with coverage of the referendum? Management ooze confidence or, is it, perhaps, given the track record, complacency? MSPs would seem to think it is the latter. Members of Holyrood's Education and Culture Committee have said they are "far from reassured" over the issue. Following evidence sessions to the committee, it intends to monitor the BBC's performance every six months.[11]

But who will be scrutinising the politicians? As a nation, we are ill equipped for the coming debate. I recognise I have concentrated on the BBC in general and radio in particular when dealing with the electronic media. These are the creatures whose ways I understand best, and I know the same problems of economic cut backs and consequent loss of talent face STV and the commercial radio sector, as recession bites into already dwindling advertising revenues. Never has there been a greater need for a robust and intelligent Scottish Fourth Estate to hold the body politic to account and act as a forum for reasoned debate. Never has it been in such a sorry state.

---

[10] Christopher Harvie, 'The battle for the Scottish media', *Comment is free (The Guardian)*, 5 September 2008, <www.guardian.co.uk/commentisfree/2008/sep/05/scotland>.

[11] BBC News Scotland, 'MSPs to monitor BBC Scotland's output', 8 May 2013, <www.bbc.co.uk/news/uk-scotland-scotland-politics-22459896>.

Educating for a Green Europe

Noel C. Spare

Introduction[1]

Suggested aims for a green Europe (from a regional perspective):

- To commit to accelerating the development and introduction of new forms of energy that are characterised by maximised sustainability and are clean and ethically viable. This will require advanced products, processes and infra-structure capable of ensuring efficient and cost effective manufacture and distribution.

- To create real jobs in which people can take pride, thus enhancing the social capital that is necessary for the viability of a modern democratic, competitive, prosperous and equitable society.

- Take a systemic approach to the creation of mixed economies embracing industry, services, finance and welfare underpinned by universal education and training and committed to research and development and technological innovation to ensure/facilitate continual process improvement.

The challenge is immense and will not diminish, especially against a background of ever-depleting finite resources. Never ending economic growth, the mantra of politicians the world over, cannot, by definition, in the long term save us on our most finite of planets! A way will have to be found therefore, of going beyond the UN *Brundtland Report* (1987), which called for 'sustainable development'. The term is unfortunately an oxymoron, and the report was more about economic development than sustainability. A more appropriate view of sustainability might be that proposed by John Ehrenfeld,

[1] The author wishes to acknowledge the help and support of his colleague, Andrew Forde in the preparation of this paper. And to Hanna for her research and presentation.

emeritus Professor of Industrial Ecology at MIT, who defines sustainability as 'the possibility that on Earth all life, human and nonhuman, will flourish forever.' The right question is not how to achieve growth. It is how to have a strong economic system that does not require incessant growth.[2]

Assertions will not do it, the market will not achieve it, and it will not be driven by the imposition of arbitrary numerical targets. Exhortations and words alone will not suffice. A green Europe will need to be built on foundations of profound knowledge for which we will require a fundamental and applied scientific approach, upheld by all-encompassing and widely available education and training (education for knowledge, training for skills). Whatever technologies are found to be appropriate for a Green Europe, it will not hang by sky-hooks, nor be run by magic elves,[3] it will need rock solid foundations provided by vast knowledge resources that are constantly under proof.

We have no model to which to refer, no Utopian vision to show us the way, but we must start somewhere. This chapter lays out the proposition that a starting scenario for educating in a Green Europe might look something like present-day Baden-Württemberg (BaWü). This approach was to some extent inspired by numerous references and statements by Christopher Harvie, and research by Stefan Büttner revealing that BaWü produces orders of magnitude greater numbers of graduate engineers and skilled technicians on a *per capita* basis than Scotland. For a country that aspires to making its contribution to a green Europe by harnessing the power of the mighty Atlantic to be transmitted to an energy hungry mainland Europe, this must be highly worrying.[4]

A former German President, Theodor Heuss, indeed referred to BaWü as a 'Model of German possibilities'[5]. So what is it about BaWü that recommends it as a model for a green Europe?

Model Baden-Württemberg

It is one of the youngest of the German Länder (federal states) being established in 1952 by the amalgamation of the states of Württemberg-Baden, Württemberg-Hohenzollern and Baden. It occupies the south-western corner of Germany, bordering France in the west and Switzerland in

---

[2] H. Thomas Johnson, (Professor of Business administration, Portland State University, Portland, OR), 'Lean Management and True Sustainability,' *Lean Manufacturing 2008: The Foundation of Success* (Society of Manufacturing Engineers), pp. 97-103.

[3] Christopher Harvie, *Broonland:The Last Days of Gordon Brown*, London: Verso, 2010, p.53.

[4] Christopher Harvie, 'Europe's Energy: Extreme Engineering and Scotland's Future', presentatrion at Freudenstadt Colloquium XX, 2010.

[5] See <www.regleg.eu/index.php?option=com_content&view=article&id=52<http://www.regleg.eu/index.php?option=com_content&view=article&id=52>.

the south. It has a landmass of 35,751 square kilometres and a population of 10,7 million, making it the third largest and most populous of Germany's 16 federal states. The state has, with sound planning, hard work, an unshakable belief in education and training, a commitment to technological research and advanced manufacturing, developed into one of the most prosperous regions of the world.

It has a robust mixed economy with a per capita GDP of 32 000 Euro (2009: cf. Germany as a whole – 29 406 Euro). It is renowned for its advanced manufacturing facilities; its R&D and innovative flair make its products recognisable and respected the world over. Its top ten companies have a combined turnover of over 300 billion Euros and employ around 1,1 million people (See Table 1).

If these world-class organisations provide the economic powerhouse of BaWü, then it is in the engine room that the strength-in-depth of the BaWü economy is to be found. This is the renowned and formidable German *Mittelstand* which is constituted by companies that roughly translate to SMEs – of which there are at least 80,000. Around a half of the state's GDP is provided by its SMEs.

Table 1: Top Ten Companies in BaWü in 2007 by Turnover

Rank	Name	Location	Branch	Turnover (Billion Euros)	Employees (2007)
1	Daimler	Stuttgart	Automotive	99,4	272 382
2	Schwarz-Gruppe	Neckarsulm	Retail	50	260 000
3	Robert Bosch	Stuttgart	Automotive	46,32	271 000
4	Celesio	Stuttgart	Pharmaceutical	22,35	37 516
5	Phoenix	Mannheim	Pharmaceutical	21,6	22 000
6	EnBW	Karlsruhe	Energy	14,71	20 499
7	ZF	Friedrichshafen	Automotive	12,65	57 372
8	Heidelberg Cement	Heidelberg	Building products	10,86	67 916
9	SAP	Walldorf	Software	10,24	44 000

€300bn combined turnover, employing 1,1 mio people

About 5.5 million people are gainfully employed in BaWü. Unemployment stands at 5,4% (Q1 2010). Of those in work, 41% are engaged in some form of production, with 59% in services. BaWü's SMEs are reported to be employing ca. 240,000 people in management positions alone.

The state is endeavouring to bring its innovative and manufacturing prowess to bear in the field of renewable energy by placing much greater future emphasis on what it terms 'Environmental Engineering'. Green will mean different things to different people, but its definition will inevitable be occupied by energy and how it is produced, transmitted and consumed. The current renewable energy production mix in BaWü and its future projections are shown in Graphs 1-3:

Graph 1: Development of the proportion of renewable energies in gross electrical production for heating and primary energy in Baden-Württemberg

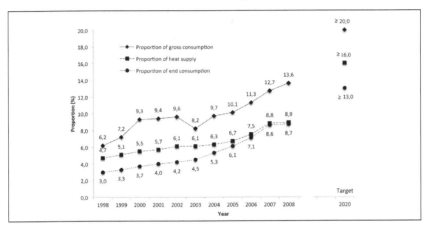

Great emphasis is being placed on increasing the share of renewable forms of energy both at a State and Federal level, and Germany can now claim to have established a €9bn renewables industry, employing some 160,500 people in 2004, which increased to 278,000 in 2008. In the period 2005-2010, a federal research budget of 800 million Euros was established. BaWü boasts

Graph 2: Development of the proportion of renewable energies in German electrical power supply

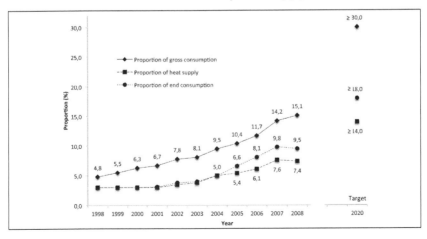

a plethora of major green projects, perhaps the most famous and high profile of which is the solar village near Freiburg with its 'PlusEnergy' communities and homes that produce an excess of energy which is fed back into the grid.[6] Interestingly enough, this project was inspired by protests against the building of a fifth nuclear power station near to the city of Freiburg.

BaWü could therefore be described, even by German standards, as prosperous; it offers its population a quality of life, in terms of real jobs in which people can take pride, premium social services and support and low crime levels, to which most Europeans can only aspire.

This, however, was not foreordained, it had to be created and it has to be nurtured. Such a society can only be sustained in this modern, competitive, energy-hungry world by ever increasing levels of fundamental thinking, innovation, competency and interdependence, the bedrock of which is the education and training of its people.

Graph 3: Development of the proportion of renewable energies in EU electrical power supply

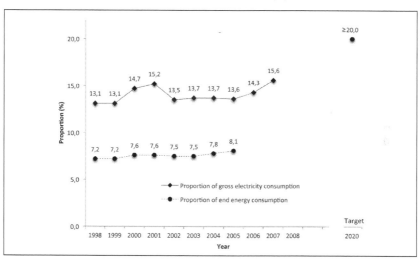

It is important to stress that the BaWü model is not something that could or should be *copied* by other regions; for is certain that what works in southern Germany would not necessarily work in south Wales or mid Scotland, for example. Rather, it is a model that, whilst not perfect, has a good track record in striving for environmental responsibility and which provides its citizens with the education and training required to maintain a high quality of life. As such it ought to be worthy of study by other regions so that lessons might be learned and hypotheses for improvement developed that are compatible with their own geo-political, economic and cultural restraints.

---

[6] <www.solarregion.freiburg.de/solarregion/freiburg_solar_city.php>.

Higher Education in BaWü

The following is a summary of higher education in BaWü:

BaWü engages in an holistic classic systemic approach to education; in other words it does not regard any one part of the education system as being more important than another and endeavours to give equal weight of support to all its parts. In this way it aims to create a system that is more than just the sum of its parts. Few fall through the educational net, and the system is flexible enough to ensure that, for example, late developers and under achievers are not lost to the system. Only about 3% of school leavers do so without some form of qualification.

In the area of higher education, BaWü maintains nine universities, six teacher training colleges and 23 colleges of technology (*Hochschulen*, some of which have the status of Universities of Applied Science), as well as two internal administrative colleges. Added to this are five music colleges, two art academies, the College of Art and Design, the Film Academy, the Pop Academy and eight vocational academies. There are also an additional 18 privately run colleges. In the Winter Semester 2009/10 around 275,000 students were attending colleges of technology.

Overall, Baden-Württemberg and its local authorities spend around €10bn on the education system every year.

Research in the region is conducted in at least 40 locations throughout the region (Box 1). BaWü expends about 4.2% of its gross domestic product on research and development – well above the EU average (1.9 %) and the German national average (2.5 %), and even well out in front of the USA (2.6 %). More than one quarter of all outlay expended by German industry on research and development originates from Baden-Württemberg. This makes perfect sense, as the standard of living and incomes can only be sustained in the long term through the continued development of sophisticated products and their sale in world markets.

In the field of training BaWü is also a leader. School-leavers not going into higher education aim for the much-cherished apprenticeships (Ausbildung) offered by employers that provide for formal training in numerous crafts and trades in a network of training colleges throughout the region. BaWü weighs in at a full 12% above the German average for apprenticeships. In 2009, 16,500 apprentices formally qualified as craftsmen, tradesmen (*Handwerker*), technicians or specialists.

Sustainable Carbon Free Energy Production

Ever since man lit his first fire, our dependency upon carbon based fuel materials has increased exponentially. The time is now upon us when we must reverse this curve and generate the energy we require by sustainable carbon free technologies. The vision of this new system is there, but who is to achieve it?

Box 1
Research Locations in Baden-Württemberg

Research Universities
Universität Freiburg
Universität Heidelberg
Universität Hohenheim
Universität Karlsruhe (tH) and Karlsruhe institute of technology (Kit)
Universität Konstanz
Universität Mannheim
Universität Stuttgart Universität Tübingen
Universität Ulm
University Hospitals

Special Types of Universities
Universities of education
Universities of Arts and Music
Universities of Applied Sciences
HtW Aalen
Hochschule Albstadt-sigmaringen
Hochschule Biberach
Hochschule Esslingen
Hochschule Furtwangen
Hochschule Heilbronn
Hochschule Karlsruhe
Hochschule Kehl
HtWG Konstanz
Hochschule Ludwigsburg
Hochschule Mannheim
HfWU Nürtingen-Geislingen
Hochschule Offenburg
Hochschule Pforzheim
Hochschule Ravensburg-Weingarten
Hochschule Reutlingen
Hochschule Rottenburg
Hochschule für Gestaltung schwäbisch Gmünd
Hochschule der Medien Stuttgart
Hochschule für Technik Stuttgart
Hochschule Ulm
Centres of Applied sciences

External Research
Max-Planck-Gesellschaft: institutes, international Max Planck research schools
Helmholtz-Gemeinschaft: forschungszentrum Karlsruhe, German Aerospace center,
German cancer research center
Leibniz-Gemeinschaft: institutes
Fraunhofer-Gesellschaft: institutes
contract research institutes
International research institutes:
Institute for transuranium elements, european Molecular Biology Laboratory
Heidelberg Academy of sciences and Humanities

Who will lead it and who is to make the great technological breakthroughs that will set us free from our carbon dependency? One thing is certain: realisation of the vision requires people educated in engineering and the sciences, people who understand a system, who have an appreciation for profound knowledge and who have the education, training and skills to make it happen.[7] Knowledge will be the single most important component in the creation of a green Europe, without it we can only fail.

---

[7] Noel C. Spare, 'A Revolution in Thought', presentation at Freudenstadt Colloquium XIX, July 2009.

"O Caledonia! Stern and Wild – Meet Nurse… "[1] For a Fledgling Green Energy Sector[2]

Irene Quaile-Kersken

Stormy winds, high waves – Scotland is a country known for its rugged landscape, wild coastline and its unpredictable weather. That might put off tourists in search of sunshine – but it could help provide the country and Europe with a secure, climate-friendly energy supply in the coming years. The government of Scotland has given top priority to the development of renewable energies. The country is home to several of Europe's largest onshore wind farms. Off-shore wind is developing at a rapid pace. Marine energy also plays a key role. Plans were recently unveiled for the world's biggest wave energy farm off the coast of Lewis.[3] By 2020, Scotland wants to cover 100 percent of its electricity consumption from renewable sources – and export excess power.

Devolution has played a key role in the expansion of green energy, according to a recent study, *Delivering Renewable Energy Under Devolution*.[4] It looked at how the development of wind, wave, solar and biomass energy had been affected by the establishment of the Scottish parliament and the other devolved administrations in Wales and Northern Ireland. The study is based on a two-year research project undertaken by Robert Gordon University, Cardiff University, Queen's University Belfast and Birmingham University. The initial findings, published early in 2013, say Scotland leads the way in renewables deployment across the UK, and that devolution is a

---

[1] Sir Walter Scott: *The Lay of the Last Minstrel*, Edinburgh: Birlinn (Bowhill Edition), 2013, Canto VI, Stanza 2: *O Caledonia! stern and wild, / Meet nurse for a poetic child! / Land of brown heath and shaggy wood, / Land of the mountain and the flood!*

[2] Much of this material was first published online by Deutsche Welle <www.dw.de>; Thanks to Chris Harvie and Stefan Büttner, who helped make the contacts for my reporting trip in 2009. Thanks to David Scrimgeour DS Consulting GmbH Munich for facilitating the reporting trip in 2012.

[3] David Ross, 'World's biggest wave energy farm gets go-ahead', *The Herald*, 23 May 2013.

[4] Richard Cowell *et al.*, *Delivering Renewable Energy Under Devolution*, A research project funded by the Economic and Social Research Council (RES-062-23-2526), Cardiff University, 2013, <http://cplan.subsite.cf.ac.uk/cplan/sites/default/files/DREUD-SummaryReport.pdf>; see also: David Toke *et al.*, 'Scotland, Renewable Energy and the Independence Debate: Will Head or Heart Rule the Roost?', *Political Quarterly* 84 (1), 2013, pp.61-70.

driving force in the growth of the sector:

> Key aspects of energy policy are executively devolved, which gives Scottish Ministers full control over major energy consents and planning, onshore and offshore, and operational control over aspects of market support systems.[5]

The study attributes Scotland's success in becoming a leading player to unique political and institutional conditions. It says Scotland has offered the long term and consistent political and business support to the fledgling industry, looking at renewables as an important motor for economic growth.

It's an ill wind...

When I first looked at Scotland's push towards renewables in 2010, I visited Whitelee Wind Farm, at that time the biggest onshore wind farm in Europe. Just 15 minutes drive from the city of Glasgow, suburbia gives way to wide, open spaces and rolling hills. The conservation village of Eaglesham with its whitewashed cottages, the odd farmhouse, and sheep on the moors looks like the Scotland of the tourist brochures. Then come the wind turbines, like giants striding across the moor, three arms rotating in the fresh Scottish breeze. This is the latest technology in the heart of traditional Scotland.

Today, Whitelee is Europe's second-largest onshore wind farm, with 215 turbines which can generate 539MW of electricity, enough to power more than 300,000 homes.[6] At a time when some people are sceptical about having wind turbines in their 'backyard', Whitelee has identified one of the key issues in promoting renewable energies: educating the public, especially the younger generation.

In conjunction with the local authorities and the Glasgow Science Centre, Scottish Power Renewables, who run the wind farm, have developed a Visitor Centre as well as site tours. Game shows, 'build your own turbine' workshops, a mini-wind tunnel to experiment with – a combination of education and entertainment makes the wind farm a popular destination for school trips and family outings.

During a visit to Whitelee I met Christine Balloch, science coordinator at the local school, Eaglesham Primary, and some of her pupils. The teacher is enthusiastic about the chance to teach her pupils about renewable energy 'hands-on'. Elizabeth, a year 6 pupil I talked to, enjoyed the tour of the turbines and finding out how they work and how high they are. "It's better for our planet. It's much better than using batteries," quips the environmentally aware ten-year-old, who also likes to walk her dog amongst the turbines on the moor.

---

[5] Cowell *et al.*, p.4.

[6] See < www.whiteleewindfarm.co.uk>.

Luke is in year 7. He, too, has become a fan of renewable energy, thanks to the lessons on the wind farm:

> It's much better than ordinary electricity, because that produces too much greenhouse gas which can affect the earth. The wind is renewable. That means you can use it again and again and again. And it doesn't hurt the planet at all.

Recently Hannah, a young relative from the area, told me she and her class had a great day at Whitelee and had "hugged a wind turbine".

Perhaps there is some hope after all that the next generation of Scots will grow up with a stronger awareness of the need to preserve the environment by using renewable energy and keeping development sustainable.

The latest win in the 'lottery of life'

In 2010, Jim Mather was the Minister for Energy, Enterprise and Tourism. Mather told me Scotland had won the "lottery of life" with regard to energy:

> We've had in the past coal, hydro, North Sea oil and gas. Now in renewables, we're in fantastic shape. 25% of Europe's wind potential, 25% of Europe's tidal potential, 10% of Europe's wave potential, even solar is relevant here because of our long summers with the long daylight. There's a lot of scope – and we're pushing on all these fronts.

Developments indicate that there was more to this than political rhetoric. "Scottish governments have the most sustained record of setting targets above the UK norm and of meeting them," according to the 2013 study.[7] The current energy minister, Fergus Ewing, told me in an interview in 2012 he was confident that the present target of matching 100% of Scottish electricity consumption with renewable energy by 2020 was "ambitious but achievable," and cited figures showing the country well on track to meet its renewables and emissions reduction targets.

Ewing believes working with industries and universities as well as seeking to build and maintain a constructive relationship with the UK government were the keys to success. The study *Delivering Renewable Energy Under Devolution* would appear to confirm this. It refers to "a high level of elite coherence and consistency over energy development in Scotland which helps legitimise and rationalise assertive use of the powers available, and reinforces – with the political leadership – a sense of commitment."[8]

---

[7] Cowell *et al*, pp.3-4.

[8] *Ibid.*, p.5.

The other key future energy sector where Scotland has taken a leading role is marine energy, both wave and tidal. The idea of harnessing the power of the waves to produce electricity has been around for hundreds of years. Now this renewable energy source is finally making a breakthrough. Pioneers are feeding wave power into the grid off the coast of Scotland. One major factor in this success was the establishing of EMEC, the European Marine Energy Centre in Stromness, Orkney. It was set up by the Scottish and British governments and the European Commission in 2003 as the world's first facility for testing wave and tidal energy in real sea conditions, but with a direct link to the national grid.

Different technologies to create wave and tidal energy are being tested in berths off the coast. These include Scottish inventions. The 'Oyster', developed by Aquamarine Power, a Scottish company with its headquarters in Edinburgh, is a hydro-electric wave energy converter. At a depth of fifteen metres, a platform, ten by eighteen metres, is attached to the seabed. A flap is joined to it by a hinge and moves up and down in the waves. This power pumps water at high pressure to shore, where it produces electricity for the grid using a turbine.

'Pelamis', the 'sea-snake', is a floating mini power-station, four metres in diameter, 180 metres long – the size of five inter-city carriages, invented by Richard Yemm, now also Director of the company Pelamis Wave Power. Pelamis consists of several segments, linked by joints. As they are moved by the waves, generators inside the device produce electricity, which is transferred to shore by sub-sea cable. At the company's headquarters in Leith outside Edinburgh, Yemm's team monitor the output with data transferred by optical fibre cables. For maintenance or repair, the 'sea snake' can be unplugged and towed to the coast.

Scotland surfs ahead

"Every developer who produces electricity from the sea here is able to sell it," explained Eileen Linklater, marketing manager at EMEC, which I visited in 2012. "The challenge is to make machinery to survive in a very hostile environment," according to Neil Davidson from Aquamarine power. Off Orkney, the devices can be tested in stormy weather and waves of up to 17 metres. EON, Scottish Power Renewables, Vattenfall, ABB, Kawasaki – all the big international names in the power sector are investing in the promising technologies being tested at EMEC. Energy Minister Fergus Ewing views that as a sure sign that wave energy is on the way to commercialisation.

The Pentland Firth, between Orkney and the Scottish mainland, where the North Sea meets the Atlantic Ocean, has a huge potential for wave and tidal energy. Companies are planning to install 1.7 gigawatts of marine power here, Ewing confirms: "a massive quantity, around a quarter to a fifth of the total electricity consumed in Scotland." Other large-scale projects are in planning off the country's west coast. The United Kingdom was the first country in the world to grant leases for the building of wave farms on designated areas of the sea. In May 2013, full consent was given for the world's largest commercial wave farm off the north-west coast of Lewis. The energy will be generated by Aquamarine Power's Oyster devices.

Energy Minister Ewing recently announced that Scotland will be the first part of the UK to have a dedicated fund to help develop the wave energy sector. "Marine energy is to play a role in the clean energy mix. The country is benefitting here from its expertise in the North Sea oil and gas sector," says Fergus Ewing.

Research and development for new technologies involve high investment costs. The rapid progress that has been made in Scotland would have been unthinkable without massive support from the government. A combination of grants, loans and feed-in tariffs, alongside the provision of well studied developments sites along the coasts, provided developers with incentives. Wave energy is still too expensive to compete with other renewables. "The costs will have to decrease for the new power source to be competitive with on-shore wind," says Roy Kirk from Highlands and Islands Enterprise, HIE, the government agency promoting the economic development of the region. The next step would be for marine energy to bring its price into line with that of offshore wind, which is still considerably more expensive than onshore wind.

Island electricity to power the British mainland

One prerequisite for the success of marine power is the upgrading of the British national grid. "It was constructed around fifty or sixty years ago to transport power from coalfields in the industrial heartlands of Scotland and England," explains energy minister Ewing. At that time it was a matter of providing small, remote communities with electricity. Orkney is at the northernmost point. Now these areas are to become large-scale energy providers. The grid will have to be upgraded to transport energy in the opposite direction. At the moment, the island communities also have to pay much higher charges for grid access – a bone of contention between the Scottish National Party government and the Conservative-Liberal coalition in London.

Northern Scotland could reap considerable economic benefits from the development of marine energy and offshore wind. The remote region of Caithness once owed its prosperity to the development of nuclear energy at Dounreay. Now wind and wave energy are set to take over. Dounreay, more than 800 kilometres north of the British capital London, was chosen as the site for a nuclear facility back in 1955, to test the fast breeder reactor. While protesters in the cities warned of the risks of the technology, many people in the region were grateful for thousands of new jobs and the investment that came with the project. Fishermen sold their boats and turned to the new plant for financial security.[9]

---

[9] See William A Paterson, *50 Years of Dounreay*, Wick: North of Scotland Newspapers, 2008.

Now Caithness is about to enter a new era. Dounreay is to be completely decommissioned by 2023.[10] More than 2,000 jobs will be lost – in a region with a population of just 26,000. "One job in three is dependent on Dounreay one way or another," says Trudy Morris, Chief executive of the Caithness Chamber of Commerce.

The decision to decommission Dounreay was taken back in 1994. At the end of 2011, the final contract to close down the nuclear site was awarded to the Dounreay Partnership, a joint venture by the British company Babcock and the US firms CH2MHill and URS. They have committed to the ambitious goal of closing the site completely by 2023. Charles McVay is the senior manager responsible for disposing of waste from the Scottish site. As well as the huge challenge of dealing with highly toxic radioactive material without harm to humans or the environment, McVay has another more immediate problem:

> Because we have such a highly skilled work force, lots of industries are very interested in Dounreay staff, especially the North Sea oil sector. So we have to ensure that we maintain an attractive work environment versus some of our competitors. So we are going to put in place a retention programme to encourage folk to keep working at Dounreay during the period of decommissioning.

New jobs in green energy, not nuclear

Making sure the highly qualified work force has prospects to stay in the region after the closure of Dounreay has top priority for Roy Kirk, who heads the Caithness section of HIE. He sees the wind parks being set up off the coast and the development of marine energy as key sources of employment for the coming years. HIE is working hand-in-hand with the local chamber of commerce to make sure as many Dounreay employees as possible stay to help transform the region into a centre for the growing offshore renewables sector. Chamber head Trudy Morris secured funding from the Scottish government, the European Social Fund, the Nuclear Decomissioning Authority and Dounreay to make the transition work. "We have to make sure we capture the opportunity and that it doesn't go elsewhere", says Morris.

A leap of faith

Scrabster harbour on the Caithness coast is gearing up for the green energy revolution.[11] 19 million pounds have been invested in refurbishing the port to

---

[10] 'Dounreay decommissioning process takes significant step forward', *STV News*, 22 May 2013, < http://news.stv.tv/highlands-islands/226417-dounreay-decommissioning-process-takes-significant-step-forward/>.

[11] 'Minister: Scrabster has central role in green revolution', *STV News*, 5 July 2010, <http://news.stv.tv/scotland/185616-minister-scrabster-has-central-role-in-green-revolution/>.

cope with the transport of large, bulky, heavy marine devices. 1,500 square metres of pier will be extended to 11,000, according to Sandie Macke, the port manager for Scrabster Harbour Trust. "Just one marine energy device can take up a whole area of pier. We also had dredging done, to ensure access and water depth at all states of the tide, and heavy lifting equipment put in." The Harbour Trust wants Scrabster to be involved in the fledgling industry from the very start and become a centre for repair and maintenance. Preparing for an industry that is not yet in operation involves a "leap of faith," Mackie admits. "There are still technical issues to be proven, but we will be ready in a couple of months and we hope to see first test arrays, then commercial arrays of marine devices."

The Scottish government's marine energy target of 1.6 gigawatts from the Pentland Firthis daunting: "If you translate that into actual devices, we would have a massive volume of activity, which all the ports in the area will struggle to cope with." But that is a problem Mackie is happy to face.

The companies reliant on business with Dounreay are already feeling the effects of the gradual decommissioning. Will Campbell is the Director of JGC engineering and technical services. "The biggest problem is we can't get enough skilled labour," he says:

> Dounreay used to train 35 apprentices a year, but in the last 15 years, they have not been investing any more. Now we train our own people and become a magnet for the offshore industry. The young guys are lured away.

And that in spite of the fact that wages are high and the cost of living low in Caithness. In retrospect though, Campbell says, the closing of the nuclear plant was the "best thing that ever happened" to his company: "We were probably 85% dependent on Dounreay 5 years ago. When that dried up, we found we can do work elsewhere. The skills are transferable."

Will the renewables industry provide enough business to replace what the engineering firm has lost? "Technically, it should be a lot more. But when will it happen? Marine energy is still a bit off from having commercial plants in the water. But there should be no problem. You have to be upbeat, don't you?" quips Campbell, the successful businessman.

Hi-tech 'made in Scotland'

Bill Baxter is another local entrepreneur hoping to benefit from the wave of green energy. His factory in Wick manufactures underwater cameras for the Norwegian company Kongsberg Maritime. Many of their customers are in the oil and gas industries. Baxter says most of them are also getting involved in renewables, which helps him make contact with the new industry. Although the basic engineering is the same, cameras for marine energy applications still require innovation, because they will be used in shallow water, says

Baxter. "The seals work better in deeper water, when they are pressurised. Another problem is bio-fouling. That is not a problem in deep water, but in shallow water with ambient light, lots of little crustaceans like to latch on to the camera and interfere with your viewing."

Science under pressure

Finding out about the interaction between the marine environment and equipment installed for marine energy has become another economic factor in Caithness. In 2000, the University of the Highlands and Islands opened ERI, the Environment Research Institute in Thurso. Research Fellow Dr. Angus Jackson looks into how new structures in the water attract algae or crustaceans. They can affect the performance of the wave converters or, for instance, cause problems for fish-farms, if they clog up equipment or nets. Invasive species can also drive out indigenous marine organisms.

Caithness is under pressure to find out about these impacts as quickly as possible. The first wave devices are already producing electricity at the EMEC sites off Orkney. "The political agenda for developing these energies is very strong, and the will to do it in Scotland is probably better than anywhere else in the world," says Jackson. But he also sees it as a real challenge for companies aiming at full-scale commercial development, and for the researchers who have to provide the data in time for that development to happen on the time scale envisaged by the government in Edinburgh. Together, they have to succeed, so that Scotland can become a model for the transition to renewable energy.

Minister Ewing quoted US President Obama to me: "We know the country that harnesses the power of clean, renewable energy will lead the twenty-first century." Scotland may still have a long way to go before reaching that status. Nevertheless, Ewing finds it inspiring: "It sounds like quite a good prospect to aim for."

Reflections on Energy Self-Sustaining Islands in Ireland: with some Scottish and wider European inspirations

Frank Conlan

Introduction

During the early 1990s, the Structural Funds of the European Communities provided a systematic approach to developments in the four fields of the funds – the Regional Development Fund, the European Social Fund, the Agricultural Guidance Fund and the Fisheries Fund. Ireland was a major beneficiary under the Community Support Frameworks agreed during that period. Indeed, since the beginning of the Freudenstadt Seminars, Ireland has been a recurring topic discussed in the annual review from the *Zollernblick*.

Of particular interest during the past twenty years has been the evolution of energy policies in parallel with infrastructural developments. This contribution is a reflection on a number of strands arising from a study which was carried out in Ireland at the beginning of the 'nineties with the support of the Structural Funds. This focused on the Irish and Danish islands and was later the stimulus for a series of initiatives particularly in the field of energy. In the intervening years since that study, contacts developed with the Scottish islands offered the potential of role models to Irish counterparts. In particular the initiative taken by the Western Isles Council in setting up the ISLENET network has been a focal point for European islands and their efforts to develop sustainable energy policies and practices. This contribution retraces some of the steps in Ireland which have contributed to the greater awareness of the role island communities can play and reflects on some small achievements.

The Structural Funds have been a major stimulus for developments in the Member States, and the particular aspect which is worth recording is how they have provided for innovation which has yielded some interesting results for the islands in Ireland. The starting point for this narrative is the project funded under the Regional Development Fund measure for Innovatory Actions – the SAPIC (Special Action Programme for Interregional Co-operation) programme, as it was then called. This allocation of funding amounting to 1 per cent of the overall European Regional Development Fund allocation and was intended to provide "support for studies or pilot schemes concerning regional development at community level." The funding awarded to the proposed Small Islands Study was a modest IR£120,000

(€152,000), and the study was undertaken in 1992-3, incorporating the Irish Islands, including Rathlin Island in Northern Ireland, and the Association of Small Danish Islands, based on the island of Avernakø in Denmark. The participants in Ireland included representatives of four island communities, their respective County Councils (Donegal, Mayo, Galway and Cork), the Social Science Research Unit of University College Galway and Údarás na Gaeltachta, the Regional development agency for the Gaeltacht – the Irish-speaking regions. The Rathlin Island Trust represented the population of Rathlin Island in Northern Ireland, and the Association of Small Danish Islands, representing 26 small Danish islands, was the third national partner.

The Small Islands Study 1992-3

The initial aims of the study were to examine the socio-economic problems of the islands, particularly with regard to access and transport issues; to look at the administrative structures in the three jurisdictions – Ireland, the United Kingdom and Denmark – and, finally, to examine the potential for the development of telecommunications and information technology on the islands. At that time, the question of energy was not a major topic of concern, and it was at the follow-up stage that a more focussed approach was taken to the task of auditing the energy demand and supply on the islands.

   At the time of the study it was shown that there was a trend of declining population on the Irish islands. The 1986 Census of Population had listed 75 inhabited islands with a total population of over 10,000 people. However, the succeeding census results for 1991 showed a continuation of the decline and the persistence of an age profile characterised by an absence of the working age cohorts in the population and a high level of dependence on state supports. The subsequent 1996 census confirmed the trend.[1]

   The Danish small islands are specifically recognised in Danish law, and there is a special parliamentary committee which oversees all legislation to ensure that there are no adverse impacts on small island populations. This was based on the Danish Parliament's Island Support Act, passed in 1984, later amended in 1987. This provided, *inter alia*, for financial subventions for the ferry services to the islands, support for investments in new ferry services and funding for projects and experiments on the islands for the improvement of living conditions for their inhabitants. Denmark was considered an excellent role model for the study programme because of its integrated structure of national, regional and municipal government. The Danish small islands, however, did not find representation through this structure, but were integrated by an alternative parliamentary and administrative route.

---

[1] Unfortunately, the deterioration has continued to this day. The latest census returns for 2011 show that there are now only 26 inhabited islands, with a total population of fewer than 3,000 inhabitants.

In Ireland, the situation was one of envy on the part of islanders for the progress the Danish islands had achieved. Islanders were not represented in local government. Their numbers were too small and the islands too scattered to provide for a single county council representative. Nor was there, until the early 'nineties, any significant recognition of the islanders' special needs. A Ministerial Islands Committee which had been established in 1987 was considered by the islanders to have been ineffective. Islanders had tried to establish a representative body to lobby on their own behalf. The Federation of Islands (*Comhdháil na nOileán*) had been formed in 1984 by twelve Irish island communities with the aim of promoting the development of the islands and their communities, especially in the fields of social, economic and cultural development. They sought to establish "one Authority with total responsibility for islands and recognising Comhdháil na nÓileán, the Federation, as a consultative body to that Authority". Between 1984 and 1986, the membership increased from 12 to 16 islands. Unfortunately, due to lack of progress and the scarcity of resources to continue, the campaign for official recognition was abandoned.

Nevertheless, this short effort highlighted two of the intrinsic weaknesses afflicting the Irish islands. On the one hand the democratic deficit already mentioned – the island population being too small to elect its own representative to either a local government or a national government body. In addition, the national policy with regard to the support for the Irish language, and the Gaeltacht regions where it is spoken, has resulted in greater support being given to those islands where the dominant language is Irish. This has had the effect of dividing the islanders, even though they are dealing with the same economic and social challenges.

In Northern Ireland, the situation of Rathlin Island was and remains different. As the only inhabited island in Northern Ireland, it comes under the administrative jurisdiction of the Moyle District Council. The island has traditionally associated itself with the other Irish islands without prejudice to its status in Northern Ireland or within the United Kingdom. Rathlin had also been a participant in the earlier attempt to establish a representative body for the Irish islands in the short-lived *Comhdháil na nOileán* 1984-87. It might also benefit from European sources of funding through the association with the other Irish islands as a transnational partner.

The outcome of the study helped to mobilise the island communities and provided a launching pad for further co-operation with other island communities elsewhere in Europe. The island representatives had seen in Denmark the operation of the Small Islands Association and its interaction with the Ministry of the Environment, responsible for the administration of the Island Support Act, and the Danish Parliamentary Islands Committee. One of the first steps undertaken, following the completion of the study, was the restoration of the Islands Federation under the new name of *Comhdháil Oileáin na hÉireann* (the Irish Islands Federation). The island representatives who had taken part in the study programme invited representatives of all inhabited islands in Ireland to Galway. At the meeting in Spring 1994, a new constitution was adopted, based on the constitution of the Danish Small Islands Association. In addition, at government level, the Minister of State for the Marine, Gerry O'Sullivan T.D., established an interdepartmental committee to examine how better coordination could be achieved in the light of the report's recommendations and drawing on the experience elsewhere in the European Community.[2] Mr O'Sullivan was later appointed as the first Irish government minister with direct responsibility for island affairs.

The recommendations of the study were conveyed to the European Commission in Brussels and, in the course of reviewing proposals generated from the work and the vision of the islanders for their future development, a Commission official made suggestions for immediate short-term steps. This included the use by the newly established Federation of a 'Global Fund' made available to the Irish Government. This enabled the new organisation to employ its first development officer, Pádraig de Búrca, who made a successful funding application on behalf of the Irish islands in the second round of the LEADER programme. This approval was given in 1994. The islands have continued to participate in the LEADER Programme since that time.

The ISLENET Network of Islands

During the course of the Small Islands Study 1992-3, contact was established with the Islands Commission, one of the Commissions of the Conference of Peripheral Maritime Regions (CPMR), which is based in Rennes, Brittany. One of the Island Commission members, the Western Isles Council (*Comhairle nan Eilean Siar*) had co-ordinated the drafting of a proposal to be submitted in 1993 to the Energy Directorate (DG XVII) of the European Commission under the call for proposals for the PERU Programme for regional and urban energy planning. At the Islands Commission meeting where this proposal was being finalised, the European Commission official endorsed the idea of a separate Irish proposal which would address some of the issues affecting the island population such as had been reported in the Small Island Study. This encouragement resulted in the establishment of a link with Brittany (and its islands) and an energy planning project for the West of Ireland.

Two significant results emerged from the final call for proposals in 1993 of the European Commission under the PERU Programme for energy planning. A proposal was drafted which included the role of Galway County Council and its island population. This was combined with an application from EOLAS/Forbairt, the predecessor organisation of the Irish Energy Centre, for an examination of the potential for renewable energy developments in

---

[2] *Dáil Report*: Vol. 431 No. 2 p. 68 20 May, 1993: Written Answer – Offshore Islands, Living Conditions.

the western region of Ireland. This included the counties of the province of Connacht – Galway, Mayo, Roscommon, Sligo and Leitrim – and, in addition, the counties of Donegal and Clare. The result of this project proposal was the approval by the European Commission of the Connacht Regional Energy Planning Study (1993-95). This was to be the first sub-national energy audit in Ireland. At the same time, the European Commission approved the proposal prepared by the Western Isles Council for the establishment of the European Islands Energy Charter – ISLENET.

ISLENET, as a network of European Island Authorities, was thereby created in 1993, and the Charter was adopted at the Annual Conference of the Islands Commission held in the Isle of Wight in the same year. The network has been hosted since that time by the Western Isles Council (*Comhairle Nan Eilean Siar*) in Stornaway, which has provided both the administrative and financial support for the network. It has coordinated many projects and initiatives among ISLENET members who have agreed to adhere to the objectives of its Energy and Environment Charter.

The network has also acted as host to other island representatives, such as the small islands of Ireland or regional groupings of small islands like the Breton islands association APPIP (*Association pour la Promotion et la Protection des Îles du Ponant*). As the number of European Community Member States increased with the accession of new Member States, so too did the complexity of problems confronting small island communities. Sweden has more than 200,000 islands, with an island population of approximately 50,000. Finland is similar to Ireland in having a language issue: for example, the Swedish-speaking inhabitants on the 50 or so islands in the Turku archipelago. Scotland has traditionally been well represented on the Islands Commission through the active involvement of the Councils of the Western Isles, Orkney and the Shetland Isles. Elsewhere in Scotland, Argyll and Bute take care of their 26 inhabited small islands which do not have island councils of their own. In general, the problems of these communities continue to increase. A common difficulty is the provision of adequate healthcare services. The declining trend in population means in some cases schools are no longer viable, and children have to attend boarding schools on the mainland, separated from their families. Traditional economic activities on islands such as farming and fishing are also in decline so that the dependence on seasonal tourism activity has become more important. Although tourism is in many cases a welcome seasonal activity, the attraction of island life for city-dwellers means that in many cases, when it comes to their purchasing a holiday home on an island, the prices are driven beyond the capacity of the islanders to buy their own homes, and this is increasingly a problem. The solution may be the provision of social housing, but there are only rare cases of social housing being provided on small islands, the Breton islands being one of the few eceptions.

The ISLENET network has acted as a catalyst for the islands, large and small, to discuss these issues and has hosted events to encourage their participation in collaborative projects in the fields of energy and the environment.

The Connacht Regional Energy Study

The Connacht Regional Energy Study was the second outcome of the 1993 call for proposals. The project was in cooperation with partners in Brittany and Galicia, where similar co-ordinated studies were undertaken. The Connacht study provided an energy audit for the region, broken down by county and the various sectors of energy consumption. It also included estimates for the development of renewable energy resources in the region across a range of technologies. These included wind power, small hydro schemes, combined heat and power (CHP) and biomass. At the time of the study, the only wind farm in Ireland was located at Bellacorrick in County Mayo, with an installed capacity of 6MW.

The energy audit was based on the situation for the calendar year of 1992, which was the latest year for which a full set of data was available. Nevertheless, the data was not sufficiently complete to avoid the need for estimations. Energy consumption in the region was estimated as 35 per cent for Transport, 38 per cent Residential and 15 per cent Industrial. The remaining 12 per cent was divided between Agricultural, Commercial and Public Sector consumption. This result corresponds with the lack of major urban concentrations in the region, a settlement pattern of rural dispersion and a low level of industrial activity. A large proportion of the electricity generated in the region (89 per cent) used coal in the Moneypoint Power Station. This contributed to the high level of electricity exported from the region (69 per cent). On the import side, the relatively large import of oil was attributed to the demand for road transport fuel, reflecting a higher dependence on private transport.

The study also carried out energy audits on two of the offshore islands – Cape Clear in County Cork and Inis Oírr in County Galway. Each had permanent populations of about 200 inhabitants, with a dependence on small scale agriculture and fishing and with a seasonal influx of tourist in the summer. The audits were carried out using the template of the regional audit for the year 1992. Both islands, at the time of the study, had electricity networks isolated from the national grid and supplied from diesel generating sets with a high cost of generation. In the case of Cape Clear a demonstration project, funded partly by the European Commission under a Research and Development programme of the late 1980s, had used a 150kW wind turbine in combination with battery storage. The German Government provided additional funding for the research project from their national Research and Development budget. German companies supplied some of the key elements of technology being tested; one supplied a control software programme to optimise the balance between the diesel generation, the variability of the wind power and the demand from the system, another company supplied the battery storage which acted as a balancing accumulator. The system worked well and had a high level of involvement by the island community in the management and maintenance of the project.

Unfortunately, when the research period was completed, the ESB, the national electricity utility company, was offered the opportunity of adopting the system as a permanent arrangement for the island's electricity network. However, the plans were then well advanced for connecting the inhabited Irish island to the national electricity grid.

Based on the experience gained with the research project on Cape Clear island, the next generation of the German diesel/wind/battery storage system was installed on Rathlin Island in Northern Ireland.

Outcomes of the Connacht Study

The detailed results of the Connacht Energy Planning Study are of little significance to-day. The pattern of energy consumption has changed significantly. For example, the high dependence on peat as a fuel for residential heating has considerably decreased and has been replaced by oil and, in some areas, natural gas. Nevertheless the quality of the housing stock, including that constructed since the base year of the study, still leaves considerable room for heeding the recommendations in the report regarding the awareness raising among consumers about energy consumption.

Two major outcomes are clear from the work undertaken. The first was that the results and the methodology of the study provided a template and a set of data on a county by county basis which enabled a number of counties to take part in the later SAVE Programmes of the European Commission. The first county was Donegal, which was quickly followed by Galway and then Mayo. By now, all of the counties which were part of the study have established Local Energy Action Teams along the lines promoted by the European Commission's concept of a bottom-up approach to addressing the local agendas in the fields of local advice on energy management and the introduction of renewable energy appropriate to the circumstances of the different region. This has been done by networking different regions across the European Union and a process of actively exchanging experience.

The second benefit was the opportunity opened to some islands to take part in further development work in renewable energy. The Connacht report, in dealing with the island energy audits, identified a number of key areas requiring attention. These included the need for a more detailed examination of the housing stock to ensure that low-cost improvements could be introduced for the benefit of the householders. The report recommended the formation of energy teams who should be given low-tech training in energy saving measures. A recommendation that there should be a training programme for island Co-operative Managers was the subject of a later ALTENER project funded by the European Commission. A number of the participants followed this step by achieving higher qualifications which brought them onto new career paths.

Inter-island Exchange

A further recommendation was that the networking instigated through the ISLENET network should be intensified so that island communities were encouraged to learn from the solutions found on other islands to address common problems and opportunities. This was particularly the case with Inis Meán, one of the Aran Islands in County Galway, which benefitted from the contact with the island of Samsø in Denmark, where a renewable energy academy has been established on the basis of their active programmes of introducing a variety of renewable energy projects on the island. Samsø was an ideal role model for an island population with an interest in developing renewable energy and at the same time improving the efficiency of the island's energy consumption. However, the Danish islands have a number of distinguishing differences over the small island cohort such as the Irish islands. The typology of islands in Denmark covers the range of devolved administrations typical of the country's administrative system. Samsø, for example, with a permanent population slightly less than 4,500 permanent inhabitants, is a Municipality with its own elected council of 13 members. The island has become popular with retired people from the cities, and it has about 1,000 holiday residences or second homes. As a popular holiday destination, the population during the season can rise up to 30,000. Nevertheless, there are no large holiday facilities, because the islanders decided to feature their natural environment and have provided for outdoor activities and the facilities needed for active ecotourism.

There have been a number of visiting groups from Irish Islands to Samsø, attracted there by the progress made by the community in the linkages between renewable energy and the sustainability of the island community. It was in this connection that the Irish island of Inis Meán was partnered with them in a sustainable islands project. Samsø had developed a number of community owned projects which have acted as templates for other communities in Europe. These included the community's development and investment in the offshore wind project near Samsø. They have also installed a district heating system on the island, and a number of wind turbine projects operate on the island, including some 'neighbourhood' wind turbines where groups of households have come together to install a single turbine. These projects provided a stimulus for the community co-operative on Inis Meán to address one of their most pressing problems.

During the late 1990s, Inis Meán's influx of tourists during the summer months was putting a severe strain on the ability of the island's water supply system to provide an acceptable standard of service, in both quality, to the required health standard, and quantity, to meet the needs of those on the island. The permanent population of the island was less than 200 inhabitants, but this number was exceeded during the summer months with tourists, including day visitors, all of which added to the demand. The geology of the Aran islands is Lower Carboniferous Limestone and, as a result of glacial action, there is a very little soil coverage on the island. The island's water supply was based on the collection of surface water which eventually discharged from a number of seeps in the limestone. This was piped into storage tanks from which the water was treated and distributed to the households and other consumers of the island. Attempts at drilling deep-bore wells in the limestone have been unsuccessful because of salt water ingress from the sea.

In the mid-'90s, water had to be severely rationed during the summer months as a result of growing demand and lower than usual summer rainfall. This had obvious consequences for the development of the island's tourism, one of the few sustainable economic activities on the island. Inis Meán, as all the larger inhabited islands, had been supplied with electricity since the 1970s with stand-alone diesel generators. These were eventually connected to the national grid, with Structural Funds support, from 1995 onwards, including some islands with small populations which had up to then had no electricity supply.

The visits to Samsø, and other islands, by representatives of Inis Meán stimulated an interest to address the problem of their water supply, using the available wind resource of the island and their link to the national grid. Together with a number of Danish partners, the Island Co-operative made an application under the European Commission's 5th Framework Programme for Research and Development. The proposal was to utilise wind energy to provide power for a desalination plant. The project was approved by the European Commission in 1999 as a Demonstration Project in community ownership. The local community ownership was structured through the island co-operative (*Comharchumann Inis Meáin Teo*), a limited company which provided services on the island. A separate subsidiary company was set up to manage and operate the wind/desalination project. The project was supported by Galway County Council for its innovative approach to solving the water problem of the island. *Údarás na Gaeltachta*, the Irish Government's regional development agency for the Irish-speaking regions, also supported the project with financial assistance.

The original plan was to install a single 650kW wind turbine on the island, but when the site had been selected, on the western unpopulated side of the island, it was discovered that the difficulties of delivering the turbine to the site would involve too great a disruption and require severe reconstruction of the island's narrow roads. Eventually, planning permission was obtained for three smaller 225kW turbines which were to be located on the same site. The remainder of the equipment, including the desalination plant, a pumping station and the grid connection plant room were also constructed on this site. The desalination plant was fed with raw seawater and, by a process of vacuum distillation, produced potable water which was fed into the island's water mains. The excess brine from the desalination process was drained back into the sea. The remainder of the island's water system continued to operate as before, so that it was not necessary to run the desalination plant permanently. The process required less than 20 per cent of the electricity the wind turbines were capable of generating, and the balance of the electricity was sold into the grid on the basis of a 15 year power purchasing contract with the national grid.

The site work commenced in 2001, and the system was commissioned for operation during the summer of the following year. The project eventually completed all the commissioning trials. Technically, each of the component parts functioned correctly and to specification. A major snag arose with the saltwater intake, which may have been designed for calmer Baltic Sea conditions rather than the wild Atlantic seas experienced in Inis Meán. An alternative and more robust saltwater intake had to be constructed, and this delayed full operation for some months. A further difficulty emerged in the course of time, and this was due to the scarce manpower resources on the island. The delays involved in having repairs and maintenance work carried out on the desalination plant, in particular, highlighted the lack of skilled labour among the island population. These difficulties added to the running cost of the project but, more importantly, delayed repairs unduly and added to the downtime of the plant.

Early in 2004 a group from the Scottish island of Gigha came to Inis Meán to learn about the ownership structure of the wind farm. The Gigha Heritage Trust was proposing to install three similar wind turbines on their island, but without the complication of a connected desalination plant. The group was pleased with the progress they saw on Inis Meán and returned home encouraged that their project was confronting fewer difficulties than had been encountered in Ireland.

An Island Laboratory of Sustainability

The continued operation of the small wind farm on Inis Meán gave rise to an interesting proposal, which relates to the intensification of wind energy development in Ireland. At the present time, there is more than 1,600 MW of wind energy capacity installed in the south of Ireland. Northern Ireland has a further 400 MW of capacity, with an interconnector which allows for export and import of electricity, depending on demand. The peak winter demand in the south reached in the past winter was over 5,000 MW. The currently installed capacity of wind generation, combined with the queue of applications for connections to the grid, is already coming close to the 2020 target that 40 per cent of electricity generation should come from renewable sources. It is anticipated that such a high dependence on wind-generated electricity will create new challenges for the management of a stable supply grid. The traditional methods of responding to changes in demand is dependent on having access to fast response generation capacity, such as hydro power or more recent developments with gas-fired turbine generators. The variability of wind power and the seeming lack of control makes it important that methods should be developed to respond to the evolving scenario when wind generation targets for 2020 are eventually achieved.

In anticipation of these circumstances, the Sustainable Energy Authority of Ireland designed a study in 2007 which used the Aran Islands as a test bed to act as a model for the national network. The test was designed to incorporate all consumers of energy on the islands. In order to cover new technology options, a pilot scheme was introduced to make available a number of electric vehicles on the islands for the period of the study. In addition, heat pumps, which are already in use in some households and other buildings, were incorporated into the data to be collected and analysed. The small wind farm on Inis Meán already provides a high proportion of the electricity demand of the three Aran Islands, when it operates at normal capacity. The concept of the study was to determine the possibility of reducing, or even eliminating, the need to import electricity from the mainland grid to the islands by managing the demand, making use of storage techniques. In other words, the island's energy demand could be managed by controlling the charging of car batteries and the use of heat pumps by individual consumers. The study was designed to provide consumers with real-time information, based on actual demand, forecast consumption and the expected availability of wind power. The model will be used to generate cost benefit scenarios in terms of CO_2 reduction and system operational cost. The final results of the tests are not yet available, but the information gathered from the analysis of the demand management will have implications for achieving the 2020 target. The expectation is that the Aran Islands will be able to achieve the aim of being zero importers of electricity as a result of this study.

This is but one example of the constraints experienced on small islands providing a basis for innovative approaches to finding solutions for the benefit of the wider community. The networking between islands initiated by the establishment of ISLENET has had wider benefits than those originally foreseen. Not all trials are successful, but the learning process involved is an important element in making progress. In the two decades since this networking activity was started, much progress has indeed been made, and as the Irish proverb goes – *Tosach maith, leath na h-oibre* – a good start is half the work!

Sustainable Energy for All

Stefan Büttner

This is a proposal which stems from participating in meetings around the Energy Efficiency (EE) Global Forum in Washington,[1] and brainstorming sessions/conversation with Ashok Sarkar, Mark Hopkins, Amit Bando, Martin Hiller, Wolfgang Mostert, Thomas K. Dreessen, and many others from different governmental levels, administrative/regulatory bodies, corporations and countries across the world. While I felt inspired by them, and they may share many if not all the points I am going to make, I do not write on their behalf.

At present, many committed people are taking initiatives – whether local, national, regional or international, from NGOs and/or from Parliaments – and are working hard towards improving energy access (EA), energy efficiency (EE) and the share of renewables (RE) in the overall energy mix.

This proposal shows how the new term 'energy productivity' and a holistic approach promise to link up and strengthen the general message, here focusing on energy efficiency.

There are 12 main reasons for it:

1. There is an ever-growing orchestra – as stated above, many people on many levels work to advance EE/RE/EA around the world – but orchestras are disciplined bodies, and 'ever-growing' contradicts this. So there is a lot of duplication in information-exchange; collaboration on testing solutions becomes difficult. This happens at the international level (conductors, soloists), at the national (string sections) and local (brass, drums) level. Just as if in an awkwardly growing-and-changing orchestra, the musicians also have headphones on, not hearing the overall tune. The goal is to have all the headphones connected through a switchboard, with the 'sound symphony' being the goal. This proposal wants to introduce such a symphony-enabler, ideally plugged-into the SE4All secretariat of the SE4All EE Hub.[2]

2. At multinational levels, exchange often happens through commonly-understood targets, overall energy performance, and policy databases. But targets are *not*

---

[1] See <http://eeglobalforum.org>.

[2] See <www.sustainableenergyforall.org>.

solutions, or even a manual about how to find solutions. Energy performance depends on the sectoral structure of the economy and the human interaction that makes people co-operate to find or exchange solutions. This is the crucial means to achieve global goals rapidly.

3. In contrast to the one-way structure of commercial product marketing, near-environment solutions and implementation strategies are usually devised and customised at the 'lower level': in town halls, local governments or local agencies and initiatives which are close to consumers of energy. But these do not usually tell the world about how they work or fail, by publishing solutions in English language manuals/descriptions/ journals. The result is that wheels – whether they work or not – are being re-invented far too often.

4. Apart from the language-barriers and financial problems of global exchange, the necessary trade skills and financing approaches can often act as prohibitors or as catalysts. Without high-level tradesman skills, energy-neutral buildings can be planned, sure, but they will not be built; without suitable financing schemes, they can also not be realised. And that goes particularly for SMEs and private customers, but also affects the public sector. Wherever there may be good policies, very often they only tackle aspects, rather than presenting a holistic solution which can be embraced and developed by all the groups which could potentially benefit.

5. Whatever solution there is, it cannot replicate existing initiatives, but needs to link them together, at least for purposes of efficiency and for giving them a stronger voice: a sort of uniting of the nations.

6. I want to argue that talking about Energy Efficiency (EE) almost intuitively makes one think about single items, such as lighting, buildings, appliances. Further, in most cultures or the business world, EE sounds rather negative, implying dilution of business success, particularly as it is often paired with 'climate protection' and 'carbon emissions'. We can get rid of that 'baggage' by changing EE into Energy Productivity – getting *most value* out of each unit of energy consumed. Thus the responsible citizen realises

that everything that consumes energy is part of this, as well as everything that causes, or prevents, the use of energy, putting the wasteful consumption of energy on the spot. So, improving EE will be seen as actually benefitting business competitiveness, fostering employment, reducing household expenditure and lowering public debt. The Alliance Commission on National Energy Efficiency Policy (ACNEEP)[3] has found a holistic solution, involving stakeholders in a broad-based project to double US Energy Productivity by 2030. President Obama has taken it on board, as it shows how we can disconnect *real* economic growth from energy consumption.

7.   Most current comparisons are in themselves problematic, as sectoral splits differ between countries. Statistics indicate that the UK is most energy-productive. But what if we factor in the *overseas* carbon cost of supplying the UK, with its huge financial/retail sectors, but less than 10 per cent in manufacturing? Germany generates around 30 per cent of its GDP in manufacturing and appears to be overall more energy efficient (third in that world wide league table of energy productivity). No one country will lead in all sectors. So there needs to be a comparison of energy-productivity by sector, comparing transport with transport, manufacturing with manufacturing. Sector champions will be the countries whose 'good' outcomes can start a process, similar to the ECS II (European Currency System), where the 'worst-performing' were motivated to catch up. For example, setting a practical target, increasing energy-efficiency by 10 per cent annually to catch up with the strongest performers, can start a race to the top in absolute and relative figures through positive peer competition. Besides sectors, this needs to be directed at SMEs as they have much 'sleeping' potential due to the lack of means to fully harvest their energy productivity potential.

8.   This exchange can happen through governments, but things will move faster when a wide range of agents active in one geographic area (players in that 'section' of the orchestra) are included in a holistic approach, such as ACNEEP developed. If a common denominator for action is fixed, before things go to parliaments and councils,

---

[3] See <www.energy2030.org>.

this will encourage suitable, effective government action. Currently, the most common 'adaptation' approach tends to be hit by government portfolio/parliamentary committee overlaps: hardly ever helpful to holistic ideas. Ideally, the commission approach would be exercised in each country, with people from other countries involved in an international advisory council.

9. Energy technology is thought about a lot. But what still lacks attention is its embedding in social, educational, historic, philosophical and the wider ethical-economic meanings. These 'soft' fields need to be understood, if we are to achieve behaviour change, adoption, and policy/entrepreneurial solutions to implement existing technologies – which still need to be linked up by smart integration of all suitable systems.

10. Rather than forcing consolidation on the musicians in the orchestra, if we link them up with each other without duplication or taking anything away, we will gradually create a 'Ricardian economy' of comparative advantages in which groups will join forces or share specialisations, or find common points – all of which strengthen the voice and make 'the field' more efficient.

11. Through this, local collaboration networks can be established, e.g. to apply for EU research funding, or to work together more intensively in a given country or continent towards holistic action/solution plans that are ready for implementation by businesses, people and governments.

12. Such an efficient 'web' could have its meeting-point where all these players can come together once a year in person, at least in the EE area. Without competing with events and activities of others, an Energy Efficiency Global Forum could be co-hosted by all the groups that are active in the continent where it takes place in that year. This could be 'tweaked' to resemble the global ownership and the partnership between mature and developing regions, with exercises as well as meetings that tackle characteristic problems.

This energy efficiency/productivity global alliance is best placed with SE4All as it truly 'Unites the Nations' in its holistic approach, comprehensively spanning from efficiency to access and renewables – while involving everybody, whichever country or continent, who wants to contribute constructively towards a world with sustainable energy for all.

Five Days in Malawi
18-23 March 2013

Sarah Boyack

In March of this year, the Scottish Parliament celebrated the bicentenary of the birth of David Livingstone and hosted a visit by the President of Malawi, Joyce Banda. We reaffirmed a commitment made in 2005 by the then First Minister Jack McConnell and the Malawian President Mutharika to commit to work together and share expertise. Their agreement pledged engagement on 'civic governance and society, sustainable economic development, health and education'.

In a Parliamentary debate initiated by my colleague James Kelly MSP,[1] who represents David Livingstone's Scottish birthplace Blantyre, we recorded Livingstone's key role in ending slavery and his enormous contributions in the field of education, healthcare, trade and commerce. As part of our celebrations, singer Annie Lennox OBE visited the Scottish Parliament to speak about her work as Special Envoy to the Commonwealth Parliamentary Association Scotland Branch.

MSPs across the Parliament's political parties also reaffirmed the positive impact of Livingstone's on the people of Malawi through their stories of civic links between Scotland and Malawi. They spoke of school links, health partnerships, church links and youth exchanges. During the debate it was noted that there are over 85,000 people across Scotland involved in project work and links with Malawi.

Those links are hugely appreciated by Malawians and are strengthened through the Scotland Malawi Partnership. Our relationship is based on a desire that Scotland makes a positive contribution to people's lives in one of Africa's poorest countries. Our relationship is one based on partnership, and on the commitment to sharing experience.

In our most recent debate on Malawi, there was also a focus on equalities and climate change. The commitment of President Banda to do more to promote the education of young girls and, more generally, to support women's equality was welcomed. We also debated climate change, an issue where Scotland supports knowledge transfer on water quality, agriculture and renewable energy in Malawi.

At Parliamentary level the commitment is to work with the Malawian National Assembly through our Technical Assistance Programme, which is managed by the Scottish Branch of the Commonwealth Parliamentary Association. That has led to links between the two Parliaments, enabling

---

[1] The debate was held on 27 March 2013; see <www.bbc.co.uk/democracylive/scotland-21961096>.

clerks to exchange best practice on issues such as committee work and research to support the work of Parliamentarians. As a relatively new institution, the Scottish Parliament aspired to emulate best practice from across the world, with a focus on openness, transparency, accessibility and accountability.

In addition to links between Parliamentary staff, there is also a twinning programme between Parliamentarians. That project has provided a good illustration of the disparity of resources available to representatives to carry out our work and the different realities in which we operate. MSPs have state funds provided to enable us to be supported by dedicated staff, with offices in our constituencies to support our work with constituents, to enable us to engage with civic society and to assist us in operating in the Parliament on committees and our policy interests.

The Scottish Parliament is not responsible for international relations or foreign policy, so our focus has been on adding value to the work carried out by the Department for International Development (DFID) and to focus on the areas set out in the 2005 agreement on civic governance and society, sustainable development, health and education.

In my blog I wanted to highlight the impact our contribution is making. There is no doubt that Malawi faces huge challenges, but I am proud of the work taking place across Scotland which is making a real difference, whether through the commitment of individual citizens, by NGOs and charities, or through our schools and hospitals.

Their work is inspiring and is both a continuation and celebration of the work started 200 years ago by David Livingstone.

As Michael Barrett, Professor of Biochemical Parasitology at the University of Glasgow, commented in an article in the New Statesman this year:

> It was this notion of integrating people who could bring sustainable development to Africa that was Livingstone's dream, a far cry from the cruelties of so many white European colonialists.
>
> He learned to speak the languages of those among whom he tried to spread the gospel. He wished to treat Africans with respect; he tested their medicines and embraced many of their customs. He gave his life in the fight against the slave trade. Few European place names were preserved in post-colonial Africa but it is still possible to visit the towns of Livingstone in Zambia and Blantyre in Malawi.
>
> When Kenneth Kaunda, the former president of Zambia, described David Livingstone as the first African freedom fighter, he might just have had a point.[2]

---

[2] Michael Barrett, 'What is David Livingstone's legacy, 200 years after his birth?', New Statesman, 28 February 2013.

As part of the Scottish Parliament's partnership with the National Assembly of Malawi, 10 parliamentarians in each institution have been paired. To coincide with celebrations of the bicentennial of David Livingstone's birth, Alex Fergusson MSP and myself visited Malawi for five days, from 18 to 23 March 2013.

While we were there, the plan was to meet groups which have links with Scotland and to meet with parliamentarians. In addition to visiting constituencies we were providing a one day workshop in the audit and accountability processes used by the Scottish Parliament to scrutinise the work of the Scottish Government, and we both participated in a one day conference run by the Active Learning Centre on promoting the participation of women in politics.

Here is what I noted in my Blog at the time[3]:

Day 1 – Cutting the Ribbon

The secondary school I visited with Christina has 400 students. It's a state school with no dedicated accommodation for students, many of whom have to walk long distances to attend classes. During the rainy season or in the blistering heat that will be a challenging journey.

After meeting the chiefs, the PTA and teachers at the school, I was given the job of cutting the ribbon on the new house that has been built for the head teacher through the Mapuyu North Constituency Development Fund. Later in the day I also visited a new market that had also been built to provide stalls for farmers and traders to sell their produce.

Day 2 – Malawi: The Warm Heart of Africa

Last summer I attended a Mary's Meals fundraising event in Edinburgh.

Today I met the staff of the Joyful Motherhood project, one of the recipients of fundraising by Mary's Meals. Beatrice, the project's manager, introduced me to the aims of the project: to support the development of young babies who have been orphaned or who have lost a mother at childbirth. The project is based at Bwaila Hospital in Lilongwe and has over 100 babies on their books at any given time.

Although Malawi's maternal birthrate has improved, there are still many children whose mothers die while giving birth. HIV/AIDS is prevalent and women in villages often live many miles away from hospital with no transport. Getting to a hospital safely is therefore a major issue.

Malawi's inflation means that the project's costs have rocketed in recent months. Diesel has doubled in price in the last year and currently costs 718 kwatcha (about £1.40) a litre. Although the nurses who visit foster mothers use buses and bicycles as often as possible, some journeys are too far to be made without a car.

---

[3] See <www.sarahboyack.com/?paged=3<http://www.sarahboyack.com/?paged=3>.

A tin of formula milk now costs 1,600kw (£3.30) and a baby will need 6 tins a month. The project provides milk and regular visits by nurses for the first year, to give children the best chance of a healthy start. To get this in perspective, a private hire driver gets just over 5,000kw a week in pay.

After the briefing, we set off to meet the family of a newborn who had been born two days ago. Her mother had been admitted with complications and in being transferred to another hospital had died in the ambulance. The journey to her village took us an hour and a half, to the Mapuyu South area, again on the border with Zambia.

As we got close to Mdamvayani, once off the main road we met no other vehicles. The road had huge potholes as a result of the heavy rains. When we arrived, the mother's female relatives were still grieving and what should have been a joyous occasion, the birth of a baby, was very emotional and a time of sadness for everyone.

All of the family came to see nurses Verina and Nitta who examined the baby and took the family through how best to care for the baby. As we sat there, it seemed like the whole village had come. There are only six families in the village, so the mother was close to everyone.

Luckily the little baby has a family, with two brothers and a father who, although he walks with difficulty, was on hand to hear what the foster mothers would be doing to care for the child. The baby is the grand-daughter of the Chief of the village, and he was very keen to tell us about the food he grows to support his villagers.

Like many smallholder farmers in Malawi, although they are growing enough food to feed the family in a good year, they are too far from markets to be able to get a decent price for their produce and are not able to earn any money or develop the range of products they grow.

It was a very human example of the vulnerability of so many Malawians. They are not able to add value to their produce, are vulnerable to bad weather affecting their crops and have no other source of income. Tackling rural poverty is the issue which is being addressed by the Women's caucus who we will meet on Thursday.

Day 3 – Theatre for Change

Theatre for Change aims to tackle the problem of HIV/Aids by producing interactive theatre productions which educates communities in Malawi.

The top three groups of people most vulnerable are sex workers, police and teachers.

Shockingly, before the project started, two teachers a day died of HIV/Aids. Nation wide testing suggests that the rate of infection is less than 1% when student teachers start college, but rockets to over 23% when they graduate from college. So Theatre for Change works with teacher training colleges and schools across Malawi to promote safer lifestyles.

I was really interested in the project's use of radio drama to spread its message. It's a very effective way to communicate across the country although radios are still hard to come by for many people.

We visited a local bar and saw the appalling conditions where sex workers live, then attended a performance about the real life experiences of a young woman who had ended up as a sex worker. The drama attracted a huge crowd, and villagers got involved in a very effective role play which was true to life, credible and clearly enjoyable to the audience.

It's a real life issue as young girls aged 11 or 12 are being forced into sexual work. They live and work in bars as they have no accommodation, having been forcibly moved from their village.

In addition to awareness raising, the project provides micro credit schemes to give young women, which follow on from training run by the project, and it distributes condoms and health advice across the country.

The project's patron is Stephen Fry, and it has been given great support by Annie Lennox.

Day 4 – Workshop with Parliamentarians on Financial Scrutiny and Audit

Our meeting with the Finance Committee and chairs of subject committees in the Malawi National Assembly provided the chance to debate financial scrutiny and audit processes across the Parliament. While the topic might seem dry, the things we take for granted were of great interest to the parliamentarians we met.

We were quizzed in detail about the ability to require ministers to give evidence to committees and to be able to scrutinise the government's budget proposals properly.

Our system of subject committees reporting to the Finance Committee was seen as a good way to shed light on issues such as health and education. We illustrated our presentations with examples of issues that the Scottish Parliament had dealt with. We also discussed the importance of having an independent audit function to scrutinise expenditure. I used the examples of the Gathering Report and the more recent Accounts Commission Report on Local Government Capital Projects to illustrate how Parliamentary scrutiny and transparency work.

One specific proposal we have been asked to take back home was the question of transparency of donor aid and development projects. Malawian MPs expressed interest in knowing how funding allocations were made by our Government, and the expected outcomes of projects in their constituencies.

Day 5 – Empowering Women

Yesterday was the joint seminar between Scotland's Active Learning Centre on Empowering Women. The event was the culmination of a three-year Scottish Government funded project on empowering women.

The walls were covered with posters outlining the work that had taken place with women MPs and local communities in their constituencies.

As with all aspects of life in Malawi, resources are scarce and limit the capacity of community involvement and engagement. The MPs were therefore very positive about the local workshops they and their local communities had participated in. One of the developments that the Malawi Parliament is currently planning would see parliamentary offices being established, which would support more local engagement with constituents.

Since I was last in Malawi in 2008, the numbers of women parliamentarians has increased, with 44 women members elected in 2009. However, only four women members of the 193 Malawi National Assembly were re-elected. This has created a debate about retention of women members, as people focus on next year's elections.

While in the UK there is an acceptance by parties that elected representatives who have worked hard and built up support will be generally allowed to fly the flag for their party again, there is no similar expectation in Malawi.

The workshop was therefore a chance for the parliamentarians to debate how to empower women and discuss strategy with NGOs and donor Government representatives. It was also open to the media and Malawi's main TV channel and newspapers. Our attendance at the seminar alongside the Minister for Gender was newsworthy.

My speech was on the Scottish experience and highlighted the difference that Labour's twinning and zipping of candidates for the Scottish Parliament and all women shortlists for MP selections have made to political culture in Scotland. I also argued that creating a higher proportion of women MSPs had seen women emerge into leadership positions, too, with the last decade seeing women leaders of parties for Labour and Conservative groups as well as a Deputy leader for the SNP. In addition to having a Deputy First Minister, we have also had a raft of women ministers and committee conveners, and now a Presiding Officer – again across the parties.

My colleague Alex Fergusson MSP outlined the work of a constituency member in Scotland and highlighted his local campaigning work for constituents – regardless of their political affiliation.

We had a lively discussion with some practical recommendations for attracting new women into politics and on retention. For retention, it was argued that NGOs should be working with women on practical projects in constituencies, and that the women MPs would also have to work harder at communicating what difference they had made to the lives of their constituents.

We were delighted to get feedback after the women's caucus that in a meeting with all Malawi's political parties a commitment to stronger support for women was given. While next year's elections will be the acid test, this is definitely a positive sign.

Regional Cultures and Cultural Connections

Scotland in Europe:
Europe in Scotland

Richard Demarco

In early June 2013, I returned with Terry Ann Newman from the Venice Biennale, after having presented the exhibition 'Scotland in Europe: Europe in Scotland' in the Demarco European Art Foundation's Pavilion on The Giudecca in Venice.

The exhibition, as its title indicates, brings up-to-date my work as Kingston University's Emeritus Professor of European Cultural Studies. My Foundation's contribution to the Biennale further strengthens my firm belief that Scotland's cultural heritage is defined, to a large extent, by the cultural and political history of Europe, from the time when the north-western extremity of the Roman Empire was defined by the Antonine Wall stretching from the shores of The Firth of Forth to those of The Firth of Clyde. In the centuries that followed, through the heroic travels of Celtic missionaries, saints and scholars, through to the Middle Ages, the world of the Celts helped define the concept of Christendom and, indeed, helped Christianise the peoples of Middle Europe, particularly those living on the banks of the great European rivers – the Seine, the Rhine, the Danube and the Rhone. This is the world of Saint Serf who was sent from Rome to Christianise those who lived on the shores of the Firth of Forth. In Scotland, he was known as St Serf, but in Rome, he was St Servanus. The Empire of Charlemagne is defined by the Christian church in the shape of The Temple of Jerusalem at Aachen. It is juxtaposed with the Schottische Kirk of St Serf who is well-known in that world where history and mythology meet in Scotland as The Slayer of The Dragon of Dunning.

The Rule of Saint Benedict originated out of the world from whence generations of Italo-Scots have followed in the footsteps of Roman Legionaries, from the Val di Comino dominated by the mountain of Montecassino and its monastery as the motherhouse of the world-wide Benedictine Communities. The monasteries of Scotland, with their famous libraries, kept alive the heritage of the Greco-Roman culture, together with that of the Christo-Judaic cultural identity which defends the concept of Christendom. The history of the great monastery and cathedral of St Andrews was second only in importance to St Peter's in Rome. The Scottish Border abbeys, even in their ruined state, cannot be fully appreciated without identifying them with those in England, Ireland, Wales and all over continental Europe – as far south as Puglia and Malta.

This short essay is illustrated by a map I felt obliged to draw, showing how all the programmes devised by the Demarco Gallery's experimental Summer School – 'Edinburgh Arts' – were designed to attract artists, art students, academics, scholars and practitioners of all the arts to consider Edinburgh, not just as the world's most famous Festival city, but as a place of learning, in collaboration with Edinburgh University's Schools of Scottish and Extra-Mural Studies, and the Schools of Fine Art, History and Architecture of the University of Malta.

Among the Edinburgh Arts Faculty were Buckminster Fuller, who was one of the luminaries of Black Mountain College, the American off-shoot of the Bauhaus, Sir Roland Penrose, the founder of London's Institute of Contemporary Art, the Scottish poets Hugh MacDairmid, Norman MacCaig, George Mackay Brown, and Sorley Maclean. They were part of a faculty with included George Melly, the unique expert on Surrealism, Michael Spens, the editor of Studio International, the artists Wilhelmina Barns-Graham, Patrick Heron, John Wells, Arthur Watson, Doug Cocker, Sandy Moffat and George Wyllie.

Among the Edinburgh Arts participants as artists and students and art patrons were Sandy Nairne, Mark Francis, Tina Brown, Charles Stephens, Sally Potter, Jackie Lansley, Neil Bartlett, James Marriott, Jay Jopling, Jimmy Boyle, Lord Balfour of Burleigh, Colin Lindsay MacDougall, John MacQueen, Clare Street, Anne Goring, Jane Chisholm, Terry Ann Newman, Howard Hull, Janet Treloar, John Hale, Trevor Thorne, Jonathan Phipps, Jane MacAllister, Justin Dukes, John Latham, Andrew Nairne, Lawrence and Mary James and Howard Walker.

Among the Romanian artists were Paul Neagu, Ion Bitzan, Horia Bernea, and Ovidiu Maitec, who all managed to survive the madness of Ceaucescu's dictatorship. Then there were the Polish artists led by Tadeusz Kantor and his Cricot 2 Theatr company of fellow-artists, and the Polish gallerists Ryszard Stanislawski and Wieslaw Borowski, as well as Polish artists such as Zbigniew Makarewicz and his wife, Barbara Kowslowka, and the Polish artist, Sonia Rolak who lives and works in Venice.

There were Americans and Canadians, such as Professor Robert O'Driscoll, Head of Celtic Studies at the University of Toronto, Jack Burnham, acknowledged expert on Marcel Duchamp, the sculptor Edwin Owre, and Professor Peter Selz, the American art historian, John David Mooney, Pat Martin Bates, David Bellman, Jon and Magda Schueler.

Among those representing the Former Yugoslavia were Marina Abramovic, Mladen Materic and his Obala Theatre company, and Marjian Susowski, Director of Galerija Grada in Zagreb. Among the Welsh and Irish participants were Michael Scott, Sean and Rosemarie Mulcahy, the art critic Dorothy Walker, and Ted Hickey, Director of Ulster Museum, and Robert McDowell.

The German art world provided the commanding figures of Joseph Beuys, Klaus Rinke, Dieter Roth, Gerhard Richter and Günther Uecker; the French art world was led by Caroline David, Director of F.R.A.C. in Lille, and Alain Bourdon, an outstanding director of The French Cultural Institute, and his wife, Catherine Chevalier; the Italian art world was represented by Gabriella Cardazzo and her Galleria del Cavallino artists inspired by the life and work of Gabriella's father, Carlo Cardazzo, and her brother, Paolo, as well as Count Giuseppe Panza di Biumo and Giuliano Gori, as Italian art patrons unique in the world of art, the artists Mario and Marisa Merz, Paolo Patelli, Giudo Sartorelli, Picolo Sillani, Gian Carlo Venuto, and Cristina Gnoni, the art historian and expert on the Renaissance art of Florence, Siena, Prato and Pistoia.

Among the Scots were Ian Hamilton Finlay and his wife, Sue Finlay, George and Cordelia Oliver, Margot Sandeman, Jim Howie, Margaret Tait, the Orcadian poet and film-maker Gunnie Moberg, the Swedish-Orcadian photographer, and her American-born husband Tam MacPhail, and Iain Noble, the founder of the Gaelic University on Skye.

The Road to Meikle Seggie

These are just a fraction of the participants who can be defined as 'Edinburgh Arts' participants. They were all invited to explore what can be defined as 'The Road to Meikle Seggie', the road to all the villages and farms and crofting communities that are in danger of being left off the map of modern Scotland, and not being celebrated as they should be as nodal points on the road which takes you from Scotland to the shores of the Mediterranean, from the Pennines to the Apennines, to the shores of the Black Sea, from the Hebrides to the Cyclades, from the centre of Europe to its farthest European peripheries. 'Edinburgh Arts' focuses upon the migrations of Europeans, from pre-historic times to the present day.[1]

The Edinburgh Festival and the Venice Biennale are two energy points on 'The Road to Meikle Seggie', defining places where the arts can be seen striking a festive note. However, it should be noted that 2014 will mark the hundredth anniversary of the beginning of The Great War which began in 1914 and ended, not in 1918, but in 1945. This gave birth to The Cold War which divided Europe by The Iron Curtain and which led, inevitably, in the post-war years to the creation of The European Union and its enlargement and Euro economics.

Among the outstanding Edinburgh Arts participants was Frank Ashton Gwatkin who died in the Seventies. He was among the last of Britain's Edwardians; he was a poet, novelist, diplomat, President of the International Arthurian Society, expert on Japan and creator of Britian's Ministry of Economic Warfare. He participated in Edinburgh Arts all the way from The

---

[1] See Richard Demarco, 'Too Rough to go Slow', in: Paul Henderson Scott (ed.), *Spirits of the Age: Scottish Self Portraits*, Edinburgh: The Saltire Society, 2005, pp.87-122.

Cyclades to The Hebrides, to the monastic world of Inchcolm Abbey and Culross Abbey. His essay for the 1975 Edinburgh Arts Expedition publication is the definitive description of Edinburgh Arts. Any descriptions of Edinburgh Arts and its cultural, political and educational significance must involve quotations from this essay:

> So Edinburgh Arts has embarked upon the great Gulf Stream of European History which has moved across the centuries, too and fro, from the four rivers of Paradise to the waters of Guadalqivir, the Tagus, the Douro, the Loire, the Severn, the Shannon and the Clyde. It was the course of Pytheas of Marseilles, when Greek genius first discovered the British Isles, those Celtic islands. They were discovered, of course, many centuries before Pytheas by Phoenician, Carthaginian, and perhaps by Cretan merchantmen seeking for tin...
>
> The Crusaders and their followers kept the stream flowing from West to East, carrying in their luggage the Celtic mythology of the Arthurian Legend, and they returned with a mixed bag of Persian manicheism with Buddist undertones.
>
> Then The Plague, The Black Death, wrecked Europe, and Islam struck back, still along the main Gulf Stream, capturing Constantinople and reaching out as far as Vienna. Meanwhile, the traditional pattern had burst – eastward and westward. Westwards to the two Americas and eastwards to India, China and Japan. Thus the European influence spread over the whole world, but the main artery remained along the original line of the historic stream, extended now, by emigration to North and South America. This is still the main line of art and culture and learning; and it is into this stream that Edinburgh Arts has plunged.[2]

In July 2012, I was privileged to be invited to deliver a key address at a conference which celebrated the Germano-Scottish cultural and educational dialogue under the aegis of Edinburgh University's Institute of Governance. Eberhard Bort and Professor Christopher Harvie made key contributions, along with Allan Massie and Robert McDowell. These contributions dealt effectively with the long-term relationship between the universities of Edinburgh and Tübingen.

My key address related to the exhibition which the Scottish Government commissioned the Demarco European Art Foundation to present in Scotland House, in Brussels, to representatives of the European Union. The exhibition's title 'Scotland in Europe: Europe in Scotland' is tailor-made for the exhibition

---

[2] Frank Ashton Gwatkin, in: *Edinburgh Arts Expedition 1975*, Edinburgh: The Richard Demarco Gallery, 1975.

which the Demarco Foundation has presented as its contribution to this year's Venice Biennale in what was the very first Italo-Scottish Biennale Pavilion. The exhibition relates the Demarco Archive to the programmes devised and directed by Professor Federica Pedriali, the Head of Edinburgh University's School of Italian Studies.

This was a welcome addition to the theme of 'Scotland in Europe: Europe in Scotland' exhibition. It enabled the exhibition to anticipate the implications of the Demarco Foundation programmes which will commemorate the hundredth anniversary of the beginning of the First World War in 1914.

Professor Pedriali invited me to participate in the programmes she devised this year at the Scottish Parliament at Holyrood, as well as in the University of Cassino, and the British Embassy in Rome, to take on board the significance of the work of Italian and Scottish school children, inspired by the writings of Carlo Emilio Gadda. His writings were influenced to a great extent by his experience of the First World War. As an Italo-Scot, I must take on board the significance of his work.

I have been deeply involved in helping to strengthen the Italo-Scottish cultural dialogue since the 1960s. Therefore I am planning an exhibition at Summerhall in Edinburgh as part of my contribution to the 2013 Edinburgh Festival. The exhibition will have a related two-day conference. This will be focused on the implications of the Italo-Scottish dimension to Scotland's future and the interface between the Venice Biennale and the Edinburgh Festival since 1968.

This exhibition would make use of the Demarco Archive which records how, over a period of more than fifty years, Scotland has been in fruitful dialogue with European countries which had found themselves on both sides of The Iron Curtain, with special reference to Belarus, Hungary, Bulgaria, the Former Yugoslavia, and The Baltic States. The attached map illustrates the Demarco Foundation's programmes since the early sixties. It shows clearly how those cultures which define Europe's peripheral landscapes are inextricably joined to any idea of Europe's culture located in the heartland of the European Union in Brussels and in Strasbourg. The map also shows clearly the impact of migration upon Scotland, with particular reference to the impact of Polish and Italian immigrants and, in the foreseeable future, the impact of immigrants from Bulgaria and Romania.

OPPOSITE PAGE: Richard Demarco, Expeditions over Land and Sea: Exploring Europe from Edinburgh & Kingston

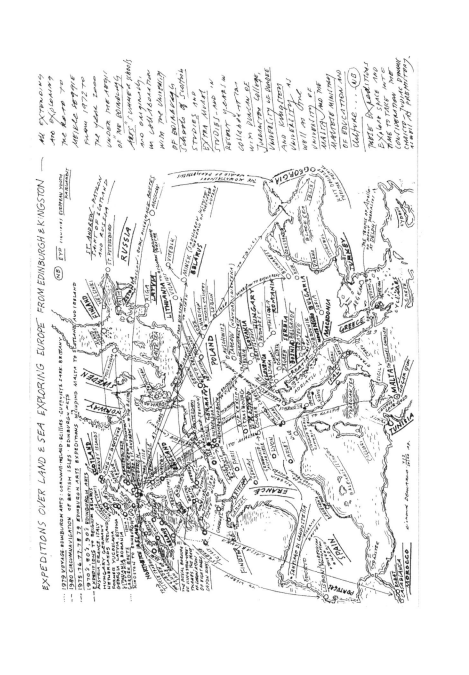

EXPEDITIONS OVER LAND & SEA EXPLORING EUROPE FROM EDINBURGH & KINGSTON —

God and the Regions

Owen Dudley Edwards

John Kennedy's victory at the Democratic Convention in 1960 was anything but inevitable, and one very awkward moment happened when a careless aide, sending out requests to all state delegations that they invite Kennedy to address them, included the Texas delegation in his summons. Lyndon Johnson, numerically Kennedy's greatest rival, accepted the request, counter-inviting Kennedy to debate him before the combined Texas and Massachusetts delegations. Kennedy, fearing that a refusal would be trumpeted abroad by Texas larynxes, appeared with a handful of Massachusetts delegates. Wiser heads than mine thought Kennedy won, but to me Johnson's opening had a touch of immortality: "No person should be denied the Presidency for his race, for his religion, or for his region."[1]

I remember the gasps from some of the more traditional Texas delegates, for the word 'race', and most of us discounted it as a mere token profession of belief in a comfortable impossibility. We were very wrong. Of the three, it was the first which mattered most to Johnson, as his Presidency would prove. The second and third were clever tactics. In these weeks Kennedy gained because of resentment against anti-Catholicism and Johnson was arguing that the same liberalism should oppose prejudice against a region, meaning the South rather than the West which, when needed, he would also claim. He was quite right. There was an ugly readiness in 1960 to denigrate the South by sanctimonious persons who exerted themselves very little to help blacks win civil rights. Condemnation was much easier than compassion.

A few years later John Kennedy was dead, Lyndon Johnson was President, Robert Kennedy was trimming his sails to see what breeze would be the most effective to shipwreck Johnson. At this point he was playing with intellectualism, which meant in practice flying world-renowned intellectuals to his home in Hickory Hill to do their thing in sixty minutes, with ensuing discussion. The English philosopher A. J. Ayer was imported for the purpose and explained what he meant by philosophy within the Procrustean time-constraint, and then Ethel Kennedy said, "Gee, Prof Ayer, where does God come into this?" There was a slight pause, and then came her husband's voice: "Can it, Ethel!" We may reflect on Johnson's perception that regions win hatred in their own right, and wonder with Ethel Kennedy where God comes into it.

God first. A few years ago, when the European Union Constitution was chasing itself through forms of adoption or rejection, Cardinal Joseph Ratzinger, as he then was, expressed displeasure that God made no

---

[1] See <www.historyplace.com/speeches/johnson.htm<http://www.historyplace.com/speeches/johnson.htm>>.

appearance in the Constitution. Apart from the obvious fact that Valery Giscard d'Estaing declined to share the limelight with God or anyone else if he could help it, I wondered if Ratzinger would be as ready to make the same complaint against the US Constitution, given American sensitivity and American financial support for Papal Christianity. It is true that the US Constitution separated church from state not because of zeal for Godlessness as much as awareness of competition in Godliness. The EU gives much less reason to suspect it of preoccupation with God in 57 varieties. And it did not, as it should have, alert us to realise Ratzinger's extraordinary innocence in the assumption that what he regarded as a university class would note down the professor's conclusion and rectify the error like good students. One feels he would have been a kindly magister: he would never have kept Giscard d'Estaing back to write out his Constitution fifty times.

Ratzinger, grown into Benedict XVI, showed that in any case he was a profound scholar, but his period was two millennia ago. His books about Jesus are worth any number of reflections on constitutions. But in the vague way that historians specialising in Charlemagne manage to direct a tutorial on Louis XIV, he had a point worth meditation. Europe, one way or another, has had rather a lot to do with God, and God's rivals.

Denys Hay's *Europe: the Emergence of an Idea* (1957) opens with Europe and Japheth, thus formally examining the development of Greek and Jewish origins of Europe, to merge in Christianity. Understanding Europe, or the Atlantic, or the Mediterranean, is impossible without thought of the religious beliefs of its inhabitants throughout formative history. But we speak with apparent confidence about them, while surreptitiously glancing over our shoulders to largely pre-Christian origins, geographical as well as theological. After the late Papal Conclave, TV watchers saw and heard some commentators in varying degrees of ignorance, who informed us that Pope Francis was the first non-European Pope. They might be pardoned for ignorance of Pontiffs in the first millennium, but had they ever heard of St Peter, or where he came from? How many of them realised that Jesus Christ never set foot in Europe? The Glastonbury faithful may insist he lived there as on sabbatical from a Phoenician voyage, just as the American Mormons require Him to have described a parabola on flight from Olivet to refound His church on the future American soil: both are fascinating cases of local patriots deifying their countries, if little more. In any case, Ignorance can conquer far beyond Faith. So presumably the mass of Europe TV commentators, and at least some of the public, assume Jesus must have been in Europe, or He could not have existed.

But then (outside of Glastonbury) you have the English who deny being part of Europe, and get rather religious about it, in tone and even in piety. It is fair enough to say that the twentieth-century roots of Anglo-Europhobia have a pious reason, the folk-memories of holding out alone against a Europe run by Hitler, Stalin, Franco, and Salazar, and what folk-memory does not answer, the chauvinist media, gasping for survival, will whip up. But in any case Anglo-Europhobia has older roots – splendid isolation in the nineteenth century, grabbing empires while losing Europe in the eighteenth, disguising a successful Dutch invasion as an English national resistance against the late French in the seventeenth, God (according to Elizabeth I) blowing with his breath, and the Spaniards were scattered in the late sixteenth. Anyhow, contrary to general assumptions, God has been under summons from all Europe, as J. C. Squire noted in World War I:

> God heard the embattled nations sing and shout
> "Gott strafe England!" and "God save the King!"
> God this, God that, and God the other thing –
> "Good God", said God, "I've got my work cut out."[2]

So we can give Ethel Kennedy one answer: God is alive and well as a receiver of human mutual hostilities. Her father-in-law said of her husband, "I love that kid. He hates like I do." And Bobby Kennedy was a good Catholic, however uncertain the piety of his brother Jack. Look at the number of children Ethel had to bear.

Nevertheless, someone slightly less self-absorbed than A. J. Ayer might have been inclined to enquire how far the Kennedy God, at least from old Joseph P. Kennedy's perspective, resembled the compassionate and clement Jesus, forgiving His murderers and mockers. Denys Hay's commencement of the origins of idea of Europe with Europa and Japheth among much else drives us back to the pre-Christian origins of what fate shaped our Europe and what it colonised/ethnically cleansed as it went. He warns us against undue fixation on the European symbolism:

> When artists in classical antiquity represented Europa it was with the maiden they normally saw, devoid of any continental overtones, a symbol of passion rather than politics. Pictures of the personified continent are rare. Only one seems to possess any emotional content. This is a first-century B.C. marble relief commemorating the battle of Arbela, where Alexander the Great defeated the Persians in 331 B.C. The picture should thus be linked with the brief period of interest in the political character of Europe which we have at the time of Isocrates.[3]

Passion in the story puts Zeus's rape and abduction of Europa at the heart of European existence, which we may easily render as a parable of Man's greedy destruction of the environment. But as Herodotus pointed out in the beginning of his *Histories*, such rape and abduction lie at the heart of so

[2] J C Squire, *Epigrams*, 1916.

[3] Denys Hay, *Europe: the Emergence of an Idea* (1957), second, revised edition, Edinburgh: Edinburgh University Press, 1968, p.5.

many ancient Greek myths including the *Iliad*, most of them causing wars between Europeans and Asiatics.

Such myths were thus at their most influential when they could be invoked in battle and conquest connection. Here Europa was undertaking what would be in much use among her fragments. Local gods were pressed into service in time of war, and at the other end of Europe from Europa (whose amorous adventures ended by settling down in Crete) Irish saints ultimately took the place of local gods with equal power in military assistance. Noah's son Japheth was assigned mastery of Europe, with his brother Shem's descendants getting Asia, and brother Ham's Africa, after Ham and his progeny had been cursed by a hangover Noah, enraged that Ham had laughed at him when the old gentleman had danced and slept in the nude while drunk.[4] But Japheth's hold on Biblical attention was firmly secondary, for all that Noah prophesied that he would be enlarged and dwell in the tents of Shem, which would be a fair prophesy of European imperialism in Asia. What ultimately interested European and European-descended divines was the apparent justification of enslavement of Africans, by the curse of Ham. Once again, the origin of the idea of Europe was turned to underwrite acts inimical to Christianity – whether slaughter or slavery. And it was Christian priests and ministers who provided the pious language of rationale for that justification. Europe, however secondary, was identified with Christendom/ Christianity. Christianity began in the conflict of two Asian high priests, Caiaphas and Jesus. And so it has continued. Caiaphas is the religion that repays its Royal or Imperial user by enforcing his rule with assertions of its morality. Jesus is Belief for its own sake, with neither destructive nor perpetual opposition for the sake of opposing.

George Bernard Shaw began his exhilarating Preface (1915) to his even more exhilarating play (1913) *Androcles and the Lion*:

> Why not give Christianity a Trial?
>
> The question seems a hopeless one after 2000 years of resolute adherence to the old cry of 'Not this man, but Barabbas'. Yet it is beginning to look as if Barabbas was a failure, in spite of his strong right hand, his victories, his empires, his millions of money, and his moralities and churches and political constitutions.
>
>   'This man' has not been a failure yet; for nobody has ever been sane enough to try his way. But he has had one quaint triumph. Barabbas has stolen his name and taken his cross as a standard. There is a sort of compliment in that. There is even a sort of loyalty in it, like that of the brigand who breaks every law and yet claims to be a patriotic subject of the king who makes them. We

---

[4] Genesis ix, 20-29.

> have always had a curious feeling that though we crucified Christ
> on a stick, he somehow managed to get hold of the right end of it,
> and that if we were better men we might try his plan.[5]

This was to identify Caiaphas with Barabbas, which in their roles in the Crucifixion of Jesus was true. Indeed Caiaphas's anxiety to see Jesus crucified meant that the High Priest and his Temple soldiers and followers were (probably quite wrongly) taken to be part of the mob yelling for Barabbas to be released. Such a mob could do its work much better without being encumbered by Temple personnel rigidly bound to do nothing which would desecrate the Passover. Their equivalent would have been the mobs who venerated mass murderers in Northern Ireland in the recent Thirty Years' War. Mr Gerry Adams's literary complaints about priests' failure to give sufficient whitewash to IRA murders capture the situation quite neatly. Mr Adams is all for Caiaphas, whom he requires to know his place and do his job. Shaw's finale restored Caiaphas to his proper place:

> ... Jesus never suggested that his disciples should separate
> themselves from the laity: he picked them up by the wayside,
> where any man or woman might follow him. For priests he had
> not a civil word; and they showed their sense of his hostility
> by getting him killed as soon as possible. He was, in short, a
> thoroughgoing anti-Clerical.[6]

Since Caiaphas made himself acceptable to the Roman rulers of Judaea who had previously fired his father-in-law Annas and Annas's sons from the office of High Priest, Shaw might concede that Caiaphas knows when to be Barabbas, and *vice versa*. We have only to think of Bishops, whether Protestant or Catholic, blessing cannons to extirpate the State's enemies, or blessing fires (or executions preceded by disembowelling) to dispose of rebels. Jesus is the Yogi, Caiaphas the Commissar. Jesus's progress is among fishermen, and tax-gatherers, and women, and children, and dying thieves. Caiaphas's progress is through the State's adoption of his religion, or his own adoption of the State's, it does not matter which. Caiaphas may well save lives by his politics: his justification for his intended destruction of Jesus probably seeks to conceal jealousy, rivalry, the wish to eliminate an all too popular dissident from his orthodoxy in superficialities and hypocrisies, but we can take his word to convince his fellow councillors (probably reported to John by Nicodemus):

[5] George Bernard Shaw, *Androcles and the Lion* (1916), preface, in: Dan H. Laurence (ed.), *The Bodley Head Bernard Shaw: Collected Plays with their Prefaces*, vol. 4, 1972.

[6] *Ibid.*

Ye know nothing at all,
Nor consider that it is expedient for us, that one man should die
for the people, and that the whole nation perish not.[7]

Caiaphas in fact exhibits here a generic mixture of bullying and reasoning, in which countless clerics of Christian churches have followed him.

Dr Rowan Williams's TV film 'Farewell to Canterbury' is an aesthetic masterpiece in filming, a most powerful repudiation of Caiaphas in its script. The Church of England is a Caiaphas church to order, if we look back to its annexation by Henry VIII for his marital purposes. Thomas Cranmer was Henry's foremost ecclesiastical instrument in that annexation. He came more directly into his own under the more Protestant Edward VI and his successive guardians or regents, the Dukes of Somerset and Northumberland, and then was martyred by the Roman Catholic Mary I, having first apparently repudiated his Protestantism and then repudiated his repudiation. Cranmer is thus a saint, because a martyr for Jesus, who should be obvious enough to Roman Catholics like myself as well as to Protestants. He is in fact a very comforting kind of martyr to most of us. We would like to think of ourselves as constant, like the Papists John Fisher and Thomas More, or the Protestants Hugh Latimer and Nicholas Ridley, none of whom seemed to waver in their readiness to die for what they thought Jesus would want. But if we have the guts to face martyrdom, it is much more likely to follow our ignominious attempts at compromise or concealment like Cranmer's. Yet Rowan Williams, thinking back on his predecessors as Archbishops of Canterbury, made no mention of Cranmer, nor indeed of any Protestant holders of the see. His hero was St Thomas Becket, martyred in 1170 by what his knightly assassins took to be Henry II's orders (with his shrine desecrated by Henry VIII). Rowan Williams claimed Becket's inspiration in his own readiness to defy Prime Ministers and denounce what he saw as policies violating what Jesus would wish, whether in taking their people into illegal wars, or injuring the poorest while insuring the wealthiest. The Church of England was still the State Church, marrying heirs to the throne or burying prime ministers as required. The belief had been widespread that it was there spiritually to affirm the righteousness of State policy as it had done ever since Henry VIII (for, apart from the Cranmers, Latimers and Ridleys, the Church of England accepted Roman obedience under Mary about as readily as it had conformed to the Protestantism of Edward VI and the vagaries of Henry VIII). When the Church of Scotland in 1988 demanded a constitutional convention and opened the doors of its General Assembly Hall to participants, the then Secretary of State for Scotland, Malcolm Rifkind, told it that as the State church it was expected to do what the State told it, only to have the Church of Scotland educate him in the dangers of imagining a Union too far; conformity of state wishes was no doubt the political theory of the Church of England, but the

---

[7] John xi, 49-50.

Church of Scotland told the State what it was supposed to do. But Rowan Williams declared an independence as firm as that proclaimed against Thatcher by the Church of Scotland, and however different the theological authorities – John Knox for the Scots, Thomas Becket for the English – in Thatcher and Thatcher's heirs they faced the same thing, rulers ready to give them pride of place provided they were Caiaphas. Thatcher, Blair, Cameron wanted a Caiaphas stealing Jesus's name and cross, but the apparel may now be what it likes and the names what they may choose, provided the priorities are Caiaphas's, to serve the State and in it to ensure the survival (and where possible the benefit) of clergy.

Caiaphas, having claimed the identity and the legacy of Jesus, then turns his natural instinct for self-preservation by persecution into supposed enforcement of Christian orthodoxy: it is expedient that one man should die for the people, and another, and another, and another. Caiaphas may indeed believe that in so doing he is fulfilling the wishes of Jesus, or if they were not, then they ought to have been, and he is protecting Jesus and his work by rectifying its regrettable omissions. I am arguing in terms of Christianity, since however little competence I have in that, it is much more than I have elsewhere, but the lesson can be all too easily applied to Judaism itself, to Islam, and so forth. Once you hold the State, you have won. From a truly spiritual viewpoint you have almost certainly lost, but you seldom admit or even realise that, and where you do, and continue in sheer cynicism, you will probably end up hollow in your own eyes and everyone else's, as did the clergy in most of France at the outbreak of the Revolution of 1789. Caiaphas of course will wait until the extent of Jesus's success, in sheer numbers of votaries, is unquestionable, persecuting Jesus and his followers as much as he can until it becomes necessary to join them. Caiaphas in this epiphany is no longer himself Jewish but Roman, which is where most of our self-notions of State rule have descended, either directly or via approved forms of classical study. If there had been no Livy, there would have been no Machiavelli, so to speak.

The State came into being from Romulus or Aeneas, Romulus the original myth among the obscure Latins telling of the twin baby suckled by a wolf and destined to kill the grandfather who had doomed him, and to kill his own twin, Aeneas the supposed survivor of Troy when the growth of the Roman empire required a change of myth for more suitable tailoring. Presumably the need for Aeneas felt itself when the enlarging Roman state came up against the ethnically Greek inhabitants of southern Italy and Sicily, *Magna Graecia*, 'great Greece' (just as Britain became 'Great' to distinguish it from Brittany), and a clear Region. Rome thus had already managed its own takeover by the theological culture of the region it was taking over and thus, culturally, was peculiarly vulnerable to subversion and conquest by Christianity. It knew it had to have a State religion. Macaulay captures this very vividly in *The Lays of Ancient Rome*, which would help the British and Irish discover pseudo-Roman ethics, particularly the ethics of force, where their Christianity was proving too Christian for their imperial purposes. But what he was trying to do was to conjure up the successive folk cultures of different ages, so that 'Horatius' is supposedly a product of several generations after his defence of the bridge against the Etruscans (whether real or imaginary), when the Roman gods were local, above all the river Tiber, worshipped as potential saviour or destroyer; 'The Battle of Lake Regillus' is the alleged product from several generations later still, by which point Greek culture is washing the original Roman theology away so that the heroic high point of the poem is the intervention of Greek heroes, now gods, Romanised into fighting for Rome and apparently speaking Latin, but when the enemy flee the poet forgets his new duty to be Greek and exults "by our sire Quirinus," Quirinus in fact being the most notable of the old Roman gods now in the process of being superseded by the Olympians and their progeny. The legend of Lake Regillus's saviours being the Great Twin Brothers Castor and Pollux ties it in with Homeric tradition, as Virgil would do in producing a National poem for the Roman Empire in the *Aeneid*. Macaulay simply worked up the 2000-odd-year-old legend, but it might seem anomalous that a state religion working itself into existence by adoption of Greek culture while insisting on descent from the Greek epic enemy, the Trojans, should pride itself on protection by two brothers whose sisters were Helen, the cause of Troy's destruction, and Clytemnestra, wife of the Greek commander-in-chief Agamemnon. Yeats, on whom Christopher Harvie was already writing so remarkably at the very beginning of his literary career, probably comprehended the reality of the mythological mix in his 'Leda and the Swan' (1923):

> A shudder in the loins engenders there
> The broken wall, the burning roof and tower
> And Agamemnon dead.[8]

In lesser words, Leda's impregnation by Zeus or, Romanised, Jupiter, spoke ruin on all fronts, Troy fallen, and the Greek leader murdered, the one because of Helen, the other by Clytemnestra. Yeats seems to ignore the twin brothers in the other egg, but Rome was buying in (or actually stealing out) Greek theomythology, and Castor and Pollux are thereby annexed, and simplified for better military comprehension (if Macaulay read Roman popular culture right, and if anyone did, he probably did). Yeats himself would have been dominated by the still waging Irish civil war, following the supposed defeat of Britain and taking the life of Ireland's iconic commander Michael Collins.

If we turn to another of the thousand fields enriched by Christopher Harvie, John Buchan (whose *The Thirty-Nine Steps* received its best edition from his hands) defined the problem of State religion and its popular context

---

[8] William Butler Yeats, 'Leda and the Swan', in: W B Yeats, *The Poems* (*Collected Works of W B Yeats, Vol.1*), edited by Richard J Finneran, London: Prentice Hall, 1997, p.220.

as well as anyone: Denys Hay in his *Europe* picked up two ballads to show that in 'Tam Lin' Christendom – the high medieval equivalent of Europe – could be held synonymous with Christianity:

> "O tell me, tell me, Tarn Lin", she says,
>   "For's sake that died on tree,
> If eer ye was in holy chapel,
>   Or christendom did see?"[9]

But 'Kinmont Willie'[10] shows what Hay called "a totally different use":

> He is either himsell a devil frae hell
>   Or else his mother a witch maun be;
> I wadna have ridden that wan water
>   For a' the gowd in Christentie.

So 'Christendom', being an identification of faith with the lands that professed it, then comes to mean the lands themselves, even though it is still used as synonymous with 'Christianity'. But it leaves unanswered Buchan's pretended ninth-century 'Wood Magic':

> I will walk warily in the wise woods on the fringes of even-tide.
>   For the covert is full of noises and the stir of nameless things.
> I have seen in the dusk of the beeches the shapes of the lords that ride,
>   And down in the marish hollow I have heard the lady who sings.
> And once in an April gloaming I met a maid on the sward,
>   All marble-white and gleaming and tender and wild of eye; –
> I, Jehan the hunter, who speak am a grown man, middling hard,
>   But I dreamt a month of the maid, and wept I knew not why.
> Down by the edge of the firs, in a coppice of heath and vine,
>   Is an old moss-grown altar, shaded by briar and bloom,
> Denys, the priest, hath told me 'twas the lord Apollo's shrine
>   In the days ere Christ came down from God to the Virgin's womb.
> I never go past but I doff my gap and avert my eyes –
>   (Were Denys to catch me I trow I'd do penance for half a year) –
> For once I saw a flame there and the smoke of a sacrifice,
>   And a voice spake out of the thicket that froze my soul with fear.
> Wherefore to God the Father, the Son, and the Holy Ghost,
>   Mary the Blessed Mother and the kindly Saints as well,
> I will give glory and praise, and them I cherish the most,

---

[9] 'Tam Lin', Frances James Child (ed.) *The English and Scottish Popular Ballads*, Vol.1, Mineola: Dover Publications, 2003, p.340.

[10] *Ibid.*, p.469.

For they have the keys of Heaven, and save the soul from Hell.
But likewise I will spare for the lord Apollo a grace,
    And a bow for the lady Venus – as a friend but not as a thrall.
'Tis true they are out of Heaven, but some day they may win the place;
    For gods are kittle cattle, and a wise man honours them all.[11]

The poem is charming and perceptive in its innocent wisdom: published in Buchan's *The Moon Endureth* (1912), it complemented 'The Grove of Ashtaroth' in which the protagonist fights in horror against a surviving pagan influence and ends in grief at having destroyed it.

Buchan uses the theme in various other ways, appropriate enough for the Pan-haunted quarter-century before the First World War (the supreme artistic achievement in Pan-theophany is surely at its zenith of love in Kenneth Grahame's *The Wind in the Willows* of 1908, its nadir in Saki's 'The Music on the Hill'[12]). Wilde captured the mingling of Christian and pagan loyalties in one of the stories he told (recalled long after his death through Robbie Ross and included in Margery Ross's letter-collection *Robert Ross Friend of Friends* (1952). It turns on a repulsively ugly statue of the Blessed Virgin Mary in a grotto above the sea which at night throws away its dull garments and tawdry paint and goes down to the sea-shore where it is Venus, playing with her fellow-immortals and above all with her son Cupid but when daybreak is at hand and she turns to go, he cries why must she leave him, and she answers *"Parceque j'ai un autre Fils qui a beaucoup souffert."*

Wilde and Buchan were (for all of their intense sophistication in their differing conquests of London) major conductors of folklore from the Regions, or more exactly the regions of the Regions, Wilde having learned his folklore and his Gaelic from Galway and Mayo and his folklore-gathering parents, Buchan from the Borders and Highlands, and both with a curious awareness of the sea as conservator of lost gods. It will not do to label their awareness of ancient survivors beyond the Christian frontier as 'Ireland' or 'Scotland': we will not originate Wilde's 'The Fisherman and his Soul' in Merrion Square, or Buchan's 'The Outgoing of the Tide' in the Manse, though the former may well have been inspired by talk in the Wildes' house in the Square, and the latter is ostensibly written in a manse. The omnipresence of pre-Christian supernaturalism may have made its way most testily into the twentieth century in the person of the farmer whom Yeats recalled saying, when asked whether he believed in fairies, "Of course not, but they're there." The farmer was not merely being Irish: in fact he was being somewhat English, the Victorians using the term 'believe in' as 'trust'. Christendom saw dangerous compromises being made, if the existence of fairies were acknowledged, even though the speaker denied 'believing in' them. It had a point.

---

[11] John Buchan, 'Wood Magic', in: J Buchan, *The Moon Endureth: Tales and Fancies*, Edinburgh: Blackwood, 1912, pp.206-207.

[12] In Saki (H H Munro), *The Chronicles of Clovis* (1911).

When priests were allowed to return to Ireland in the mid-eighteenth century after some fifty to eighty years of efforts to exterminate them, they found penitents in confession showed no sign of succumbing to Protestantism (having declined the obvious socio-economic betterment awaiting them if they did). Paganism on the other hand was alive and well, often in the most charming local, supposedly Christian, devotions. Many a saint on inspection looks more like a pagan descended through two millennia. Modernising clerics had every reason to prohibit pilgrimages to holy wells, for instance. It becomes easy to see this everywhere, once it is admitted. Here Angus Wilson's *Anglo-Saxon Attitudes* (1955), probably the best novel written about historians, gives us a salutary warning. The supposed evidence as to pagan devotional survival found in the tomb of a seventh-century Christian missionary proves to have been faked by an iconoclastic rebel son of a historian who then covers up the proof of his son's malice when the son is dead. The ultimate proof of the fraud sends another historian insane, rather than accept it. Only a couple of years earlier Orwell. in 1984, gave a highly convincing portrait of the manufacture of a wholly imaginary working-class hero who would then become a standard authentic item in ruling party hagiography. In 1920, Hilaire Belloc could write that "The Faith is Europe. And Europe is the Faith."[13] Then the Regions are primarily disputable lands, whose frontiers may not necessarily be at European limits. Nor does the long division of Europe between Communist and non-Communist negate this. Just as Orwell's invention of a young Communist could have been written about Catholic or Protestant inventions of the same edifying kind, Communism itself was in many ways an obvious evolution of Christianity, however perverted, much more of an evolution from it than Fascism or Nazism. To say this in the security of a sanctum (actually a kitchen) long after them is not to imply that contemporaries saw it the same way. Spain, for all of the unifying effects of medieval conflict against the Moors, remained regionally highly conscious from the marriage of Aragon's Ferdinand and Castile's Isabella onward. The Spanish Civil War of 1936-39 clearly divided Regions in quest of autonomy from centralising authoritarians. But the Basques supported the Republic, while retaining full Christian devotion, and Catalonia seemed to a gratified Orwell to have killed its Catholicism stone dead. Whatever Regions may have been and are, they are not interchangeable.

The most obvious basis for a Region is as a survival capsule. This may mean either a refuge against conquerors or as a haven untroubled by them. In post-Roman Britain the German, Pictish and Irish invaders forced the indigenous, but over-civilised British into diminishing regions – Wales, Cornwall, Strathclyde, Lothian – and the vanishing of the last two from the physical map is offset by the survival of some of the poetry of Taliesin and Aneurin. Ireland was apparently immune from Roman conquest (or else what happened there was so humiliating for the Romans that they

---

[13] Hilaire Belloc, *Europe and the Faith*, New York: The Paulist Press, 1920, p.viii.

subsequently eradicated all allusions to it). Yet Ireland became a survival capsule from the Roman civilization and its attendant Christianity. And here we return to Caiaphas and Jesus. St Patrick is our chief witness, but it seems probable that Christianity reached Ireland not simply through the work of one enslaved Christian, but of several, escaped or otherwise. Also, it replicated one Roman feature. It meant that Christianity entered Ireland, as it entered Rome, through the lowest classes: slaves, fugitives, and vagrants. St Patrick's *Confession* (whose consciousness of its bad Latin renders its forgery extremely unlikely) makes it clear that his objects in return to fifth-century Ireland were evangelisation of Christianity and extirpation of slavery. He succeeded so well in the first that Operation Caiaphas went into forward drive, Christianising official Druids in many minor kings' courts. He failed in the second. In its way the success in antislavery might have helped us to measure the depth of Christian conversion, as against secret but surviving paganism. Yet it is clear that Christianity, however adulterated, held its own, perhaps because Ireland lacked an organic central kingship.

The Reformation bargain '*Cujus Regio ejus Religio*' (whose the Region, his the Religion) did not apply here. Oxbridge historians who speculate that Irish Catholicism would have perished had Cromwell's regime won a longer lease are talking nonsense from comfortable chairs and tables, especially tables. *Religio* in Ireland meant something uncontrollable, let the *Regio* be *cujus* it might. The prime reason for resistance was that its backbone was female, priests or no priests. The women held firm and brought up the children to remain Catholics or Presbyterians, regardless of male legislators, soldiers, administrators. So we have to rethink Region from the bottom up. Control of the mind is surely the final proof of rule, and the women in the region, remotest from metropolitan male power, determined the mind-set of the future.

My argument would be that on religious questions the women were the ultimate power all the more because they did not claim authority, save over the children at their breasts and under their feet. Regional power is at its strongest the smaller the unit. Women in fact exerted far more power than they ever flaunted, whether in region or kingdom, and the horror of men at the contemplation of female power shows itself in the much more cruel punishments against women when both sexes were found in the same rebellion. Woman Power was so distasteful, (all the more because it might be true in the domestic life of the male ruler) that it became easier to target the clergy as leaders of disaffection, once they were visible in sufficient numbers. Caiaphas had indeed been so successful in displacing Jesus throughout Catholicism and Protestantism that clerical power not linked to the State seemed painfully unnatural to Erastians, whether English Protestant Episcopalian or French Catholic Gallican. In Scotland the new Union from 1707 made it clear that Caiaphas might be Presbyterian if he liked, so long as he was the magnate's man, and thus under State control.

Ireland had produced martyr bishops in the seventeenth century, MacMahon of Clogher leading Papist rebels in arms in 1652, and Plunkett of Armagh being hanged, drawn and quartered at Tyburn in London in 1681. Come Victorian imperialism, and its fear of a Caiaphas out of control spread itself to the imperialist's perennial battle against the witch-doctor, the Mad Mullah, Greenmantle, and whoever as spiritual leader might seem capable of frustrating the administrative intent of the State used to the apparent subservience of Caiaphas at home. If the State rulers, whether regal or merely manipulative, found the region rejected their control of clerics, it could result in even greater disillusionment when Caiaphas and his master are of the same religion as the rebels, and the rebel priests or ministers. The Dutch revolt against Philip II of Spain lined up many north-eastern Catholics alongside the rebels. The Basque hostility to Franco would be a comparable case. Sometimes the rejection of Caiaphas by his co-religionists would be all the greater because they saw his capitulation as treachery to their spiritual beliefs. Such was Andreas Hofer's revolt in the South Tirol against Napoleon when the Austrian Empire had yielded its imperial title and imperial daughter.

Regions are kittle kattle, as Buchan would say. They may be the meek results of imperial lines drawn on maps. But they may also (although never fully realised as such) be the work of God. There is a touching moment in the film *Chariots of Fire* when the future King Edward VIII slowly realises, from the refusal of Eric Liddell to race on Sunday, that God does not exist purely to save the King, at least in the view of this one of his subjects, and that Liddell's anxiety to save himself (however incredible) outweighs his readiness to save the King. This problem was compounded by Caiaphas's having always assured successive monarchs that God saw His duty to them as His primary and perhaps sole function. It took Tom Paine to point out in *Common Sense* that God had thought Kings a perfectly rotten idea from the first, and had told Samuel in fine proto-Marxist style that kings would merely create worthless courtiers, administrators, leeches to exploit the people.[14]

From all this the question naturally arises, where did the Region begin? If the Religion was to be the property of whoever owned the Region – and that is what the Reformation settlements of Augsburg (1555) and Westphalia (1648) amounted to – how did it come into existence? In some instances the Region might be owned or claimed by a figure alien in religion, birthplace, language or ethnicity, as the Bohemians of 1618 felt in resisting the imposition of an Austrian Catholic ruler, thus supplying one origin of the Thirty Years' War. But the Region discovered its own identity and expressed, as best it could, its autonomy when a people migrated to it or recognised sufficient common ground amongst themselves, environmentally as well as theologically, ethnically, or whatever. Principal William Robertson, the founder of modern historical archival-based writing in the English language, argued (perhaps with a fleeting grin) that the Huns were the most democratic

---

[14] 1 Samuel viii.

people in History. Certainly they showed one basis of Regional formation in having got themselves thoroughly (although not universally) disliked. Attila, their leader, was declared 'the Scourge of God', yet on Robertson's reading of them, they are in the tradition of Jesus rather than Caiaphas. They also raise questions as to how far the Region is the product of religious identity, economic rivalry, or other differences and, however deeply associated with the persecution of Christians, it is hard to pigeonhole the Huns as motivated primarily or even visibly by religious motives. They certainly do not seem to have hated Christians as Christians – the Byzantines were the most sophisticated Christians of the fifth century, and their ambassadors got on quite well with the Huns. Professor John Corrigan's useful essay on 'Religious Hatred' quotes Rousseau's *Contrat Sociale*:

> It is impossible to live in peace with people whom one believes are damned. To love them would be to hate God who punished them. They must absolutely be either brought into the faith or tormented.[15]

But Rousseau had his own targets for damnation, such as Religion. At the end of the Thirty Years' War in Northern Ireland a Government was formed, led by the Revd Dr Ian Paisley and the comparably pious Martin McGuinness. Dr Paisley has given us every reason to assume he believes Mr McGuinness and all his coreligionists such as myself are damned. Mr McGuinness may or may not hold the converse for all Protestants, but his ancestors certainly did. Yet they worked together with evident mutual regard. Mutual hostilities from their ethno-religious groups show more evidence of being grounded in Protestant occupancy of former Catholic land. Even the atrocious Catholic massacres of Protestants in 1641 were about land, and Cromwell's foremost impact on Ireland was not in the massacres of Drogheda (where he took himself to be punishing English-led supporters of the recently executed Charles I) and Wexford (where he could not control his own army and could not admit he could not) but in confiscating most of Irish land which, in any case, the Long Parliament had designed for appropriation long before Cromwell had come into prominence. The continued degradation of Irish Catholics by Irish Protestants was chiefly in the conviction that, once emancipated, they would gouge their former lands out of the current owners. The English control of Ireland was chiefly dictated by security fears as well, initially in fear English settlers would grow too powerful for the English State while profiteering from such a happy hunting-ground, and later, when Tudor Ireland began to look a dangerous back door for invasion of the British Isles by Spain, Stuart Ireland by France. God was more a convenient label

---

[15] John Corrigan, 'Religious Hatred', in: J Corrigan (ed.) *The Oxford Handbook of Religion and Emotion*, Oxford: Oxford University Press, 2008, p.337.

by which land confiscation could be pietised. The first such confiscation had been by the Catholic Mary Tudor and her husband Philip II of Spain. When an increasingly devolved Ireland changed county names back from Queen's County to Laoighis or Leix, King's County to Offaly, few Irish Catholics were likely to realise that the King they were thereby scrapping was Spanish, and implacably Catholic.

God may get back into the tale of Regions and their enemies as we remember Lyndon Johnson's declaration of racial, religious and regional right to rule. The widespread American hatred of the formerly Confederate South could be deemed religious, however atheist so many of its practitioners, when what was at stake was genuine anger at white Southern degradation of the African Americans: there was a neo-evangelism in these heirs to the old religiously-motivated enemies of slavery. But in 1960 few Northerners were ready to take the drastic steps to make racial integration a reality. The integration programme sounded dangerously like Socialism, the still revered J. Edgar Hoover was ready to label most integrationists as Communist or member of 'Communist-front' organisations. Hating the South was cheaper and easier. And here what was involved may have been a secular religion. There really was a religious element in American devotion to the American flag. The Confederate flag was thus abominable in most American eyes. Today this would be so because it would be taken to justify slavery, Jim Crow, and victimisation of African Americans. But in 1960 the Stars and Bars was still the banner of the greatest opponents of United States identity that it ever knew, branded as un-American for putting the Union in danger, and for being defeated. In their unsuccessful attempts before the US Supreme Court to free themselves from what they saw as a religious act, pledging allegiance to the Flag, Jehovah's Witnesses made a case which may well have had validity, but was very unwelcome during US participation in World War II. They are probably not classifiable as Christians, but they were in fact in the tradition of Jesus against Caiaphas .

There is a class issue here. Jesus may have inherited a carpenter's business, Peter, Andrew, James and John may have owned their fishing-boats, Matthew may have brought his own private enterprise into tax-gathering, Judas was clearly an accountant, but Jesus's is a story of have-nots, a faith in tune with a lower-class world. Caiaphas sleekly radiates substantial income and social position. Subsequent evangelists in Jesus's tradition would be martyred until and unless they won the dubious benefit of success. The crusades started with obvious worshippers of a real Jesus, not simply of vestments for Caiaphas: Peter the Hermit, and Walter the Penniless. Then came profit, whence takeover by Caiaphas, reaching the lucrative stars in the Fourth Crusade, when Venice led the plunder of Constantinople, whose pleas for aid had initially elicited the crusades. A Region on any useful analysis must surely start out as poor, or defeated, or disadvantaged in some visible way. Also its identity must initially attract opprobrium, most obviously if it involves scorning the prevailing culture of the nation which enfolds it or tries to. And Region may even be landless. Gypsies and Tinkers have shown that both in their integrity and in the hostility they create. Like the fox they may win initial hostility by plundering livestock, but like the fox they become objects of mob pursuit (in pink coats or otherwise), and the hunt by the end is for its own sake rather than for the rape of hens. It may be that the Region when congruent with a specific land-mass will actually exhibit much less basis for representative conflict than representative figures of the Region who are themselves isolated far from it. French Canadians outside Québec receive far more hatred and contempt than do the Québécois in Québec. But they are not necessarily Québécois. Some will be the descendants of the Acadians, brutally scattered by their British conquerors in the beginning of the eighteenth century. The Region may be of greatest importance where it is invisible. So, of course, is God.

Lyrical Links:
The Scottish Poetry Library and Europe

Tessa Ransford

The Scottish Poets Tour of Germany took place from 7 to 14 June 1985. Iain Crichton Smith and Aonghas MacNeacail, Willie Neill and Rory Watson, Joy Hendry and I were the poets who went, each giving readings, Joy singing, Rory discussing, all of us meeting and socialising with those teaching Scottish Literature at the various ports of call in Germany. We gave readings in Köln, Aachen, Germersheim, Mainz, Tübingen and Munich. Christopher Harvie in Tübingen had been the prime instigator, but Iain Galbraith in Mainz was also enthusiastic, as was Horst Drescher in Germersheim. Harold Fish was the British Council director in Köln who welcomed us and helped to make the contacts. Peter Marsden was in the Anglistik department in Aachen where we performed.

My memories are of enthusiastic audiences and long dinners in restaurants with our hosts, of the British Council's regional offices in Germany at that time being excellent, but of having to keep my head all the time and make sure the whole group was where it was meant to be on the tour, at the stations to catch the trains, at the theatres and universities, at the right lodgings. We were a congenial band, however, and I enjoyed it all, despite the responsibility that was upon me before, during and afterwards.

After the performance at the University of Tübingen, Christopher Harvie wrote:

> Everyone I've met since agreed it was a very fine evening's performance. Professor Ludwig said that he had found it 'erstklassig'... All the students thought it great and a marvellously varied programme.

That tour, generally deemed a great success, was also a showcase for the Scottish Poetry Library, which had been established not long before in Edinburgh, and whose genesis and remit I would like to present as an example of a Scottish cultural institution making links across Europe and beyond. Just as Christopher Harvie, through his teaching at the University of Tubingen, was a means of introducing and representing Scotland in Europe, past and contemporary, so, during the same period, as this essay will demonstrate, the Scottish Poetry Library was giving Europe access to Scotland's literature.

Poetry Survey

In my kitchen one day in the Spring of 1982 I received a phone call from the European Commission in Brussels asking me to attend a conference about poetry in Europe and to bring statistics, under various headings, about the poetry situation in Scotland: a tall order, given that no-one kept any statistics. Scotland was to be represented for/as itself at this conference – or would be if I could get there with the information by the Autumn. I asked Douglas Mack, of Stirling University Library, who had been to some of our committee meetings for the Library, if I could do the research from there, in order to give it more status. Day after day in a very wet and dismal summer, I drove to Stirling and worked on the research, sending out questionnaires and collating the answers into what would become the *Scottish Poetry Library Association, Action for the Promotion of Poetry in the European Community, Preliminary Data.*

The final document ran to twenty-eight pages, typed out by me, with appendices. The findings make astounding reading now, when few people will remember the situation for poetry and poets in the decades before the founding of the Scottish Poetry Library. In some respects things were better then. For instance, there were fifteen literary reviews publishing some poetry, and seventeen small presses. In Edinburgh alone there were Canongate, Gordon Wright, Paul Harris Publishing, The Ramsay Head Press, The Salamander Press, Stramullion Cooperative Ltd, William Blackwood & Sons, and Macdonald Publishers, Edinburgh.

The questionnaire was sent to seventy-seven poets in Scotland, out of which forty-three replied, of which three were under thirty, thirty-three male and ten female. Seventeen of these had published themselves at some time between 1975 and 1982. The point is made that "even well-known Scottish poets have not had their collected works published until after their death, e.g. Robert Garioch, Sydney Goodsir Smith, Hugh MacDiarmid." It lists occasional translation work – Garioch, Edwin Morgan, Alistair Mackie, Derek Bowman, Stephen Mulrine – but the research found no anthologies had been translated. One hundred bookshops were circulated and eighteen claimed to stock an average of 3 per cent poetry, of which 32 per cent was contemporary. All, except for two in arts centres that occasionally ordered from Scottish publishers, ordered only from the main English publishers. There is the bald statement that "there is no central organisation for the promotion of poetry in Scotland."

The document states that all Library Headquarters were sent the questionnaire and 57 per cent replied. "They keep no records whatever of poetry books bought or lent." Newspapers supported poetry better than they do now. Six newspapers published poems on an average of twice a month. Three papers had staff who acted as poetry editors. Seventy-eight books of poetry were reviewed in all the papers in one year, which was 10%

of all books reviewed. Radio and television admitted that no records or statistics for poetry programmes were kept, nor was any audience research done for these programmes. There were sixty sound recordings at the Mitchell Library, 25 of which were of twentieth-century poets. Seven poets were on video.

There are sections on schools showing that, on average, Scottish and contemporary poetry represented 20 per cent of the poetry syllabus, which is 10% of the English literature syllabus. Eight universities ran courses in Scottish and/or modern poetry for undergraduates, and three ran such courses for postgraduates. The Scottish Arts Council spent 1.2 per cent of its total budget on poetry. Poetry spending between 1975 and 1982 was £447,862. At the first Edinburgh Book Festival in 1983 there were a total of 74 events, one of which was Sorley Maclean reading his poetry. Other Scottish events featured naturalists, novelists, short-story writers, children's books and whisky. Of women there is the statement: "Only one woman poet has been a writer-in-residence or had a writer's fellowship or travel exchange for poetry between 1975 and 1982." (That was Liz Lochhead)

The document covers research into 'the reading population', and 'reading through libraries and through secondary school libraries'. There is also an assessment of income and 'the social situation of professional poets.' Strategies for pilot projects are then suggested. Of these, festivals, university courses, poetry workshops in arts centres and the Scottish Poetry Library have to some extent been developed since the research in 1982.

Although the research was only a beginning, it represented a step forward for poetry in Scotland. I went to the conference in Brussels, made my report and enjoyed meeting representatives from Wales and Ireland. The effort was not wasted, because it gave me a realistic picture of the poetry scene and contact with librarians, teachers and others involved in poetry before I started my work in the Scottish Poetry Library. That was invaluable. It gave me an authenticity that I could not otherwise have had.

Establishing the Scottish Poetry Library

In January 1982 I had sent a letter to the Scottish Arts Council asking for £10,000 to establish a Scottish Poetry Library. It was refused. Alan Taylor, at that time a librarian in the reference department of Edinburgh's Central Library, heard about this and suggested to me that I write a piece about my proposal for the Spring issue of the Scottish Library Association News (SLAN) of which he was editor.[1] My article set out the plan quite clearly, even at that early stage; for example:

> We will build up a careful information system and develop a
> network of contacts all over the country and beyond; in due

---

[1] It was printed by Callum Macdonald's Macdonald Printers, Loanhead.

course there may be a travelling van to take books and poets on tour and visit groups wherever they exist; the existence of the Library as a building will give poetry a little more tangibility and credibility; to come and browse in the library you won't need a university entrance, you won't need to have heard of any poets or be knowledgeable, you won't even need to know of a book or author; you will be encouraged to ask and talk, to share what you know with others and feed the library with information about local poets, small presses and unknown talents.

After the *SLAN* article, two people contacted me to assure support and encourage my taking the idea forward. They were Dolina MacLennan, the Lewis-born singer and actress, and Anna Smith, novelist and journalist with a weekly *Scotsman* column.

A steering committee got underway and met for the first time on 24 May 1982. It consisted of Alan Taylor, Paul Scott of the Saltire Society, Tom Fenton, the publisher of Salamander Press, and Joy Pitman, poet, archivist and a founder of Stramullion Women's Press. We sent a letter to two dozen key people and organisations, with immediate support. I opened an Abbey National Account and received cheques for £1 and £5 from 278 people over that summer of 1982. Among the earliest donors were Tom Scott, John Herdman, Edwin Morgan, Iain Crichton Smith, with Norman MacCaig, Callum Macdonald, Marjorie Stark, Deric Bolton, Duncan Glen, Hamish Henderson, Norman Wilson (of the Ramsay Head Press), the Scottish Publishers' Association under the direction of Judy Moir, the Heritage Society of Scotland (represented by Billy Wolfe), the Scottish Civic Trust (Maurice Lindsay), E.F.D. Roberts (Librarian of the National Library of Scotland), James and Janet Caird, Bill and Norah Montgomerie, Sue and Ian Hamilton Finlay, and Trevor Royle.

Professor John MacQueen of the School of Scottish Studies and Joy Hendry of *Chapman* joined the committee at the second meeting on 28 June 1982. The third meeting, on 4 August, saw John Bate join, the poet and librarian at Napier College. After that meeting we sent out a letter to thirty people, asking if they would give their names to a promotional leaflet, which would also invite the public to an inaugural meeting, where we would set up an official Scottish Poetry Library Association. That inaugural meeting was planned for 23 November 1982 at the Appleton Tower, where Norman MacCaig was billed to give a lecture in memory of Sydney Goodsir Smith. Alastair Fowler, professor of English literature at Edinburgh University, gave us permission to use this occasion to launch the Association. I asked Iain Crichton Smith if we could print one of his sonnets from the sequence *The White Noon* on the leaflet. I had found the poem in *Chapman 16* and felt it expressed the constructive energy of what I imagined. The last line of that sonnet is now engraved on the glass balustrade in the new building we built for the Scottish Poetry Library, which opened to the public in April 1999.

> And lastly I speak of the grace that musicks us
> into our accurate element till we
> go gowned at length in exact propriety.
> I speak of the glowing light along the axis
> of the turning earth that bears the thunderous sea
> and all the chaos that might learn to wreck us
> if the chained stars were snapped and the huge free
> leonine planets would some night attack us.
>
> I speak of the central grace, that line which is
> the genesis of geometry and of all
> that tightly bars the pacing animal.
> Around it build this house, this poem, this
> eternal guesthouse where late strangers call,
> this waiting room, this fresh hypothesis.

I love that poem. I suppose that 'the central grace', at the heart of all great poetry and great buildings and great people, is what I knew we needed. The last line is now engraved on the glass balustrade of the new Scottish Poetry Library building. It ties in with Gerard Manley Hopkins' line: "The just man justices;/ keeps grace, that keeps all his goings graces".[2] I wrote to my fellow steering committee members saying:

> I like the poem for being an excellent poem and suitable length and by a representative poet for Scotland. Also it talks of building around the grace that holds the creation together, and goes on creating it anew, which is what the Library's all about really.

In our committee meetings for setting up the poetry library, which were held downstairs in the Music Library on George IV Bridge, I remember Ian Campbell, always impishly eager and smiling; Cairns Craig, also from Edinburgh University's English Department and up to date with computers; Derek Bowman, poet and translator from the German Department; William Wolfe, former SNP chairman, chartered accountant and businessman; Angus Calder from the Open University and Joy Hendry of *Chapman*. Douglas Mack came from Stirling University library, partly because there was talk of housing a collection of books from the Poetry Society in London and we

---

[2] Gerard Manley Hopkins, 'As Kingfishers Catch Fire, Dragonflies Draw Flame', G M Hopkins, *The Major Works* (Oxford World Classics), Oxford: Oxford University Press, 2009, p.129.

Tom Hubbard, the first librarian of the Scottish Poetry Library, in Tweeddale Court.
(Roddy Simpson)

discussed where that might be possible. There were others, and so many came and went on the committee over the years that it would be difficult and tedious to try to name them all. Martin Eckersall of Scott Oswald, Chartered Accountants, a friend of Joy's, together with Bill Balfour and Ethel Houston of Balfour & Manson, solicitors, took care of our finances and legal affairs, the latter also proving generous benefactors.

As the Scottish Arts Council continued to dither over whether to support us, I received a letter from the representative in the UK for the Calouste Gulbenkian Foundation to whom I had written. A charming, bright and intelligent Simon Richey invited me for a drink at the Caledonian Hotel in Edinburgh's West End during the Edinburgh Festival of 1983. I remember a long, pleasant conversation, when I felt really listened to for the first time. Not long after, the Calouste Gulbenkian Foundation offered us £9,000 pump-priming money for our first year. It was a breakthrough moment and tipped the scales with the SAC, who then offered a further £10,000. We had discussed whether the library should be in Glasgow or Edinburgh, or indeed Stirling, but from a practical point of view it more or less had to be Edinburgh where most of us on the committee lived and worked. Meantime I had looked at possible premises to rent and early on explored Tweeddale Court. Robin Hodge, formerly an employee of Canongate, had bought the derelict buildings there and was beginning to restore them. He showed me round. The buildings were full of dry rot and in much decay. Next door, the building work on the site of the demolished New Palace cinema made Tweeddale Court a far from attractive place. I did not see the mess but saw only my longed-for library.

Our opening party was such a memorable and epic occasion that I cannot do justice to it here. Suffice it to say that it took place on 23 January 1984 in St Cecilia's Hall in a white-out blizzard but was attended by some 200 people, with eight poets giving readings, five Scottish and three from abroad. We opened in Tweeddale Court, in the former packing room of Oliver and Boyd (former publishers) on 6 February 1984. Tom Hubbard wrote about the early days:

> outside, a heap of bricks, rubble, planks; scurrying of feral cats, fed by an auld wife who hobbled down the Close. We shivered through that February of 1984, emptied boxes, arranged them on the few shelves in the middle of a bare room. We were powered by a naïve existentialism, not asking ourselves how long this venture would last... A year later, we were still miraculously there and we had before us a palpable reconstruction of modern world poetry.

Making Connections

The opening of the Scottish Poetry Library's first Festival Poetry Week was on Sunday, 19 August 1984 at the North British Hotel, (now the Balmoral). It was entitled 'Not the North British'. Our exciting poster was designed by Tom Scott's daughter, Marina. We had invited Herbert Kühner (half American) from Austria, who translated from various languages of the Balkans and edited anthologies. I had met him while on holiday in Vienna in June. Kühner was introduced to me by James Wilkie, a Scotsman in Vienna who edited *Austria Today* for the English- speaking world. I found myself boldly walking into the Ministry for the Arts in Vienna, without appointment, was taken to the Minister, where I asked if they would send a poet to the Edinburgh Festival. I cannot imagine myself daring to do something like that now, but the atmosphere of 1984 was such that anything seemed possible. The answer was, virtually, 'no problem Madam'. We also invited David Dabydeen from Warwick, then emerging as an exciting Caribbean voice in Britain. Added to these was the scholarly, classical, impassioned, poetic voice of Julia Budenz from Cambridge, Massachusetts, published in *Akros, Chapman* and *Lines Review*, a friend of mine and of Emily Lyle of the School of Scottish Studies.

"Full house," I wrote then, "excellent atmosphere." And so it was, with the presence of Liz Lochhead, Sorley MacLean, Norman MacCaig, Edwin Morgan, Iain Crichton Smith, Derick Thomson, Donald Campbell, Catherine Lucy Czerkawska, Willie Neill, Ellie Macdonald, alongside relative newcomers such as Sheena Blackhall, Ian Stephen, Ian Abbott. I remember the singing and the music during that week of events: Nancy Nicolson, Jo Miller, Sheena Blackhall, Richard Matthewman, Dolina MacLennan and many others. Night after night for a week we held these extraordinary events in the hotel. Scotland had its own poetry at the Festival for the first time and was enjoying it. We took our guests on sightseeing tours of the city and down to Abbotsford, where we swam in the Tweed. We gave them a dinner at L'Auberge, a French restaurant in St Mary's Street, and invited Walter Cairns, literature director of the Scottish Arts Council. Everyone was in a haze of unbelief and happiness that we could do it, that it was working. The events were recorded too, but not without problems. The person doing the recording was something of a non-starter, who had wormed his way into the Saltire Society that year. It was all done reel to reel and I remember long hassles thereafter and am not sure if we did ever eventually acquire the tapes.

On 27 October 1984, Miroslav Holub visited, for which occasion our Librarian, Dr Tom Hubbard, had put on an exhibition of Czechoslovak and East European poetry – not an easy task as that time. Holub said, "I wish we had something like this in Czechoslovakia." It was a wish we heard repeated over and over in subsequent years by poets from all over the world. In some cases attempts were made – e.g. in Germany and Denmark. But none succeeded.

In addition to the German tour initially mentioned, we were also planning a conference of poets and composers in liaison with Raymond Monelle, music critic and teacher, who was a warden at Pollock Halls, where we held the conference in the autumn, supported by Edinburgh District Council. For the Edinburgh Festival in 1985 we were planning a visit from Michel Deguy from France in liaison with a young graduate from Oxford called Robert Crawford and his friend David Kinloch. They had links with *Verse* magazine in Oxford, which in turn was publishing and promoting Michel Deguy.

Alexander Hutchison went to represent Scotland at the Leuven international poetry conference in 1986, which led to more and continuing contacts with overseas poets (including Roberto Sanesi and Grete Tartler), and the attendance by a delegate from Scotland at all the future Leuven conferences – among them John Glenday and Tom Hubbard. Tom prepared a talk for the Leuven conference on 'dùthchas' and duende. He felt that the Gaelic concept of 'dùthchas', described as "all that is passed down by heredity, one's natural inclinations, one's land and one's language"[3] has affinities with the Spanish-Andalusian concept of 'duende' as described by Lorca: "a power, not a behaviour, a struggle not a concept ... not in the throat of a singer but it surges up from the soles of the feet."[4] Tom reported enthusiastically about the conference, where he met poets from all over Europe, including Gyozo Ferencz from Hungary, who was later to spend a few months on an Arts Council Grant at St Andrews as a guest translator. He reported that "people had never heard of Scots or Gaelic, and this was a revelation to them; they wanted to know more."

We had always built up the Library's collection as an international one, and Tom's knowledge of European poetry helped to make ours possibly the best collection open to the public of European poetry in Europe. This conference inspired Tom with a high regard for poetry traditions in Europe. He said his life would be dated as BL and AL – before and after Leuven!

That summer was when Anette de Gott from Mainz first came in to start work on her thesis on Norman MacCaig, and Rebecca Wilson from America researched her anthology of Scottish and Irish women poets: *Sleeping with Monsters*. Both benefited from Tom's knowledge, since there were no appropriate bibliographies that they could use and no index to any Scottish poetry magazines.[5] There was no cuttings file for reviews or interviews. In short, it was almost impossible to study Scottish poets, as no records had been kept to provide the resource materials for such study.

We were planning two St Cecilia's Hall Festival events for the Festival of

---

[3] See Tom Hubbard's introduction to the anthology *The New Makars*, Edinburgh: Mercat Press, 1991.

[4] Federico Garcia Lorca, *In Search of Duende*, New York: New Directions, 1998, p.49.

[5] Apart from *Lines Review* up to number 60 in 1977, prepared by its editor of that time, Robin Fulton.

1986, with Lassi Nummi, from Finland, and Derick Thomson, and another with Tom Paulin and Douglas Dunn. A BBC producer from Northern Ireland visited in connection with the Tom Paulin event and was very impressed with, for instance, our list of poets who write in Scots, saying there were weekly readings at Queen's University arranged by Edna Longley and he would tell them about us. I remarked, "Maybe BBC Northern Ireland will tell BBC Scotland about us!" We found it impossible to persuade Radio Scotland to take an interest in our events involving important overseas poets, even though at that time they were included in the official Edinburgh International Festival Programme.

Lassi Nummi was charming and gave us twelve beautiful, large posters illustrating the Finnish epic poem *The Kalevala*. I read the English versions of his poems at the event, which entailed hours going over them with him, so that I could read them with understanding. The event was a success, with the Lord Provost attending, as well as Iain Crichton Smith, Paulin and Dunn, and Walter Cairns from the Scottish Arts Council. Angus Calder, always helpful on the entertaining side, presented Lassi Nummi with the *New Testament in Scots*, which had been published in 1983. We remained in touch for many years, and I recently learned that the Scottish poet Donald Adamson, who went to live in Finland, has translated some of Nummi's work.

A Swiss woman, unknown to us, named Annabel Seidler, who had a Scots mother, gave us a donation of £1,000 from her father's estate. "O my God," I wrote "It is a miracle". It did often feel as if the Library's whole existence was a miracle.

We had a constant flow of international visitors, researchers, students or student groups, brought by their own staff, the British Council, publishers, the University, the City Council (a large group of Russians were brought in by the Lord Provost himself) – all of whom we personally looked after in the Library. Often enough we put on impromptu readings and recordings for them.

The Danish Institute in Edinburgh held a conference for Danish and Scottish women writers, which led to a return visit of Scottish women writers to Denmark in 1989. The day in May 1987 at the Danish Institute was a memorable one, at which elderly Norah Montgomerie, artistic folklorist, editor, wife of poet William Montgomerie, read her own work for the first time in her life. Nothing to compare with it has been held since in Scotland for women writers. That summer we invited Marianne Larsen from Denmark as our main guest for the Festival. She read with Sheena Blackhall, a Scots writer and singer from Aberdeenshire, and the Gaelic poet Catriona Montgomerie in an event we called 'Fjord and Firth'.

Steinnun Sigurðardóttir, the Icelandic poet who was due to come to read at the Festival 1987 for us, cancelled at the last moment, due to a muddle over her ticket. We had spent many days writing letters, finding sponsors, making posters, finding lodgings and generally arranging her visit, so this was a major blow at the very last minute. Professors Paul Edward and Hermann

Palsson, who had translated her work, agreed to read some of her poems in English and an extract from the *Orkneyinga Saga*. Strangely enough, this same troublesome Steinnun was our first poet in residence in 1992, when an Icelandic festival was taking place in Scotland.

Just before the end of the year we had an effusive letter from an Italian student, Romano Rivolta of Milan, who had apparently visited the Library in August. He thanked "every people who did my holiday so happy and surprising" and ended: "you did me knowing something about Scotland that I didn't find in one month."

I had to fend off the suggestion that we change the name of the Library to 'The National Poetry Library of Scotland'. The new obsession with marketing and image-making (later to be horrendously called 'branding') was beginning to rear its ugly head. My response was, "If your work is solid and honest, that is its image. You only need to work at your image if you have no solid work behind you." Duncan Glen had returned to Scotland after early retirement from being Professor of Graphic Design in Nottingham, and he agreed to take over the design and editing of the Newsletter. That was indeed the beginning of a new image, and a very desirable one.

Roberto Sanesi arrived from Milan, and Alexander Hutchison, who [I took over as chair of the International, Inter-Arts and Events subcommittee in January 1989] worked closely with him on translations and the programme for our Festival event of 1988 at St Cecilia's Hall, which also featured Edwin Morgan Sanesi, was interviewed by Joe Farrell, Italian lecturer at Glasgow University, both on radio and for *The Scotsman*. Aonghas MacNeacail had undertaken to arrange a second event in the evening, after the main Sanesi events, but downstairs in St Cecilia's Hall (whereas the main event was always upstairs in the oval chamber.) Aonghas's event was to be called 'The Music of Meaning' and had a large line-up of performers in ceilidh style, mainly friends of Aonghas. Stephen Watts, an award-winning poet from London, himself half Italian, read his marvellous poem 'Caruso and Gramsci'. He presented us with a bibliography he had produced of contemporary Italian poetry.

Our fifth anniversary party took place on Monday 13 February 1989. It was marked by a party attended by about a hundred folk, including visitors from Canada, America, Japan, Finland and Denmark.

'Migratory Birds'

In April 1989 I was part of a group of Scottish women writers invited to Denmark, as a return visit for the one from Danish women writers that we had helped with. Joan Lingard was the big name, Anne-Marie di Mambro came as a playwright, and I was the poet. We spent a week in Denmark, visiting schools and groups of writers and publishers. I met Pia Tafdrup and Marianne Larsen again and went with Marianne to 'Café Victor' for a reading on the Sunday, where I had my photograph taken for the magazine, *Maskinfabrik*, in number 21, where two poems of mine appeared in translation by Marianne. We were mainly in Copenhagen but were also taken to Odense and Svendborg.

We learnt how much importance is given to translation in Denmark and the relatively better arrangements for writers to earn their living. It was in Denmark that I first learnt of the newly-opened school for translation in Norwich at the University of East Anglia. The Danish Authors' Association welcomed us. We discovered that MacDiarmid was the only Scottish poet they had heard of. They did not know of the 1954 translation of Danish ballads into Scots, published by Edinburgh University Press, entitled *Forty and Four*, by Alexander Gray, a former professor of Economics at Edinburgh. One of the Danish schools had a group of pupils sing me a Ronald Stevenson setting of one of my poems ('Chanticleer'). They gave me a copy of it on cassette. It was beautiful. They had previously visited the Scottish Poetry Library and by chance met Ronald Stevenson. We had some happy further visits to Edinburgh from Danish school groups as a result of this trip.

When we returned, I wrote a piece for *The Glasgow Herald* in which I referred to 'migratory birds':

> The Danes are great sailors and yachtsmen. All along the coast ships are thick as thieves. Danes seem to glide serenely through life, like swans, in a pleasant unruffled manner. Sophus Claussen (known as the Danish Yeats) wrote a poem 'Do not awaken the swans', which describes the danger of migratory birds causing unrest. We found Danish cities, trains, schools, offices, homes, elegant and simple in design, open, sunny and human. Design is more easily translated than literature, but it is probably we who need to be awakened to the riches in the contemporary literatures of Europe.[6]

Edinburgh University Press published a book of translations of European material by Scottish poets,[7] and the SPL was recognised in the acknowledgements. I had some translations from the German of Hölderlin in the book. It was a landmark in recognising the richness of translation in the Scottish literary tradition.

Our internationality was kept apace by Peter France bringing Gennady Aygi into the Library and arranging a reading for him, and by mixed nationality groups from the Applied Language Centre coming in on arranged visits. Aygi was taken on a special visit with Peter France, Duncan Glen, Ian Revie and Alexander Hutchison to Dumfries to the Robert Burns mausoleum, where he sprinkled some soil from the grave of the Chuvash national poet

[6] Tessa Ransford, 'How literature is food and drink to the Danes', *The Glasgow Herald*, 30 May 1989.

[7] Duncan Glen and Peter France (eds), *European Poetry in Scotland: an anthology of translations*, Edinburgh: Edinburgh University Press, 1989.

and admirer of Burns, Vasley Mitta, who was incarcerated by the Soviets. We had another visit from Roberto Sanesi, our festival guest of the previous year, who was invited back again by the Italian institute.

In those days the Edinburgh Festival was still run from London. I had to phone London to find out the theme and discuss our contribution. With Frank Dunlop as Festival Director, our Scottish Poetry Library international poetry event in St Cecilia's Hall was included in the official Festival brochure. After Brian MacMaster took over in 1990, we were relegated to the Fringe, along with the art galleries. 1990 was the beginning of the time of bureaucracy over 'accessibility'. I gave a long interview about this to a researcher, sent by the Arts Council, Vi Hughes from Oxford, who "kept praising us and saying Alastair Niven and Mary Enright in London thought we were marvellous." However, we had to fill in more and more complicated three-year-funding applications to the Scottish Arts Council, in order to receive our grant of £15,000. If we wanted more, we had to qualify for a special 'development fund', which meant going through yet more hoops.

Tom Hubbard was constantly in touch with Europe, its major and minority language poetry, sending out material from Scotland and receiving their books in return. He had a vision of the Library as 'a pan-European Poetry Centre'. 'We're for a celebration of world poetry, in the spirit of MacDiarmid's 'In Memoriam James Joyce'," he wrote in the *Newsletter*.

There was a big symposium: 'Pier Paolo Pasolini: Film, Poetry and Art' which we ran in collaboration with The Edinburgh International Film Festival, the SAC and the Italian Cultural Institute, etc at the Filmhouse in August, 1989.

By 22 February 1990 we were negotiating our visiting poets for the Festival. We wanted to invite Greta Tartler and Daniela Crasnaru from Romania, with their translator, New Zealand poet Fleur Adcock, who lived in London. By March we were discussing with Paolo Vestri, culture spokesman for the District Council, events for the European Commission meetings planned for 1992 in Edinburgh; and the British Council had agreed to pay the fares of the Romanian poets.

Our guest German writers had now arrived for the conference 'Civilising the City'. They were Katrine von Hutten and Barbara Bronnen, both from Munich, which is a twin city of Edinburgh. We held a reception for them in the Library at lunch time with about twenty people, including George Bruce, Duncan Glen, Alexander Hutchison, Colin Nicholson and others. On the Friday evening we held a reading at the City Chambers, featuring our guests and also poets involved in *Makars' Walk*, a book Duncan had written and published, featuring walks around the Old Town connected with literature. On the Saturday there was a unique event in Greyfriars' Kirk, which was packed out with delegates from the conference. Katrine von Hutten herself remarked: "This is a very unusual occasion. I've never read my poems in a church before to an audience of civilised architects." Barbara's father had been a friend of Brecht. She was a novelist. Both visitors were surprised at our standard of living in Edinburgh. They were staying in the university residence at Pollock and found it dismal by their West German standards. We took them for lunch to the pub, The Judge, in the Lawnmarket, where they explained how Edinburgh struck them as downmarket – more like eastern Europe – and we thought we were giving them such a good time!

Tom Hubbard had prepared a Hungarian and Romanian poetry display for the visit we were expecting from George Szirtes. George was impressed by our efforts, and he gave material to Alexander Hutchison, who was going with a group of poets to Poland. We were constantly, every day providing information of this kind, acting as enablers and intermediaries. We were given a donation of books from a Russian library, adding to our remarkable European collection.

Alastair Reid, poet and translator, wanted a recording of Pablo Neruda reading his own work to use as part of his talk and reading in St Cecilia's Hall. By a miracle we managed to find one at the Mitchell Library, a 1967 Caedmon cassette. The Alastair Reid/Nerdua event on 21 August was at St Cecilia's Hall – a full house. Deirdre Keaney, chair of the literature committee of the Scottish Arts Council was there, and Catherine Lockerbie, literary editor of the *Scotsman*. We then prepared for the Romanian event on 23 August, entitled *The Flying Carpet*. That, too, enjoyed a full house.

In October 1990 I was in Tübingen or, more precisely, Blaubeuren conference centre near Tübingen, to join in a conference with German poets and critics and English-language poets and critics. This was set up by the English Department at Tübingen. It was an exciting time because German poets from east and west were meeting each other for the first time. The title of the conference was *Regionality, Nationality and Internationality in Contemporary Literature*. Participants were asked to submit a paper. Mine was on 'India and Scotland as Emotional Force-Fields in the Making of my Poetry'. Other contributors were Cairns Craig from Edinburgh University, Michael Hamburger, Charles Tomlinson, Anne Stevenson, Gillian Clarke from Wales, and John Montague from Northern Ireland. On the German side were Elmar Schenkel, Ursula Kimpel, Heinz Czechowski, Wulf Kirsten, Uwe Kölbe and Werner Dürrson. The papers were subsequently published in Germany and a copy donated to the Scottish Poetry Library.

The following year I edited an issue of *Lines Review* (no. 119) featuring German poets from former east and west in translation and invited Heinz Chechowski, Werner Dürrson and Michael Hamburger to read at the Festival in Edinburgh for the Scottish Poetry Library. I made friends with Elmar at the conference and kept in touch afterwards, inviting him to contribute to *Lines Review*, and he published some of my work in the magazine he edited, *Chelsea Hotel*. I also made friends with Germanist academic Raymond Hargreaves from Leeds, who helped with the translations for *Lines 119* and later produced a book with his own translations of modern German poets.

The event at the Festival was called *The Other Half* (referring to the halves of Germany now being re-united). It was an exquisite occasion with an appreciative audience, despite the lack of interest from the press. We held a dinner afterwards in the Doric, with Karin MacPherson from Edinburgh University German department joining us, who was a friend of Heinz Czechowski's from former East Germany. It was the first event in Britain representing the newly united Germany, and *Lines Review* 119 was timed to coincide with it, featuring poets from both sides.

In September I went to Montpellier to see Patrick Gedde's *Collège des Écossais* there, where I was taken round by André Schimmerling, who had known Geddes. He took me up the tower, saying that Valéry and Tagore, two of my favourite poets, had been there before me. I felt I was seeing the two emotional force-fields of my life symbolised in the *Collège des Écossais* and the *Collège des Hindus*, flourishing in the 1930s when Geddes lived there, side by side on the 'garrigue' above Montpellier.

In October 1990 I took part in a Slavonic conference organised as part of the City of Culture celebrations in Glasgow. I attended the conference to assess the atmosphere because I was to chair a ceilidh in the evening. I remember a Polish editor, who was one of the speakers, saying that if you take care of the aesthetics you will also take care of the politics. There were Czech writers who had re-opened their PEN centre and had encouragement from President Vaclav Havel. I did my best with the ceilidh, but it was clear that some of the Russian writers had been flown in and were being flown out again and hardly knew where in the world they were.

Tony Andrews, the Director of the British Council in Edinburgh, came to the SPL in November 1991 and agreed to help prepare a good brochure, advertising our poet-in-residence scheme, which the BC would make known abroad. We had a series of poets in residence over the next two years from Singapore, India and Botswana as well as Iceland. Then we had to give over the space to computers! The School of Poets was flourishing, with people coming from far beyond Edinburgh, and with Sophie Bentinck, from Holland, joining for the first time. Sophie spoke Dutch, German, French, Spanish and Italian as well as English, and wrote poetry in all these languages! She became a devoted friend to me and to the Library.[8] Jay Hamburger, a poet from New York, attended the School of Poets one evening and reported that he had "never been to anything as informal and yet as intense."

We had visits from librarians from many different countries wanting to find out about InSPIRe (International and Scottish Poetry information Resource), our subject-indexed poetry cataloguing system, and librarians' groups across Scotland were asking for talks from us and visits. In 1992 I proposed a book of translations of Scottish poetry into the languages of the

---

[8] Sophie recently published her Second World War diaries which she had re-discovered in the early 2000s: Sophie Gräfin von Bentinck, *Mein Hunger nach Leben: Kriegstagebücher zwischen Adel und Arbeitsdienst*, München: Bucher, 2012.

EC as a high-quality gift to delegates for the coming EU summit to be held in Edinburgh under John Major. I was given free estimates, specified paper and typeface, format and other details by Tom Dalgleish, print production manager at Macdonald's publishers and printers, Loanhead. The book never materialised. No money for poetry as usual.

In the midst of the panic and chaos following a break-in at the Library in March 1992, Karin MacPherson from the German department at Edinburgh University called in with the distinguished East German poet Sarah Kirsch. I later attended her reading at the University and had dinner afterwards with members of the department. It was the first time I witnessed the low morale among University lecturers about bureaucracy and commercialism taking over the University's ways of managing its affairs.

At this time I had the idea of buying Abden House, the house of the principal of Edinburgh University, which was on offer for sale at £600,000. I had a vision of a European Poetry Centre with bookshop, café, seminar/reading room, library, parking, children's room, residency and lovely garden. Looking back, now that Edinburgh has claimed the title of 'Unesco City of Literature', it would have been a wonderful investment.

I had heard about the British School of Literary Translation that had been opened in Norwich at the University of East Anglia. I wanted something similar in Scotland. But I also realised that we needed a bibliography, to tell us what Scottish literature had been translated over the centuries into foreign languages. This was the instigation of the idea that finally came to fruition in BOSLIT: *Bibliography of Scottish Literature in Translation*, about three years later.

Tom Hubbard was growing restless and looking out for other jobs. His part-time, underpaid job with us could not continue forever and his children were all now at school. He told us he would apply for a research assistant job at the Adult Education Department in Glasgow University. In fact he was offered a visiting lectureship in Grenoble, teaching Scottish literature, starting in January. Keith Dixon, who taught Scotlit at the University in Grenoble, visited the Library that autumn. He contributed to *Newsletter* no 20 in February 1993, describing his courses in Grenoble.

In December 1992, we had helped to arrange a big international event at the National Library. This consisted of readings from European poetry in a variety of languages translated into Scots, Gaelic and English, as a contribution to the European Festival at the NLS. Over ninety people attended and enjoyed an evening of humour, lyricism and internationalism. It was devised by Duncan Glen and Peter France. George Bruce, Christopher Whyte, Sandy Hutchison and I joined Duncan and Peter for the reading. All the publicity for this was done by the SPL in collaboration with the NLS. The event was covered by the BBC.

The European Summit was about to take place that December, at Holyrood Palace, so the Canongate was full of police and traffic barriers.

Considering the state of the Canongate in those days, and that it was winter, it was a strange decision. The street was derelict and ill-lit, culminating in a public toilet opposite the palace. It had no shops except the odd newsagent, sandwich or chip shop. Moray House lurked on the right and the Canongate Kirk and graveyard on the left. Chauffeur-driven saloon cars cruised up and down with European heads of state, while Edinburgh just went about its business. No fireworks, no fuss, no special Christmas decorations. There was a certain austere dignity about this find-us-as-we-are approach, which I prefer to the razzmatazz to which we are subjected in the twenty-first century!

The year ended with my staying 'till the small hours' to send out the SPL Christmas cards, designed by Rose O'Connor, especially poignant with Tom Hubbard being 'demobbed' and writing "au revoir, mes braves et bravesses". It was undoubtedly the end of an era, since Tom and I had begun everything and worked out our policies and practicalities, our ethos and ideas, our working and personal relationships from the first cold start in February 1984. Tom's academic knowledge and brilliance, his self-learnt depth of knowledge, not just of Scottish but of international literature, his dedication to the cause, his unwavering belief in the absolute necessity of our work for literature in Scotland, his dogged hard-work, his wit and sense of humour would be irreplaceable.

We helped to organise an event on translation at the Italian Institute in June 1993, involving Edwin Morgan, Christopher Whyte and Duncan Glen. On Tuesday, 1 June 1993 the first (historical) meeting on a Translation database was held in the SPL. Present were Shonagh Irvine from the SAC, Ian Mason from the Heriot Watt School of interpreting and translation and Peter France. There was a lot of brainstorming and a few clear ideas were taking shape. The journalist and writer Anne Smith wrote a piece about the proposals in the *Sunday Times* of 11 July. This new initiative resulted in the setting up of BOSLIT: *Bibliography of Scottish Literature in Translation*, which twenty years later was not only well established within the National Library, but had also achieved its aim of having catalogued the bulk of the material going back several centuries.

It was in 1993 that Brian McMaster, the director of the Edinburgh Festival, decided that only music and drama could be part of the Festival, excluding the art galleries as well as groups such as the Scottish Poetry Library and the Saltire Society. I reported in the *Newsletter* that "we have no overseas visiting poets this year, since the new policy has left us without any funding from the official Festival. Last year the European Festival supported our event." This policy of McMaster's continued throughout his reign and made the Festival of virtually no interest to vast swathes of Scottish cultural society. It was a hard blow to us, because our visiting overseas poets had always been performing at the Edinburgh International Festival. Henceforth it was as part of the Festival Fringe, for which we had to pay, rather than being ourselves subsidised. The events, though, were no different.

We were planning a visit to Edinburgh of the Polish poet Tadeus Rozewicz with his translator Adam Czerniawski, then based at the University of East Anglia's School of Translation (he had been warden for a time at Hawthornden Castle writers' retreat). I decided to try a collaboration with Scottish PEN and to hold an event in October at the Traverse Theatre. We found that Christopher Whyte had translated Rozewicz into Gaelic, so we were able to add that to the programme for the event, which took place on Wednesday, 21 October 1993. Alexander Hutchison was chair, and he also reading his translations into Scots of some of Rozewicz's poems.

The Importance of Translation

I prepared a 'talk' on the Scottish Poetry Library for its tenth anniversary in 1994 and it is probably worth quoting extensively from it as a way of summing up our ideas and practice:

> The Scottish Poetry Library is unique and many of its activities are new in the field of poetry. It opened its doors in February 1984 and began lending from the premises and by post within a month. Since then it has grown to 14,000 volumes, cassettes and magazines. (Of course it swiftly rose to well over 20,000 plus CDs, cuttings, pamphlets and ephemera.) It lends from its eight branches too (Dundee, Glasgow, Paisley, Kilmarnock, Ayr, Ullapool, Stornoway and Lerwick). [This later became ten branches with Grangemouth and Selkirk added]. It also runs a van-service, touring the country with a choice of some 300 books for lending and magazines for sale. The Fieldworker, Stuart Reid, has proved popular with children, writers' groups, prisoners, the elderly, the disabled, when he gently introduces books of poetry as offering a path of inward adventure, paralleled by outward adventures such as skiing and climbing.
>
> Patrick Geddes (1854–1932) adopted the triad: folk, work, place, to stand for the enmeshment of these factors in all human endeavours. Situated in a courtyard off the Royal Mile with an open door to the public six hours a day, six days a week and presenting poetry throughout the community, the SPL caters for the aspiring poet, the academic, the creative artist, the literary activist, the broadcaster, and people of all backgrounds and tastes. The SPL is a fine example of Scotland's 'democratic intellect' in practice. The SPL is run according to principle: that poetry is an essential dimension in the life of every human being. Therefore anyone who wishes can borrow from us freely wherever they live and whether or not they know exactly what they want to read.
>
> The practices of the Scottish Poetry Library introduce poetry in new

ways through the use of specially-devised computer programmes, bringing up-to-date technology naturally into the medieval precincts. The cataloguing system invented in the SPL is known as InSPIRe: International Scottish Poetry Information Resource. This accurately describes the nature of the SPL's stock. The primary concern is with Scotland's own poetry, beginning with the present day but comprehending poetry in Gaelic, Scots and English throughout the centuries. This may sound obvious but it is revolutionary. It is the first time there has been any public effort to collect and record Scotland's poetry per se, to index and catalogue it, to make it known and accessible. For the first time the literary magazines, full of extraordinary treasures, are being indexed and put 'on-line' for the public. For the first time the sheer number of poets writing nowadays, and in previous eras, in a variety of dialects, styles and subject matter, is made visible and brought to consciousness in the national psyche.

As the poetry itself demonstrates, Scotland is not alone in the world but culturally interacts constantly with other nations, just as poetry is not alone among the arts, but interacts constantly with other forms of creative expression. Therefore there is a deliberate policy to stock a selection of poetry, mainly in translation and mainly twentieth century, from other countries, particularly those that have a strong cultural link with Scotland. We also stock general books on music and ballads, painting, myth and legend and Scottish history. We put on colourful, movable exhibitions on differing themes, which we rotate around local libraries.

The importance of translation is emphasised in the SPL and our pioneering work with creative ways of cataloguing has led to a literary translation database being initiated in Scotland (BOSLIT: Bibliography of Scottish Literature in Translation). In the SPL itself we can trace poetry under the entry-point 'translation' as we can also under thousands of other key words, whether names, languages, eras, categories or subject matter. This innovative approach, transcending the normal bibliographic one, allows people to find poetry without necessarily knowing the names of poets.

We reverse the stultifying emphasis on the importance of a few poets per generation; and instead of poems being known because of the poet, we make it possible for poets to become known because of their poems. Again, it seems logical and obvious but in practical terms it is revolutionary. It puts poetry on a par with music and painting where it is normal for people to enjoy the work and then discover the name of the composer or artist. This approach to poetry also means it can be introduced through the education system in a cross-curricula and broad-based manner, thereby rescuing poetry from its obscure marginal position as 'a tiny fraction of English Literature' (I quote from a conversation with Scotland's foremost Professor of Education).

In the Scottish Poetry Library, poetry is not 'on the shelf'. It is in the hands and hearts, the minds and the making of people whoever they are. During the Edinburgh International Festival we make our medieval courtyard available for spontaneous gatherings and readings as well as dancing. Our international policy is not only reflected in the materials we stock but also in our actively inviting overseas poets to Edinburgh. This we have done every year for ten years, putting on a high quality formal reading during the Festival. We also began an international poets-in-residence policy for purposes of cultural dialogue with long-staying guest poets from Iceland, Singapore, India and Botswana within two years.

A figure of eight represents the energy pattern of the Scottish Poetry Library, as the work within the premises feeds into the work beyond the premises which, in turn, in a dynamic loop, feeds back into the work within. Thus we work with energy patterns, with volunteers and committed staff, with love for the common weal.

We went on to hold Festival events for Scottish Literature abroad, for Italian, Danish, Hungarian, Irish and Catalan poets in subsequent years, often supported by Kenneth Munro of the European Commission in Scotland. At the Italian event one, Hamish Henderson read some of his translations of Italian poets, with Carla Sassi, Christopher Whyte and Marco Fazzini in attendance, and Guiseppe Conte came from Italy. This was also linked to an issue of *Lines Review* (no 130). Gyozo Ferencz came from Hungary, Inger Christiansen from Denmark, with Soren Ulrik Thomsen and Francesc Parcerisas from Catalonia. Following on from this, Anna Crowe subsequently went to Catalonia and began translating Catalonian women poets.

We obtained funding from the European Commission to acquire even more European poetry, what we called our EPIC project: European Poetry Information Centre. After my retirement, I sent packs of 60 issues of *Lines Review* with a sound tape of Scottish poetry to fifteen universities in Eastern Europe, with the help of the British Council and, on a travel scholarship from the Society of Authors, I visited Leipzig and translated five poets from Saxony, published by Shearsman Books as *The Nightingale Question* in 2004.

The New Building

In the *Newsletter* number 26, published in February 1996, I wrote on the front page about the 'good news':

> We have good news for SPL members: The Scottish Poetry Library is delighted to announce the award of National Lottery for the Arts funding towards the building of a new library. A

George Bruce, laying the Foundation Stone for the new Scottish Poetry Library building, 1 August 1997. (Roddy Simpson)

sum of £506,301 has been allocated. With ever increasing use and growth of holdings, the SPL is full to capacity, and expansion is an urgent necessity to meet the needs of users, improve access and to provide for the long-term future.

I then continued with a description of the proposed site – off the Canongate in Edinburgh's Old Town and quoted Malcolm Fraser's assurance that many of the attractive features which make the SPL a living centre of creative energy would be found in the new building: e.g. a place for courtyard readings, with a forestair acting as seating; the main Library on the ground floor, with a members' room on the mezzanine. But there would be more space to circulate, to study and browse quietly, better access for the disabled and more functionality for administration and cataloguing systems. I finished by explaining that the fundraising target was £100,000 as our share of the new building costs and that this was £100,000 over and above the sum that might be raised by the sale of the Tweeddale Court premises, which of course we could not do until the new building was ready.

Getting to that stage in 1996 had taken two years since I first went to a talk on the new lottery funding when it was becoming available in 1994. Ours was the first lottery application for the arts in Scotland and the first building for the arts to be assisted by the lottery. It then took a further three years and never-ending effort to raise the funds and manage the building process. We were on time and within budget. The building won many awards. We moved in during March-April 1999, opening to the public in April. We held our official opening on 22 June 1999. I retired at the end of that year.

For much of this period, Iain Galbraith worked to compile *Beredter Norden*, a generous anthology of twentieth-century Scottish poetry translated into German.[9] During this time, as he observes in his introduction, the social, literary, and political landscape of Scotland has been changing. He senses that Donny O'Rourke's edited anthology *Dream State: New Scottish Poets*[10] marked a turning point in the sensitivities of poets writing in Scotland. O'Rourke himself claimed in 2001 that writers had contributed more to a new Scotland than had the politicians. Galbraith suggests that during the 1990s the poets were aware of a role almost imposed on them to represent and speak for the national culture, whereas after devolution (and the death of major literary figures such as Tom Scott, Norman MacCaig, Sorley Maclean, George Mackay Brown, Iain Crichton Smith, and Hamish Henderson), with that burden as it were taken over by elected politicians, they felt free to be more personal, various, self-contemplative, or linguistically athletic. New language-inclusive anthologies, new histories, and international conferences now abounded.

---

[9] Iain Galbraith (ed.), *Beredter Norden: Schottische Lyrik seit 1900*, Berlin: Edition Rugerup, 2011.

[10] Donny O'Rourke (ed.), *Dream State: The New Scottish Poets*, Edinburgh: Polygon, 1993; rev. ed. 2001.

New building of Scottish Poetry Library at 5 Crichton's Close, Edinburgh EH8 8DT
(Allan MacMillan, May 2013)

Snippets in Couplets

1984:   We open, six, two, eighty-four
         they're demolishing the old cinema.

1985:   We're lending books all over the country
         all over the world, of Scottish poetry

1986:   Laboriously we go on listing
         catalogues, bibliographs persisting

1987:   Still the old-fashioned typewriter
         and 'give us more hell' photocopier

1988:   Touring from Galloway to Inverness
         in the time-expired post-office bus

1989:   The courtyard clear, we fix a striped awning
         readings and dancing and singing till evening
1990:   We begin to devise the system, InSPIRe
         in a cupboard with nothing but 'wordstar'

1991:   A united Germany comes to call
          for festival readings in St Cecilia's Hall

1992:   At last we can welcome visiting poets
          in our flat upstairs for a Scottish experience

1993:   From Iceland, Singapore and India
          but this year Seboni, 'the Man' from Botswana

1994:   Our ten-year anniversary party
          haggis, poetry and whisky

1995:   Gordon, most trusted of volunteers
          still keeps the Library on Saturdays

1996:   Will we ever manage to raise the money
          to match our grant from the Lottery?

1997:   The foundation stone, a people's ceremony
          and St Columba's 14-hundred centenary

1998:   Tessa's sixtieth birthday, a cheque arrives
          for £60,000 from the Lady Marks

1999:   Dust on dust, we claim our building
          suddenly folk are seeing, believing

2000:   A new era starts, all is in place
          our long struggle over, money flows, a new face

2001:   It was Eric's devotion, Tom's integrative vision
          those Friday afternoons of discussion

2002:   The pamphlet cause now well underway
          in memory of Callum, his generosity

2003:   Dorothy launches her women's anthology
          in Tweeddale Court she breastfed her baby

2004:   He has started at university
          where now they teach Scottish poetry

CODA:

> Hundreds have given their time and skill
> their hope, enthusiasm, goodwill
>
> poetry's for people and not for money
> prestige or pride or bureaucracy
>
> may we keep humble, may we keep true
> to the pain that made beauty, the love we all knew

That is what I wrote for the *Newsletter* celebrating the twentieth anniversary of the Scottish Poetry Library on 6 February 2004. And the SPL continues to act as a treasure trove and living movement for poetry in and of Scotland in relation to Europe and the wider world.

'The Postman Rings Again':
Alexander Trocchi's *Young Adam*

Mario Relich

I am sure I would rather be a bargee than occupy any position under Heaven that required attendance at an office.[1]

Much ink has been spilled on the confrontation between Alexander Trocchi and Hugh MacDiarmid at the 1962 Edinburgh International Writers' Conference. James Campbell's account tells us that "Hugh MacDiarmid was on the platform, as usual promoting his own work, denigrating everything English, dismissing *all* contemporary fiction out of hand, proclaiming Scotland's potential as an international force" (italics in original). He describes Trocchi's famous intervention as follows:

> When MacDiarmid had finished, a tall young man with a hawk's profile and bristly black hair got up to respond. Trocchi had published one little-read book in Britain, *Young Adam*, but some of the writers present, such as Lawrence Durrell and Norman Mailer, knew him as a drug addict and a friend of Burroughs, who was sitting next to him. Trocchi answered the locally revered poet by first saying that the best modern poetry had been written by novelists anyway, then dismissed the work of MacDiarmid and his clan as "stale, cold porridge, Bible-clasping nonsense. Of what is interesting in Scottish writing in the past twenty years or so, I myself have written it all."[2]

To put it mildly, while Trocchi wildly exaggerated his literary prominence as a Scottish writer, he certainly shook things up in Scotland and elsewhere, and at the time MacDiarmid possibly needed to be taken down a peg or two. It is now also indisputable that his first novel, *Young Adam*,[3] and *Cain's Book*[4] are

---

[1] Robert Louis Stevenson, *Travels with a Donkey/ An Inland Voyage/ The Silverado Squatters*, edited by Trevor Royle, London: J. M. Dent, 1993, p.14.

[2] James Campbell, 'Alexander Trocchi: The Biggest Fiend of All', *Antioch Review*, vol. 50 (Summer 1992), p.458.

[3] Alexander Trocchi, *Young Adam*, introduced by John Pringle, Edinburgh: Rebel Inc., 1999.

[4] Alexander Trocchi, *Cain's Book*, introduced by Richard Seaver, London: John Calder Publisher, 1998.

among the finest twentieth-century novels, and surely by now canonical so
far as Scottish Literature is concerned and, at the very least, "interesting".

It is a toss-up whether *Cain's Book,* first published in 1960, or *Young Adam*
is Alexander Trocchi's best novel, even if Campbell and other critics prefer
the former. *Young Adam* first appeared in 1954, but in a version which added
pornographic material at the instigation of the Olympia Press publisher
Maurice Girodias[5] – no doubt a rare example in literary history in which
the overly erotic first version constituted a kind of inverse bowdlerisation.
Cain's Book looks forward to drug addiction as a major theme in Irvine
Welsh's *Trainspotting* and subsequent works. Welsh himself, however, is on
record preferring *Young Adam,* for reasons which will be examined in the
conclusion. Trocchi's 1966 revised edition of *Young Adam*, while very much
a Scottish variation of existentialist writing – particularly Albert Camus'
L'Etranger, usually translated as *The Outsider* –,[6] its key appeal lies in its
being firmly grounded in the social realities of 1950s Scotland. John Pringle's
introduction to the 1996 edition of Trocchi's novel, published by Rebel Inc.
and based on the 1966 edition, tells us that when Trocchi wrote his first draft
of *Young Adam*, as early as 1947, he "perhaps felt this was over-influenced
by Camus' *The Outsider,* since he rewrote it in Paris in the early 1950s to
resemble the current version."[7] Trocchi's first novel, moreover, unlike the
more relentlessly self-conscious *Cain's Book,* is a hybrid one in which the
subjective perspective of the amoral 'Joe' is combined with a strong sense
of the still highly industrial reality of 1950s Scotland.

Much of the novel takes place on the Forth and Clyde Canal, part of which
is the Union Canal; and this is significant, because Trocchi combines Joe's
sense of existential alienation with a hard look at the environment in which
he lives and acts, the canal at times almost acting as an 'objective correlative'
for his state of being:

> ... everything was silent except for the ambiguous presence
> of the canal itself. There is a noise that is peculiar to inland
> water at night, a kind of radiation that is not exactly sound and
> not exactly smell; it is closer to touch; its being touches one at
> the pores (p. 68).

But the canal, as I shall go on to argue, is not merely symbolic of Joe's state
mind at various stages of the novel.

Young Adam begins with Joe, the first-person – and possibly 'unreliable'
– narrator, doubting his own individuality. On the very first page he looks
at his 'chromium plated' steel mirror and questions his own individual

[5] John Pringle, 'Introduction', in *Young Adam*, pp. x-xi.

[6] Albert Camus, *The Outsider,* translated by Stuart Gilbert, introduced by Cyril
Connolly, Harmondsworth: Penguin Books/ Hamish Hamilton, 1961.

[7] John Pringle, p. x.

consciousness and memory. As he puts it, "... there existed between the mirror and myself the same distance, the same break in continuity which I have always felt to exist between acts which I committed yesterday and my present consciousness of them." (p.1) It soon emerges that he and Leslie, his work-mate in a barge, have dragged the body of a young woman from the Clyde, and called the police. We learn that he is a drifter, although a middle-class one, in contrast to Leslie, and for five chapters in Part One (of three) he plots to seduce Leslie's wife, who actually owns the barge. He succeeds in doing so. But it is only in Part Two, ch. 1 that we have reason to suspect he may have had something to do with the body found floating, which he later reveals is that of his estranged girlfriend Cathie. The language employed for signposting this shift of narrative is very reminiscent of a film-script: "**GO BACK TO** the beginning" (p. 73, bold italics in the original).

Up to this point, Joe sounds like he is entirely driven by lust for Ella, Leslie's hard-bitten but highly-sexed wife, and entirely unsentimental in his views about other people. At a particularly tense, indeed claustrophobic moment, this is how Joe describes the dynamics of his relationship with Ella and Leslie:

> Ella's back was still towards us. Looking at her now I realised that you had to think in terms of two women, his and mine. His was hard. I could understand his dumb frustration, even sympathise with it. Mine he had probably never known. It was difficult to square what I supposed was his experience of her with the woman who, half an hour previously, had bared her belly for me against the boarding and then sunk downwards through my arms on the grass. (p.51)

Joe's shrewd, sardonic assessment of what is almost a 'menage a trois' runs counter to his more existentialist musings about himself as an outsider against society, and is arguably reminiscent of pulp thrillers like James M. Cain's *The Postman Always Rings Twice.* There is a hint of this earlier on, and very much before any attempt at seduction from either of them: "For I seldom talked to Ella, who appeared to dislike me and who gave the impression she only put up with me because of him: a necessary evil, the hired hand." (p.5) The operative phrase here is 'hired hand'.

While it is a moot point whether Trocchi had read any 'pulp fiction' before writing *Young Adam,* chances are that he would have seen the Lana Turner-John Garfield *film noir* of James M. Cain's thriller. In that film, Garfield as the 'hired hand', working in her husband's garage, makes the first move in seducing Turner, who finds her husband too old and unexciting; similarly, Trocchi has Joe, sensing that her marriage is not very fulfilling, communicating his desire for Stella by touching her legs underneath the barge's kitchen-table while they are having dinner. This is rather well conveyed by Ewan McGregor and a poker-faced, yet also alertly sensitive, Tilda Swinton in David

McKenzie's fine 2003 film version. Joe in Trocchi's novel tells us that Ella has social ambitions after his first, unsuccessful attempt at seducing her:

> (s)he had probably thought it over during the afternoon and decided no good could come of it, perhaps that I was getting ideas above my station, for I had known for a long time that Ella was a snob and she had set her heart on leaving the canal one day to live in a 'nice little bungalow', as Leslie called it, in one of the quieter suburbs of Edinburgh. (p. 39)

The Lana Turner character is similarly ambitious in the Hollywood film. It was released in 1946 and, according to Trocchi's biographer Andrew Murray Scott, Trocchi began work on his novel in 1948. Scott maintains that "(i)n a small notebook, titled after Eliot, 'Butt-ends' the original idea for the novel that would eventually become *Young Adam* was taking shape," even if "vastly different from its first published form in 1954 and its 'definitive' version in 1963."[8] But the 'vastly different' version initially projected emphasised the 'crime' aspect, further confirming the novel's 'pulp fiction' genesis: "The central character, not the narrator, was Jo Henfield … a reporter from the *Lairs Gazette* investigating a sex-crime." Murray Scott further observes that it "derived some of its solipsistic structure from Simenon,"[9] thereby suggesting that it is rather less metaphysically existentialist than *The Outsider*.

Ultimately, it is how Trocchi portrays Joe himself that matters. He is entirely self-obsessed and pretty much lives for the moment, and nothing else. Even if we have to 'trust' him on this one, it is unlikely that he has murdered his girlfriend, although he is at least partly responsible for the 'accident' which leads to her death by drowning, since it was the direct result of their coupling in the dark and her slipping into the waters of the river Clyde, which is connected to the Forth and Clyde Canal. He begins to describe the aftermath very directly to the reader as follows: "Say I was involved in a state of quiet shock, at the edge of apprehension, soothed by the water." This is followed by "I felt a sense of personal danger. … as though a trapdoor all at once opened into a deeper consciousness of the situation …," leading to this confession about his own vulnerability: "I felt very alone then, an alien, an exile, society already crystallising against me, and only my own desperate word for what had happened." (p. 78) And it is his very alienation that allows him to shirk responsibility for his girlfriend's death: "My responsibility in the matter was simply a convenient social fiction, one which had shamed God knows how many men into assisting at their own murder." (p. 87) The profound ambivalence of this statement reverberates throughout pretty

---

[8] Andrew Murray Scott, *Alexander Trocchi: The Making of a Monster,* second edition, Kilkerran: Kennedy & Boyd, 2012, p.25.

[9] *The Making of a Monster,* p.128.

much the second half of the novel, since he therefore does not report the accident (if it was an accident) to the police, the consequence of which is that an innocent man is arrested for murder and eventually convicted and executed for his 'crime'.

But, however Joe's feelings of existential angst may be defined, Trocchi presents him as a very much a product of his own society, more specifically a product of a grimly 1950s Scotland in industrial decline – at least in retrospect we realise that it was a part of the UK at the fag-end of industrialisation. One example of how Trocchi's novel achieves this effect occurs when Joe recalls walking aimlessly in a Glasgow street and making this observation:

> A coal-cart moved slowly towards me at the other side, but there was nothing special about the Clydesdale horse which hauled it nor about the man who walked beside it, who, as it had now begun to rain, wore an empty coal-bag like a monk's cowl at his head and shoulders. He walked in front of the horse and slightly to one side of it, shuffling his big boots along the gutter. (p. 88)

There is nothing very dynamic or all that modern about the coal-man and his cart, and the 'monk's cowl' even gives us a hint of the medieval. The coal industry, which we now know was in steep decline at the time, nevertheless accounts for his casual job on the barge. His job is to help Ella's husband Leslie with transporting anthracite coal from Glasgow to Edinburgh, and eventually Leith. Readers at the time would have known that it was primarily used for heating fuel.

One aspect of what makes Joe tick, as it were, is that he lives by his senses, cultivating a kind of spontaneous sensuality. This is evident in his descriptions of Ella, but he is also very much subject to the grimy physicality of handling coal. This is how he describes it:

> It was a dirty job for Leslie and me. After each load of anthracite had been emptied into the hold, he and I had to get to work with shovels and spread it evenly to prevent the barge listing. It wouldn't have been so bad working at the other end, but all the dust and grit in the world was down there in the hold and it got into our eyes and our noses and into the orifices of our ears. I never liked coal or anthracite. (p. 15)

On the other hand, only a few pages later, he is very positive about navigating the canal itself, considering it the most enjoyable part of his job:

> Of all the jobs I have been forced to do I think I liked being on the canal best. You are not tied up in one place then as you are

if you take a job in town, and sometimes, if you can forget how
ludicrously small distances are, you get the impression that you
are travelling. And there is something about travelling. (p.28)

Paradoxically, although Joe evidently likes the canal because it steers him
away from the presumably dull, sedentary jobs in 'town', by which elsewhere
in the novel it is clear he means Glasgow, the canal is actually the Forth and
Clyde Canal, merging into the Union Canal, and it is this canal setting which
roots him to history.

The importance of the Canal for the economic development of Scotland
has been emphasised by Tom Devine:

> In the central Lowlands, where, by the early nineteenth
> century, the majority of the population lived, the construction
> of the Forth and Clyde Canal was ... crucial, enabling, for
> example, the booming commercial metropolis of Glasgow to
> be supplied with grain and meat from as far away as the farms
> of the Lothians and Fife.[10]

Interestingly, for Devine as an economic historian this is no matter of Joe's
dismissal of 'ludicrously small distances.' His view is applied to more
specifically industrial development by T.J. Dowds in his history of the Forth
and Clyde Canal:

> Without the Canal, it is difficult to imagine the growth of
> industry in the central belt. It is doubtful if the Lanarkshire coal
> deposits could have been successfully exploited without the
> facility to transport the coal to Glasgow and from there to the
> rest of Scotland and beyond.[11]

The Union Canal was particularly vital for Edinburgh, and the machinations
of the coal industry have been succinctly described by Guthrie Hutton:

> Edinburgh was at the mercy of a cartel of coal merchants who,
> like all monopolies, fixed high prices. They were not noticed
> for their honesty either. Coal was sold by the cartload and by
> judicious spreading of the loads two carts could miraculously
> become three. Householders bought large, carefully mined,
> lumps of coal known as 'big' coal which they would then break

---

[10] T. M. Devine, *The Scottish Nation, 1700-2000*, London: Penguin Books, 2000, p. 141.

[11] T.J. Dowds, *The Forth and Clyde Canal: A History*, East Linton: Tuckwell Press, 2003,
p.71.

up themselves in preference to spending less on an uncertain mixture from dubious traders. The canal changed all that. Suddenly people could be reasonably confident they were getting what they asked for at a price they could afford.[12]

The canals, as Trocchi's novel indicates, still had a substantial economic function in the fifties. They did stagnate from the sixties to nearly the end of the century, but by the late nineties British Waterways and other bodies, governmental and non-governmental, attracted funding which completely changed the economic prospects, now orientated towards leisure and tourism, of the now renamed Millennium Canals. As Hutton puts it, "... high-level lobbying kept the issue on the boil until April 1998 when the Secretary of Sate for Scotland, Donald Dewar, announced that funding guarantees were in place."[13] On 12 March 1999, Dewar in his Glasgow Anniesland parliamentary constituency, "watched by invited guests and bemused local residents ... dug the first spadeful of earth."[14] The Falkirk Wheel was key to this development, and it was opened by the Queen on 24 May 2002.[15]

Christopher Harvie has pointed out in his book *Mending Scotland* that the Millennium Canals "could rival Ireland's money-spinner, the Shannon, with the techno-bonus of the Falkirk Wheel," although, writing in 2004, he still felt that much more development was needed to realise the full economic potential of the Millennium Canals.[16]

Part of what makes *Young Adam* more rooted in history than may be expected from an 'existentialist thriller' is that it reminds us of what is now a long-forgotten commerce in coal that the Union and Forth and Clyde Canals provided. For Joe, despite the hard graft of his job helping to transport the coal, the canal to some extent offers an escape from city existence: "When we went on deck, the rain was off, but over the fields and the canal gusts of

---

[12] Guthrie Hutton, *The Union Canal: A Capital Asset*, Glasgow: Richard Stenlake, 1993, p.7.

[13] Guthrie Hutton, *Scotland's Millennium Canals: The Survival and Revival of the Forth & Clyde and Union Canals*, Catrine: Stenlake Publishing, 2002, p.145.

[14] *Scotland's Millennium Canals*, p. 147.

[15] See photograph in *The Forth and Clyde Canal*, p. 49.

[16] Christopher Harvie, *Mending Scotland*, Glendaruel: Argyll Publishing, 2004, p.103. In the past years, the situation has continuously improved – the Bowling end (Lock 39 on the Forth and Clyde Canal officially) saw a major refurbishment; including a new picnic area and sculptures overlooking the Clyde. There are quite a few permanent boats/houseboats around the harbour, and a well-kept old stonewashed harbourmaster's house. There is also a bike-shop and a large nature reserve nearby. And now there is even talk of building the first new canal in Scotland since 1818, connecting Loch Lomond with the River Clyde. See Emma Cowing, 'Canal to unlock Lomond for Clyde sailors', *The Herald*, 28 April 2013.

whiteness blew, not rain, but damply and wild, visible only when thickened under the force of the wind, making the atmosphere bracing and uncertain." (p.57) It does not take long before Joe, reveling in the 'bracing and uncertain', turns his thoughts to imagining about Stella that "(t)he barge would have rocked gently as she climbed naked on to the bunk for me." (p.58)

Once the wrong man, Daniel Goon, a Glasgow plumber, is charged with Cathie's supposed murder, the barge becomes very claustrophobic for Joe:

> I had become part of a situation which seemed to protect me against another, less enviable one, the one in which I would have been involved had I gone to the police. But the more I became involved in the small world of the barge, the more I felt myself robbed of my identity. (p.100)

It is part of Trocchi's great distinction as a novelist that, at one stroke, Joe here describes both his own 'existential' or 'metaphysical' alienation, involving loss of personal identity *and* a very real situation, so much a staple of pulp fiction, or *film noir* for that matter, that could culminate in his arrest as a criminal suspect.

As he puts it in relation to Stella at this point of the novel, when she settles in with him: "I was still the hired man." (p.102) Earlier on, he even welcomes 'passing' for working-class, but in rather derogatory terms: "... that day I was wearing one of Leslie's cloth caps as a badge of my insignificance." (p.88)

Regarding Cathie, Joe is surprised when he discovers that Goon, who is wrongly incriminated in her death, had an affair with her, but his observations sound very much like those of a snob:

> It puzzled me. A plumber, Goon. Married with four children. And Cathie, whose father had been a minor civil servant with the Post Office or something, an eager representative of possibly the most class-conscious of all British classes, whose influence she had never quite thrown off. (p.89)

Whether Trocchi intended Joe to sound snobbish at times, this kind of comment on his part is arguably not what one would expect from an existentialist anti-hero – it sounds more typical of pulp fiction or any number of Scottish and English social realist or naturalistic novelists. Trocchi's depiction of Scotland in the fifties at times gives the impression that it could be re-titled *The Coal Barge with the Curtained Windows*. Above all George Orwell, about whom Trocchi wrote an essay, with grimy early novels like *A Clergyman's Daughter*, *Keep the Aspidistra Flying*, and *Coming Up for Air*, comes most prominently to mind.

Joe, at any rate, tries to wriggle out of this entrapment with Stella's sister Gwendoline, who is socially less ambitious and recently widowed.

After making love to Gwendoline "very coldly and mechanically in a field" (p.114), Joe returns with her to the barge, moored at the end of the canal in Edinburgh, and a hint that even she, like Stella before him, is likely to try to lure him into a conventionally respectable relationship, this time in Leith rather than Stella's posher, suburban Edinburgh:

> We walked slowly back to the barge talking in a desultory way about Leith, where we had both lived. She liked Leith, she said, and she thought she would go back there and settle down when the damages came for her husband's death, as he died in an accident. (p.115)

Leith is the final destination of the coal transported in Stella's coal barge.

It is Gwendoline who reinforces his determination to leave Stella, and he perhaps pays her his greatest compliment, albeit only revealed to the reader when he observes that: "I doubted whether she had ever felt righteous." (p.110) This contrasts with his finding, only a few pages previously, that Stella with her "aura of respectability" personifies "a moral judgement smelling of eau-de-Cologne." (p.106) An exchange between Joe and Gwendoline tells us much about how his life on the barge is purely an expedient:

> "Don't you ever get bored with the canal, Joe?"
> "Sure I do, sometimes."
> "I thought you would. You don't look the type."
> I didn't contradict her.
> "You've got to be born to it," she said.
> I flicked the ash from my cigarette in reply.
> "And even then," she continued, "if you're like me you wouldn't want any part of it."
> "Why not?"
> "It's no life," she said. "I could tell the first time I saw you you weren't cut out for it." (pp.110-11)

Arguably, what Gwendoline detects in Joe is that he is in no way working-class, and indeed we do learn later, when he recalls his relationship with Cathie, that he is a university drop-out with writing ambitions.

And it is his inability to successfully write a book which causes the disruption in their relationship. He remembers her reproaching him as follows: "I don't know why you can't write an ordinary book, one other people will understand. It's been eight months now. I get up early in the morning, sit in a lousy office all day, and when I get home you're either drunk or asleep!" (pp.123-24) Although this leads to sexual shenanigans between the two, involving his flinging some custard at his girlfriend, her accusation only confirms what he says much earlier in the novel, not only about himself, but most cruelly about the plumber accused of murder, and eventually hanged in a dreadful miscarriage of justice: "As a representative of the industrious working classes he was in a sense my enemy. I dislike people who make a virtue out of work." (p.86) Trocchi himself, as Gavin Bowd points out in his monograph on Trocchi and Kenneth White, disparaged work in his counter-cultural Sigma manifestos: "There is ... something tediously negative about Trocchi and White's scathing comments about work."[17] Quite possibly, as well, Trocchi reacted against Carlyle's 'gospel of work' and, in an essay like 'Invisible Insurrection of a Million Minds', even sounds almost like a social prophet in the Carlylean mould, at least in polemical style if not in substance. Here is an excerpt:

> At the present time, in what is often thought of as the age of the mass, we tend to fall into the habit of regarding history and evolution as something which goes relentlessly on, quite outwith our control. The individual has a profound sense of his own impotence as he realises the immensity of the forces involved. We, the creative ones everywhere, must discard this paralytic posture and seize control of the human process by assuming control of ourselves.[18]

Chances are that Carlyle would have agreed with such a stance – even if Trocchi seemed to think that creativity is incompatible with any kind of 'work' – at least in the implication that only if you reform yourself can society itself change for the better.

Joe himself appears to be incapable of such self-reformation, and it may not be insignificant that he is a failed writer. He is portrayed not only as an 'alienated outsider', but very much in terms of how he fits into his social environment. He is, for instance, very much aware of himself as a Glaswegian, well aware of the St. Mungo legend, when he throws away his potentially incriminating lighter in the dead Cathie's purse: "I wiped it carefully with my handkerchief and hurled it as far as I could. I listened for the plop, thinking of St. Mungo and the fish. Mouth open, fish." (pp.82-83) Such awareness contradicts what seems to be his 'existential' or 'absurdist' refusal to accept responsibility for the 'accident' in which his nearly-naked

---

[17] Gavin Bowd, 'The Outsiders': Alexander Trocchi and Kenneth White, Kirkcaldy: Akros Publications, 1998, p.20.

[18] Alexander Trocchi, 'Invisible Insurrections of a Million Minds', in Andrew Murray Scott, ed., Invisible Insurrections of a Million Minds: A Trocchi Reader, Edinburgh: Polygon, 1991, p.178. Trocchi goes on to add that "(w)e must reject the conventional fiction of 'unchanging human nature'. There is in fact no such permanence anywhere. There is only becoming." (italics in original) I expect he would have found Nietzsche and Heraclitus good company, but it is the kind of thing that can be found in, for instance, Italian Futurist manifestos.

girlfriend slipped into the night-time darkness of the Clyde: "I felt vaguely that the whole incident had taken place out of time, that there had been a break in continuity, that what happened was not part of my history. It was pervaded with the unreality of fiction, dream." (p.83)

He also justifies his decision not to inform the police of her fatal mishap with the way that any jury from the deeply conservative Scotland of the time, as Trocchi perceived it to be, would believe his story. At the same time, the reader is also in a quandary, because he, or perhaps especially she, cannot be sure that Joe is being entirely candid, since we are also eventually informed that she was pregnant. As Joe puts it near the end of the novel: "I remembered Cathie talking very quietly, persuasively, after we had made love, telling me she was pregnant, that I was the father, and asking me to marry her." (p.102) Her death, therefore, seems to be very convenient for him.

Joe even goes so far as to declare that "(m)y responsibility in the matter was a convenient social fiction, one which had shamed how many men into assisting at their own murder." (p.87) His vision of justice and police procedure, at a time when the ultimate penalty was capital punishment, seems to be paranoid, but it is based very much on a sociological, not merely an 'existential' one, of the justice system at the time. Significantly, Trocchi through Joe deploys the metaphor of the impersonally bureaucratic machine:

> The anonymity of the men who at that very moment might be working against me not because they had a personal grudge against me but because they were part of an impersonal machine whose function it was to maintain order, to explain the presence of an ambiguous thing like a corpse, to see that, if foul play was deduced, someone atoned for it that the moral structure of the system might be preserved – that was horrifying. (p.87)

His scepticism about the justice system includes not merely individualised, but cultural mistrust of the jury: " … and if I were very lucky, I might get off with manslaughter, though the temper of the good people, the Presbyterian city of Glasgow, their moral appetites already whetted, made me have a second thought about that." (p. 90)

This is not so much a Kafkaesque vision of the Scottish justice system – Trocchi does not suggest that the Scottish system of justice is arbitrary, rather that it is repressive and loaded against 'disreputable' behavior – but it startlingly foreshadows the sixties youth revolts in the West. An extract from a famous speech in Dec. 1964 by Mario Savio at Berkeley University makes this evident:

There is a time when the operation of the machine becomes so odious, makes you so sick at heart, that you can't take part; you can't even passively take part, and you've got to put your bodies upon the gears and upon the wheels, upon the levers, upon all the apparatus, and you've got to make it stop. And you've got to indicate to the people who run it, to the people who own it, that unless you're free, the machine will be prevented from working at all![19]

Of course, Joe is no political activist, and only formerly a student, yet his analysis is that of a Trocchi who would indeed become a cultural, if not quite a political activist. His culturally revolutionary clarion call was that

... by a kind of mental ju-jitsu that is ours by virtue of intelligence, of modifying, correcting, polluting, deflecting, corrupting, eroding, outflanking ... inspiring what we might call *the invisible insurrection.* It will come on the mass of men, if it comes at all, not as something they have voted for, struck for, fought for, but like the changing seasons; they will find themselves in and stimulated by the *situation* consciously at last to recreate it within and without as their own (italics in original).[20]

Gavin Bowd and Martin Gardiner have written extensively on Trocchi and the Paris Situationists.[21] Here, suffice it to say that Joe's existential pessimism was later converted to a more radical, and radically optimistic, vision of cultural change. It is almost as if Trocchi reversed Marx's view of class struggle leading to political change, indeed revolution, to a non-Leninist elite, one partial to the insights supposedly derived from drug-taking, shaking things up culturally so much that a profoundly cultural revolution will be the result. Joe in *Young Adam*, however, only ends up in various cul-de-sacs, and the canal, which provides for his livelihood for a while, is both the product of industrial history, and yet at the same time offers opportunities that he grasps for sexual and escapist freedom. For Joe, indeed, the canal is a kind of sanctuary.

Joe himself arrives at a moment of clarity and self-recognition, almost if not quite like the 'anagnorisis' of the tragic hero in ancient Greek drama, when he becomes aware of the social origins of his existential malaise, and

[19] Mario Savio's speech is readily accessible online; e.g. <www.fsm-a.org/stacks/mario/mario_speech.html>.

[20] *A Trocchi Reader*, p.179.

[21] See Bowd's *Alexander Trocchi and Kenneth White*, pp.3-14, and Michael Gardiner, *From Trocchi to Trainspotting: Scottish Critical Theory Since 1960*, Edinburgh: Edinburgh University Press, 2006, ch.4, pp.73-107.

also why he cannot be convinced of the existence of the individual 'I' that he was so sceptical about at the beginning of the novel. Here is how he puts it:

> My sudden need of Ella the day after Cathie died and after many months of living close to her in a state of detached unaffection, and the fact that the power of seduction came with the need, that I discovered in every successive response a sense of control in myself and of her permissiveness – this complex knowledge gave me a sense of vast gravitational forces which went beyond any 'I' I was conscious of, of a complexly woven matrix within which my own conscious decisions were mere threads. (p.90)

He is talking here about social and cultural determinants, and this is one way that he is very different from Meursault in *The Outsider*. Conor Cruise O'Brien has argued persuasively that while Meursault in Camus' novel is admirable in many ways, particularly the way he is so true to his own feelings, and refuses to lie about them, there is something unconvincing in the way the French Algerian court convicts him of gratuitously murdering an Arab. Here is what O'Brien says about such an 'unreal' situation:

> And just as Meursault is scrupulous in regard to his own feelings and indifferent to the society around him, so Camus is rigorous in his treatment of the psychology of Meursault ... and lax in his presentation of the society which condemns Meursault to death. In practice, French justice in Algeria would almost certainly not have condemned a European to death for shooting an Arab who had drawn a knife on him and who had shortly before stabbed another European. And most certainly Meursault's defence counsel would have made his central plea that of self-defence, turning on the frightening picture of the Arab with a knife.[22]

Young Adam, on the other hand, portrays how his protagonist relates to Scottish society in the fifties very scrupulously, even if Trocchi's perspective is a jaundiced one, and the miscarriage of justice at the end of the novel is all too believable. On the other hand, the fact that Joe has a 'lucky escape' from the draconian justice system of the time, and an innocent man 'takes the rap' for him, to put it in pulp fiction terms, perhaps indicates something of a failure of nerve on Trocchi's part. Just like Meursault, he needed a good lawyer if he wanted to clear himself, rather than let an innocent man be convicted, but such a reaction misses the point of Trocchi's hostility to 'the system' in Scotland at the time.

Some critics, Michael Gardiner and Gavin Bowd among the most prominent, seem to value Trocchi rather more as a kind of prophet, or counter-cultural

---

[22] Conor Cruise O'Brien, *Camus*, Glasgow: Fontana, 1970, p.22.

critic, than as *primarily* a novelist; hence for them his real masterpiece is *Cain's Book.* Gardiner even dismisses the earlier novel as "the single most tedious text written by Trocchi."[23] But he does not explain why he holds this opinion, so – equally subjectively on my part – it could be said that his own book on 'Scottish critical theory' strikes me as rather turgid. Bowd's view is more nuanced, and he does warn against pigeonholing Trocchi "as a precursor of the junkie literature of Irvine Welsh et al."[24] Edwin Morgan observed that *Young Adam* is a "thinner and less impressive book than *Cain's Book*," but also pointed out that the former has a story "that does stick in the mind."[25] Irvine Welsh, on the other hand, dismisses the latter as follows: "I thought it was just a sub-Burroughs junkie type thing; it didn't appeal much," and excoriates Trocchi in this as "just an existential, middle class figure mythologising drugs and the junkie experience." Yet Welsh can also be accused of 'mythologising' drugs for his own generation. But his case for preferring *Young Adam* has polemical bite:

> I read and enjoyed *Young Adam.* There was a real cynicism in the outsiderness of his voice, which was attractive. It was a breath of fresh air after all those horrible, sickly celebrations of Scottishness which some Scottish writers feel obliged to do. They feel that because of Scotland's relationship with England they've always got to be nice and watch what the neighbours might say; but the neighbours don't care. He seemed to have a vision which wasn't constrained by other people's narrow definitions of Scottishness. He was off in his own world.[26]

This begs the question of whether Welsh has 'kailyard' writers in mind, or more recent ones, but he does remind us in his own partisan way that *Young Adam* is just as much an incisive portrait of Scotland in the fifties, as it is about the existential angst of its protagonist.

Harking back to the clash at the 1962 Writers' Conference, James Kelman recently observed:

> The 1962 thing was important in Scotland, without overrating the thing which happened with MacDiarmid and Trocchi, but it has its place in the contemporary context, not a thing we

---

[23] *From Trocchi to Trainspotting*, p.89.

[24] *Alexander Trocchi and Kenneth White*, p.39.

[25] Edwin Morgan, 'Alexander Trocchi: A Survey', *Edinburgh Review*, no. 70 (1985), p.57.

[26] Irvine Welsh, 'A Scottish George Best of Literature', in Allan Campbell and Tim Niel, eds., *A Life in Pieces: Reflections on Alexander Trocchi*, Edinburgh: Rebel Inc., 1997, p.17.

should all think was great, because it certainly wasn't and we shouldn't glamorise it. I don't think either MacDiarmid or Trocchi came out of it particularly well, to be honest, but there was more to it than that. There is definitely room for a healthy debate about these issues, what it is to be a writer in Scotland, to create within an inferiorised culture, the dangers of nationalism.[27]

However, it is Edwin Morgan who best articulated what could be called Trocchi's Scottish internationalism:

> ... it should be remembered that in his famous public clash with Hugh MacDiarmid during the Writers' Conference at the Edinburgh Festival of 1962 – an international event if ever there was one – Trocchi's claim was not a stateless or cosmopolitan claim: he was there on the panel of Scottish writers, and he claimed (if we strip off the colours of rhetoric) to have contributed more to Scottish literature during recent years than Hugh MacDiarmid had done. The argument was not so much a simple nationalism v. internationalism debate as it seemed at the time; it was an argument about how, in the early 1960s, a Scottish writer should go about his business, and whether a change of direction was due, whether it was time to take a closer look at what was happening elsewhere, whether openness of spirit rather than hugging of certainties would be good for Scotland.[28]

If Morgan was right in his assessment, then Alexander Trocchi in *Young Adam* steers us on a voyage in which uncertainties are embraced, and the canal leads to the open sea.

---

[27] James Kelman Interview, *Scottish Review of Books*, vol.8, no.3, 2012.

[28] 'Alexander Trocchi: A Survey', 56.

The Way of the Hand-Loom Weaver

Allan Massie

In his novel, *All That Is*, James Salter has his main character reflect that "The power of the novel in the nation's culture had weakened. It had happened gradually. It was something that everybody recognized and ignored."[1] He was writing about the USA, but the same thing might be said about the status of the novel this side of the Atlantic and throughout Europe. Of course we still write novels and many read them. If you measured the health of the literary novel – horrid but inescapable phrase – by the number published, you might persuade yourself it was in good health. You might still do so if you dwelled on the quality of the best fiction now being written. There is no need to list the names of fine living novelists. We could all do so, and some of our lists would be long.

Nor is it a valid criticism of the modern literary novel to remark that popular fiction – crime, romance, and blockbusters – sells very much better. This has almost always been the case, and most popular fiction does not last. Who now reads Edgar Wallace, for example? Bestsellers are often short sellers, while a novelist like Conrad, whose sales were wretched for much of his life, may fairly be called a long seller.

It is more a matter of how much attention is given to even the best novelists. How many may be called public figures, as Scott and Dickens were in the nineteenth century? Both, in their own lifetime, were among the most famous men in the country. They were seen as speaking for it. Tolstoy held the same position in Russia, likewise Balzac and Hugo in France. It was not even necessary to sell lots of books to have such a position. André Gide was never a popular author, but his moral influence on France in the first half of the twentieth century was great. I suppose Günter Grass has had a comparable status in Germany. But who else, and where?

No doubt there are many reasons for this. In one way it is surprising as well as depressing, for there are far fewer illiterates than there were, even in advanced countries, in the nineteenth century. In Europe, almost everybody now receives secondary education, and anything between a third and a half of young people go on to college or university. In absolute figures, the market for literature is bigger than it has ever been. And yet few novelists can make a living from their novels alone. The question must be: do we still need them?

In his last collection of essays, *Fractured Times*, Eric Hobsbawm writes:

> The word has for some time been in retreat from the image, and the written and printed word from that spoken on the

---

[1] James Salter, *All That Is*, London: Picador, 2013, p.26.

screen. Comic strips and picture books with minimal text are
by no means aimed at beginners still learning to spell. What
carries much more weight, however, is the retreat of the
printed in face of the spoken and illustrated news.[2]

The consequences for the novel are evident. It is not only that it has more
competitors. It is also that these competitors are less demanding. It is easier
to watch a movie than to read a book – and as for television... Films are
intended to be watched by a lot of people at the same time, and this is true,
even though modern methods of reproduction can enable you to watch a
movie in solitude. Consequently, films are aimed at the audience's common
denominator; this is part of their charm. Compare anyone's list of the Ten
Greatest Films with a list of the Ten Greatest Novels, and you cannot fail to
be struck by the intellectual disparity. A film such as *Casablanca* will appear
on many such lists – and why not? It is delightful, it is thoroughly enjoyable,
it has memorable scenes, smart dialogue, even wit. Yet we all know that it is
really an absurd caper, which bears no relation to the real life circumstances
of the time and place it pretends to deal with. There are comparable novels
of course – *The Prisoner of Zenda* perhaps – but they are not listed among
the great ones.

The novelist, however ambitious, must now concede that his has become
a minority art. Its appeal is narrow. How often has he heard people say, "I
get no time for reading now"? He does not contradict – what is the point?
– even though he knows that the speaker will spend hours surfing the web,
on the computer, on iPhone or iPad, or engaging in the social media. If he is
sensible, he will say nothing and get on with his own work.

Yet the message is clear. What he writes matters only to a few. The few
may be numbered in thousands, or even, if he is lucky, in tens of thousands,
but in comparison with the audience that a reality TV show may attract, the
number is negligible. Strangely, however, as the literary novelist reflects
that his sales are lower than those of an author of similar standing might
have been fifty or sixty years ago, he finds that, unlike his predecessors, he is
expected to make public appearances at book festivals, of which there seem
to be more every year. His publisher, who used to take full responsibility for
selling his authors' work, now expects the novelist to engage in promotion
and be in effect his own barker. So while the novelist may have a lower public
profile than of old, he is better known to the fairly small number of people
who attend his events – but nevertheless do not necessarily buy his books.
Some of them are there only to be entertained. But he will be glad of their
presence.

The novel is not alone in being demoted in the market-place today. Poetry
has already suffered the same fate and become a minority art form. Like the

---

[2] Eric Hobsbawn, *Fractured Times: Culture and Society in the Twentieth Century*,
London: Little, Brown, 2013, p.10.

novelist, the poet will be expected to put himself on show at festivals and for poetry readings. Sometimes it seems probable that more people write poetry than read it, more certainly than buy books of verse. Be that as it may, poetry, which was the principal literary art form in Europe from the time of Homer, is, in market terms, utterly unimportant. And the value of modern culture is determined in the market place, like it or not.

Other art forms cling on. Classical music may not be on a life support machine, but very few new works are added to its repertory. The world is awash with music; it is hard to escape from it. Yet much of the music we listen to is manufactured by electronic means; the mixer is as important as the original maker. As for classical music itself, Hobsbawm remarks that "the potential concert audience, even in a city of more than a million inhabitants consists of about twenty thousand elderly ladies and gentlemen" and "is hardly replenishing itself."[3] The classical repertory, like that of the theatre, is one of the common strands of European culture, but it would appear to be withering.

Painting is in like condition. Art schools turn out thousands of graduates. Many paint well, in traditional style; they draw (though some art colleges no longer teach drawing); they paint portraits, landscapes, still-lifes. Few attempt religious, mythological or historical subjects, all of which have been staples of western art for two millennia. The most fashionable art in the twentieth century has been abstract, then 'Pop', then conceptual. The last of these is often not regarded as art by traditionalists. Tracey Emin's tent and Damien Hirst's cow in formaldehyde may be Art – this is obviously a matter of opinion – but they would not have been recognised as such a hundred years ago. One may hold that such art represents a retreat. No longer seeking to attain the sublime or create the beautiful, these artists see their task as to provoke and disturb.

One may sympathise – and not only because it is natural that artists should respond to the demands of the marketplace. There is a deeper reason: the fear that the individual artist is in danger of becoming as redundant as the factory worker who has been displaced by a robot. Trains run without drivers; cars are beginning to do so too. So the obvious question is: do we need artists to create works of art? The answer may soon be that we do not. There is no technical reason, I believe, why dead film stars should not star in new films. Computer technology can effect their resurrection. The old line about monkeys with typewriters coming up with a bit of Shakespeare no longer seems absurd. After all, anyone versed in their work can produce a passage of Miltonic or Wordsworthian Blank Verse; the computer might do this more effectively.

I have the horrid fear that, astutely programmed, a computer might write a characteristic Allan Massie novel. Typical characters, themes, settings, turns of phrase, might be assembled, the programme set to run, a button

---

[3] Hobsbawm, p.14.

pressed, and there you would have a novel that might satisfy such readers as I have. I might even wonder if I had written it myself, and forgotten it.

Reaching this conclusion – whether cheerful or gloomy – it seems that the fears and regrets expressed in my opening paragraphs are pointless. The world moves on. The individual artist will go the way of the hand-loom weaver, surviving only as a worker in an economically insignificant cottage industry. He is faced with the prospect of redundancy. "Vivre? Les serviteurs feront cela pour nous!"[4] Write? The computers will do that for us. Already they do most of the research, for historians and others. The next step will be for them to write the history.

Fortunately, we are not there yet – not quite – and so, Chris, you are still, thank heaven (which may not exist), at work.

---

[4] Auguste Villiers l'Isle-Adam, *Axël* (1890) ["Living? Our servants will do that for us."].

Memories of Amikejo
Europe's Pasts and its Possible Future

Neal Ascherson[1]

The death of the contemporary forms of social order ought to gladden rather than trouble the soul. Yet what is frightening is that the departing world leaves behind it not an heir but a pregnant widow. Between the death of one and the birth of the other, much water will flow by; a long night of chaos and desolation will pass.

Those resonant, vatic words come from Alexander Herzen, the Russian democratic exile, and he wrote them shortly after the failure of the 1848 Revolutions in Europe. The old empires had reasserted control. But Herzen knew that 1848 spelled their ultimate doom, even though it was not to come for another seventy years and more. What that doom would be, and what kind of new order would replace the empires, he could only guess and fear.

Like many things Herzen said and wrote in his exile, that prophecy about the pregnant widow seems on the face of it to say more about Russia than about Western and Central Europe. He once contrasted the traditions of the Russian and Polish revolutionary émigrés around him in London. The Poles, he said, looked back for inspiration to countless holy relics. But the Russians had only 'empty cradles'. Even after the rise and fall of the Bolshevik revolution, whose consequences dominated the short 20th century, even after an enigmatic decade with Vladimir Putin, we still do not know what sort of infant the Russian pregnant widow will finally set in her cradle.

But when I reread Herzen's words, I can't help also setting them against the big 'matryoshka' Europe which reaches from the Atlantic to beyond the Dniepr, containing a smaller EU which in turn contains an even smaller Eurozone – which may get smaller still. Two forms of social order died in our big Europe during the years after about 1980: the Communist system embedded in the fifty-year continental order of the Cold War, but also the regulated, social democratic welfare order developed in the nations of Western Europe after 1945. One of these deaths should gladden the soul. But the second should trouble it.

'A long night of chaos and desolation' to follow? You could hardly describe the last quarter-century in Europe as desolation, except for the losers from neoliberal capitalism. But chaos: that we have in abundance, European and

[1] This piece was first published in *The London Review of Books*, vol.34, no.6, 22 March 2012. It is here reproduced with the kind permission of the author.

global, from the financial crash to the continuing political upheavals set off by the melting of Cold War discipline. And, twenty years on, as the enthusiasm for free-market deregulated economies begins to wither, we have that Herzen feeling of living in a dimly lit corridor, a transition between orders. The widow's first painful contractions may not mean that a birth is anything like imminent. But those pains are already felt in Europe and Eurasia.

There is a story, maybe a fable, about a Displaced Persons camp somewhere in Germany at the end of the war. Red Cross and UNRRA ladies are interviewing survivors from the concentration camps. "Well, Mr Lemberger, and where would you like to go now?" "New Zealand." "New Zealand? But that's awfully far away!" "Far away from what?" To me as a wartime child, Europe meant nothing good. It was where the Heinkels and Dorniers came from. It was a hostile place beyond the sea which required Operation Overlord to open it. There was shocking suffering and cruelty there, and also brave Resistance movements, but the word 'Europe' stayed ominous for me and for many other Brits for years after the war. In the 1950s, I went to hear Oswald Mosley (that rhetoric – cheap but giddying, like a fairground chairoplane) preaching the need for a United Europe to save civilisation from Bolshevism. Later, vaguely Bevanite, I and most of my friends thought plans for European unity were a plot by Catholic conservatives (most of them, we assumed, wartime collaborators) to revive a German army and pelt the Soviet Union with atom bombs.

But later still, I went to live in West Germany and learned not to sneer when young Germans said earnestly that they felt European, not German. Europe to them meant neutrality, reconciliation, open frontiers. A few years before, some of them had gone to the bridge over the Rhine at Kehl/Strasbourg and set about demolishing the frontier gates in the name of the new Europe; they were immensely surprised when the French guards, instead of embracing them as brothers, walloped them over the head and threw them into police vans. At that time, remembering pictures of jolly Wehrmacht soldiers wrenching down the red and white Polish border gates, I felt quite protective about frontiers. But then I read a Polish novel. An allegory contrived to lull the censor, it described a tiny sliver of land between Belgium and Germany which had been overlooked by the surveyors as they drew new European frontiers after the fall of Napoleon. In this splinter lived a handful of free people, untroubled by military service, identity papers, taxes or censors. Happy, stateless Europeans.

For forty years, I thought this was a sentimental fiction. Then I discovered that it wasn't, and last month I went to see the sliver. Now securely part of Belgium, it has had a lot of names. The one I most fancy is 'the Akwizgran Discrepancy'. More often, it was called 'le Moresnet neutre' or Kelmis or La Calamine. The name it wanted to have was 'Amikejo'.

The Polish novelist wanted the place to be a pure discrepancy – one of those map-drawing mistakes which leaves a little white triangle where lines should meet. In reality, the Prussian and Dutch diplomats chopping up Napoleon's empire at the Congress of Vienna couldn't agree who should have a nearby zinc mine, and declared its fragment of countryside to be 'neutral'. In 1830, the Kingdom of Belgium was created. The four territories – Prussia/Germany, the Netherlands, Belgium and le Moresnet neutre – all met on a forested hilltop, where their frontier pillars still stand.

Not much bigger than Hyde Park and Kensington Gardens combined, the triangular Discrepancy is covered by pretty green woods in summer, with the small, drab town of Kelmis/La Calamine in one corner. For a century, the inhabitants lived mostly by smuggling booze into the Netherlands, especially after the zinc mine gave out; the little strip contained seventy bars and cafés. In time, as refugees and fugitives from other European countries arrived, the population grew ten times larger. Dr Wilhelm Molly, a whiskered physician, issued a set of postage stamps in 1886, an initiative squashed by the Prussians and the Dutch, who ruled that the Code Napoléon, under which postal services were an imperial monopoly, was somehow still in force in the enclave seventy years after the empire's collapse.

In 1908 Dr Molly and friends declared le Moresnet an Esperantist state, to be named Amikejo ('Friendship'), and the inhabitants set to learning the language with enthusiasm. Soon there was a flag and an anthem. But by now imperial Germany was raising claims to the territory, making its point by recurrent severing of electricity and telephone lines. In 1914 German troops invaded le Moresnet neutre on their way into Belgium, allegedly shot some Esperantists, and annexed Amikejo to the German Empire. After the war, the Versailles Treaty awarded the place and the districts around it to Belgium, ending a century of furtive independence.

Today, hardly anyone there remembers that lost freedom: no souvenir Amikejo flags, no reproduction postage stamps, nothing. The inn where the inhabitants took their solemn decision for Esperanto became the Skyline Disco, which is now a rain-filled hole in the ground. Only the stone border markers in the woods survive, topped with snow and laced with dead brambles. There's a reason for the amnesia. This corner of Belgium is a patchwork of linguistic communes, Francophone or Germanophone, where the traffic signs can change language every kilometre. Kelmis, or La Calamine, is bilingual, though most people speak German. But in contrast to the bitter feuds between French and Dutch-speaking areas of Belgium, there's no strife here. In the *friterie* on the Liège road, they say: "Nobody cares what you speak in this place." They want it to stay that way, and history might not help.

Yet there's European significance in this story. It proved that a tiny Europe could exist *sans frontières*, or at least without enforcing them. It says that there was a time when nation-states did not abhor a vacuum or panic about sovereign discrepancies. In the 20th century, the Discrepancy whispered that Europeans living in tyrannies could dream of slipping away to a no-man's-land between the armed camps where they could live miniature but authentic lives. And le Moresnet/Amikejo was also a wormhole through time into our Europe of the Single Act and the Maastricht Treaty. No customs barriers, no closed frontiers, military conscription almost a memory, no national currency, no danger of arrest for playing bizarre identity politics.

But in the mid-20th century the last airholes in the European pressure-vessel were sealed up, and the heat turned up high. Fortunately the vessel burst before it could reduce everything, all our cities, all our persecuted peoples, to ash. And yet even now, in diligently humane times, Europe is a place in which pressures, some creative and some destructive, repeatedly build up.

Visualise Eurasia, that enormous, shaggy outline beginning in the space between China and the Volga but narrowing towards an untidy mass of tentacles protruding into the ocean. Think of a fish-trap, a conical wicker one as plaited by a woman from the Mesolithic Danube or Victorian Orkney. She secures it across the path of the shoals and soon it's filled with flashing, struggling creatures, the fish nearest to the apex thrashing most frantically as the force of those behind thrusts them against the barrier.

We don't know at what moment in the Holocene the first big westward migrations began, out of Asia and then across the Volga and Pontic steppes into the European peninsula. It was probably sometime in the second millennium BC, only much later appearing in the literary record when pastoral nomads of Indo-Iranian and then Turkic or Mongol cultures entered the Black Sea region and then the eastern fringes of the Roman and Byzantine Empires. There followed more than a thousand years in which invading groups or displaced populations from settled cultures pressed ever more tightly into the narrowing fish-trap whose apex was the sea, driven on and compressed by the sometimes ferocious and always land-hungry peoples following on their heels.

Would it be fanciful to suggest that the desperate pressure of human societies crammed and squeezed into the trap's narrowing Western European tip has something to do with the peculiar intensity of European behaviour, its obsession with change and its capacity to release psychopathic blasts of destructive energy? Well, yes, it would be fanciful: I have offered a 19th-century metaphor incapable of proof or disproof and therefore without scientific interest. Nonetheless, the migrational background of Europe since the Iron Age has left many traces. In the west, the sheer pressure of growing populations combined with a shortage of resources, land above all, has encouraged communities to fuse and cohabit. The old 'culture-historical' approach to archaeology was obsessed with identifying supposedly distinct ethnic groups by their material culture. Now it's clear that they weren't necessarily distinct at all. I well remember the annoyance of German scholars when a dig near Berlin revealed Slav and Germanic settlers living together using the same gear in the same squalor.

So in the west the pressure of the demographic fish-trap – backs to the sea, nowhere to go – forced incoming groups towards accommodation, hybridity and fusion. Further east, where the land broadened and the pressure was lower, it was different. To this day, you can find settlement patterns which are pointillist rather than solid colour, where the ethnic settlements remain distinct. You can see it in parts of south Russia: a Cossack village here, an Armenian village there, then a small town that was a Jewish shtetl before the Holocaust, then a village planted by Catherine II where the farmers still speak an archaic Swabian, or a settlement of Pontic Greeks returned from forced exile in Kazakhstan. They trade with each other – Armenian vegetables, Cossack vodka – but guard their prejudices. This sort of landscape is hard to understand in terms of the Western nation-state, with its idea of 'imagined community' and its anxiety about homogeneity and cohesion. But pointillism is European too.

Europe is something that should not exist: a quadrilateral with three sides – Mediterranean, Atlantic, Baltic. Europe from the Atlantic to where? Old Konrad Adenauer, as West German chancellor, used occasionally and reluctantly to travel to West Berlin by night train. As the wagons rumbled over the Elbe bridges, he is supposed to have turned over in his bunk and muttered: 'Ach, wieder Asien!' De Gaulle, on the other hand, announced that Asia began at the Urals.

It was in the late 18th and early 20th century that this game of denying European identity to neighbours began, as an aspect of modern nationalism. It was to end in the almost comic phenomenon of 'bulwarkism'. It started at the ocean with the French, who imagined themselves as the defenders of Christian civilisation against the barbarous denizens of the forests across the Rhine. But then it turns out that the Germans also saw themselves as the front-line defenders of Europe against primitive uncultured Slavs, in particular the untidy, untrustworthy Poles. Poland in turn erected a perfect cult of its national mission as the outermost bastion – *przedmurze* – of Catholic Christianity and civilised values against the brutal Asian hordes of schismatic tsars or Bolshevik atheists. And why stop there? One of the most powerful nerves in Russian nationalism has been the notion of standing as a bulwark protecting Europe against the Asian onrush – Mongol or Chinese.

The strangers come from the East; they want what we have; they are Other. In the early period of westward migration, Otherness often resided in the encounter between settled farmers and nomadic pastoralists, those who had no centre, who were *aporoi* and constantly in motion across the grassy plains with their herds and wagons. For a long time, it was supposed that mobile pastoralism was an early human phase and that more advanced lands would evolve into settled agriculture. Now it's clear that the reverse is true: the sort of pastoralism practised on the steppes by great moving nations like the Scythians or the Golden Horde was a specialised way of life which had long ago emerged from even earlier Neolithic farming societies.

The antipathy of settled communities to travelling communities or individuals is still hard-wired into Europe. Anthony Pagden, discussing Diderot's opinion on this, remarked that his disapproval of travel 'belongs to an ancient European tradition, one which locates the source of all civility – which is after all a life lived in cities (*civitates*) – in settled communities, and which looks on all modes of nomadism as irredeemably savage'. The first encounter between Greek urban colonists and Scythian nomads took place on the north shore of the Black Sea from the seventh or sixth century BC. At first, as Herodotus suggests, the Greeks registered this difference as amazing and unfamiliar, but did not express it in terms of human 'value'. It was the Athenian playwrights during the Persian Wars who demonised non-Greek peoples, attributing to them vices – cowardice, uncontrollable passion, excessive luxury, deceit – that were the inverse of supposed Greek virtues: courage, moderation, austerity, candour. From that opposition emerged the long discourse of civilisation and barbarism, which has never quite been detached – not in northern Europe, anyway – from the discourse about 'respectable' farmers and 'rootless' clans of wanderers.

When I mentioned psychopathic blasts of destructive energy I didn't mean large-scale outbursts like the wars the Europeans inflicted on themselves in the 20th century. More interesting is the capacity in Western Europe for what could be called *furia* – the entry by one individual or a small group into a passion of reckless, murderous violence exerted with what seems to be superhuman strength. At least one of the Cuchulain legends from Gaelic Ulster describes the hero growing to twice his own height as his chariot hurls into battle, his head spinning round on his shoulders with his eyes shooting flame. The word 'berserker', as it came to be used, conveys the same image.

Furia, the sudden and shattering use of extreme aggression and cruelty, served Europe well in early ventures into the outside world. The Crusades can be seen as the last of the 'barbarian invasions', this time heading south-eastwards into the Balkans and the Levant. But long before 'Europe' replaced 'Christendom' as a recognised political term, the Crusaders were often able to overawe superior enemies by showing a blind, even crazed ferocity which had little to do with the Lamb of God. A most striking example of *furia* is the behaviour of Vasco da Gama and his company of Portuguese warriors when they reached the Indian subcontinent at Calikut in 1498 and again in 1502. At first made welcome by the ruler, whose armies far outnumbered them, the Portuguese fell out with him and the local Muslims. To make their point, they set fire to a pilgrim ship, locking nearly four hundred passengers in the hold to burn and then drown. After that, da Gama and his gang hanged and dismembered 38 local fishermen under the ruler's eyes. Calikut had not seen or imagined anything like this, and the Portuguese got much of what they wanted.

Vasco da Gama also gave the kindly king his first experience of being bombarded by a new European device: the cannon. As time passed and

Europe's military technology outstripped that of its rivals, the need and
capacity for *furia* grew obsolete. It belonged to times when European
invaders and indigenous armies could seem almost evenly matched, bows
and spears against swords and unreliable matchlock firearms. But why be
a berserker when you could simply turn the crank of a Gatling gun? None
of this should imply that mass murder and atrocious cruelty were European
monopolies. A look into Aztec or Mayan history, or into John Roscoe's early
20th-century history of the Buganda kingdom, will correct any such error.
What seems to have been a specially European capacity, from the early
medieval period, was the resort to instant, frantic aggression as 'shock and
awe' to break an adversary's will to fight. Remember the Emperor Wilhelm
II's appeal to his German troops, during the 1900 Boxer Rising, to behave like
King Attila and his Huns in order to "open the way for civilization".[2]

So an intimidated world received what Europe chose to bestow. Scottish
steamships, German artillery, cotton goods from Lille or Manchester, French
electrical engineering, cognac, whisky and the White Fathers. We know
all that. But what strikes me, when it comes to the export of institutions
rather than hardware and colonists, is the slight but pervasive sense of the
inappropriate. To reach the Jhelum or the Zambesi and build a bridge over it
to carry the railway – that's a problem provided with a solution. But to found
a girl's public school in Uganda, to draw frontier fences across southern
African plains seasonally crossed by herds and herders, to standardise a
confederation of related Congolese peoples into a single 'tribe' with a 'chief'
and impose a single dialect as the only written language for its schools: here
we are looking at wandering solutions seeking a hospitable problem. One
could say the same about Communism, another European export which has
always proved hard to fit over local needs. Fascism, an equally European
solution, has occasionally been imitated in style on other continents, but
never really found an overseas market.

Long before Europe began to export solutions, there was an internal
market for schemes to make the continent a safer place. These schemes
implied an awareness that its inhabitants could imagine their empires and
kingdoms and city-states to be part of some larger unity. Sometimes that
unity was ghostly: the thought that the half-remembered Roman Empire had
merely gone into recess and could be reconvened. Sometimes it referred to
the international reality of the medieval church. The word 'Europe' was not
widely used as a political reference until the 16th or 17th centuries, when
Renaissance and Reformation humanists found it possible to define the
continent in new laic ways, independent of Church dogma. In the Strahov
monastery in Prague there is a 16th-century map which shows Europa as
a woman: Hispania is her brain and Bohemia her heart. She also tells us,
through this trope of nations as parts of one body, that the thought of

---

[2] <http://germanhistorydocs.ghi-dc.org/sub_document.cfm?document_id=755>.

European unity and the interdependence or complementarity of Europe's Christian nations had already taken hold.

So, can we identify a period when Europe was somehow most truly, authentically itself? Perhaps a devout Catholic historian might chance a date. But most of us would take the question in the ironic, slightly postmodern way Gwyn Alf Williams intended in calling his best book *When Was Wales?* If European enthusiasts see a Golden Age in the continent's past, a moment of definition from which all subsequent history has been a decline, what contemporary political needs edged them into such a delusion? And there have been a fair few delusions, many of them archaeological. Euro-exhibitions have suggested that the EU's ancestor is the Bronze Age, depicted as a time of a single market, no frontiers and busy trade routes carrying amber, gold, furs and ceramics between the Baltic and the Mediterranean. One exhibition, *I Celti* in Venice, used the la Tène design style from the European Iron age to evoke a continent politically, culturally and linguistically united by its Celtic population.

It is mostly nonsense, but the 'Celtic Europe' myth has taken some demolishing. And, like many sugary myths, it has put on some political weight. A few years ago, visiting the Svet Knihy book fair in Prague, I was astonished to encounter a widespread Celtomania. The stand for Scottish and Welsh writers was sought out by parties of young Czechs in kilts with Braveheart face-paint. Artists showed us paintings of the god Lugh, and invited us to celebrate Beltane at nearby cairns. They explained gravely that the Czechs had never really been Slavs; the language had been forced on them in the first millennium by marauding war-bands. Instead they were ethnic Celts. Roman writers had identified the Celtic tribes of central Europe, including the Boii (Bohemians). Now was the time to rediscover these Celtic roots. At the book fair, shelves were packed with the Dark Age bodice-rippers of Anna Bauerová, bestsellers about Celtic romance and heroism at the court of the kings of the Boii. Tickets for Bauerová's lectures were sold out.

Czech nationalists in the 19th century had been passionately Slavophile, rescuing and fostering their language to avoid the disaster of becoming Germanised. Russia had been the great cultural protector for generations; many Czechs believed that the Soviet Union would have rescued them from Hitler if Britain and France had stood firm at Munich. But all that ended in August 1968, with the Soviet-led invasion. After 1968, the Czechs – remembering that Bohemia had once been 'the heart of Europe' – looked west with a new passion. The Europe they now longed to join, rich and free, seemed to have nothing to do with the Slavdom which assigned its members to the shabby despotism of the East. The Celtic fantasy had always lurked in corners; after the 1989 Velvet Revolution, a section of Czech intellectuals used their freedom to promote it. To be European you had to be Celtic, not Slav. So an identity migration beckoned: the migration of a hermit crab scuttling across the sand from one shell to a new and more comfortable one.

How far the movement will go, I have no idea. Probably not very much further. But the idea that people can opt voluntarily to change ethnicity is very European, very cheering. At a low level, the inhabitants of borderlands have often had flexible identities, depending on which uniform is banging on the door. Villagers in the forest regions between Poland and Belarus, challenged to confess their nationality, used to say: 'We are *tutejszy* – from-here people." A better answer to that question is another question: "Who's asking?"

Europe's diversity is what strikes us most in our own times. But Perry Anderson, in his indispensable, shrewd book *The New Old World*, shows this was not always the case. Enlightenment critics, unlike us, were excited by resemblances and symmetries between European nations. They thought of Europe as one body, much like the green lady in the Strahov library. The limbs of the body were nicely proportioned, a coherence made possible by broadly similar religion, manners, customs and laws. Voltaire spoke of Europe as "a single republic divided into several states",[3] with a balance of power not to be found elsewhere in the world. Gibbon thought that the balance fluctuated a bit, but remained beneficial. From Edinburgh, William Robertson described the nations of Europe as a single community with a general resemblance and a "great superiority over the rest of mankind." Only Rousseau, nastily but perceptively, choked on this invention of the universal European. "Nowadays we have only Europeans," he wrote in 1770, all with the same tastes, the same passions, the same mores, all speaking of the public good and all thinking only of themselves; all affecting moderation and wanting to be Croesus ... what do they care which master they serve, the laws of which state they obey? Provided they find money to steal and women to corrupt, they are everywhere at home.

The French Revolution, or more correctly the Napoleonic Wars which followed it, changed the old Enlightened perspective sharply. No natural balance in this postwar Europe: after Bonaparte, schemes for unity were usually also alliances to contain any overmighty and expansionist state. But the 1815 settlement endured precisely because it was an alliance composed of Europe's overmighty and expansionist states, committed to dynastic absolutism and to the suppression of all kinds of revolution, social or national. Vienna allowed tiny le Moresnet to appear, but paved over most of the space where an independent Poland had once stood. Intellectuals and some politicians continued to sketch plans for European union, but now – in contrast to their 18th-century predecessors – they generally took the disparities of Europe, rather than its symmetries, to be its virtue. François Guizot, the most effective politician in 1830s France, thought in a quite dialectical way that the clash of these disparities was the source of Europe's collective energy. Jakob Burckhardt and Leopold von Ranke were among German-language historians who took a similar line: Burckhardt wrote of

---

[3] Quoted in Perry Anderson, *The New Old World*, London: Verso, 2009, p.476.

Europe's 'unprecedented *variety of life*' since the Renaissance; he was well aware of the continent's capacity for annihilating violence, but insisted that 'history should rejoice in this profusion' of conflicting ideas, individuals and nations.

These were all broadly conservative figures. The European left was also to enjoy dreams of a United States of Europe during the 19th century, but here the emphasis of republicans and early socialists was on unity – or federation – as a way of preventing war. The catastrophe of 1914-18 gave fresh force to this pacifist strand in the left's European thinking, an element so prominent and passionate that it obscured debates about what the economic and social policies of a united Europe should be, and distracted practical plans for bringing it about. There was no shortage of vast federalist visions 'between the wars', but it was the French government which took positive action at the League of Nations in 1929 to propose a European union.

Nothing came of it at the time. But it had at least three elements that were retrieved from the rubble after 1945. The first was that a European union's political strategy must be to construct an international framework – which would include Germany – to contain German strength. The second was that any union had to start with some deal over economic and industrial integration between France and Germany. The third, that 'the construction of Europe', institutional and economic, would have to be a top-down affair carried out by international technocrats under political protection. The notion that 'the people of Europe' should play an active part or be consulted was not entertained. After all, a European people did not exist. Maybe one day it would, making possible a true American-style federation based on democracy. But there was no point in waiting for that.

Anderson traces this 'technocratic line' back to the work of Saint-Simon in the early 19th century. As Anderson writes, "it was enough that Europe itself should be secured from war, and devoted to the growth of industry and the progress of science, for the well-being of all its classes." Whatever its ancestry, the assumption that European integration could only be imposed from above won out when projects for a united Europe emerged again after the Second World War. Rather than reciting the history of the EU, from Monnet to van Rompuy. I want to bring up three contentious, revisionist ideas about that history, only one of them mine.

The first is that historians of 20th century Europe have lost a whole distinct episode. You could call it the 'Resistance Spring'. It was an upsurge not just of defiance against fascist occupiers but of hope and idealism for the future. It mobilised men and women in nations all over the continent. It produced programmes for social justice and change, at first strikingly similar in different countries. Its texture, or context, was national-patriotic, and for that reason it quite clearly belongs in the sequence of national upheavals which began with 1848 and culminated – for the moment – in 1989. The Resistance Spring could be said to begin in about 1943 and to peter out – or be overlaid – in about 1948. By then, the Cold War was taking shape and forcing new allegiances. The Soviet Union directed Western Communists to end wartime solidarity and break with their comrades in social democratic, liberal or Christian Democratic movements. The Americans, concerned above all to keep Soviet influence out of West Germany, also wanted those links broken.

The consistent elements in Resistance postwar thinking were two. First, that the prewar order in these nations – forms of liberal capitalism – had failed to defend democracy or national independence. Their collapse was partly due to the corruption, verging on treason, of the prewar elites; indeed, some of their members had collaborated with the Nazi occupiers. So liberation must involve sweeping institutional and social change. Second, the Resistance programmes from Poland through Italy or Greece to France or the Netherlands framed those changes in statist, welfarist forms of democracy which were 'socialistic' but far from the Soviet model. There would be plural political democracy, with all the 'bourgeois liberties' guaranteed. There would be steeply progressive taxation, a planned economy, public health insurance and widespread nationalisations of industry, finance and transport. (At the founding congress of Angela Merkel's Christian Democratic Party in 1947, the Ahlen Programme declared that "the capitalist system has failed to meet the national and social needs of the German people," and called for part-nationalisation of heavy industry.)

On a postwar united Europe, the Resistance leaders and the London governments-in-exile were more ambiguous. After all, their followers were fighting and dying in order to destroy a United Europe, Hitler's new continental order. Pro-European passions were mostly heard from people who wanted to join the Waffen-SS Nordland Division or the Légion des Volontaire Française to defend 'Western European civilisation' against the Bolshevik hordes. The Resistance movements certainly hoped for a fraternal, anti-fascist continent, including Britain, in which rebuilt nations could live together in peace and prosperity. But their institutional visions for it were vague.

It would be nice to think that the boys and girls in the forest were dreaming of a European economic community as they waited for the next parachute-drop of weapons. But they were not. They were fighting to liberate their countries. Old-fashioned patriotism drove them, the longing to free and then cleanse and rebuild their violated nations. And that brings me to my second contentious, revisionist idea.

It comes from the late Alan Milward, iconoclast of recent European history. His book *The European Rescue of the Nation-State* (1992) knocked the wheels off conventional accounts of how the European Community arose, and it is still angrily argued over. Milward derides the received idea that the saintly founders of this Europe set out to overcome and transcend the nation-state. Just the opposite. The purpose and the effect of the early

EEC was to rescue, re-equip and restore legitimacy to the nation-states so damaged physically and morally by the last war. Supranational institutions were a means to those national ends – not an end in themselves. Milward writes:

> Far from renouncing the nation-state as the foundation of a better European order, they [the founding fathers] achieved prominence and success because they were among those who developed an accurate perception of the positive role it would play in the postwar order, and who also recognised or stumbled upon the need for those limited surrenders of national sovereignty through which the nation-state and Western Europe were jointly strengthened, not as separate and opposed entities, but within a process of mutual reinforcement.[4]

I am sure this is right. The priority for the post-liberation governments, as it had been for Resistance fighters, was the nation, the need to restore a discredited state with a better one which could regain legitimacy in the eyes of the public. And that went also for the People's Republic coalitions in Eastern and Central Europe, in the year or so before full Sovietisation was imposed by terror. But to fulfil even the basic requirement of legitimacy – getting food and clothing into the shops, repairing shattered transport networks – international pooling of production would be needed.

So it went on. Jean Monnet did not organise the European Coal and Steel Community because he had a dream of union. Whatever he and his admirers said later, he did it to keep the French steel industry going, and to give France some purchase on German production. And it worked. Economic and political integration over more than fifty years has restored a multiplying pack of mostly confident and stable nation-states nourished by a spindly Brussels bureaucracy.

So do the 27 states of the EU, most of them healthy until hit by the swine flu of sovereign debt, really need the institutions of union any more? Milward thinks that the EU's wide-screen historical boasts are largely bunk. Yes, in the 'trente glorieuses', the thirty years or so which ended in 1975, Western Europe enjoyed the longest period of peace and soaring real incomes in its history. But how much of that peace and prosperity do we owe to the old Community? "We made war between European nations unthinkable," they said, but wasn't it the Americans and Cold War discipline that ensured it? Prosperity? The dismantling of tariffs and the free movement of goods, money and people were certainly a precondition for the boom. But Brussels, if Milward's deconstructive *furia* is to be believed, directly contributed very

---

[4] Alan Milward, *The European Rescue of the Nation-State*, London: Routledge (second ed.), 1992, p.319.

little. The investments and the risks belonged to those restored nation-states.

Those thirty years were the epoch of the social-democratic consensus: strong interventionist states with large public sectors, committed to full employment and the redistribution of wealth. As the late Tony Judt insisted, we should not remember the 20th century only for its horrors. The stability and social justice achieved in postwar Western Europe was one of humanity's triumphs.

But there followed three very different decades of neoliberal dogma, now withering, which landed us in the mess we are in. Obviously enough, nation-states lost hard-won legitimacy as they privatised the public services which affected people's lives. Voters lost interest in the democratic process as the state withdrew from them. Only now are European governments trying to rebuild their authority. And, significantly, one of the ways they do this is by increasing, not reducing, the pace of supranational integration.

My own sense of the Europe we have is that it is like a sponge, a living sponge of squashy texture and uncertain outline, a rich and beautiful collective creature into whose open pores countless visiting organisms swim or stay to breed. It will never be a clanking metallic superstate, capable of instant peace and war decisions. It will always, in reality, be dependent on someone else to defend it. The legal philopher Samuel von Pufendorf described the Holy Roman Empire as "monstro simile – 'like unto a monster'. Seek not to understand, only to preserve!" Centuries later, Pufendorf's phrase was often used to describe the mad honeycomb of rules and exceptions which was the legal status of West Berlin. This gentle European monster of ours has some pre-modern precedents. One was the Polish-Lithuanian Commonwealth, the old Rzeczpospolita. Although it was eventually murdered by authoritarian neighbours at the end of the 18th century, the Commonwealth lived as an ill-defined, inefficient, hospitable, decentralised, rather tolerant federal and multicultural realm for nearly four hundred years – for much of the time, the largest state in Eastern Europe.

Its own democracy – or distaste for authority – helped to bring it down. The Polish Sejm worked by unanimity: the Liberum Veto of one member was enough to block any bill or indeed to cancel all the previous work of the session. As we know all too well, this is also how the main organs of the European Union work – monstro simile. The point was pounced on by Radek Sikorski, the Polish foreign minister, in the extraordinary speech he gave in Berlin last December. The Commonwealth, Sikorski warned, had left reform too late to stave off partition. In the Eurozone crisis, the European Union must act at once. As he said, he was the first ever Polish foreign minister to admit that he feared German power less than he feared German inactivity. The choice for the EU was now between deeper integration and collapse, and his choice – speaking for a country outside the Euro but committed to entering it – was full speed ahead for a federal, integrated union.

It is a cavalry charge of a speech. I do not agree with the bold Radek about everything – he is still a passionate neoliberal, for example – and I do not foresee a Brussels army which would frighten anybody more than its own accounts department. But I believe he is right about further integration. That's why the Euro crisis will get much worse but then find a solution: Europe without a common currency has become unthinkable. And a suggestive part of Sikorski's speech takes him close to Milward's sense that European Union and the nation-state are not antithetical but complementary. "The more power and legitimacy we give to federal institutions," he says, "the more secure member states should feel that certain prerogatives" – he means the whole field of identity, lifestyle and culture – "should forever remain in the purview of states."[5] Odd that a free-marketeer should say that, because it implies that closer integration will once again help elected governments depleted by twenty years of small-state claptrap to regain their self-confidence and find their way back to their own citizens.

What about Britain? Everyone in the EU – well, almost everybody – is mournful about British semi-detachment. But it seems to me now that the Union and the Eurozone would both be better off without Britain. The partner they need is another country: England. Scotland would easily find its own small-nation place in the EU and in a reformed currency. But England, stripped of its Great British pretensions, its archaic view of sovereignty and its Special Relationship delusions, might eventually find its way to a leading European destiny.

It's more than thirty years since that old Cold War, social democratic order began to die. But at last Herzen's pregnant widow is feeling some warning contractions. A new birth of so-called 'reformed capitalism'? An unexpected litter of small brothers and sisters as old states subdivide? Or a European order of rediscovered liberty, equality and fraternity in which, to take Tony Judt's words, 'we can remake the argument about the nature of the public pod'?[6] I'd wave an Amikejo flag for that.

---

[5] See < www.warsawvoice.pl/WVpage/pages/article.php/24386/article>.

[6] Tony Judt (with Timothy Snyder), *Thinking the Twentieth Century*, London: William Heinemann, 2012, p.388.

Two Poems

Keith Armstrong

Song for Northumberland

Drifting in moonlight,
the dunes sing their songs.
Wings of old battles
fly all night long.
Cry of the seagulls,
curse of the ghosts;
aches of dead warriors
scar this old coast.

Hover the kestrel,
sing out the lark,
we will be free in our time.
This air is our breath,
this sea is our thirst
and our dreams are sailing home.

Wandering through castles,
their walls are our lungs.
Searching for freedom
in country homes.
Forbears and old cares
blown in the wind;
pull of loved harbours
draws our boats in.

Surge of the salmon
and urge of the sea
leaps in our local blood.
Peal of the bluebells
and ring of bold tunes
reel in all those grey years.

Slopes of the Cheviots,
caress of the waves.

Shipwrecks and driftwood
float in our heads.
Pele-stones and carved bones
hide in these hills,
roots of new stories
in ancient tales.

Dew on our lips
and beer on the breath,
drinking the countryside in.
Bread of the landscape
and wine of this earth,
flows on these river beds.

Drifting in moonlight,
the dunes sing their songs.
Wings of old battles
fly all night long.
Cry of the seagulls,
curse of the ghosts;
aches of dead warriors
scar this old coast.

Hover the kestrel,
sing out the lark,
we will be free in our time.
This air is our breath,
this sea is our thirst
and our dreams are sailing home.

***

After the UK

Shreds of the UK
flapping in the downturn,
decayed Britain
broken into smithereens.
No Kingdom now,
no United State.
We are
citizens
with no obligation
to genuflect
in front of an overstuffed Queen.

Get the UK out of your system,
no going back.
We take the power
to rule ourselves,
make community,
build our own spaces.
Break
the hegemony
of dead parties,
lifeless institutions,
let debate flower,
conflicting views rage.

We want to breathe
and strip away
executive power,
share
the beauty and culture
of these islands around.
Make good things,
good love.
Empower ourselves
with an autonomous freedom
in a new England,
in a new Europe,
in a New World
of real ownership
and delicate emotion.

Appendix

Christopher Harvie:
A Select Bibliography

Books

1. Ed., with Graham Martin and Aaron Scharf, *Industrialisation and Culture, 1832-1914: A Source Book*, Milton Keynes and Basingstoke: Open University and Macmillan, 1970.
2. *The Lights of Liberalism: University Liberals and the Challenge of Democracy, 1860-86*, London: Allen Lane, 1976.
3. *Scotland and Nationalism: Scottish Society and Politics, 1707-1977/ 1707-1994*, London: George Allen and Unwin, 1977; new, extensively revised, edition, Routledge, 1994, fourth revised edition, London: Routledge, 2004. Contributing Editor, with Arthur Marwick, Charles Kightly and Keith Wrightson, *The Dictionary of British History*, London: Thames and Hudson, 1980.
4. *No Gods and Precious Few Heroes: Scotland 1914-1980* (Volume VIII of *The New History of Scotland*), London: Edward Arnold, 1981. Revised edition, *No Gods and Precious Few Heroes: Scotland Since 1914*, Edward Arnold, 1987; new edition, Edinburgh University Press, 1993, fourth, revised edition Edinburgh University Press, 2013.
5. With Arthur Marwick, *Britain Today: The Economy*, Hagen: Deutsches Institut für Fernstudien, 1985. Revised edition, with Eberhard Bort, 1993.
6. With Martin Holmes, *Britain Today: Politics and Society*, Hagen: Deutsches Institut für Fernstudien, 985. Revised edition, with Eberhard Bort, 1992.
7. Ed., with Iain S Wood and Ian Donnachie, *Forward! Scottish Labour from 1888 to the Present*, Edinburgh: Polygon, 1989. (Responsible for two sections, 'Before the Breakthrough, 1888-1922' and 'The Recovery of Scottish Labour, 1939-51').
8. *The Centre of Things: Political Fiction in Britain from Disraeli to the Present*, London: Unwin Hyman, 1991.
9. *Cultural Weapons: Scotland and Survival in a New Europe*, Edinburgh: Edinburgh University Press/Polygon, 1992.
10. *The Rise of Regional Europe*, London: Routledge, 1993.
11. *Fool's Gold: The Story of North Sea Oil*, London: Hamish Hamilton 1994, and (revised edition) Penguin Books, 1995 (further edition in preparation).
12. *Travelling Scot: Scotus Viator: Essays on the History, Politics and Future of the Scots*, Glendaruel: Argyll Publishing, 1999.
13. With Colin Matthew, *Nineteenth Century Britain: a Very Short Introduction*, Oxford: Oxford University Press, 2000.
14. With Peter Jones, *The Road to Home Rule: Images of Scottish Nationalism*, Edinburgh: Polygon, 2000.
15. *Deep-Fried Hillman Imp: Scotland's Transport*, Glendaruel: Argyll Publishing, 2001.
16. *Scotland: a Short History*, Oxford: Oxford University Press, 2002.
17. *Mending Scotland: Essays in Regional Economics*, Glendaruel: Argyll Publishing, 2004.

18. 'Engineer's Holiday: L.T.C. Rolt, Industrial Heritage and Tourism', in: Hartmut Berghoff, Barbara Korte, Ralf Schneider and Christopher Harvie, eds., *The Making of Modern Tourism*, Basingstoke: Palgrave, 2002.
19. *A Floating Commonwealth: Politics, Culture, and Technology on Britain's Atlantic Coast*, Oxford: Oxford University Press, 2008.
20. *Broonland: The Last Days of Gordon Brown*, London: Verso, 2010.
21. *Scotland the Brief: A Short History of a Nation*, Glendaruel: Argyll Publishing, 2010; second, revised ClanScotland edition (with QR code, online links to history, museums, transport, etc), Colintraive: Argyll 2012.
22. *1814 Year of Waverley: The Life and Times of Walter Scott*, (ClanScotland, format as above), Colintraive: Argyll, 2013.

Pamphlets etc.:

1. *Military Power and Technological Change*, Adelphi Paper, 1978, and reprinted by Macmillan.
2. With Gordon Brown, *A Vote's Guide to the Scottish Assembly*, Dunfermline: David Watt & Sons, 1979.
3. *Against Metropolis*, Fabian Tract No.464, 1982.
4. *Imagining an European Future*, Scottish Council: Development and Industry, October 1988.
5. *Europe and the Scottish Nation*, Centre for Scottish Economic and Social Research, 1989 (new editions, 1990, 1991).
6. *Language and the Decay of Politics*, (The Donaldson Lecture), Edinburgh; SNP, 1992.
7. 'The Folk and the Gwerin: Popular Political Culture in Scotland and Wales, 1815-1930', London: The British Academy, 1992.
8. *Europe and the Welsh Nation*, Aberystwyth: National Library of Wales, 1995.
9. *Boundaries and Identities: The Walls in the Head*, Edinburgh: International Social Sciences Institute, 1996.
10. Ed., with Eberhard Bort, *The Borders and the Waverley Route*: Transport Problems and Solutions for an Excluded Region, Edinburgh: International Social Sciences Institute, 1999.

Book Chapters and Articles

History

1. 'John Boyd Kinnear: Passages in the Life of a Scottish Radical, 1828-1920', in: *Scottish Labour History Journal*, 1970.
2. 'Ideology and Home Rule: Dicey, Bryce and Ireland, 1880-1887', in: *English Historical Review*, 1976.
3. 'Ireland and the Intellectuals, 1848-1922', in: Owen Dudley Edwards, ed., *The Committed Historian: a*
4. *Festschrift for Victor Kiernan*, Edinburgh: New Edinburgh Review, 1977.
5. 'Labour and Scottish Government, 1939-1945: the Age of Tom Johnston', in: *The Bulletin of Scottish Politics*, No.2, Spring 1981.
6. 'Scottish Labour and World War II', in: *The Historical Journal*, 1983.
7. 'Revolution and the Rule of Law, 1780-1850', in: Kenneth O Morgan, ed., *The Oxford Illustrated History of Britain*, Oxford: Oxford University Press, 1984.

8. 'Scotland in 1946', an introductory essay for *The People's Story*. London: BBC Network, 1987.

9. 'Legalism, Myth and National Identity in Scotland in the Imperial Epoch', in: *Cencrastus*, No. 26, 1987, pp. 35-41.

10. 'The Politics of German Railway Design', in *Design History*, 1989; a German translation published in *Design Report*, 1989.

11. 'Henry Fawcett as Politician', in: Laurence Goldman, ed., *Henry Fawcett: the Blind Victorian*, Cambridge: Cambridge University Press, 1989.

12. 'Gladstonianism, the Provinces, and Popular Political Culture', in: Richard Bellamy, ed., *Victorian Liberalism*, London: Methuen, 1990.

13. With Graham Walker, 'Popular Culture in late Nineteenth Century Scotland', in: Hamish Fraser, ed., *People and Society in Scotland*, Vol.II, Edinburgh: John Donald, 1990.

14. 'John Ruskin', in: Bernd-Otto Lange ed., *British Social Critics of the Nineteenth Century*, Frankfurt: Peter Lang, 1990.

15. 'The Scottish Countryside and the Scottish City', in: *History Teaching Review Yearbook*, 1991.

16. 'Modern Scotland: Remembering the People', in Rosalind Mitchison, ed., *Why Scottish History Matters*, Edinburgh: Saltire Society, 1991; revised version, 1996. Translation into Japanese, 1998.

17. 'Nineteenth Century Scotland: Political Unionism and Cultural Nationalism, 1843-1906', in: Ronald Asch, ed., *Three Nations - a Common History*, ADEF 1993, and in: Christian Civardi, ed., *Proceedings of the Annual Conference of English Scholars in French Higher Education*, Paris 1993.

18. 'Scottish Industrialisation, c.1750-1880', in: Rainer Schulze, ed., *Industrieregionen im Umbruch / Industrial Regions in Transformation*, Essen: Klartext Verlag, 1993.

19. 'Scotland: Enlightenment to Renaissance: Scottish Cultural Life in the Nineteenth Century', in: Claus Bjorn, Alexander Grant and Keith Stringer, eds., *Social and Political Identities in Western History*, Copenhagen: Academic Press, 1994.

20. '"These Islands" und ihre Nationen: Das Dilemma "britischer" Geschichte', in: *Blätter Deutscher Geschichte*, Bd. 130/1994.

21. 'Comparative Studies on Governments and Non-Dominant Ethnic Groups' (review article), in: *European History Quarterly*, Vol. 25, 1995.

22. 'Reform and Expansion, 1854-1871', in: Michael Brock, ed., *The History of Oxford University*: Vol. 6, Oxford: Oxford University Press, 1998.

23. 'Cleveland, Selborne and the Statutes of 1882', in: Michael Brock, ed., *The History of Oxford University*: Vol. 7, Oxford: Oxford University Press, 1999.

24. 'Federalism and Confederalism in Scottish Political Culture', in: Richard English and Charles Townshend, eds, *The State: Historical and Political Dimensions*, London: Routledge, 1998.

25. 'Industry, Identity and Chaos', in: *Scottish Affairs*, No. 32, Summer 2000.

26. 'The Moment of British Nationalism, 1939-1970', in: *The Political Quarterly*, Vol. 7, No. 3, July-September 2000.

27. 'The Folly of our Fable: Getting Scottish History Wrong', in: *Scottish Studies Review*, Vol. 1, Winter 2000.

28. 'Scotland since 1979', in: R A B Houston and William Knox, eds, *The Penguin History of Scotland*, Harmonsworth: Penguin, 2001.

29. 'Men who Pushed and Went: West Britain, War and Fiction', in: Barbara Korte and Ralf Schneider, eds, *War and the Cultural Construction of Identities in Britain*, Amsterdam: Rodopi, 2002.
30. 'Contrary Heroes: Modernisation, Religion and Ireland in 1848', in: Eberhard Bort, ed., *Commemorating Ireland: History, Politics, Culture*, Dublin: Irish Academic Press, 2004.
31. 'James Viscount Bryce, 1838-1922' (and other shorter entries on Joe Westwood, Arthur Woodburn and John Maclay, Viscount Muirsheil), in: *The New Dictionary of National Biography*, Oxford: Oxford University Press, 2005.
32. 'Robert Finlayson 'Robin' Cook, 1946-2005', in: *The New Dictionary of National Biography*, 2009.
33. 'Scottish Transport and Communications: an Overview', in: Kenneth Veitch, ed., *Scottish Life and Society: Transport and Communications*, Edinburgh: John Donald, 2009.
34. 'Reimagining Fife', in: *Pathhead Review*, issue 1 (Spring 2011)
35. 'The image of a ship', in: Don Leggatt and Richard Dunn, eds, *Inventing the Ship: Science, Technology and the Maritime World, 1800-1914*, Aldershot; Ashgate, 2012.

Literature

1. 'The Sons of Martha: Technology, Transport and Rudyard Kipling', in: *Victorian Studies*, 1977.
2. 'MacDiarmid the Socialist', in: *Scottish Labour History Society Journal*, 1981.
3. 'Behind the Bonnie Brier Bush: the Scottish Kailyard Revisited', in: P N Furbank, ed., *Proteus*, Summer 1978, an amended version published in *The Scottish Review*, No.27, August 1982.
4. 'The Politics of Stevenson', in: Jenni Calder, ed., *R L Stevenson and Victorian Scotland*, Edinburgh: Edinburgh University Press, 1981.
5. 'Scott and the Image of Scotland', in: Alan Bold, ed., *Sir Walter Scott: The Long-Forgotten Melody*, Vision/Barnes and Noble, 1983, reprinted in Raphael Samuel, ed., *Patriotisms*, London: Routledge, 1989.
6. 'The Barrie who never grew up: The Little Minister Reassessed', in H W Drescher, ed., *The Nineteenth Century Scottish Novel*, Frankfurt: Peter Lang, 1986.
7. 'Second Thoughts of a Scotsman on the Make: Politics, Nationalism and Myth in John Buchan', in: H W Drescher, ed., *Literature and Nationalism in Scotland*, Frankfurt: Peter Lang, 1989. Reprinted with alterations in *Scottish Historical Review*, 1991.
8. 'Industry, Religion and the Matter of Scotland', in: Douglas Gifford, ed., *The History of Scottish Literature*, Vol.IV, *The Nineteenth Century*, Aberdeen: Aberdeen University Press, 1989.
9. '"J D Scott's *The End of an Old Song*" and the Scottish Predicament of the 1950s', in: *Ideas and Production*, 1989.
10. 'Introduction' to John Buchan, *Witch Wood*, Edinburgh: Canongate 1989.
11. 'Nationalism and Literature in Twentieth Century Scotland', in: Peter Zenzinger, ed., *Anglistik und Englischunterricht*, 1989.
12. 'Political Thrillers and the Condition of England', in: Arthur Marwick, ed., *Society and Literature*, Methuen, 1990.

13. 'J G Frazer and John Buchan', in: Robert Fraser, ed., *Sir James Frazer and the Literary Imagination*, Macmillan, 1990; and in: *The John Buchan Journal*, No. 9, Winter 1989.

14. 'Introduction' to J D Scott, *The End of an Old Song*, Edinburgh: Canongate, 1991.

15. 'Alasdair Gray and the Condition of Scotland Question', in: Robert Crawford and Thom Nairn, eds., *The Arts of Alasdair Gray*, Polygon, 1991.

16. 'British Perspectives on European Regionalism', in: Lothar Fietz and Hans-Werner Ludwig, eds., *Studien zur zeitgenössischen englischsprachigen Lyrik*, Tübingen: Attempto-Verlag, 1992/Cardiff: University of Wales Press, 1995.

17. 'Thomas Carlyle and the Scottish Mission', in: Jens-Ulrich Davids, *et al.*, eds, *Britische Regionen, oder: Wie einheitlich ist das Königreich*, in: *Gulliver Deutsch-Englische Jahrbücher*, Band 31, Hamburg: Argument Verlag, 1992, revised version in *Scotlands*, 1997.

18. 'Gnawing the Mammoth: History, Class and Politics in the Modern Scottish and Welsh Novel', in: Gavin Wallace, ed., *The Scottish Novel, 1970-1991*, Polygon, 1993.

19. 'Introduction' to John Buchan's *The Thirty-Nine Steps* (World Classics), Oxford: Oxford University Press, 1993.

20. 'John Bull's Other Irishman', in: Eberhard Bort, ed., *Standing in their Shifts Itself: Irish Theatre from Farquhar to Friel*, Bremen: European Society for Irish Studies, 1993.

21. 'The Democratic Intellect: Philosophy, Theology and Hugh MacDiarmid,' in: Hans Ulrich Seeber and Walter Göbel, eds., *Proceedings of the Anglistentag 1992*, Tübingen: Niemeyer 1993.

22. 'Kultur und Gesellschaft', in: Hans Kastendiek, Karl Rohe, Angelika Volle, eds, *Länderbericht Großbritannien: Geschichte. Politik. Wirtschaft. Gesellschaft*, Bonn: Bundeszentrale für politische Bildung, 1994; revised edition, Frankfurt: Campus Verlag, 1998.

23. '"My country will not yield you any sanctuary"': A polemic by way of preface', in: Hans-Werner Ludwig and Lothar Fietz, eds., *Poetry in the British Isles: Non-Metropolitan Perspectives*, Cardiff: University of Wales Press, 1995.

24. 'North Sea Oil and Scottish Culture', in: Susanne Hagemann, ed., *Studies in Scottish Fiction: 1945 to the Present*, Frankfurt: Peter Lang, 1996.

25. 'British Studies in Germany: Some Practicalities', in *Proceedings of the German Anglistentag*, Greifswald, 1995, in: *Anglistik*, 7:1, 1996.

26. 'Studying Wales from Germany: the Welsh Studies Centre at Tübingen University', in: *The Differences Between*, Vol. 2.2, *The Journal for the Study of British Cultures*, 1996.

27. 'The Welsh Studies Centre at Tübingen University', in: *European Planning Studies*, Vol. 4, No. 1, 1996.

28. 'Anglo-Saxons into Celts: the Scottish Intelligentsia, 1760-1930', in: Terence Brown, ed., *Celticism*, Dublin: The Royal Irish Academy, 1996.

29. 'Garron Top to Caergybi: Images of the Inland Sea', in: *Irish Studies*, Vol. 19, 1996.

30. 'The Challenge of the New Eastern Europe for British Studies and German Universities', in: Wolfgang Mackiewicz and Dieter Wolff, eds, *British Studies in Germany*, Trier: Wissenschaftlicher Verlag, 1997.

31. 'Radical on the Run' (on William Godwin and Caleb Williams), in: *The London Magazine*, Spring 1998.

32. 'Stereotypische Schotten: von Deutschland aus gesehen', in: Uwe Zagratzki and Winfried Siebers, eds., *Deutsche Schottlandbilder*, Osnabrück: Universitätsverlag Rasch, 1998.

33. 'Introduction' to John Buchan, *The Thirty-nine Steps* (translated by Carola Ehrlich), Ditzingen: Reclam-Verlag, 1998.

34. 'The Celts and the Atlantic: Three Themes from the Culture of the Western Seaboard, 1880-1920', in: *Proceedings of the Nation and Region Conference*, St. John, New Brunswick, 1998.

35. 'Sacred Lambencies and Thin Crusts: Symbolising the Scottish Problem in the Epoch of Industrialisation', in: *Cultural Values*, Lancaster, 1999.

36. 'Introduction' to John Buchan, *The Leithen Stories*, Edinburgh: Canongate, 2000.

37. 'John Buchan and The Northern Muse: the Politics of an Anthology', in: Barbara Korte, Ralf Schneider and Stephanie Lethbridge, eds., *Anthologies of British Poetry: Critical Perspectives from Literary and Cultural Studies*, Amsterdam: Editions Rodopi, 2000.

38. 'Hugh Miller and the Scottish Crisis', in: Lester Borley, ed., *Hugh Miller and his Time*, Cromarty: Cromarty Arts Trust, 2003.

39. 'Hamish Henderson: The Grand Old Man of Scottish Folk Culture', in: Eberhard Bort, ed., *'Tis Sixty Years Since: The 1951 Edinburgh People's Festival Ceilidh and the Scottish Folk Revival*, Ochtertyre: Grace Note Publications, 2011.

Politics

1. 'The Labour Campaign in Lothian', in: David Denver and Allan Macartney, eds., *The Referendum Experience*, Aberdeen: Aberdeen University Press, 1981.

2. 'Liturgies of National Decadence: Wiener, Dahrendorf and the Decline of Britain', in: *Cencrastus*, 1985.

3. 'Scottish Politics since 1900', in Christopher Haigh, ed., *The Cambridge Dictionary of British History*, Cambridge: Cambridge University Press, 1985.

4. 'Grasping the Thistle', in: Ken Cargill, ed., *Scotland 2000*, Glasgow: BBC, 1987.

5. 'Thoughts on the Union between Law and Opinion, or Dicey's Last Stand', in: Allan Macartney, ed., *Self- Determination in the Commonwealth*, Aberdeen: Aberdeen University Press, 1988. An altered version in: David Marquand and Colin Crouch, eds., *The New Centralism*, Oxford: Political Quarterly/Blackwell, 1989.

6. 'A Nation Once Again?', in Kenneth White, ed., *Ecosse*, Paris: Editions Autrement, 1988.

7. 'Towards a New Scotland', in: *Cencrastus*, 1989.

8. 'Regionalismus in Großbritannien'. Stuttgart: Landeszentrale für politische Bildung Baden-Württemberg, 1991, republished Stuttgart: Kohlhammer Verlag, 1992.

9. 'Living with Federalism: the German Experience', in *Scolag*, July 1991.

10. 'English Regionalism: the Dog that Never Barked', in: Bernard Crick, ed., *National Identities: The Constitution of the United Kingdom*, Oxford: Political Quarterly/Blackwell, 1991.

11. 'Nationalism, Journalism and Cultural Politics', in: Tom Gallagher, ed., *Nationalism in the Nineties*, Edinburgh: Polygon, 1991.

12. With Stephen Maxwell, 'North Sea Oil and the Scottish National Party, 1970-79', in: T C Smout, ed., *Scotland and the Sea*, Edinburgh: John Donald, 1992.

13. 'Scottish Politics, 1914-1989', in: James Treble, ed., *People and Society in Scotland*, Vol.III, Edinburgh: John Donald, 1992.
14. 'The English Railway Enthusiast', in: Stephan Kohl, ed., *Englishness* (special edition of *Anglistik und Englischunterricht*), 1992.
15. 'In Time of the Breaking of Nations', in *Scottish Affairs*, Vol.1., 1992.
16. 'Sport and the Scottish State, 1880-1924', in: Grant Jarvie and Graham Walker, eds, *Scottish Sport in the Making of the Nation*, Leicester: Leicester University Press, 1993.
17. 'Historical Perspectives on European Regionalism', in: Udo Bullmann, ed., *Die Politik der dritten Ebene: Regionen im Europa der Union*, Baden-Baden: Nomos, 1994.
18. 'The Culture of the Region', in: Léonce Bekemans, ed., *Culture: Building Stone for Europe 2002*, Bruges: College of Europe, 1994.
19. 'A Letter to the Scottish Minister of State', in: *The Differences Between, The Journal for the Study of British Cultures*, Vol. 2.2, 1996.
20. 'Wales and Europe', in: Horst W Drescher and Susanne Hagemann, eds., *Scotland to Slovenia: European Identities and Transcultural Communication*, Frankfurt: Peter Lang, 1996.
21. 'Take your Think Tanks off my Lawn', in: *Agenda*, December 1996.
22. 'Lord Home, 1903-1995', in: Graham Walker, ed., *British Prime Ministers*, London: Routledge, 1996.
23. 'A Costly but Noble State of Tension', in: Andrew Morton and Jim Francis, eds., *A Europe of Neighbours: Religious Social Thought and the Reshaping of a Pluralist Europe*, Edinburgh: Centre for Theology and Public Issues, 1999.
24. 'Beyond the Sovereign State: An Afterword', in: Eberhard Bort and Neil Evans, *Networking Europe: Essays on Regionalism and Social Democracy*, Liverpool: Liverpool University Press, 2000.
25. 'Scotland goes to the Polls: Elections and Cabinet-Making', in *Journal for the Study of British Cultures*, 2000.
26. 'The Cultural and Commercial Representation of Scotland in Europe', in: *Scottish Affairs*, Spring 2001.
27. 'The Moral Sentiments of Inspector Rebus', in: Eleanor Bell and Gavin Wilson, eds, *Scotland in heory*, Amsterdam: Rodopi, 2004.
28. 'Labour and Society in Scotland', in: Gerry Hassan, ed., *The Scottish Labour Party: History, Institutions and Ideas*, Edinburgh: Edinburgh University Press, 2004.
29. 'Devolution and Nationalism in Twentieth Century British History', in: Paul Addison and Harriet Jones, eds, *Blackwell Companion to Twentieth Century British History*, Oxford: Blackwell. 2004.
30. With Eberhard Bort, 'After the Albatross: A New Start for the Scottish Parliament', in: *Scottish Affairs*, No.50, Winter 2005.
31. 'Bad History', in: *Political Quarterly*, Vol. 77, No. 4, 2007.
32. 'Diary of a Candidate', in: *Scottish Affairs*, No. 60, Summer 2007.
33. 'A Year with Salmond', in: *Scottish Affairs*, No. 65, Autumn 2008.
34. 'National Identity in Scotland and Wales', in: Matthew Flinders, Andrew Gamble, Colin Hay and Michael Kenny, eds, The *Oxford Handbook of British Politics*, Oxford: Oxford University Press, 2009.
35. 'Europe's Energy and Extreme Engineering: Scotland's Future', in: *Scottish Affairs*, No.75, Spring 2011.

36. 'The Official History of North Sea oil' (review article) in: *Northern Scotland*, May 2013.

Papers not yet published

Literature

1. 'Carlyle and the Conjurer: Islam and the Scots', read at ESSE Conference, Bogazice University, Istanbul, September 2012.
2. 'The Wizard and the Man of Destiny: Sir Walter Scott and Napoleon', delivered at the Historical Novel symposium at Summerhall, April 2013, to be published in *The Arts Journal*. 'Love and Freedom: the Democratic Poetic' address to Burns and the Diaspora conference, July 2009.
3. 'John Arden and the Matter of Britain' in: *Essays for Eckhard Auberlen*.

History

1. 'A Blast of Annandale Grapeshot: Carlyle and the Heroic', part of a symposium on Heroes and Hero-worship, edited by David Sorensen.

New Editions of Books

1. *Oxford Short History of Scotland, second edition, new final chapter covering 2002-2014.*
2. *No Gods and Precious Few Heroes: Scotland 1914-2014, Edinburgh University Press, fifth edition, being rewritten from 1979 to date*
3. *Fool's Gold and the New North Sea, new edition (covering renewables and counter-inundation), Edinburgh: Birlinn, 2014.*

New Books

1. *'International Men'; Liberalism and European Union from the Victorians until Today.*
2. *The Top of the Tide: A Romance of the Bourgeois Clyde, 1912-1957 (a novel).*
3. *with Allan Massie, Alex's Castle: Salmond and British Politics.*

Open University

For the Open University, Chris Harvie wrote teaching units and made associated BBC television and radio programmes, among them, **1969-70**, three units for A100 Humanities: A Foundation Course on 'The Industrialisation Process, 1830-1914' and 'The Debate on Industrialisation'; two television programmes 'Brunel, the Technocrat as Hero' and 'Glasgow: the Industrial City', and three radio programmes on factory life, strikes and social criticism. Also joint editor of course reader Industrialisation and Culture (Open University/Macmillan); **1970-71**, three units for A202 The Age of Revolutions on 'The Industrial Revolution, 1750-1830' and 'Restoration Europe 1815-30'; one television programme 'The Machine in the English Cotton Industry, 1720-1820' and two radio programmes, on T S Ashton as an economic historian and John Wilkinson, the 18th-century ironmaster; **1971-73**, five units for A301 (equivalent of junior honours) War and Society on 'War and Technology in the 19th Century', 'War and Social Adaptation', 'War and the Idea of Progress', 'Rudyard Kipling: War and the Imperial Mind' and, dealing with the 20th century, 'War and Ideas'; one radio programme on war and society in the 19th century; **1973-74**, four essays for A401 (equivalent of senior honours) Britain 1750-1850: Sources and Historiography on 19th century social policy, commercial and governing elites, and party politics; two television programmes 'Landscape, Maps and the Historian' and 'The Press in a Provincial Town', and a radio programme 'The Scottish Administrative State'; **1974-76**, two units for A321 The Revolutions of 1848 on 'The European Economy in 1848' and 'The Austrian Empire, 1848-49' with an essay on 'The Revolutions and the Balance of Power'; three television programmes 'The Media in 1848', 'Students and Revolution', and 'Land and Race in the Austrian Empire', and one radiovision programme 'Transport in 1848'; **1976-79**, three units for A101 Arts Foundation Course: Unit 21 'The Key Concepts of Industrialisation'; Units 24 and 25 'The Experience of Industrialisation: The West Riding of Yorkshire, 1750-1850'; Unit 32 (Section 1) 'John Ruskin: Ideas and Influence'. Two television programmes 'The Harris Tweed Industry' and 'The Yorkshire Woollen Industry'. The radio programme 'Alfred Williams and Swindon' was the only such programme from A100 to be retained in A101; **1979-80**, three units for A309 Conflict and Stability in the Development of Modern Europe, 1789-1970 on war and technology from 1848 to 1918, and political ideas from Marx to Weber and Pareto. One television broadcast on modernisation and nationalism in the Austrian Empire; **1982-83**, one unit as consultant for AST281 Technology and Society 1750-1914 on the rise of the British textile industry; **1989**, participation in a BBC-TV programme for the Social Sciences Faculty Foundation Course, on 'Nationalism and Society in Scotland'; **1994**, one unit 'Wales and the Wider World' for Welsh History and its Sources; **1998**, one unit 'Culture and Identity' for Modern Scottish History.

Journalism

Chris Harvie has contributed short articles, journalism and reviews to dozens of print and online newspapers papers, journals and magazines, from *Bella Caledonia* to *Die Zeit*. He was transport correspondent for *Tribune*, 1973-78, regular history book reviewer for *Scotland on Sunday*, 1988-89, as well as European feature writer for the *Scotsman*, 1989-97; he writes frequently on Scottish and German affairs for *The Herald* and *The Scotsman*, occasionally for the *New Statesman*, and the *Guardian*. He is also a frequent contributor to opinion forums such as *openDemocracy*, the *Scottish Review of Books*, *Scots Independent*, the *Guardian's Commentisfree* and the *Scottish Review*. Many of his comment pieces can be found at <www.chrisharvie.co.uk/index.php?option=com_content&view=article&id=231&Itemid=15>.

Parliament

Chris's parliamentary speeches (2007-2011) can be found at <www.theyworkforyou.com/search/?s=christopher+harvie&from=3rd+May+2007&to=31+Matrch+2011&person=christopher+harvie&section=sp&column=>.

Broadcast Work

For BBC OU, 1969-80: Half-hour TV films on 'History and Art' with Tim Benton, 'I K Brunel' with LTC Rolt, 'Glasgow Industries' with J R Hume, 'Cardinal Newman' and 'Textile Industries' with Nuala O' Faolain; 'Austrian Imperial Railways', 'Maps and History in Yorkshire', with Patricia Hodgson; 'Harris Tweed' with Paul Kafno; 'German Universities in 1848' with Ed Hayward. Radio: 'Thomas Carlyle' with Geoffrey Best; discussion with colleagues on T S Ashton. 'Life in a Railway Factory' with Gary Watson (1969) as the poet-blacksmith Alfred Williams was the only programme to feature on two successive foundation courses.

For BBC Scotland, a 50-minute television documentary, 'Grasping the Thistle', on Scottish politics in the Scotland 2000 series, 1987, (made by the Tutti-Frutti camera crew) with associated TV and radio programmes. A 60 minute radio doc on Tom Johnston, Secretary of State, 1941-45; with Fenner Brockway, Naomi Mitchison, William Ross, etc.; broadcast 21 December 1983. 'The Camsteerie Rose', similar format, on the General Strike of 1926, May 2, 1986. In summer 1997, two two-programme radio series for the BBC: 'Whitehall and the Boffins' for Radio Four and 'The Fourth Reich?' for BBC Scotland. Much general interview, discussion stuff throughout Europe. Covered the fall of the Wall for BBC from his Tübingen parlour on excellent German TV.

Fairly regular commentaries on politics and history. Consultant to Harlech TV/S4C on 'Divided Kingdom', documentary series, 1988-89, and to Agenda Productions on a projected series, 'Frontiers'. Consultant to/appeared on Agenda/BBC Wales, 'Europe of the Regions', 1991 and BBC-TV Scotland, 'Hitler's Celts', 1994; RTF 3rd prog on the Duke of Rothesay 2011.

Consultant/writer to Fine Art Productions on North Sea oil 'Wasted Windfall', made for Channel Four in 1994. For Radio BBC Four: consultant/part-narrator on 'The Long View: the Tay Bridge Disaster', September 2001; interviewee on 'The Heat is On', December 2001, and 'John Buchan', September 2006, interviewee on 'The Union that never happened', consultant/ interviewee on Brian Cox's TV series 'Sweet Addiction', 2012.

Contributors

Keith Armstrong was born in Heaton, Newcastle upon Tyne, where he has worked as a community development worker, poet, librarian and publisher. Keith Armstrong is a pioneer of many creative writing and community publishing enterprises, like the Northern Voices Community Project's creative writing and community publishing enterprise, specialising in recording the experiences of people in the North East of England. He has visited Tübingen some 30 times since he first spent a month there in November 1987 as poet-in-residence supported by Durham County Council and the Kulturamt, and he has performed his poetry in the city's Hölderlin Tower and, on several occasions, as part of the annual Book Festival.

Neal Ascherson is a Scottish journalist and writer. He was the Observer's Central Europe correspondent based in Germany from 1963 to 1969. He is the author of Games with Shadows (1988), Black Sea: The Birthplace of Civilisation and Barbarism (1995) and Stone Voices (2002), among other books.

Eberhard 'Paddy' Bort is a Lecturer in Politics at the University of Edinburgh and the Director of the Academy of Government's Parliamentary Programme. For the past 23 years, he has co-convened the Freudenstadt symposia with Chris Harvie. With Neil Evans, he edited the first volume of Freudenstadt papers, *Networking Europe: Essays on Regionalism and Social Democracy* (Liverpool University Press, 2000). More recently, he published three edited volumes on Hamish Henderson and the Scottish Folk Revival (*Borne on the Carrying Stream*, 2011; *'Tis Sixty Years Since*, 2011; *At Hame wi' Freedom*, 2012) with Grace Note Publications.

Sarah Boyack was brought up in Edinburgh where she was amongst the first female entrants at the Royal High School. She went on to study at the University of Glasgow in 1979, gaining an MA Honours degree in Modern History and Politics. She then did a Diploma in Town and Country Planning at Heriot-Watt University. Her father was an important figure in the Labour Party and the campaign for Scottish devolution. She was elected to the new Scottish Parliament in 1999, and she was Minister for the Environment, Planning and Transport in the Scottish Executive from 1999-2000 (visiting Freudenstadt in 1999), then Minister for Transport 2000-2001 during which time she introduced one of Scottish Labour's flagship policies of free bus travel for people over 60.

Terry Brotherstone is a Honorary Research Fellow in History at the University of Aberdeen; former president (2007-09) of UCU Scotland; member of the STUC General Council, 2009-10. He was the STUC nominee on the Scottish Government Review of University Governance panel, chaired by Ferdinand von Prondzynski, 2011-12.

Stefan M. Büttner, an Economics graduate of Tübingen University and former member of the University Senate, is a Parliamentary Advisor and Researcher at the Scottish Parliament; he worked first for Chris Harvie MSP, and is now working for David Torrance MSP.

Frank Conlan is a graduate of University College Dublin in Mechanical Engineering; University College Galway MBA. He has industrial experience in the United Kingdom, Germany and Ireland. He is the former Director of the community-owned wind-desalination project on Inis Meán. He is currently a PhD candidate at the Centre for Irish Studies in the National University of Ireland, Galway, with the research topic of 'The Trade Loans (Guarantee) Act 1924 in the period 1924-1939 – an 'economic experiment'?'

Patricia Conlan is a graduate of University College Galway (BA, LL.B), National University of Ireland (LL.M) and Eberhard-Karls-Universität, Tübingen (Dr. jur.). She is a Member of the Institute for the Study of Knowledge in Society (ISKS), the Faculty of Arts, Humanities and Social Sciences (FAHSS) at the University of Limerick (UL). She has published in a range of areas, including Irish accession to the European Union; European Social Charter and Irish labour and welfare law; free movement of persons, citizenship, internal market; parliamentary scrutiny of European affairs; economic empowerment of women; legal regulation of the movement of cultural objects.

Peter Conradi, who celebrated his eightieth birthday in 2012, has been a member of the Social Democratic Party of Germany for more than 50 years, and represented a Stuttgart constituency in the Bundestag from 1972 to 1998. An architect by profession, he has been an ardent critic of the 'Stuttgart 21' project and a member of the mediation team on the side of the opponents to the mega project to put Stuttgart's main railway station underground.

Henry Cowper was Senior Counsellor at the Open University in Scotland, 1970-1994. He taught History at Napier University in Edinburgh from 1995 to 2010. Prior to joining the Open University in Scotland in 1970, Dr Henry Cowper taught in further education.

Richard Demarco was a co-founder of the Traverse Theatre in Edinburgh in 1963. Three years later he and other organisers of the theatre's gallery space left the Traverse to establish what became the Richard Demarco Gallery which, from 1966 to 1992, doubled as a performance venue during the Edinburgh Fringe. For many years, the Demarco Gallery promoted cultural links with Eastern Europe, as well as establishing outgoing connections for Scottish artists across Europe. His involvement with the artist Joseph Beuys led to various presentations, from *Strategy Get Arts* in 1970 to Beuys' hunger strike during the *Jimmy Boyle Days* in 1980. Since the early 1990s, Richard Demarco's activity has continued under the auspices of the *Demarco European Art Foundation*.

Helmut Doka is a Stuttgart Social Democrat. He served as an elected member on the City Council of Stuttgart 1976-89 and 1992-94, and as an elected member of the Stuttgart Regional Assembly, 1998-2004. He has worked extensively with neighbourhood associations and grassroots initiatives before and during his time as a councillor.

Owen Dudley Edwards, born in Dublin as the son of Professor Robert Dudley Edwards and brother to the Irish writer, Ruth Dudley Edwards, was Reader in Commonwealth and American History at the University of Edinburgh. He edited the Oxford Sherlock Holmes series, and is a renowned expert on Sir Arthur Conan Doyle, P. G. Wodehouse and Oscar Wilde, about each of whom he has written.

Tom Gallagher is Emeritus Professor of Politics at Bradford University. He is the author of *Glasgow: The Uneasy Peace* (Manchester University Press, 1987), three volumes on the politics of the Balkans: *Outcast Europe* (Routledge, 2001, 2003, 2005), and *The Illusion of Freedom: Scotland Under Nationalism* (Hurst & Co, 2009).

Alison Harvie, Chris's daughter, is responsible for the management of the Young Foundation's external affairs – overseeing all media relations and events as well as their website and social media. Prior to joining the Young Foundation, Alison was the producer for a public arts collective. She has also worked for the think tank Demos. She holds a degree in Politics from the University of Newcastle upon Tyne.

Paul Gillespie is a former foreign policy editor with The Irish Times. He currently writes a regular column for the newspaper entitled 'World View'. He has also lectured on European Politics in the School of Politics and International Relations at University College Dublin.

Christopher Harvie, born in Motherwell, was educated at Kelso High School and at the Royal High School in Edinburgh. He studied at the University of Edinburgh, where he graduated in 1966 with a First Class Honours degree in History. He joined the Open University in 1969 as a history lecturer, and from 1978 he was a senior lecturer in history. In 1980, Chris was appointed Professor of British and Irish Studies at the University of Tübingen. He initiated the Freudenstadt symposia in 1991. Formerly a member of the Labour Party, he left it for the SNP in 1988. He is Honorary President of the Scottish Association for Public Transport and holds honorary chairs at the University of Wales, Aberystwyth and the University of Strathclyde. Between 2007 and 2011, he was a Member of the Scottish Parliament for the Mid Scotland and Fife region, and served on the Economy, Energy and Tourism Committee. In 2008, he received the Free Spirit of the Year accolade at *The Herald* 2008 Scottish Politician of the Year awards.

Tom Hubbard, a native of Kirkcaldy, Fife, gained his first degree and subsequent PhD from the University of Aberdeen, and a diploma in librarianship from the University of Strathclyde. He was the first Librarian of the Scottish Poetry Library, from 1984 to 1993, before leaving to take lecturing posts in the United States, France and Hungary, which have been followed by visiting professorships in the same countries in the twenty-first century. He was the Editor of BOSLIT (the Bibliography of Scottish Literature in Translation) from 2000 to 2004, and worked on a bibliography of Irish literary criticism at the National University of Ireland, Maynooth. He is the author of the novel *Marie B* (2008); his collection *The Chagall Winnocks* (Grace Notes, 2011) comprises his own poems about Europe along with his transcreations into Scots of European poetry, and *Parapets and Labyrinths: Poems on European Themes* (Grace Note, 2013) reinforces that internationalist outlook.

Thomas Leuerer is a Senior Lecturer in Politics at the University of Würzburg (Akademischer Oberrat am Institut für Politikwissenschaft und Soziologie). He received his PhD in 1996. His research interests include the American Forces in Germany, Anglo-German relations, Devolution, and Montesquieu.

Douglas Macleod is a former journalist who worked as a reporter and news presenter in the Highlands before moving to Glasgow in 1986 where he joined the editorial staff of BBC Radio Scotland's 'Good Morning Scotland'. He also wrote and produced a large number of historical and scientific documentaries for Radio Scotland, Radio 4 and BBC Five Live.

Allan Massie was born in Singapore, but spent his childhood in Aberdeenshire. He was educated at the private schools Drumtochty Castle preparatory school and Glenalmond College in Perthshire before going on to attend Trinity College, Cambridge where he read history. He is a prolific journalist and book reviewer and has, as one of Scotland's foremost Scottish novelists, written around 30 books, from his series of reconstructed autobiographies or biographies of Roman political figures, including *Augustus*, *Tiberius*, *Mark Antony*, *Caesar*, *Caligula* and *Nero's Heirs*, to crime novels set in Bordeaux during Vichy France. His 1989 novel about Vichy France, *A Question of Loyalties*, won the Saltire Society Award for the best Scottish Book of the Year.

Robin McAlpine graduated from Glasgow University to work as a journalist. He then moved to London to become Press Officer to George Robertson, then Shadow Secretary of State for Scotland and leader of the Scottish Labour Party. Returning to Scotland to work in policy development, Robin became employed as Public Affairs Manager for Universities Scotland. Robin is also the Editor of the *Scottish Left Review*, Scotland's leading left-of-centre political magazine. In 2004 he set up the Scottish Left Review Press, a publishing arm of the *Scottish Left Review*. It published his *No Idea: Control, Liberation and the Social Imagination* in 2005.

Peter McCarey was born Paisley and brought up in Glasgow. He lives in Geneva. His work is accessible on <www.thesyllabary.com>. His *Collected Contraptions* was published by Carcanet in 2011. *Find an Angel and Pick a Fight* is available from Molecular Press as of August 2013, on paper and on screen.

James Mitchell completed his first degree in political studies at Aberdeen University. He first met Chris Harvie while completing his doctorate – a study of the Scottish Office – at Nuffield College, Oxford and has benefitted from that initial encounter ever since. As with so many others, his work has been informed more than can be appreciated from any cursory glance at bibliographies and references by Chris's work. His latest book – *The Scottish Question* – will be but the latest example of this influence.

Wolfgang Mössinger, from Zell am Harmersbach in Baden, studied at Freiburg University and then entered a diplomatic career with the German Foreign Office. After postings in Boon, Senegal, Finland and Russia, he became, in 2008, the German Consul General in Edinburgh. Since 2012, he is Chargé d'Affaires a.i. of the German Embassy in Baku, Azerbaijan.

John Osmond is he former Director of the Institute of Welsh Affairs and has written widely on Welsh politics, culture and devolution. He edits the IWA's journal *Agenda* and also its online news magazine <www.clickonwales.org>. His books include *Crossing the Rubicon: Coalition Politics Welsh Style* (IWA, 2007); *Welsh Politics Come of Age: Responses to the Richard Commission* (Editor, IWA, 2005) ; *Birth of Welsh Democracy: The First Term of the National Assembly for Wales* (ed., IWA 2003); and *Welsh Europeans* (Seren, 1997).

Irene Quaile-Kersken is a Scots-born journalist with a PhD from the University of St Andrews who works as Correspondent for Environment and Climate Change with *Deutsche Welle*, Germany's international radio broadcaster. She has received several international journalism awards, including a United Nations gold award for outstanding radio. She was a founding member of the European radio project 'Network Europe'.

Tessa Ransford <www.wisdomfield.com> is an established poet, translator, literary editor and cultural activist on many fronts, having also worked as founder and director of the Scottish Poetry Library. Tessa initiated the annual Callum Macdonald Memorial Award for publishers of pamphlet poetry in Scotland, now in its thirteenth year <www.scottish-pamphlet-poetry.com>. She was president of Scottish PEN from 2003-6. Tessa's Not Just Moonshine, New and Selected Poems was published in 2008, two books of poems followed in 2012: don't mention this to anyone, poems relating to India and Pakistan; and a two-way translation book with Palestinian poet Iyad Hayatleh, who lives in Glasgow, of poems based on the Five Pillars of Islam, entitled Rug of a Thousand Colours. (all Luath Press).

Dr Mario Relich, who lives in Edinburgh, is Associate Lecturer in English and Post-Colonial Literature in the MA English Literature Programme of the Open University. He is also on the executive committee of Scottish PEN. His essay is a revised and expanded version of a talk he gave a few years ago to the Freudenstadt Symposium on European Regionalism, chaired by Christopher Harvie and Eberhard Bort.

Lesley Riddoch is one of Scotland's best known commentators and broadcasters – a weekly columnist for the Scotsman and Sunday Post and a regular contributor to the Guardian. She was assistant editor of The Scotsman in the 1990s and a contributing editor of the Sunday Herald. She is best known for broadcasting with programmes on BBC2, Channel 4, Radio 4 and BBC Radio Scotland, for which she has won two Sony speech broadcaster awards. Lesley runs her own independent radio and podcast company, Feisty Ltd, which produces a popular weekly podcast. Lesley is Director of Nordic Horizons, a policy group which exchanges expertise between the Nordic nations and Scotland. She was a founding member of the Isle of Eigg Trust, which led to the successful community buyout in 1997, and is about to publish her latest book: Blossom – what it takes for Scotland to flourish (Luath, 2013).

Paul Salveson is a visiting professor at the University of Huddersfield, a local Labour Party councillor in Huddersfield and general secretary of the Hannah Mitchell Foundation, which campaigns for devolution to the North of England.

Noel Spare is an independent consultant teaching knowledge-based management theory to manufacturing and service organisations and is visiting lecturer in Managing Complexity at the graduate school of the Technical University of Offenburg in Baden.

Klaus Stolz is a political scientist and Professor of British and American Studies at the University of Technology in Chemnitz. He works in the field of comparative politics (with a special focus on the UK). His research interests include territorial politics, political careers and political professionalisation. His books include Towards a Regional Political Class? Professional Politicians and Regional Institutions in Catalonia *and Scotland* (Manchester University Press, 2010) and, as editor, *Ten Years of Devolution in the United Kingdom* (Wißner Verlag, 2010).

David Walker is a former leader writer for *The Times* and *The Guardian* and a council member at the Economic & Social Research Council. With Polly Toynbee he is the author of *The Verdict* (2010) and *Dogma and Disarray: Cameron at Half Time* (2012).

Ian S Wood taught History for the Open University and also at Napier University, Edinburgh. His most recent books are *Crimes of Loyalty: A History of the UDA* (2006), *Britain, Ireland and the Second World War* (2010) and *Times of Troubles: Britain's War in Northern Ireland* (2012), which he co-wrote with Dr Andrew Sanders, all published by Edinburgh University Press.

Made in the USA
Charleston, SC
11 July 2013